Shifting Gears

SUSAN MUSGROVE

Shifting Gears

FOREST HOUSE PRESS

SHIFTING GEARS, Copyright © 1989–2008 by Susan Musgrove, Forest House Press. All rights reserved. Printed in the United States of America. No part of this book may be used or reproduced in any manner whatsoever without written permission.

ISBN-13: 978-0-9843084-0-8

Layout and design credits: © 2009 Kelly Wagner, ReDesign Creative Studio.

Cover photo by Clarke Cohu, © 1989.

Acknowledgments

First of all, Clarke Cohu, for being willing to sell his advertising agency and travel for a year. It was his idea to bicycle. A professional photographer, he took the cover photo at Winn and Jackie's garden near London.

Most, my sister Jill Barnes, a far better writer than I, who read this manuscript numerous times without complaint, always with great suggestions, an eagle eye for errors, and the same patience with which she tends the tiny seedlings in her large garden. No Jill, no book fit to print.

Kelly Wagner, lucky me, she's the niece who bicycled with us for the summer and now has forgiven me enough to design this book. A graphic designer extraordinaire and owner of ReDesign Creative Studio (www.redesigncreativestudio.com) near St. Louis, she is amazing.

Megan Davis, Kelly's best friend who rode with us from London to Frankfurt – both teenagers were sources of high drama and great fun.

My friends, who won't let me stop writing.

Although Clarke, Kelly and Megan may have totally different recollections, this story is as close to true as I can make it from my daily trip journals.

Preface

We began this adventure in February of 1989. Almost twenty years later, people still ask if they can read about it, so here it is.

Traveling was different then – no Internet to keep in touch, my twenty-four pound laptop not rugged enough for the rattles and bumps of bicycle travel, heavy steel mountain bikes with no suspension, no waterproof panniers or shoe covers. Different politics, different countries even. But the part of the trip that mattered, pedaling every mile of the way, would still be the same – and I would do it again in a heartbeat.

Chapter 1

It takes a week for two middle-aged Americans and their mountain bikes to get by train from Germany to Spain, not an auspicious beginning. The four of us just can't seem to stay together.

First, the bikes ditch us in Dallas, where Clarke and I change planes for the European leg of our flight. "Our bikes are smarter than we are," I grouse after we finally discover their whereabouts. "If they don't want to go over the Alps, why should we?"

Clarke is not amused. Day One of our European adventure is shot, neither of us has slept on the fourteen-hour flight from Denver, and we've spent a day's budget on taxi fare back and forth from the Frankfurt air cargo terminal. We haven't eaten in twelve hours. "Let's get some sleep, Susan." Clarke scrunches into a hard vinyl chair in the airport lounge as I struggle unsuccessfully to write about how it feels to leave my country for a year.

The next day, the bikes arrive as promised and we bundle them still in their boxes onto the escalator down to the subway. "Okay, you two," I admonish my aluminum friends, "I don't care if you are dismantled—you're not getting out of these boxes until you're on the train to Paris. No more running away!"

Clarke rolls his eyes at my silliness. "I'll assemble the bikes," he offers at the Frankfurt railroad station, "if you'll see about shipping them to Paris." Because it's late February, two-week Eurail passes will allow us to begin our bicycle adventure in mild weather, in Portugal or Spain.

The station agent doesn't speak English and I don't speak German, so we settle on Spanish. "I think he told me that we have to pay extra for the bikes once we cross the French border at Forbach," I explain when I return to help build the bikes.

I've missed an important word. Apparently, we're supposed to pay before we cross the border, not after, because when Clarke ambles back to the baggage car to see about paying the extra freight as we cross the French border, he finds no bikes for which to pay extra. "They must have been taken off on the German side of the border," he shouts around the corner of our compartment. "Come on!"

"Cripes, they ditched us again," I grumble, following with our passports and carry-on luggage. On the platform in Metz, all arms and legs and gestures, we somehow convince the French conductor to release our tagged-for-Paris panniers from the baggage car, and covered in packs, run to stuff everything in lockers before boarding the 8:03 back to Saarbrücken to rescue our bikes from the Germans. Instead, we board the 8:01 for Luxembourg.

By the time we realize our mistake and disembark with two passengers and the conductor in the small French village of Hagondange, the last train to anywhere is the one we've gotten off. It's nine o'clock, the station is closing for the night, and taxi fare back to Metz is sixty dollars, six days' budget. Clarke turns to me. "We've got to find the bikes tonight!"

"Hitchhike?"

The old French stationmaster shakes his head when we ask for directions to the highway. It's too dangerous to hitchhike at night, he explains; but we're more afraid of losing our bikes than of being robbed. Overhearing the exchange, the conductor who got off the train from Metz offers to take us part way, nudging us out of his tiny car at a lonely crossroads.

It's dark and cold. We've never hitchhiked, don't speak French and don't even know how far we are from Metz, reminded by the strange yellow headlights of the foreign cars just how far we are from home. I fuss at myself: just because we want to travel in Europe for a year, like idiots we sell almost everything we own, find someone to take care of our dogs, say heart-wrenching goodbyes to families and friends, then lose our bicycles in Germany and ourselves in France before pedaling our first kilometer. This is teenager stuff, not the actions of responsible forty-year-olds!

The third car stops. "Climb in," the driver whispers in English, his voice scratchy as dry sand. "You are Americans," he continues as his car lurches down the tiny road. "I've spent quite a bit of time in your country."

"Please forgive me," I say finally, "but I majored in speech pathology and am terribly curious. What happened to your voice?"

The man shrugs, a dark outline in the front seat. "My throat was cut by my enemies and I was left for dead. I was a recruiter for the Middle East wars."

I'm sorry I asked, and mentally compose my first postcard home: *Having a wonderful time hitchhiking in the middle of the night in a foreign country with a mercenary whose throat has been slit, while looking for our bikes that have disappeared for the second time in two days.*

In the front seat, Clarke chats amicably with our driver about France and America, grateful for English conversation and a warm ride, while I wait nervously for someone with a knife to jump out of the darkness for a second attempt on the man's life.

Back in Metz, we take the midnight train to Saarbrücken but the authorities won't open the baggage room until morning, and for the third night in a row, we jam ourselves in hard little chairs to sleep. It's another long night.

At dawn, the stationmaster opens the baggage room. "There they are!" I screech, spotting our bicycles in a corner, then say prayers to the train gods before tucking them onto a train to Paris while Clarke and I return first to Metz to pick up our luggage.

We and our bikes arrive at the same station by late afternoon. It feels like a miracle. We decide to head for Madrid, and as Clarke leaves to check schedules, I check out the sleek Parisian women and crisp German businessmen swarming through the station, embarrassed at my appearance: pink sweats and tennis shoes that I wore on the plane, plus a bright blue-and-yellow bike jacket, my long hair a tangled mass of wild curls. "I usually don't dress like this when I visit Paris," I explain to the bikes as Clarke returns with a you're-not-going-to-believe-this look.

"We can't catch a train to Madrid from this station," he says. "We have to go to Gare d'Austerlitz. Do you know where it is?"

"On the other side of the city, of course."

For most travelers, the transfer would be a simple cab or bus ride. For us, nothing seems to be simple. Because the assembled bikes won't fit into a cab or bus, we load our packs onto the bikes, inflate their tires with a tiny hand pump, and hustle off into the streets of Paris in the waning light of rush hour.

Clarke has dreamed of seeing France for many years. His ancestors were French Huguenots and he loves the language and the whole idea of Paris and its culture and art. He too is an artist. Now, here he is, an inexperienced bicyclist trying to stay alive instead of sightsee.

The chic and the bizarre rush everywhere; speeding Parisian Peugeots fill every inch of street space, bistros spill onto the sidewalks with checkered tablecloths and animated gossip, and behind ornate lampposts, beautiful old buildings stand stoic and mysterious in the Claude Monet evening. Graceful bridges loop the fabled Seine. At a traffic light, Clarke turns to me in despair. "My first time in Paris, and all I can think about is whether someone will open a car door into my face."

Traffic is heavy and fast. Half lost all the way through the darkening streets, we weave this way and that through the speeding cars. By the time we reach the train station, the sky is totally dark. "How do you like bicycling in a big city?" Clarke asks my wide eyes.

"Let's see," I answer, "postcard number two will say: *Wrested the bikes from the grasp of the Germans only to narrowly escape double suicide while bicycling through Paris after dark in rush hour after three sleepless nights.*"

"Just don't send that one to my mother."

Because the French can check the bikes only to the border, we decide on a night train to Irún, Spain, Basque country, and buy bread and wine and cheese for a midnight picnic on the train, settling into instant sleep in the plush seats of a first-class compartment. Jerking awake when the train starts, we watch the lights of Paris pick up speed until they thin and then disappear altogether.

The three-quarter moon washes the hills of the French countryside in blocks of silver light and shadow as the train speeds quietly past tiny villages and farms, hedges and walls shooting like black arrows past the window. Alone in the six-person compartment, we each stretch across three seats but snatch only small handfuls of sleep as the moonlight and magic of France pull us awake every few minutes.

In the morning, we discover that for the first time, we and our bikes have actually gotten on and off the same train at the same place at the same time. We're in Spain, and because I studied Spanish in high school, I'm in charge of communication; consulting the station agent, I'm glad to hear a semi-recognizable language instead of German or French. The bikes, I'm told, must take the night train that has a baggage car; Clarke and I can take the first-class day express and wait for them in Madrid. "Didn't we read that in Spain we need seat reservations, even with our Eurail passes?" Clarke asks when I return.

"The agent said they weren't necessary," I answer. "I think." But when the train arrives, it's almost full and the conductor seems upset that we have no seat reservations. "I feel like a stupid American *turista*," I complain as the first-class compartment continues to fill with smartly dressed travelers at each stop. "It's just a matter of time before the people who bought our seats kick us off the train."

"Then let's get off at the next stop and ride the night train with the bikes," Clarke suggests. "With all their mysterious disappearances, I'll feel better if we're all on the same train anyway."

Wrestling our heavy packs from the overhead racks and from under the seats, carrying everything we still own on our backs like gypsies, we lurch off the train at Aranda de Duero. "We need a basket of squawking chickens to add just the right touch," I point out. It's nine-thirty when we drag our packs into the station.

In four days, we've spent two weeks' allowance on train fare for the bikes, and I grudgingly head for the ticket window to buy seat reservations on their train to Madrid. "There are no more trains tonight," the station manager tells me in Spanish. "The baggage train does not stop here." Sighing enormously, I size up the plastic chairs that will be our beds for the night, wishing too late that we'd taken our chances on the crowded express with its soft, upholstered seats. "You must return at seven-thirty in the morning, *señora*," the agent says. "The station is closing now."

"Can't we wait here?" I plead, indicating our mountain of baggage.

"I am sorry, you must go into town. It is only two kilometers from here."

"Will this never end, Clarke?" I'm totally deflated, discouraged, tired of being a good sport, sick of my grimy pink sweats, my shoulders in knots from carrying heavy packs and draping myself over hard plastic chairs every night. Clarke doesn't respond, lost in the adventure of the trip, part of a huge board game, the world versus Clarke and Susan, the object of which is to respond to all the snaggles and traps and delays and detours with grace, humor and wit.

Keys jiggling loudly, the station master waits impatiently as we array ourselves in packs and duffels and set off down the dark and rutted dirt road in the cold and wind toward town. I walk in silence, feeling like an idiot for not buying seat reservations on the first train. Clarke takes a more useful approach and tries to decide on a course of action. "We can't afford a hotel, but we have to sleep somewhere," he begins. "Maybe the cops will let us stay in the police station."

Ignoring him, I trudge on, eyeing with guilt my bulky computer pack draped over Clarke's shoulders. Originally, I thought this trip would make a good book but now can't imagine anyone wanting to read about our stupidity.

Although I'm under the impression that I can speak a little Spanish, at the police station we might as well be on Mars. After every cop in the place asks me to repeat my request, they insist on taking us to a *pensione*. I try to explain that we can't afford a hotel, but the police either don't understand or don't believe me. Off we go, shrouded in duffel bags, with a police escort. "Let's cause a disturbance," Clarke suggests half-seriously. "Then we can sleep in the jail for free."

The hotel is seventeen dollars, almost two days' budget, and now Clarke's grace, humor and wit suddenly plummet to the gloom where my attitude already lies in a heap. That he's hardly slept or eaten in four days means nothing; it's part of the adventure. But spending money on a hotel before we've bicycled is a snaggle he doesn't like, not at all, and he's fuming. "At least we have beds to sleep in, Clarke, and water, even though it's cold." We've refused to pay extra for a shower, much as we need it, and dropping into the lumpy twin beds, exhausted but glad to be out of our clothes for the first time, if only for a few hours, we fall asleep instantly.

At six o'clock the next morning, the proprietor pounds on our door and we struggle to consciousness, trying to remember where we are. It's raining and windy. The room is dark. Lurching in a daze to the tiny sink, I quickly stick my head under the icy water to wash my hair before I can change my mind, then we pull on dirty clothes and leave the hotel, depressed and gloomy.

The whole town is gray in the pre-dawn light. Low clouds scud overhead in the high winds and the streets are slick with rain. Wet papers stick against the old buildings and the few people on the streets huddle under umbrellas, looking down at the pavement. Everything drips.

Clarke marches ahead swiftly, oblivious of his heavy load, while I struggle behind, wrestling with my packs and duffels as I hurry to keep up. "Slow down, Clarke," I call ahead, stomping through the mud, icy wet hair in my eyes. Suddenly, my right ankle turns with a painful crunch. "Damn!" Standing on one leg, my face turned up to the cold rain and wind, I cry in frustration and pain. Clarke comes back. "I sprained my ankle," I sob.

"Can't you walk?" he snaps, exasperated, grabbing as much of my load as he can.

"I have to," I snap back, limping toward the station, "and I also have to bicycle."

At least the bikes seem to be resigning themselves to the trip; they're already in Madrid when we finally arrive late that morning. A young Spaniard waiting for a train to his home in Valencia convinces us not to cross another border. "I was robbed by bandits with knives in Lisbon," he explains. "Valencia is beautiful, the weather is wonderful, and the people, they are friendly. Go there."

Why not? Anyone's opinion has to be better than ours. Besides, the train to Valencia leaves earlier than the one to Lisbon and we're tired of sitting in stations. Clarke takes our Eurail passes to arrange for the bikes to be shipped to Valencia, on the Mediterranean about halfway down the eastern coast of Spain, while I rub my ankle and mentally prepare postcard number three, something about being crippled and getting us thrown out of a train station after abandoning a perfectly good train because we were underdressed.

We miss the train to Valencia. Unlike the other stations in which we've been, trains from Madrid don't seem to leave on predetermined track numbers. As departure time nears, we position ourselves in the middle of two dozen tracks, listening carefully to the scratchy public address system, worried that all of our stuff and my ankle will prevent us from boarding our train before departure. "*¡Cinco!* Track Five!*" I shout after hearing the announcement for Valencia. "Hurry, Clarke!"

Grabbing the biggest chunk of our baggage, he bolts down the stairs like a portable mountain. I hobble after him, clinging to the banister and two packs and a duffel. By the time I enter our reserved car, Clarke has found our seats and is stowing his share of our gear. We're alone. "Are you sure this is the right train?" he asks.

I shrug. "That's what the P.A. announced, and this car has the same number as our reservation."

Clarke walks to the next car, where a surprised conductor waves his arms. "Valencia?" Clarke asks.

"*¡No, no, no, señor!*" The conductor is adamant. Again, packs and duffels and two tired travelers bundle off the train.

"I'll try again, Clarke," I sigh. "Stay with the bags. As bad as my Spanish seems to be, it's still better than yours." Steeped in self-pity, I limp up the stairs, ankle throbbing. "Is this the right track for the train to Valencia?" I ask someone in a uniform.

"*No, señora*," he answers, then runs up to me five minutes later as I try to coax an automated information machine into speaking English. "*Señora*," he shouts, gesturing wildly. "I am sorry," he continues in Spanish. "The train to Valencia was on Track Five, but it has already left."

Scanning the overhead schedule where I now realize that track numbers are listed, I discover that the next train to Valencia doesn't leave for seven hours, then reconsider Lisbon before remembering that our bikes are already on their way to Valencia on the train we've just missed.

Down by the track, Clarke paces among packs that seem to be multiplying like rabbits. "If it means anything, Clarke, I was right. It was Track Five. And yes, we missed it. And no, I have no idea why. Maybe we just got on too early. And no, I have no idea if I'll do any better with the next one, but I have seven hours to figure it out. Give me the Eurail passes and I'll go stand in line again."

Clarke reaches for the passes, then checks all his pockets. "I must have left them in the baggage area," he groans, bolting up the stairs. Postcard number four is looming large.

"They're on the train to Valencia," he explains after returning a long time later. "The baggage agent gave them to the conductor when he discovered I'd forgotten them."

"So now we have to buy tickets to Valencia as well as seat reservations," I sigh, picturing a week's groceries needlessly tossed down the drain.

"Let me finish, Susan. The agent took me to the stationmaster, the *jefe* they call him, who speaks a little English. He wired ahead to Valencia, where they'll hold our passes until we arrive, and gave us free tickets on the next train." Clarke is clearly proud of himself for slugging it out without speaking Spanish.

I'm proud of him also. "Good for you, Clarke."

"Maybe we can afford a two-dollar sandwich. We haven't eaten since yesterday." Returning with two cheese sandwiches, Clarke digs through his pack for his sketchbook and markers, drawing a colorful picture of the station for the *jefe*, his humor, grace and wit totally restored, while I massage my aching ankle and wonder whether we should just give it up and go home if and when we ever find our bikes.

As train time nears, we move us and our stuff in sight of the big departure board. Our train isn't even listed. Standing in a long line at the information counter, I understand only that I'm supposed to listen and I wonder what the *jefe* will say when we miss this one.

Just prior to scheduled departure, I stand in line again. "Why is our train not listed?" I ask again in Spanish. The answer seems to come back in Swahili. Determined to find out what's happened to our train before we have to spend the rest of our lives in the Madrid train station, I continue to question the impatient clerk until another traveler pushes up to me. "He's explaining that your train has been canceled because of a hurricane in Valencia," the man says in English. "Another will be rescheduled when and if possible."

"Ready for another postcard, Clarke?" I sigh after thanking my interpreter.

The delayed train out of Madrid deposits us and eight bags of luggage in Valencia at three in the morning. The bikes, we're told, have taken an unexplained detour—again—and will—we hope—arrive later in the morning. The Eurail passes arrived before any of us.

We finish the night in black plastic chairs. At dawn, Clarke crawls onto the floor for a catnap but is reprimanded by a station policeman. He couldn't have slept anyway. On the other side of the room, three Spaniards, two men and a woman, erupt into a loud debate over an unknown subject. All three yell and argue ferociously, then the oldest man throws up his arms in disgust and bangs out of the room. In the silence, the other travelers settle down like chicks in a hen house for a pre-dawn nap. Fifteen minutes later, the old man crashes back through the door, taking up where he left off, and the room jerks awake to the topic at hand. The argument is still raging when we leave to change into cycling clothes before picking up our bikes.

It's Sunday, February 26th. We stand silently, each holding a bicycle loaded like a fat mule, our own arms and shoulders finally free. We've had only a few hours' sleep in the past week, and almost no food. Outside is the tail of a hurricane. After all we've been through, the weather is just one more inconvenience. "How's your ankle?" Clarke asks softly, searching my bloodshot eyes.

I look at him for a long moment. "Let's find out."

Chapter 2

Six months after deciding to sell everything we own to discover Europe, Clarke and I finally feel that Day One of our trip has arrived. We thought that it would come before this – our last day of work, when we moved out of our house, the start of our short training trip in Arizona, boarding the plane, or at least when we landed in Frankfurt. But as each of these times came, it didn't bring the feeling of beginning. Always, the start of the trip loomed ahead somehow.

No more. This is it. In the cold and wind and rain of a leftover hurricane, on a Sunday morning in downtown Valencia, Spain, at the top of a wide flight of steps from the train station to the flooded street, the trip really begins for each of us.

Palm trees shake their shredded fronds like pom-pons in the gale-force wind and pelting rain flattens the beautiful old city into a black-and-white postcard. The streets are deserted. Twisted signs, bricks, broken glass and tree limbs describe the storm of the night before. Against the storm-gray day, our bright jackets and red-and-white helmets look out of place, unreal, painted on like the purple crocuses blooming out of the snow each spring at home in Colorado.

"Let's see if you can get down all these stairs with your packs," I say to myself and my bicycle, squeezing the brakes as I thump down the steps, one by one. Clarke bumps down much faster and waits at the bottom.

"We need a market and some gas for the camp stove," Clarke reminds me, "then let's get the hell out of this storm." Unable to read the storefront signs in Spanish, we pedal up and down the streets looking in windows for a hardware store and a food market. They're all closed – Spain is serious about Sunday being a day of rest.

Zigzagging down the empty streets as strong winds blow us this way and that, a blast of wind spills me in front of an oncoming car on a narrow bridge; the auto swerves as I retract my arms and legs like a turtle.

At a tiny market on the south side of town across from a church, we're able to buy yogurt and bread. It will have to do. "Which way are we going?" I yell above the wind as Clarke pedals past a flock of Spaniards heading for Mass.

"Unfortunately," he yells back, pointing at a giant black cloud that looms just off the coast, "toward that."

As we near the edge of the city, the stench of flooded sewers is overwhelming and dead animals litter the highway like Frisbees with furry feet. "Kitty litter!" Clarke shouts and I shudder as another fuzzy flat face, feet pointing to the four directions of the compass, passes next to our tires.

When we meet the black cloud mid-afternoon, it takes only moments to decide to stop at the nearest campground. Wind is one thing, rain and hurricanes another. Although our guidebooks say that two or three dollars is the going rate all over Europe, this one costs eleven. "It's high season," the owner explains, and we wish that we knew how to ask in Spanish what the weather is like in the off season.

As we pitch our tent in the howling wind, the cloud disintegrates into cold sheets of rain. Lashing our bicycles to a tree, we throw our packs and ourselves inside the tent to weight it down. "Will the tent hold?" I yell, my voice almost lost in the gale.

"I have no idea," Clarke yells back as he hands me a piece of damp bread. "Let's string our packs together in case we have to run for it."

Fully dressed, our packs mounded around us like a dike, we sleep for fifteen hours, oblivious to the worst storm on the Costa Blanca in a hundred years.

The next day, we find food and camping gas and more bad weather as we twist in and out of broken tree limbs, past demolished greenhouses and now-fenceless hotel tennis courts. Highway signs dangle, their poles twisted and bent like straws. Billboards are shredded. At dusk, we stop at a deserted campground and set up our tent near a fence. "I'm staying dressed again," I announce, haggard and frightened from fighting the winds. I've hardly thought of my aching ankle.

"Let's sleep while we can, Susan." We doze from seven to nine, then lie awake as the wind continues to strengthen. Twisting and turning in my sleeping bag, truly scared but not wanting to admit it, I attempt to take my mind off the present by remembering the events that led up to this moment in my life.

As newly married forty-year-olds, we'd decided to cash in my retirement savings to live in Europe for a year so that we could expose ourselves to more than an American view of life. Planning to travel in our VW camper, we decided at the last minute that we wouldn't have enough money for a year of driving. Yet it was too late to change our minds—as director of the chamber of commerce of a mountain town near Aspen, Colorado, I was screening a hundred applicants for my job; and Clarke, an artist and the owner of a small advertising agency, had already closed his business. We'd even been interviewed by the local newspapers. "How about bicycling?" Clarke finally suggested in desperation.

I was horrified; after three knee surgeries, I'd bicycled exactly twice in thirty years and Clarke didn't even own a bike. However, with no better solution in mind and not wanting to give up my dream of living outside my own country, I finally agreed to give it a shot, then wondered if I could actually pedal eight hours a day for a year, cook three daily meals on a camp stove, sleep on the ground every night and make do with a wardrobe of only two pairs of bike shorts and two t-shirts.

As departure neared, the trip took on a momentum of its own, leaving little time for reluctance. As we completed business obligations, we also arranged passports and visas, made airline reservations, bought camping supplies and bicycle equipment, sold most of what we owned and stored only the essentials, closed bank and charge accounts, canceled phone service and subscriptions, arranged to have mail forwarded, loan and child support payments made, dogs taken care of by friends, income taxes filed and money accessible.

In January, only three weeks before departure, after Christmas with Clarke's parents and his two teenagers, we drove to Arizona to train. It didn't take long to learn that Clarke was the stronger athlete, especially as we added heavy packs to the bicycles. "So Clarke," I said finally, "how many miles a day do you want to ride?"

"If we want to see twelve countries, which probably means cycling ten thousand miles, we can't be sightseeing in every small village," he began.

"This trip is about experiencing people and their cultures," I interrupted, "not to see how many miles we can pedal. I'd love to come home all fit and proud of myself, but I refuse to consider this trip as my private fat farm." When we realized that we both wanted the same thing, to see as much of Europe as possible without ruining my already-ruined knees, we agreed to cycle as far as we both could each day, settling on a thirty-mile daily goal to start.

After three days of thirty-mile sprints carrying full weight, we crossed the Mexican border to get a taste of foreign travel, then found ourselves lost in the desert, aliens, with no one at home even knowing what country we were in. "We'd better get used to this," I said, two days past the last town and out of food.

"If we can't find a town by evening," Clarke said, "we'll have to turn back—which means no food for three days—or miss our flight to Germany."

Thirty miles later, a dusty Mexican came around the back of a shack with three dusty chickens and explained in Spanish that the coast was twelve miles farther. "So much for thirty-mile days," I sighed, but by evening we were tucked under a telephone pole in a crowded RV park filled with North American retirees.

"How long you folks gonna ride them bicycles?" an old man asked as we folded our entire household onto the bikes in the morning.

"A year," Clarke replied cheerfully. The man's smile disappeared and he walked away shaking his head.

Now I'm not sure that we'll be alive in a year. As the wind howls outside the tent, the thin nylon shivers and pulls and I scrunch down farther in my sleeping bag, wondering how long it will take for the fabric to rip apart. At two o'clock in the morning, we hear the insistent bleat of a car horn, over and over. "Someone wants us awake," Clarke yells above the storm as the wind ups the ante by a few more decibels; clearly, our tent wants to be somewhere else. "Hang on to it, Susan—I'll be back!"

Clarke unzips the door and scrambles outside as a nearby fence flaps, ready for takeoff. I hold the top of the tent tightly to keep it from blowing away like a tumbleweed, sure that without our heavy packs inside, it and I would be smashed into a wall by now. Maybe we still will. Clarke returns after what seems like hours. "Come on!" Running through the gale to the men's cinderblock shower, we and our bikes stretch out in single file on the dirty cement in front of the toilet stalls. It's smelly, but safe.

In the morning, fragile sunshine washes the tattered landscape with the palest of light. Although the rain has stopped, the winds are strong and gusty as we tiptoe out of the men's toilets. Rain drips from broken tree limbs and flattened fences and, defeated, I consider suggesting that we go home where we belong and leave foreign bicycle touring to the youngsters. Then I imagine what it will take to retrace our steps—another week of misery chasing the bikes back to Germany with two hundred pounds of stuff on our backs—and I know that I can't face it. It's easier to go on.

We head inland. At times, the headwinds are so strong that I literally stop in my tracks, dead, an immovable object. Riding the other direction on the curving roads, we sail along without pedaling at thirty kilometers an hour as if pushed by invisible hands.

Early that evening, we decide to ask if we can put our tent in someone's field; our plan to spend two or three dollars for campgrounds isn't working and groceries alone cost almost our whole budget of ten dollars a day. After finding no one home at three houses, we discover a deserted, crumbling house tucked into an old orange grove and pitch our tent between the trees, sheltered from the wind and the eyes of the neighborhood. Captivated by the aroma of the famous Valencia oranges, I stuff fresh orange leaves into my sleeping bag before collapsing into dreamless sleep.

At daybreak, we thread down the coast looking for an edge of the depressing weather, and when we can't find one, turn inland toward the mountains, hoping they'll shield us from the wind.

Mid-morning, we're sitting on a wall next to a hospital as I finish a yogurt and wipe off the spoon with my fingers. "We need water." With four empty water bottles and our expandable plastic container, we slip past the reception area to find a restroom with what we hope is drinking water, feeling like thieves.

In a few hours, the wind quiets as the scenery changes from flat orange groves to terraced hillsides of olive and fig trees. Pedaling through a resort area, we eat lunch at the end of a hairpin turn and I lie back to enjoy the sun and the view. Tiny objects inch along a line near the top of the mountain. I sit up and point. "That's where we're going, Clarke? Up there? Cripes, you picked this route just to kill me!"

Built on a sheer wall, the road is too narrow for a centerline. Averaging two kilometers an hour for five hours, on seven to twelve percent grades, we concentrate on the difficult climb. "Water break," Clarke calls from in front, stopping on a straight stretch of road, and I chug in behind to suck down great gulps of water. From our training, we know that each of us will drink a gallon of water every day, plus one or two liters of fruit juice.

"Hold my bike, Clarke; I need a tree." Unzipping four squares of toilet paper from a front pack, I return a few moments later and straddle my top tube, glaring at

Clarke through yellow-tinted sunglasses. "You men should be a lot more thankful for what you've got."

"At least you don't have to worry about your parts falling asleep," he replies. "Ready?"

Once we get into our toe clips, we settle into a rhythm, pedaling a revolution or so per second, twenty or thirty thousand a day. We shift without thinking, almost simultaneously. "What gear are you in?" Clarke makes conversation.

"Low - low," I respond. On the steep hills, we labor on the smallest chain ring of three and the largest sprocket on a freewheel of six for me, seven for Clarke. It's a snail's pace, but it gets us and our stuff up the mountain.

At the top of the pass, we find a small restaurant, and looking east to Denia on the Mediterranean, toast our day's progress with a beer as a French couple and a tipsy Englishman assure us that the road to Benidorm is all downhill. Checking brakes, tires and packs, we slip on our leather gloves, excited. We've earned a ride down.

I'm already way out in front. There isn't much to do, really—just watch for cars on blind corners, and for loose gravel and broken pavement or potholes, keep the legs moving to avoid cool-down and stiffening. I'm in heaven. Then we find that what other people call down in an auto isn't down on a bicycle, and our delight quickly turns into despair at the bottom of another long, steep hill. It's late afternoon and we check the map for the nearest town. There isn't one. We have no food. "Who cares?" I groan. "Let's just find a place to stay for the night. We've been on the road eleven hours, sixty kilometers of it mountain passes."

"I don't see a spot unless you want to sleep on a forty-five-degree angle, Susan."

Finally, after two more steep hills, we find a grassy place to sleep, not caring if we're discovered as we put up our tent in the twilight and go to bed without dinner.

After insisting that I need a laptop computer on the trip, already it isn't working, and at Benidorm, Clarke suggests a side trip by train the next day to Madrid to get it repaired before our Eurail passes expire. We check into a campground, hoping for a sunny beach and a laundry. The beach is windy and laundry is six dollars a load, so splitting up the dirty clothes, we go to the showers and wash ourselves and our clothes at the same time.

It's our first experience with Europeans in a campground. Most are English, German and Dutch, in vans, small camping trailers and tents, and seem right at home. We aren't; it's too comfortable, too noisy and, of course, too expensive. Full of northern Europeans, it doesn't feel like Spain. As we leave the next morning, we meet a Scot who asks where we're going next. "Morocco, after a quick trip to Madrid," Clarke replies. I glance at him, wondering yet again why he wants to visit North Africa.

"Ah, Morocco, you say," the man smiles. "It's a fine place, it is. A wonderful and different place, yes it is. Good luck, mate." Clarke is all ready for the open markets, the Arab music and the veils.

From the campground, we pick our way to Alicante through bumper-to-bumper traffic for a night train back to Madrid.

Early the next morning, the shantytowns on the outskirts of the Spanish capital pass like a patchwork quilt, and the immense Madrid station evokes mixed emotions in us both. This time, we firmly declare, we'll leave under our own steam, unwilling to deal again with P.A. systems in Spanish or lost Eurail passes and hurricanes.

But we've lost track of days and dates already, and Spain runs on a different clock than America does. Stores and businesses, even in the capital, close all weekend in addition to the three- or four-hour lunchtime *siesta* each weekday. We arrive in Madrid on a Saturday; the computer store won't open until Monday, and two more nights in a crowded train station have zero appeal. "Why not bicycle around Madrid," Clarke suggests, "and then take a late afternoon train to Seville? There's a computer store there also, according to this warranty booklet."

"Let's put our packs in a locker, then, so we don't have to worry about them in town. I'll get our seat reservations if you'll wait with the bikes." I pace inside the crowded station for my number to come up for a ticket window while Clarke waits outside. And waits. Once, I come out. "There are still fifty people ahead of me," I complain. "Shall we go on?"

"We've already waited this long—let's not start over later." Clarke is irritated. By the time I return, we both are, and after walking the bikes down a steep flight of stairs to the street in silence, I check the tickets so we'll know when to be back at the station.

"No, no, no!" I bleat. "They gave me seats on the wrong train! We have to leave in an hour!" I pause for breath. "And don't say a word, Clarke. At least I hung on to the Eurail passes."

"Why didn't you check the tickets at the window, Susan? Or did you do this on purpose because you're too lazy to bicycle today?"

"Don't be ridiculous. Next time, you go speak Spanish with the ticket agent. Come on." Grumbling the bikes up the steep stairs to the freight area to check them on a baggage train to Seville, we uncheck the packs and arrive at the right track, on time, for the right train to Seville, where the bicycles are going—we hope.

The train snakes into the Seville station about eight-thirty that night, and we drag our luggage to the freight area, anxious to de-mule ourselves, then discover that the bicycles' train will arrive at another station in the morning. It's Aranda de Duero all over again. "This station closes at ten," the baggage clerk explains, "but you can take a commuter train to the other station and wait there."

The commuter train will leave in an hour, so we tuck ourselves into plastic chairs and I make notes in tiny handwriting on a ragged piece of paper, grimly determined to have a full account of the trip, with or without my computer.

As I write, a tumble of young teenagers bursts into the waiting room herded by two elderly nuns. The young people eye Clarke and me curiously when they hear us speak English, then crowd around after Clarke hands them pictures of his children. I practice Spanish while the teenagers practice English; the youngsters give me a red carnation and we all write our names and draw pictures and finger faces on each other's hands. I trade a woven bracelet I'd bought in Mexico to a girl named Susanna for a leather good luck bracelet, and as the children board their train to somewhere, we share tears and blow kisses. Susanna pulls off her pink-and-white ponytail band and throws it to me.

Clarke and I board our empty train and stand by the door, wrapped in each other's arms. "You really miss your kids, don't you?" I ask, holding him tightly. Although Chris and Jennifer have lived with their mother in California for several years after their parents' divorce, I'm sure that our being in Europe will be hard on everyone, especially since the teenagers have decided not to join us for the summer.

At the quiet station across Seville, the storage lockers are closing for the night, but one look at our baggage convinces the agent to reopen. After potato and cheese tortillas in a café across the street, our first restaurant meal in Europe, we postpone our return to the station by buying ice cream at a movie arcade. Back at the station, we ease our rears into the plastic chairs—red this time—but are awakened at midnight by the station police. "The station is closed," they explain in Spanish. "You must leave."

We can spend all night walking around the block or we can find a hotel. As we knock on the door of a tiny *pensione* down the street, Clarke says, "They probably won't even let us in without luggage. This is a Catholic country, you know."

"More important, I won't be able to change my underwear."

After showing the proprietress our wedding rings, we get a room with twin beds and a shower for twelve dollars, then kick ourselves for spending money on a restaurant meal and for not knowing about the station closing in time to get a full night's sleep and clean clothes for our money.

It's a luxury to wake up in the morning in a bed instead of on the ground or in a plastic chair. The bikes won't arrive until ten, so we have plenty of time to make love. It's been two weeks since we've had sex, and I want to feel Clarke's familiar body in this unfamiliar place. Clarke, however, dresses without a glance my way and I'm disappointed and hurt. Sulking, I take a long shower to deliberately irritate him. "What's the rush?" I say when he shouts at me to hurry. "It wasn't very long ago that you would have loved being in a hotel room with me for as long as possible." My sarcasm drips along with the water from the leaky shower.

"If you wanted sex this morning, Susan, why didn't you do something about it?" Clarke asks as I twist my hair into a threadbare towel.

"I'm tired of being turned down."

Once we began dating several months after becoming friends, Clarke and I couldn't bear to be apart, deciding that we had all the tools to do it right this time—honesty, commitment, passion, unconditional love. Although we lived a hundred miles apart, he commuted almost daily, just to have dinner. In June, we decided to marry in August.

After climbing a 13,000-foot peak in July to celebrate Clarke's fortieth birthday, unwilling to wait another minute to begin our lives together, we were married the next day, six weeks early, then exchanged vows and wildflowers again on our planned wedding date, surrounded by families and friends in a beautiful mountain meadow.

Totally committed to each other, everything we did had magnitude; we erupted from one happening to the next, filled with passion. Our fights had the same immensity as our love, with big gestures, huge fury, incredible drama. Reflecting each other's strengths and weaknesses, we put our marriage on the line every moment, risking everything; and our lovemaking was a perfect expression of a relationship that was uninhibited, exciting and tender. In Europe, we thought, we could jump off the bikes and make love anytime we wanted; with no work, no meetings and no plans, our honeymoon could go on for a year.

One night before leaving America, Clarke had asked why I never initiated sex. "Because you always beat me to it," I'd chuckled. After that, I tried to find opportunities to be the seducer but Clarke always rebuffed me, unreceptive to lovemaking unless he initiated it himself. It was beginning to be a sore spot between us.

Now, in the little hotel room in Seville, our anger flares and sputters like a campfire as we add word chips. Soon it blazes out of control, engulfing us both. The stress of the last two weeks, our frustration and fear and fatigue add even more fuel; but for the first time in two weeks, we finally focus on each other instead of lost bicycles and hurricanes, and our anger eventually turns to passion and we leave the hotel later, holding hands.

Seville, the capital of Andalucía, is a beautiful old city full of broad avenues and squares, parks and ornate twelfth-to-fifteenth century buildings. After retrieving our bikes, we pedal around and around in a maze of heavy Sunday traffic, lost, but it doesn't matter because we can't go to the computer store until the next day. "Where are we?" I ask a handsome Spaniard with gold eyes, handing him a city map.

"*En Sevilla,*" he answers, eyes twinkling.

We're looking for the largest Gothic cathedral in the world. What we find are cool tiny streets of walls, with doorways opening onto colorful tiled courtyards filled with trees and flowers. When we finally locate the huge cathedral around four, it's too late to go inside because we still have to find a place to camp outside the city.

An hour later, we discover a public picnic area not far from the highway. Pretending to be only picnickers, we fix our dinner, then pitch our tent after dark, after everyone has packed up the coolers and the kids and their soccer balls to return to the city.

"Clarke, wake up. Listen!" Motorcycles roar to a halt fifty yards from our tent. I hold my breath, listening to loud men's voices. Women's laughter and the crackle of a fire quickly assure us that the party is for making love instead of war, and we reach for each other's hands, acknowledging our vulnerability, then fall asleep, fingers clasped together. In the morning, we step out of the tent to find a dead sheep by the door.

The computer store fixes the blown fuse under warranty and we're ready to leave by noon. While Clarke exchanges money, a man warns me to keep a close eye on the bikes. "There are many thieves in Sevilla," he says regretfully.

As we pedal past the field where we slept the night before, I realize how rare it will be for us in the next year to see something familiar, to see something even for a second time. So much of our American lives are centered around familiar routines—where we live, the route to work, our offices, anticipated meetings and appointments, plans for the weekend. Even if we aren't in our daily routines, we know where we plan to be, and that's familiar also. The unexpected happens, of course, but in the framework of the physical settings of the known.

Here, nothing can be anticipated. Where or what or when we will eat, where we will sleep, what the next mile will look like. We have no route or schedule in mind other than south in winter, north in summer, and we no longer have any centers except our love and the ones we create inside ourselves one minute at a time. The feeling unnerves me, and although it's exciting, it's also uncomfortable.

A woman bicycling alone in Spain causes a bit of commotion, I discover as I pedal ahead through the small town of Utrera during *siesta*. As I pass the *cantina*, a man leaps out of the door, mouth gaping. Then, like puppies tumbling out of a box, the bar empties into the street. To their obvious disappointment, Clarke appears around the corner and waves, and the men accordion back inside. "Nobody runs to watch *me* ride by," Clarke grumbles as three men run across a rooftop shouting greetings after my bike.

"I have better legs."

Late in the afternoon, we spot a *hacienda* far ahead, atop the next horizon. "Shall we ask to stay in someone's field tonight, Susan?"

"There?" I ask, pointing to the growing white mansion as we approach the long tree-lined drive.

"You're in charge of Spanish," Clarke reminds me.

Centuries-old prickly pear cactus lines the inside road in a tall, solid mass, creating a formidable barrier as we walk the bikes slowly up the hill and watchdogs announce our arrival. The *hacienda*, we learn, is owned by a man who continues his father's tradition of raising bulls for the bullfights in Seville, Madrid and Barcelona. Apprehensive at first, Antonio nevertheless gives us permission to camp and then tells stories of his family and his wife, who once studied in America and now lives with him part-time in Seville and part-time here in the country, half an hour from the city by car but five hours by bicycle.

We sleep well, for the first time not worrying about barking dogs or leaving by first light to avoid discovery. With an abundance of well water freely offered, we wash clothes in the morning, and hang them off of our packs to dry.

I take my first over-the-handlebars spill late that afternoon. We've ridden on a rough and rutted gravel road to a dilapidated farm to ask permission to camp. No one is home except the turkeys, dogs, cats, chickens and junk cars. On the way out, I hit a deep patch of gravel and my bicycle bucks me off, dumping me in a tumble of fur and feathers. Sitting on the ground, I inspect my bleeding legs and hands as turkeys and dogs come to investigate. Relieved that my audience is only animals, I quickly sort myself out from the farmer's chickens and pedal carefully back to the highway pulling feathers from my hair.

That night, we aren't able to get permission to camp, but our tent just fits into a clearing between boulders and dense shrubbery in a construction dump. "I thought I heard you bicycling in your sleep," Clarke says as the sun rises the next morning, "but the noise was rats, trying to get at the food pack near your head."

"I thought all the animals in Spain have already been run over," I respond as we pedal off into the already-warm morning.

Starting on a steep grade, we finish on another, our Andalucían tour replete with heat and winding roads designed by the descendants of mountain goats. On one of the long, hot passes, a driver stops to tell us of a spring up ahead, flowing out of the mountain, cold and clear. In the center of most villages, water flows from a simple brass spout or the mouth of an ornate lion, always cold and fresh and good.

We head toward a national game reserve on a twelve-plus percent grade, the road so steep that it's difficult to hold our bikes when we rest. Before the end of the day, I start pushing mine on foot although Clarke shows less sense by continuing to pedal. "It's right there," he points for the tenth time. "We can't stop until we get there," he continues, panting. "There's no place else to stay."

Fatigued and nutritionally depleted, we take longer and longer breaks. Once, while we droop over our bikes, a pre-teen boy streaks past on an old ten-speed bicycle, headed for the top. Twenty minutes later, he races back down toward Ubrique, now fading into evening shadows, greeting us with a wave and taking out the curves in the road without slowing. Clarke and I look at each other, miserable, slumping down farther on our handlebars.

After two more kilometers, we hide behind a big boulder at the edge of the reserve and write letters before dinner, exhausted but proud of our day's progress. Clarke is unpacking pans when we hear gunfire from nearby hunters. "You're okay where you are if you keep your head down," he says. "A bullet just whistled over my head."

I continue my letter to Clarke's kids. "I'd rather be shot than ride farther," I respond, keeping my head down.

A herd of goats steps down a worn path, one after the other, in the early evening shadows. Others join from the deep green tangle, moving alongside, each wearing a copper bell that rings into the burnt light of the Andalucían hills. Passing close by, the goats play a song in a chorus of dozens. It ends as it began, with one bell fading into the yellow glow of a hillside farm.

Ubrique sparkles below in a light evening fog. Huddled together, Clarke and I watch the twinkling lights appear gradually in fuzzy pinpoints on the mountain across the valley, then in the safety of darkness, pitch our tent and sleep.

As usual the first to wake up, Clarke pokes his head out of the tent flap. "Sleep in if you like," he tells my dead body, "we're fog bound." I wake again in time for a hot breakfast of fried potatoes, green peppers and onions, orange juice, bread and yogurt. Shivering as Clarke opens the flap to pull his packs outside, I add long riding pants over my Spandex shorts and a sweatshirt over my t-shirt.

I always keep my panniers neatly packed on my side of the tent in a certain order. Before I go to sleep, my clothes for the next day—usually the same ones I've just taken off—are carefully folded on top of my panniers. I never have to think in the morning. Clarke, on the other hand, never packs his panniers the same way twice, and his side of the tent turns into a jumble of loose gear every night as he empties his packs looking for a spatula or his camera. Each morning, he repacks his panniers from scratch; it gives him something to do while I grab my extra ten winks. "I don't understand why that doesn't drive you nuts," I remark as he returns to the tent for another armload.

"It doesn't," he answers, sarcastic. "Is that okay with you?"

The fog lifts enough to find the road by the time we bundle our fog-drenched tent into its nylon cover. My knees stiff from the cold and humidity, I look forward to cycling to warm them and me. Clarke leads, disappearing instantly into the mist, and we ride enveloped in individual cocoons of thick, silent fog, only a few feet of road and our own bicycle tires visible to each of us. The clouds damp all noise to silence; all we can hear are our own hearts beating, and we float through the forest primeval on top of the earth, shrouded in white, cold mystery.

The cloud pulls back into the forest, trailing wispy white fingers through the trees. Ahead, the thick fog undulates along the contours of the mountain and valleys, moving and changing shape at the whim of the breezes. When the sun finally breaks through, we pedal straight into the cloud, surrounded by sparkling bright mist; it's like riding into white light and it feels like flying.

All morning, we cycle with the clouds through the woods, chasing them east toward the sea. Slowly, the fog burns off, leaving bits and pieces that float in the air and hang on the pines like spun glass. Then it's gone. We've stripped off our extra clothes as the forest stripped itself of fog, layer by layer.

The sun colors the sky azure as we pedal higher and higher to Cortes de la Frontera, tucked on a mountaintop like a star, then scream down the other side in an exhilarating dash to the valley below. As Clarke leans into a fifty-kilometer-an-hour turn, he hears a scraping noise on his front tire. His left pannier is rubbing, pulling hard on its straps to get free. "Stop!" he hollers, and brakes, front and back, leaning left to keep the pack straps out of his spokes. A bolt has worked loose in the rack that holds his panniers, and while Clarke unloads his front rack to replace the bolt, I enjoy the view and the warm sunshine. Bright white villages cling to the mountain ridges in clusters of whitewashed walls capped with ocher tile and the hillsides are dotted with flocks of sheep and goats, their bells tiny wind chimes in the distance.

The rack mended, we're back on the road, plunging down to the valley and the local train station. We stop then and look up, surrounded by peaks that tower above the valley floor, dwarfed by the scenery and by the hundreds of years that these villages, these people, these goats and sheep, have been a part of this life. Little has changed over the centuries. "How far is it from here to the mountaintops?" I ask.

Clarke consults the map. "About thirteen or fourteen hundred meters, I'd guess."

"How far in feet?"

"About four thousand. Multiply the meters by three; that's close enough."

The metric system is beginning to make sense. I can think in kilometers now—in fact, I prefer them to miles because they're shorter. Clarke still thinks in miles. Not surprisingly, we've both adjusted to weights and measures quickly because food is at stake. A thousand grams is a kilo, a kilo 2.2 pounds. A liter is just over a quart.

It's hot now, the cold morning fog a faraway memory. We cycle up the next mountain, out of the valley, winding slowly up and up, drawn to the top of the mountain like beads on a string. Drenched in sweat, the sun burns our already-tanned faces and arms as I take off my helmet to let the slight breeze from my movement cool my head and dry my hair. We cross a stream that churns and bubbles down the mountainside. "Want a bath?" Clarke asks as he looks over the side.

Arms full of towels and lunch, we lock our bikes to the bridge and climb down through the barbed wire fence to a river of pools and tiny waterfalls made by large boulders; we strip and scrub, gasping at the cold on our hot skin as we wash each other's hair, alive once again after being baked to a stupor. Clarke washes his clothes and lays them on the rocks to dry. I wash mine also, then dress to enjoy the cold wetness on my skin. Sitting close together on the rocks, we eat lunch–melted chocolate croissants, white cheese and big fresh strawberries, red and sweet. "That was the most wonderful bath of my life." I nuzzle Clarke's bare arm with my cheek. "Ouch! Your skin's hot." Shaking my wet hair, I spray his chest with a shower of water that evaporates immediately.

Trying to stretch the memory of the cold bath into the long, hot afternoon, I'm partly successful until my hair dries into a tangle of curls; then it burns my fingers when I touch it and sweat drips in my eyes and down my back as the road twists and turns in steep switchbacks, following the mountain contours. "I can't even breathe, Clarke. I have to walk."

Clarke pedals laboriously ahead, then waits when he needs a break. I ride, then walk two hundred steps, then ride again, my head down, the view forgotten, thinking only of reaching the top or of stopping for the day, whichever comes first.

We arrive in Gaucin, another village hanging in the sky, at happy hour, stopping for a cold beer and olives before deciding to ride down the mountain that evening. Clarke doesn't like to ride downhill in the cold mornings because his muscles don't warm up fast enough, and I just want the thrill of the plunge as a reward for my afternoon's work.

Falling off the mountain, we spin down and down like fall leaves in the wind. Abruptly, the highway stops. Asphalt lies in chunks across the road, and we skid to a stop just short of the tangled hunks of rock and road, then pick our way through the unmarked construction, hearts pounding. All the way down the steep mountain, the road is interrupted by non-road. That's the last time we'll ride downhill, all out, in a freefall, we decide—at least until the next day.

At the bottom, there's a clean, wide river, but all of the land is fenced. We can see a farm on the road up the third mountain of the day. "That's our only chance for tonight, isn't it?" I ask, massaging my swollen knees.

"Looks like it," Clarke answers, studying the map. "I'm tired too. Let's take it easy."

The leftover heat is manageable and we concentrate only on the steep grade, grinding up the mountain in our lowest gears, hardly moving. My knees throb and I'm short of breath. Turn after turn, up and up we twist to the hillside farm, but the gate is locked with a *"no intrusión"* sign. "Maybe there's another farm around the corner," Clarke says hopefully. "I thought I saw something around the next turn."

I've been focused on my front tire, on pushing down my pedals one more revolution, and then one more. I've seen nothing. "I'll walk from here. I'm not even sure I can push my bike." Why haven't we started somewhere flat, like Holland?

Clarke soon returns on foot. "There's a farm ahead with no gate. Here, let me take your bike. You look beat."

We walk together to the little farm and enter the yard as a young woman comes outside with three curious children hanging on to her skirts. No power or telephone poles connect this house to anything; there aren't even tire tracks in the dirt yard, only hoofprints. Two horses with neck bells watch as I ask in Spanish if we can stay in the field for the night. The woman nods shyly. *"Muchas gracias, señora,"* I smile, wishing I knew how to say more.

The children watch from a distance as we pitch our tent alongside the horses, goats, chickens, pigs and dogs, which all roam freely in the yard. After dinner, we crawl into our sleeping bags, but tired as we are, can't sleep because the horses graze by the tent most of the night; their bells, which jingle as they move their heads, alternate with the sound of their ripping up the short, coarse grass and the periodic thump of their hobbled front legs as they hop forward between bites.

Well before dawn, the roosters wake us up with the chickens. As Clarke goes up the hill with a handful of toilet paper and a plastic bag, I try to pack my bike but give it up quickly when half a dozen pigs decide on Clarke's packs for breakfast. They work as a team. As I chase two or three squealers from the panniers, others rush the packs from behind. One nibbles on Clarke's pedals and handlebar grips, rolling its eyes to keep my position in sight, then trots off grunting before I get close enough to tackle it. It doubles back as I chase away the main group again, all of us squealing, and snatches our trash sack. Holding it high in victory, the quarterback pig trots proudly off in an end run into the woods for a touchdown. Its buddies follow. I watch them go, hands on my hips, as Clarke returns laughing; he's seen the whole second quarter from the hill.

As we cinch up the bikes, the woman and her children come out of the house to wave goodbye. *"Adios,"* she calls as we pedal toward the road. *"Vaya con Dios."* The children wave, and we stop and wave back one more time.

The map shows a series of switchbacks to the crest of the mountain; from that point, the road plummets to the sea. At the top of the exposed crestline highway, we discover a strong crosswind mixed with light, chilling mist. Over and over, the wind blows me toward the edge of the narrow road; once, a strong gust knocks me over and I'm just able to catch myself with a foot before toppling down the mountain. Horrified at the close call, I'm struck inanimate by the force of the wind, unable to get back on my bike. "Let's go!" Clarke shouts.

My voice trembles. "I'll fall off the mountain!"

Clarke studies my face. "We've got to keep moving or we'll lose body heat – then we'll really be in trouble."

"I'll walk."

"Then I'll walk with you," he says gently, supporting any decision that means getting off the dangerous road.

Occasionally, the sun breaks through the cloudcast, quickly moving across the narrow highway like a spotlight, and the misty sky glows a luminous gold as sun searchlights sweep over the choppy water far below. Finally, we're off the hogback, dropping down through villages to the coast, to Gibraltar.

For days, we've discussed Clarke's desire and my reluctance to see Morocco, but he can't be dissuaded. Stopping to check ferry prices to North Africa, we check in at the first campground at San Luis de Sabinillas, ready for hot showers. Disappointed that we can't buy tokens for hot water except during certain office hours, we settle into our tent to cook veggies, jealous of our neighbors' sizzling barbecue. As the loud party continues late into the night, we decide that a stone washboard and toilets probably aren't worth the price of commercial camping, particularly since the Moroccan-style toilets are like standing in a porcelain shower with the drain screen removed. That's it. There isn't even any toilet paper.

Chapter 3

Although Clarke wants to see Morocco badly, I don't want to see it at all. I've heard of the hustlers, the robberies, the anger that erupts when travelers refuse to be part of the system. I've heard how Moroccans treat women, of the unsafe roads, of the corruption. Towns are far apart, drugs close together. I feel vulnerable, much too vulnerable, as a woman, as an American, as a bicyclist with everything I own in plain view. I feel as unprotected as the underbelly of a small wooly animal under the paw of a tiger.

As we wait at the Algeciras dock for the ferry to North Africa, I hang back. "I hope you know how much I don't want to do this," I say. Clarke doesn't respond. We've both said all there is to say on the subject, before we left America and in the evenings coming down the coast.

It's nearly dusk when we arrive at the Moroccan border south of Ceuta, a Spanish holding on the tip of Africa, taking our places behind a long line of dusty cars and pedestrians. "Welcome to Morocco!" We spin around at a booming voice speaking perfect English. It belongs to a huge, beefy Arab wearing a long brown robe and pointed white floppy slippers. "I am Hamid, from the Ministry of Tourism, and it is my job to make sure that you have a pleasant stay in Morocco. Sir, bring your passports and come with me. You, lady, wait over here. Do not take your eyes from your belongings."

Clarke and Hamid disappear into the crowd. I wait nervously, eyes darting from our bikes to where I've last seen Clarke, then to the streams of people walking into Morocco from Ceuta. The women wear long robes head to ankle, scarves covering everything but their downcast eyes, backs bent forward under bulging cloth bundles.

Not one woman looks at me; all the men do. Many men wear the caftans called *djellabas*; others wear Western clothes, including American t-shirts.

The light has almost drained from the sky when Clarke and Hamid return. Gesturing wildly, Hamid towers over Clarke, his face set in earnest folds. "No, you cannot bicycle into Tetouan at night," he is saying. "The roads are unsafe. Let me get you a taxi for two hundred *dirhams*."

"We can't afford twenty-five dollars for a cab," I rush to respond, my fear of Morocco momentarily outweighed by my fear of running out of money.

Hamid smiles sadly and melts into the crowd for a few moments, then returns as if bearing a great gift. "I found a good friend who will take you to town for one hundred *dirhams*, as a favor to me." Clarke and I look at each other and shrug, not knowing what else to do but accept. At the taxi stand, other drivers join to push our panniers into the trunk of the cab and to lash our bicycles on top as Hamid stuffs himself into the front passenger seat, filling more than his side of the old Mercedes. Turning, he speaks with the voice of a heavyweight boxer. "I will show you my city—only if you like, of course," he adds as the car bolts on to the highway and Clarke and I slide across the cracked leather seat, grabbing for armrests long ago clawed away by other hands.

The slender driver argues with Hamid in Arabic, looking at his friend instead of at the road while Clarke and I watch for approaching headlights. After an oncoming car swerves off the road, blasting its horn, Hamid finally makes a plea or a threat to the driver, who briefly looks back at the road before continuing his conversation, arms waving for emphasis.

Between horse carts and headlights, we race for the ancient border city. At the city square, Clarke exchanges travelers' checks into Moroccan *dirhams*, then hurries back to the smiling taxi driver and asks Hamid what the custom is for tipping. "If you like, then tip what you want," explains Hamid. Clarke looks at the reckless driver, then stuffs the change back into his pocket while Hamid rings for the manager of a small *pensione*.

After a few words of negotiation, bikes and packs and bicyclists bundle up the spiral marble stairs, forty feet over the plaza, third floor landing, first door to the right. Hamid carries only the empty food pack, straining and puffing his considerable weight up the stairs into our room, where he flops on the only chair and demands coffee from the manager, removing a cigarette from a pocket under his robe.

Our room is modest but only fifty *dirhams*, a little over six dollars, which includes one shower each. At Hamid's bellowing summons, the manager trots up the stairs with a wrench to turn on the communal bathroom's gas-fired boiler with a smack on the steel case and a turn of the valve. Warmish water dribbles from the rusty showerhead and Clarke and I duck under, one after the other, then wipe off most of our dirt with our dirty towel and leave muddy footprints on the dirty floor as we walk barefoot back to our tiny room to join Hamid for a tour of the city.

Tetouan is like a shoebox of junk jewelry, tangled heaps of rhinestones and beads of every color and size winding without end. Turning the colored ball of beads over and over, it always looks the same, flickering colors and shapes in the light. If an end is found and pulled, the rest of the jewelry seems to tangle in a knot, protecting itself from examination.

Matching the giant strides of Hamid through the streets to the *medina*—the old part of town, the walled city, the marketplace—feels like jumping into the shoebox. Shapes and colors whirl about and strings of white lights loop in long spans overhead. Signs in Arabic symbols speak, but we're deaf to their language. The sound of many voices speaking Arabic is like looking into a kaleidoscope of tiny glass pieces, like hearing shapes and colors instead of words.

Dark faces like bright-eyed hand puppets in dark *djellaba* robes bob and dip as we scurry down the crowded, noisy streets, trailing Hamid through one of the seven gates to the seven-hundred-and-fifty-year-old *medina*, a mouse maze of tiny streets and alleys so intricate and confusing that we're instantly lost. The miniature passageways hold hundreds of workshops. Tapping and light spills from every window, and through every door reverberates hammering and clinking as male artisans fashion leather into belts and shoes and purses and jackets, copper and brass into lamps and plates and figures and jewelry, wool and cotton into dresses and *djellabas* and shirts. The *medina* is a giant flea market, jumbled and tangled and without sense.

This is not to be a stroll through the *medina*, however; Hamid has a destination in mind. Making two more turns through cobblestone streets narrow enough to touch the buildings on both sides if we stretch out our arms, he turns to us. "You are lucky. Today is a very special market day in Tetouan. I want you to see our government's rural cooperative," he booms in his Ministry of Tourism voice. "It represents fifteen hundred mountain families."

Climbing several flights of narrow, dark stairs laid with tiny, worn mosaic tiles, he leads us to a large room with walls hung with ancient carpets and rolls and rolls of new rugs stacked around the edges. We're told to sit on an old couch and are served hot mint tea in small glasses with three sugar cubes. "Moroccans like their tea very sweet," explains a man named Mohammed. "I am here to assist you," he continues. "Hamid will return shortly."

With an assistant, Mohammed choreographs a display of carpets, made of cashmere, merino wool and silk in intricate designs of every conceivable shade of blue and red and green and peach and brown. Pressure to buy is intense, the techniques sophisticated and creative. "We're sorry, Mohammed, we're not here to buy one of your rugs. We have very little money and all of it is going for our bicycle trip," Clarke explains every way he can.

"Then buy two and sell one at a huge profit to pay for your journey," urges Mohammed as he counters our no-offer with a price reduction to tempt us. It doesn't. "You drive a hard bargain," Mohammed smiles. "I like you, you make me work hard. Look, this is the best I can do. These two rugs for half the price of one, nine thousand *dirhams*. And my government will pay shipping to your home."

Clarke laughs. "We don't have a home."

The bargaining is over. Hamid magically appears, trailed by a handsome youth. "I must return to my home," he says coolly. "My cousin Mustapha will see that you arrive at your hotel safely."

As we twist and turn back through the mazy *medina*, I ask Mustapha if he's really Hamid's cousin. He shrugs. "In Morocco, everyone is a cousin." The young man explains that he's a geography student at the university. His English, like Hamid's, is perfect, and he politely inquires about our travel plans in his country.

"After we buy food in the morning," Clarke explains, "we will ride south toward Fès."

"If you like," offers the boy, "I will pick you up at nine o'clock tomorrow and show you where the market is." We accept gratefully.

Clarke and I climb the stairs to our room. "Morocco is just as bizarre as I thought," he exclaims happily.

"I feel a lot better than I thought I would," I admit.

After a good sleep in real if somewhat lumpy iron beds, we emerge from the hotel in the morning to find, instead of Mustapha, an army of hustlers. News travels fast in Tetouan. "You're the Americans on bicycles," we're told. "Mustapha isn't coming."

"How do you know?" I'm instantly suspicious, my fear of Morocco awakening after a night's sleep.

"He would be here by now," the hustlers say simply. I try to brush the young men away, to ignore them, but they press closer. "Do you think Hamid took you to the *medina* last night as a friend? He wanted a commission if you bought a rug. Didn't he leave when you didn't?" The hustlers know as much about us in Morocco as we do. Half a dozen of them try to convince us that they're different from Hamid and Mustapha, that they just want to be our friends or to practice their English.

"Your English is already fine," Clarke tells them, steering me toward the *medina*, memorizing every turn, hoping to meet Mustapha on the way. The hustlers follow in dribs and drabs.

The food market is easy to find. Dark-skinned vendors stand behind long wooden tables stacked high with a rainbow of produce. In addition to vegetables and fruits, the stalls sell meat, fish, live poultry, cheese, eggs, nuts and spices. Colors and textures and smells engulf us as we walk crookedly through the stalls and tables and vendors sitting on the ground. A toothless old man squatting against a wall sells Clarke eggs and tries to keep the change; we also buy oranges and strawberries, bok choy and green peppers and bread. The hustlers have followed us into the market and watch with amusement as we bargain, making sure that the food vendors see them so that they can collect their commissions.

Once, as we haggle over the price of tomatoes, Clarke jerks away to my left. I turn quickly, certain that he's been kidnapped. Sure enough, Clarke's eyes widen as he finds himself stolen by a burro carrying a wide load of sticks that have impaled his shirt. He trots sideways down the street with the burro, squeezing past the bananas, the green peppers, the fish—until he makes enough ruckus that the burro's owner stops, surprised, allowing him to wiggle free of his sticky friend. His shirt gaping open from a large tear that exposes a bloody gash, Clarke struggles to look dignified as he walks back to me. Chuckling, I finish buying our tomatoes and we walk on.

Mustapha catches up with us a block from the hotel. "Please forgive me. I overslept because I stayed up late to study last night."

"We'd like to ask you about our route to Fès," Clarke says.

Mustapha leads the way to the Café Nationale, a small restaurant that appears to be frequented by important local men. "Why aren't there any women here?" I ask just inside the entrance.

"Moroccan women," Mustapha explains, "are not permitted inside. They must sit outside on the curb or go home." Clarke and I wince; Mustapha looks embarrassed. "We are not progressive like your own country."

As we crowd around a tiny table, a tall waiter greets Mustapha by name and brings an inch of thick, hot coffee in small glasses on saucers holding three sugar cubes, then fills the glasses with steaming hot milk from a pitcher. I study Mustapha as I sip the strong coffee; a handsome young man with curly black hair, he seems well bred and at ease with himself, with none of the frantic quality of the hustlers. He must be one of the few who doesn't need money, I think, beginning to trust Mustapha's open face and thoughtful eyes. Clarke spreads out our Moroccan map as the waiter politely backs away with the empty glasses. "We plan to go south to Fès, through the Rif Mountains."

"I would not advise it," Mustapha says quickly. "The roads are very steep and the villages are far apart. It is not safe to camp in Morocco – the campgrounds are deserted now. No, you should go west to the Atlantic, to Tangier, and down the coast to Kenitra. There are many small villages with safe *pensiones* along the way. Then turn inland to Fès."

"I'm nervous about being in Morocco," I admit.

"It is a country that is not always safe," Mustapha agrees, looking at me carefully. "Do not talk to anyone, do not even look at anyone's eyes. Be careful of your money and watch your bicycles every minute. When you return to Tetouan, call me at home or leave a note here with my friend," he gestures toward the tall waiter. "My parents and I would like to have you as guests in our home for a few days."

With detailed instructions on how to find the highway west toward Tangier, we return to the hotel to shuttle our bicycles to the street, leaving Tetouan at noon, me wearing long pants and a long-sleeved shirt as advised by our guidebook. The scenery is wild and beautiful but we miss our turn toward the coastal villages. "Let's not go back to Tetouan," I say when we discover our error. "I feel safer in the countryside."

"I'm sure we can find a secondary route that cuts across to the west."

As it turns out, there are no roads west and the nearest village is Chechaouen, sixty-five kilometers into the Rif Mountains, where Mustapha told us not to go. As we pedal up a desolate mountain pass, dope peddlers appear from the folds of the hills, in rusted-out vans or on bare feet, insisting that we buy, following us slowly up the steep road, screaming and shaking their fists because we won't. Each time we stop to rest on the steep grades, dusty men spit Arabic threats from the roadside. My fear rises at each encounter.

Then the children appear, moving swiftly down through the rocks as if the trees themselves have come alive, starting and stopping to arrive at the highway as we approach, waving their arms like skinny branches. They demand candy and cigarettes, which we don't have, then block the road and chase the bicycles, screaming and spitting and throwing sticks and rocks. Up the steep hills, they can easily keep up with our heavy bikes. I try to regain my sense of proportion by thinking up another postcard from hell, as I now call them, something about one of us being murdered by a five-year-old. It isn't funny.

Three boys step into the road in front of us. "Don't stop, Susan," Clarke warns. As I pedal through the children, one throws stones at Clarke, then runs after his bike, yanking it with both hands, screaming. A tour bus approaches from behind. Clarke turns as the driver stares open-mouthed, brakes squealing. Finally, the boy releases his grip and falls along the roadside as the bus roars past, honking.

We pedal as hard and fast as we can in the stifling heat, up the long, steep hills, afraid to rest, dreading each bend in the road, powering our bicycles with the adrenaline of fear and anger. My knees ache and my heart literally hurts. Short of breath, I try to exhale fear, to inhale strength. It doesn't work.

Around a long curve, three little girls sit in the rocks near a small flock of sheep. Shiny black hair tumbles over their shoulders and each wears a dress of brilliant red. I wave hesitantly and pass, followed by a stream of obscenities, spit and rocks as their beautiful faces transform into masks of hatred. It's my final straw: my camel dies of a broken back and a broken heart, and my fear of Morocco shatters me into a thousand pieces. And this is only the preview, the short subject, the newsreel.

The main feature begins at the turnoff to Chechaouen, a mountaintop village, home of the Berbers, at the end of a steep five-kilometer road off the main highway through the Rif Mountains. Exhausted, afraid, confused and angry, we've pedaled sixty very steep kilometers in four hours. Stopping a young Arab traveling toward Tetouan, we ask in fumbling French and Spanish about the children. "Just kick them away," he advises, dismissing us.

Enough. Time out. We turn up the road to Chechaouen, determined to hitchhike with the first truck up the hill, drug dealers or bandits welcome to apply, no one over the age of fifteen refused. We'll take our chances with the adults; we can't bear to encounter another violent child.

There aren't any trucks on the road, but there are children, dozens of boys swimming in the river that winds down from the village. Around the first turn, a teenager threatens us with a long knife. Clarke glances from the teenager to the boy's companion, then back at the first young man. "Hold my bike, Susan," he orders, dismounting. Walking slowly toward the boys, his eyes never leave those of the teenager clutching the knife. "What do you intend to do with that?" he asks in English as the distance closes between them. The boy looks for a long moment into Clarke's eyes and then turns away sullenly and motions his friend to follow him back down the hill. As Clarke strides back to me, I let out a long breath and relinquish his bicycle in silence. I have no words.

Within moments, we're surrounded by a group of young boys who have been watching from the river. Perhaps intimidated by Clarke's actions, they demand nothing and follow us up the hill. Too hot, too tired and too drained to pedal up the steep grade, we push our hundred-pound bikes on foot. Clarke asks the boys to help and they respond eagerly, rolling the bikes uphill with ease. I relax, grateful, and they take over my bicycle completely as I chatter in English and Spanish and they respond in Arabic and French. Clarke walks ahead, a Pied Piper surrounded by his own mice, climbing slowly in the blistering sun. Other boys join us until there are twenty or thirty, moving in clusters up the mountain like bees around two honey hives. I wonder where the girls are.

One boy tries to ride my bike, then another plays with the freewheel shifter while another flicks the chain ring shifter up and down. Suddenly, the boys swarm all over my bicycle, examining this, playing with that. "No, *basta*, enough! Leave it alone," I plead in English and Spanish. Faster and faster, my bike moves up the hill. Then the boys begin to paw my body, insistently running their hands over my thighs and buttocks. Distracted, I push the boys away angrily as my bike disappears up ahead in a mass of running boys. Imagining it at the bottom of a cliff, broken and stripped, unable to take me out of Morocco, I run in pursuit, screaming. Clarke is too far ahead to hear me, smart enough to keep a firm grip on his own bike.

A villager walking down from town assesses the situation in a glance and commands the boys to stop. As I retrieve my bike with trembling hands, the man yells at me for letting the children touch my belongings. They've been opening my packs, he explains, looking for money. It's then that I notice the boys all have pockets full of stones.

The dark lobby of intricately-designed mosaic tile is cool and safe. We sit in a low, cushioned booth around a large square table, drinking cold soft drinks and talking quietly with Mohammed, a young man who with two companions had pushed and carried the bicycles through steep streets and long flights of stairs to the center of Chechaouen. Mohammed explains about the children. "The Americans started giving cigarettes and coins to the youngsters. Now the children expect gifts from all tourists, and if they do not receive them, the youngsters are very angry." He waves a hand in dismissal. "Pay them no mind," he advises.

"That's easier said than done on a bicycle," I snap.

Mohammed looks at me curiously, then turns to Clarke. "You should not bicycle in Morocco," he said, "especially with a woman. The roads are too dangerous, too lonely. But you are here, and with your wife." After a short pause, he continues, "I advise you to continue by bus, particularly if you are traveling south to Fès. And never stay in campgrounds. Trust no one." He pauses to light a cigarette. "I know every person in my village, but I do not trust one." Mohammed looks at Clarke sternly and inhales deeply.

"I can't imagine living without trust," Clarke says softly. "What is it like?"

Mohammed shrugs. "It is the way everyone lives in Morocco."

For less than four dollars, we have twin beds in a second-floor room overlooking a narrow street, the bathroom and drizzly shower on the first floor across the lobby. I slump on one of the beds and look outside the high, tiled window, my heart crumpled and beaten, my mind ground to a halt. It's dusk, and the sounds outside seem like the sounds of any village – children playing before dinner, women returning from market leading burden-laden burros, men calling greetings in Arabic. The late afternoon sun drapes a soft golden shawl on a whitewashed maze of alleys and streets and doorways of every shape and size. White goats and old black Mercedes compete for street space, and everywhere I feel mystery and intrigue and a way of life that is foreign to my spirit. It doesn't compute.

Clarke stands at the window with his own thoughts. Children to him, I know, are humanity in its highest form – was today Morocco at its best? What kind of a system teaches hate to seven-year-olds? He too is shattered, struck ragged; we share our confusion without words. Tears of frustration and exhaustion roll down my face then, and Clarke reaches over to hold me, stroking my hair. All the life has drained out of me. "I hated today, Clarke. This was the worst day of my life. I'm sorry, but I can't bicycle here anymore."

"I can't either, Susan. Rest now. We can make plans after dinner."

Placing our one-burner camp stove on the window ledge, Clarke prepares a simple meal while I stare at the ceiling, arms crossed under my head, wondering how we'll get out of Morocco and wanting not to be there while we do. As we eat, we try to make sense of a country that seems to be based on fear, mistrust and manipulation. We find no answers, only questions. I make one decision. "I won't support this awful system by buying cigarettes for children," I declare. Clarke agrees. Talked out, our emotions shredded, we chain the bikes to our iron beds and drift into a restless sleep.

I'm already awake when Clarke stirs as the five o'clock Muslim call to prayer filters with the first yellow rays of the morning sun through the high window. The chanting is beautiful, full of mystery, an intertwining of two voices, alternating each with the other between free-form melody and a long, pure note that moves up and down the scale. "What does this religion offer these people?" Clarke wonders aloud. I can't answer.

We agree to rest for a day in Chechaouen before deciding whether to return to Tetouan or to go on to Fès by bus. Leaving for the market early, careful not to look at anyone, we find our way by following three live chickens swinging by their feet from the hand of a woman whose fingers and palms are stained black and yellow with dye.

The open market is large and busy, and we buy a pound each of potatoes, squash, tomatoes, onions, carrots, bread and oranges, all for fifty cents, discovering later that the beautiful oranges for which we'd negotiated were exchanged by the vendor for shrunken, moldy ones. Returning to the hotel, we find Mohammed in the lobby. "We've decided to return by bus to Tetouan," Clarke tells him. "We have an invitation to stay with a family there, and then we will return to Spain."

Mohammed shrugs. "Come, I will take you to buy your tickets." Escorting us through the small *medina* of Chechaouen, he says, "You are lucky. Today is a very special market day." Clarke and I wink at each other, but Mohammed seems unconcerned that we have no interest in buying the pretty local rugs. He hails a man on the street who slips money into his hand and walks on without explanation. "The *medinas* are the old parts of each village," he says instead, "where the poor people live. See this rounded doorway? It means that many families live here. A square doorway signifies only one or two." Mohammed walks a few more steps. "Most of the entrances are painted pale blue, like snow, for coolness in summer and because it keeps away the mosquitoes."

At an open doorway in the center of a long, white wall, Mohammed stops. The sign above it is in Arabic symbols; inside is a single wooden desk covered with dust and a few papers. Mohammed argues with the bus station agent in Arabic. "What's he saying, Mohammed?" Clarke finally asks.

"He is trying to cheat you. It is good that I am here to help you." Mohammed hands Clarke two scraps of paper with Arabic scribbles. "The price for each of you to Tetouan is ten *dirhams*. Your bicycles will cost thirty-five for both, which includes loading and unloading here and in Tetouan. You will leave at eight in the morning." A dollar and a quarter each, plus four-fifty for our bicycles, is a small price to pay to have metal and glass between us and the children.

In the morning, everyone in the village except Mohammed seems to be at the bus station, a large bare lot below the police station. While we wait, a man chases a small boy through the street, unnoticed by the crowd; the boy's swollen face is black and blue. Eventually, a cranky old bus sputters into the yard and we watch as the bikes are loaded under cargo netting on top next to several large woven baskets; then Clarke relays me and our packs inside the already-crowded bus and we stow our panniers wherever we can, under seats, overhead—wherever we can keep them in sight.

The baggage handler boards to collect a five-*dirham* baggage charge for the two bicycles. Clarke, between two Moroccans in dark brown *djellabas*, turns to me, two rows back on the rear bench with five men, on the end seat by the emergency door. We've already paid thirty-five *dirhams* to the station agent and presumably Mohammed, based on the amount we've been overcharged. "Collect your fee from him," Clarke gestures toward the agent outside the bus. The baggage handler shakes his fist and pounds off the bus and onto its roof, and I imagine our bikes sailing through the air to the cobblestone street, whisked away to be sold on the black market in Tetouan for enough money to support a large family for a year. The bus lurches forward before either of us can protest, and in three shocking minutes, we screech down the five-kilometer stretch of twelve-plus percent grade that had taken us ninety minutes to walk up.

I've apparently chosen the seat normally occupied by the rear door guard. He squeezes in anyway, and six men and I string across the five-person bench like squashed brown berries. At unscheduled intervals, we slow to a halt and the door guard opens the back door with a screwdriver, collecting *dirhams* instead of tickets and allowing more people on the overcrowded bus. At several posted stops, the driver passes without slowing, leaving ticketed passengers shaking their fists into a tunnel of dirt. Once, an attractive young woman boards at the back. There are nods from both sides but no money or ticket changes hands.

The man next to Clarke holds a cigarette in his mouth for twenty minutes. Then he lights it. The smoke hangs along the hooded edge of his skeletal face; he stares straight ahead. Then he smears the butt into the metal seatback and lets it fall from his fingers into his lap as Arab music weaves through the passenger seats from the front.

When the police stop the bus, Clarke and I exchange glances as the door guard motions us to be quiet and scrambles to the roof to bring down two flapping chickens by their feet. They're soon in the hands of the proper authorities and we continue on our bumpy way down the mountain.

The crotchety old bus finally shifts through Tetouan and arrives at a real bus station, our bicycles intact. Grateful, Clarke pays the baggage handler five *dirhams* while I watch another man unload woven baskets full of live and suffocating chickens. Moroccans mill about, inspecting our bikes and panniers with interest; packing quickly, we discover that the panniers at the bottom of the heap are sitting in vomit.

Unwilling to push our luck any farther, we hurry to the *pensione* where we stayed before, hoping to lock up the bikes in our room while we look for Mustapha. I want to meet his mother; I've not spoken to one Moroccan woman. Mustapha is out of the city, we are told, and we wait for his return for three days. Our room rate is twenty-five percent less than when we arrived with Hamid.

After leaving a message for Mustapha at the Café Nationale, we cook with bottled water because the water in the hotel is turned off. The next night, we eat half-raw rice and vegetables after running out of camping gas in the middle of cooking our meal. The third, we eat in a restaurant; the most expensive item on the menu is two dollars.

The first day, we stay in our room, using Mustapha's awaited phone call as an excuse; in reality, we aren't up to the hustlers. Disappointed that Mustapha doesn't call, that we might miss the other Morocco for which we long—if indeed it does exist—and feeling trapped in the tiny room, we take out our frustrations on each other. Once, Clarke throws a wet orange at me, gooping up my shirt and shorts with sticky juice; I pull off my clothes in a rage, wash them in the sink and hang them dripping on wall pegs.

We walk the streets the next day, eluding the hustlers by telling them that we aren't shopping. When I notice a small boy carrying a baby goat, his friend takes the animal and deposits it in my arms, smiling. Surprised, I hug the smelly little animal before handing it back, smiling in return. Neither boy asks for a handout.

The fight starts during our restaurant dinner the third night. We've let go of a lot of American trappings on this trip, and the adjustment has been difficult and time-consuming. "Listen, Clarke," I say earnestly as I sip mint tea, "we've learned a lot about ourselves and our ability to cope with a huge physical challenge. At least I have. We can focus and get the job done, and both give a hundred percent. But we don't have the time or the energy to concentrate on each other anymore. Can't this trip be fun too?"

"Just what would you like to eliminate from the day, Susan? Planning our route? Finding a place to sleep? Getting water or shopping for food? Eating, perhaps? Look, you're the one who had to bring a computer along to keep a journal. I'll gladly ship it home."

The conversation gets louder as we walk back to the hotel. The fear of Morocco has blown the stress of bicycling way out of proportion. "Why can't we ever just slow down?" I ask. "I hate it when we do laundry or bathe—you make us bicycle that much longer those days. You're obsessed with moving, all day, seven days a week. All you care about is miles!" Tears come to my eyes. I won't give up, or in. "One of the reasons I married you was because you were so romantic. We used to talk all night sometimes. We're newlyweds, for heaven's sake. Don't you miss that?"

"No. I'm into other things now. There's so much happening that I can't ask my life to be the way it was."

"Well, I feel like your Boy Scout buddy and I don't like it at all!"

Our nerves raw from the week, we reiterate our positions over and over, and at two-thirty in the morning, run out of words. There's nothing left to do but sleep.

At dawn, empty and lonely and unwilling to reach out for each other, we stagger out of bed to leave Morocco. It's a cold and gray day that matches our moods. Clarke goes for a taxi while I guard our packs and the bikes, dismantled for the thirty-five kilometer drive because we refuse to bicycle to the border. Clarke returns with an eighty-*dirham* quote for us and the luggage—again, twenty-five percent less than when Hamid brought us in for "half-price." An Arab in his early thirties loiters at the hotel door. "How much money do you want from me today?" Clarke snaps.

"You are my friend, I will help you for nothing," he responds. "I will get a taxi to come pick you up here."

"Then come on," Clarke says and they walk together toward the taxi stand, returning with a cab. As we load the car, the Arab tells Clarke that the driver wants another twenty *dirhams* for the luggage. "I already negotiated the price of eighty *dirhams*," Clarke responds. "That's all he gets and I'll pay him myself."

"The driver won't take you at all, then. He will throw your bags on the street." Ignoring him, Clarke pays the driver. "Give me ten *dirhams* for my help," the man demands.

"I thought you were helping as our friend," Clarke mimics. Unabashed, the man insists on payment. Clarke offers him five *dirhams*, easily a day's food.

"Fuck you, American," the man screams, throwing the coin on the street as he rips into a string of curses, calling us every name he can think of, including "*bambino*."

I laugh for the first time in Morocco. "Clarke, '*bambino*' means 'child' in Italian."

"I think you mean '*bandito*,' my friend," Clarke says coldly, eyes twinkling with amusement. As we drive off, a trail of expletives follows the old taxi like red flames.

Relieved to be on our way, able to let go of our fear, we chat with the driver in bits of English, Spanish and French. The man is friendly and kind, underscoring our growing belief that we get back exactly what we put out in life. We tip the grateful driver ten *dirhams*, glad to give instead of being taken from. "If that man in Tetouan had either offered to help for a fee or had truly meant to help for nothing, I would have given him twice what he asked for," Clarke says as we repack our bikes at the border.

As I wait by a low wall next to the sea for Clarke to clear us through Customs, my remaining anger of the night before melts into relief as I prepare to bicycle away from a land of anger and fear and wonder if I'll ever understand what happened to us there.

Chapter 4

During the rough ferry crossing back to Algeciras, we surprise an Arab woman slipping a packet of white powder to a young man who stuffs it into his sock. When the same young man approaches us later, I brace for a threat because we'd seen the drug transaction. Instead, he tries to sell us jeans.

Out of Africa, the relative safety of Spain seems like a warm blanket, but hard rain dampens our spirits and we don cheap fluorescent rain gear, flapping up the steep passes like sloppy orange crows. Back in Gaucin, we flee into a tiny bar for weak hot chocolate, wringing out our jackets in the restroom sinks before going back into the cold wind to make our first phone call to America. Our original plan had been to call my sister and give her the number where she could return our call because it's less expensive to telephone from America and because billing to Jill's phone would eliminate our need to carry heavy coins. In Spain, however, pay phones have no telephone numbers for return calls.

Crowding into a booth with a double fistful of change gathered from the bar, Clarke feeds the hungry beast while I talk as fast as I can. By the time I say, "We're okay, we made it out of Morocco in one piece," the phone is swallowing the last of our *pesetas*. "I love you!" I yell into the dead connection. The phone burps, ten dollars richer, but we have no news from home. Disappointed, we continue in the wind and rain, our rain gear already in tatters.

That evening, we find nowhere to camp on the steep, rocky hills. After starting up yet another mountain pass with no luck, we coast back down and turn onto a dirt road that winds past a discotheque and several *haciendas* with locked gates. "Down there, Susan, over that embankment, is a flat place just big enough." Unloading the bikes in silence, we quietly shuttle everything down the thirty-foot ledge and wait inside someone's fence until dark before making camp.

After dinner, I slip outside to wash dishes with water from our quart bike bottles. The sky has mostly cleared and an almost-full moon floods the valley with silver light, illuminating silhouettes of farms scattered across the landscape. Stars shine like tiny brilliant dots, and the lights of Gaucin across the ridge huddle in a twinkling cluster between the folds of the mountain. The last tatters of my Moroccan fear disintegrate in the moonlight and I crawl into my sleeping bag next to Clarke, two black caterpillars safe in our navy blue tent cocoon.

It's Palm Sunday. Pedaling up a mountain toward Ronda in cold wind, we stop for water. Leaning against an ancient wall listening to goat bells, we spot Algeciras and Gibraltar far below in the misty distance. I stare for a long minute. After seeing with my own eyes how far we've traveled in just two days, in distance and in altitude, I actually believe for the first time that we can bicycle all the way across Europe.

Amazed, I pedal with renewed energy to the top of the pass where a shepherd perches on a wall supervising his tiny flock of three. As we approach, he jumps to greet us with greasy hands full of fresh-fried *churros* and hot coffee, inviting us to stop. We can't resist. Leaning our bikes against a whitewashed wall, we follow the man through bright white streets to a narrow doorway. Inside a small room, three women squeeze batter through a funnel in swirling circles into hot grease, serving the fried dough in white paper.

The only person we see for the next two hours is an old man clutching a handful of wild asparagus as he makes his way in the wind down to a white-walled village as the barren landscape rises to rip the underbelly of the clouds.

About two o'clock, the wind too strong to make much progress, we lean our bicycles against a low wall to fix lunch. As I sit on the wall in my flaming yellow and electric blue jacket, my mouth full of yogurt, the largest bumblebee in the world lands with a thud on my right arm, buzzes around my wrist and trundles up the inside of my sleeve, breathing heavily on my arm. "It's love at first sight," Clarke surmises, looking at my bright jacket with amusement. "Just stay calm."

It's easy to be brave, of course, when there's a forty-pound bee with a twelve-inch stinger stomping up someone else's arm. When the bee emerges, I jump off the wall, unable to restrain myself for another second. Startled, my suitor flies straight at Clarke, who forgets his own advice and flails at the bee with our plastic bag of trash. Whack! He hits it full on, but the bee zzzz's back, heading for Clarke's face like a charging bull trying to eliminate its competition. Whack! It's obvious that the bee won't be discouraged, so Clarke scoops it up mid-charge in an empty yogurt cup and flings it off the mountain. Scrambling to the bikes, we make a frenzied exit, listening for the buzz of the bee bomber for at least five kilometers. My next postcard: *Survived Morocco's child rapists only to be taken out by a Bee-52 on Palm Sunday.*

We move so slowly from place to place that when we arrive, we just keep going, to arrive somewhere else. Ronda is one of the most beautiful cities in Andalucía, full of echoes of Roman, Visigoth and Moorish pasts. When we arrive, however, we pedal straight through, looking for a food market. My only vivid memory of the city is Clarke taking a spill in the middle of a busy intersection.

We choose a steep route out of town, up a 1200-meter pass. The sun is bright and hot, the wind and cold of the day before left behind the last mountain. My knees are still sore from our climb to Gaucin, and now all of my muscles seem to hurt. Mile after mile, in blistering heat, we labor up the pass, guzzling water, taking frequent breaks. Finally, unable to pedal another inch, totally done in, I stop, too tired even to walk. Clarke continues slowly up the mountain in front of me, barely moving.

Legs straddling my bike with seventy-five-pound packs, arms draped over the handlebars in surrender, I gulp hot air into lungs squeezed shut by asthma. Each breath burns my dry throat like boiling steam, and the sun lays hot irons on my back. Blood pounds drums in my ears and my knees are on fire.

Clarke is probably at the top of the pass by now, I decide, where he's lying in the cool grass, drinking water from a cold mountain stream or taking pictures. Actually, he's probably being fed frosty, sweet grapes by a beautiful *señorita* while he's wondering what I'll whine about when I catch up. If I ever do. I take a sip of hot water from my diminished supply. "Let's go, Susan," I say aloud.

Putting my left foot in the toe clip at the top of its revolution, I push down hard to get enough momentum to put the other foot on its pedal, then flip it over to slip my toe in its clip. If I don't have enough speed, this brief hesitation is enough to stop my momentum, to send my feet lurching to the ground to start all over again. On steep hills, Clarke often starts pointed downhill, but I would rather die than pedal even a foot of a steep hill twice. I always start uphill, and I always die a small death. Starting and stopping like a rusty conveyor belt, I pull myself up the mountain in the blistering sun, my mind processing only the pain and the heat and my shortness of breath, the scenery irrelevant.

In the mountains of Spain, the roads follow the contour of the countryside, stringing tiny mountain villages like white beads on a necklace. Clarke waits at the top of the mountain, rested and ready. I'm neither rested nor ready when I arrive alongside, and I refuse to be robbed of the view for which I've abused myself.

Whitewashed villages nestle on the mountaintops like white clouds, and herds of goats and sheep, neck bells singing, fold into the valleys like cream-colored moss. The noon sun washes the shadows from its light and casts mountains and valleys in pure gold. Now I'm ready. "Let's go!" I call to Clarke and am gone before he can reply.

We hurtle down the pass, sweat freeze-drying in the wind, goats and sheep and trees lost in a kaleidoscope of white and green. I squeal with delight, my pain forgotten, freshly-washed socks and underwear streaming like flags from my packs. At fifty kilometers an hour, I chicken out and squeeze the brakes to slow my freefall, backpedaling so that my knees and muscles won't lock. The bright sun lights up my heart and I feel like a real traveler, at one with my bicycle and the road and the wind. At the bottom of the pass, I slow to more human proportions and wave merrily at everyone I pass. I feel like a hero; I've made it over another mountain.

The twenty-minute fall from the sky, following a grueling two-hour climb, has ended—then the road ahead turns up yet again, sniffing and snuffing to find another mountaintop bead to add to its necklace. I balk as I stare up at our fourth mountain of the day. The map shows a twelve percent grade. "Do you realize how hard it is for me to keep pace with you, Susan?" Clarke gripes when he catches up. "Do you ever thank me for that? All you do is whine about your precious knees."

"I didn't complain once today!"

"Remember when you hit your pelvic bone on your bike frame?"

I puff up like a porcupine. "I never said a word!"

"You can whine without words!"

When we argue, we always do it right where we are, this time straddling the bikes in the middle of the road. Whatever gripe we have boils to the surface and erupts, and there it is, spilling all over the place until it's out of us, down the sides, into the dirt. This one, however, ends before it's over, as dark approaches along the steep uphill road with no place to camp in sight. Necessity forces us to go on.

That night, I lie awake in the tent feeling sorry for myself, too tired to continue the fight. Málaga is seventy-five kilometers away, forty-five miles, and I decide to ride there in one day, no matter what. If I ruin my knees, it will serve Clarke right.

But it's easy. Most of the last pass has been ridden the night before after our argument, and after one brief climb, the rest is downhill. We race down to the coast, our anger disintegrating like clouds in a high wind.

At two o'clock, I spot a clump of trees across the road from a small whitewashed house with flowers cascading like rainbows over the wall. Baskets of red geraniums dot the little garden and hang in the trees with morning laundry, and a railroad track winds through the surrounding orange and lemon groves. After asking permission to eat lunch in the garden, Clarke and I share sandwiches of white cheese, sweet onion and ripe tomato on fresh bread, and oranges and strawberries and chocolate. Immersed in the sun and flowers and clear sky and fresh food, we agree that getting to this one spot has been worth all the effort – financially, emotionally and physically. "We're incredibly lucky to have this trip, Clarke," I say, popping an unwashed strawberry into my mouth. We never rinse vegetables or fruit anymore; water's too precious.

Perhaps because the architecture of Málaga reminds me of London, the palm trees seem terribly out of place. Our sightseeing consists of looking for a campground, where we run for hot showers, dirt and weariness and soreness flowing from our bodies as we wash, and wash again. Then we scrub our clothes in cold water in a cement basin, using flat stones as brushes, and walk across the street to the market for hot dogs and potato chips as a change from our more transportable and less spoilable menu of cheese, fresh bread and vegetables.

After a restless night in the noisy campground, fumes and heavy traffic quickly convince us to turn up into the hills at Torre del Mar, leaving the flat Costa del Sol for the party hounds, a bittersweet decision. After laboring to the top of a steep pass late in the afternoon, we spot a white *hacienda* peeking through tall palms. "Let's ask if we can stay here," I suggest, wiping sweat from my face and neck.

My knock at the old wooden door brings a smiling face to a second story window. "I'll be right down, luvs," the smile says. Clarke and I look at each other in disbelief and delight, quite sure that the language we just heard was English, or to be precise, British. A moment later, a pert young woman in a cropped t-shirt and pink sweats comes to the front door in bare feet. "Yes, good," she responds to our request to camp, motioning toward the garden. "Just find a spot wherever you like. We live in London but spend our holidays here," she explains. "Excuse me, but I'm off to a party now. Just tell my mum and dad you talked with me."

Minutes later, her parents arrive home to find a tent going up alongside their house. "What the bloody hell is going on here?" we overhear. "Our fruit thieves are getting a bit bold, eh?"

Clarke and I approach quickly, hoping to avoid gunfire. "My name is Susan and this is my husband Clarke," I explain, translating my simple Spanish request back into English. The couple waits patiently, arms full of groceries. "We're bicycling through Europe for a year and asked your daughter if we could camp in your yard tonight. She said yes," I hurry to add.

"You should have picked a spot with fewer weeds," Michael replies, then presents us with fresh spring water, two bottles of local wine and an armload of freshly dug potatoes, delivering a small table and chairs for our meals. "Help yourself to oranges and lemons—the locals always steal them anyway. If you'd like to shower or use the kitchen, be our guests."

Christine stands to the side, eyes twinkling behind big round glasses. "We lived in a tent for six months while we restored this old house," she tells us as a small red car pulls into the drive, "so I know what it's like. Good for you." The car is filled with friends from Scotland and Denmark. "Join us on the patio for drinks," Christine suggests.

"You've already done too much," I answer, unwilling to intrude even more.

"You prefer that wine, or company?" demands the Danish woman.

"Company!" Clarke and I reply in unison.

We spend the evening conversing in our own language about whatever we want rather than being limited to our tiny Spanish vocabulary. Michael and Christine's friends are a merry bunch, and after Michael tells us that being absentee property owners in Spain means that their house is regularly ransacked and their orchards stripped every year before harvest, I'm surprised that they've allowed us on their property.

In the morning, Michael arrives early at the tent with a tray of buttered toast and hot coffee with milk and brown sugar. He and Christine are going to town but leave us keys to the house. For the first time in Europe, I wash dishes in hot water, while Clarke sketches the little *hacienda* for our new friends.

The memory of these people make bicycling easier all day—the mountains feel like hills, the steep grades like flat stretches of coastal highway. That night, we camp below a small village in thick, green grass near a clear, bubbling stream. Memories of the evening before, along with church bells and the musical chimes of the goats, fill us with awe and appreciation, at least for the moment, of our new lifestyle.

We follow a canal to Moraleda. The pines are very tall; the road, a car wide. A man in his auto sputters up the lane; a minute later, his dog follows, turning to observe us watching his determined pilgrimage on paws. Scattered like leaves on the road are small spots of bright sun moving with a gentle breeze as the sweet-smelling pines soak up the hot sunshine. The crisp air smells like Colorado.

We've read that the Alhambra in Granada is the number one tourist attraction in Spain, but on the day before Easter, riding bicycles into the big city is like being flung in front of the opening lap of the Indy 500.

Almost out of the anti-inflammatory pills for my knees, I buy a big box at the first pharmacy, then weigh myself; I've lost ten pounds. After leaving the store, Clarke announces that we're out of cash. It's Saturday morning and we can't exchange money until the banks reopen on Monday. We have food but no place to stay in the big city, and now a campground is out. "I've spent all our money on my stupid knees," I fuss at myself. "What an idiot!"

"If you want to think that way, you can, but it's not very productive." Clarke points out as we eat lunch in a flowery park.

"Maybe a priest would let us sleep in his churchyard tonight. I'd really like to attend an Easter service."

"Much more productive, Susan." We pedal through streets jammed with Easter weekend traffic, Clarke looking for a church, me concentrating on how to make our request in Spanish. I don't know many churchy words.

Granada is overrun by cars and pedestrians. As we approach the center of the city, traffic slows to a crawl. Then it stops in a giant tangle. Horns honk, people shout, policemen try to get things moving with whistles and grand gestures. The scene is a microscopic look at a blood clot; every now and then, a cell breaks free of the masses and bumps along the edge down the street-vein, but mostly car cells just jostle together, spouting fumes, going nowhere.

Following the signs to the Alhambra, we turn onto a very narrow and, of course, steep cobblestone street along with every other car in Granada, and weave in and out of autos and pedestrians up the hill as the sun blazes. Drivers and walkers cheer us on—applauding, flashing headlights, giving us the high sign—courteously letting us through so that we won't have to stop.

At the top, we see a long red wall, a small piece of the outside of the only medieval palace left in the world. "Do you want to go inside?" I ask, panting and sweating.

"I'd hate to leave the bikes with all our packs outside on this crowded street."

"We could take turns going in, I guess, but that doesn't sound very fun." What I don't say is that I'm uneasy about guarding everything we own by myself. Although I feel totally safe in villages, in these crowds, I feel vulnerable after our experience in Morocco.

"Let's get out of here, then," Clarke decides, frustrated. "We should have found someplace to store our packs." As we coast down the backside of the killer hill we just climbed for no reason, he calls back, "Let's celebrate Easter in a little village."

"Wonderful," I reply as we pedal past a beautiful old cathedral without stopping. Its gate is padlocked; we couldn't have asked for help anyway.

The next day is our longest yet, eighty-eight kilometers. We choose a larger road than usual, with tempered grades that host an Easter Sunday bicycle race that passes as we climb the first hill, the cyclists dressed in bright colors, skinny racing bikes shiny clean. Most of them ignore our greetings, intent on the race, but the older men, the ones near the back, wave and salute our heavy packs.

Once, as a tour bus passes, a young boy in a striped shirt jumps up and down in the back window, waving and cheering. Around the next bend, we stop for water at a service station; the same bus has stopped for fuel and out scrambles the boy to visit as well as he can for a few moments. I speak to a man from another bus, amazed at how much of his Spanish I understand. "By the time we leave Spain," I tell Clarke as we pedal back to the highway, "I'll probably be able to actually speak with these people. Your Spanish is improving also." He can by now get through the "hello's" and "how are you's" and ask questions. Understanding the answers is always the hard part—the more people try to explain, going into elaborate detail to be as helpful as possible, the harder it is for us to understand the basic point.

"I feel great today, Clarke. Let's try to make it all the way into Jaén and get a hotel so we can clean up and see if there's an Easter evening Mass. If we don't have to pay for our room until morning, we can exchange money before check-out."

Jaén is off the road several kilometers at the end of a long, steep hill. By the time we arrive, fifty-five miles from where we've started, it's almost dusk, and all the small hotels seem to be on the third or fourth floors. I feel totally inadequate speaking Spanish into street-level intercoms, realizing how much I rely on gestures to communicate. The first place we try is too expensive, thirty-five dollars, and the clerk recommends a hotel around the corner. There, the price seems just right, and we pull our bicycles inside the building to squeeze into a tiny elevator, then find that I've misunderstood the price. The sympathetic clerk lowers his rate, but it's still more than the first hotel. The third hotel is as much as the second. At a youth hostel, I blurt over the intercom, my voice full of frustration, "Doesn't anybody speak English?" I wince when I hear myself but the damage is done. We're told coolly that the hostel won't allow bicycles inside. I turn to Clarke. "I deserved that. Now what?"

"We ride back down the hill and find a farm. Guess we're not supposed to be in church this Easter." As we coast down the mountain in the growing dusk, I mentally beat myself about the head and shoulders for not finding us a hotel room.

Back off the highway along a dirt road, we find an olive farm, and as we pull into the dusty driveway, I struggle to improve my attitude before we're turned away again. A man comes out of the house at my greeting but isn't particularly inclined to grant our request. Rephrasing my question, I concentrate on the human being who stands in front of me instead of on my own frustration. *"Uno momento, por favor,"* he says then. "I will ask my father." Moments later, he returns with his father, who grants us immediate permission.

As we unfold our tent, an audience gathers. One by one, the family comes out into the dusty yard to watch: grandmother joins grandfather; mother joins father, baby in her arms and two small children behind her skirts; and three goats, three chickens and seven dogs come and go, mostly uninterested in us after formal introductions.

For an hour, we visit in Spanish and in gestures—about the bicycle trip, Spain, America, families and religion. Everyone understands everyone, because we want to. Clarke and I learn many new Spanish words simply because three generations of a family take the time to teach and because we truly desire to learn. It's better than an Easter service.

One night, near Baeza, as the air cools, clouds scud toward us across the sky, one after another, piling into a heavy black mass above our heads. No one is at home at the first three farms we find, and at the fourth, we meet only a gentle white German shepherd in the courtyard of an old *hacienda*. As we pitch our tent outside the wall after dark, it begins to rain, and the cold drizzle continues through the following day. Bicycle books say not to worry about rain. If it's raining in the morning, don't ride. If it starts mid-day, find a café and wait it out. It never quite worked that way for us, but this time we try. The rain is still with us after eighteen hours. "Let's go," I say finally, preferring the rain to cold and boredom in a six-foot tent.

"We can't dawdle much longer," Clarke agrees. "We're almost out of travelers' checks and we're still a few hundred miles from the closest American Express office in Castellón."

It's two o'clock when we toss the last of our bread over the wall to our whimpering dog friend, scanning the old *hacienda* for signs of life as we pedal off, our packs only marginally covered by the tattered orange rain jackets. It continues to rain all afternoon, and each time a car passes, we're drenched with sheets of cold water; rooster tails from our bicycle tires soak the underside of our packs and the backs of our jackets as if the rain weren't enough. After only twenty-eight kilometers, we're ready to quit.

All the roads off the main highway seem to be dirt, and soon we're bogged down on a greasy clay road. By the time we find a farm, our bikes' brakes are so mired in mud that the tires won't turn, our own shoes thick with gooey mud. A housekeeper directs us to the edge of the field, and we push the bicycles back up the road like sleds.

In the morning, neither of us wants to get out of our warm sleeping bags; our shoes and clothes are cold, wet and muddy. Our bikes wait outside, brown and slimy, tires fat with clay. My sense of humor and everything else is covered in goo, and I can't remember what a warm, sunny day feels like. For this, we sold everything? Struggling to put on cold, wet shoes huge with mud, I hunch in the tent with my goopy feet out the door, stuck in mental muck. Then Clarke sets his panniers outside in the muddy field and yells, "Porter!" I dissolve into laughter, able to get on with finding a stick to scrape mud from my brakes.

The only good thing about bicycling on a cold, wet morning is that it produces body heat. But serious rain meets us after lunch, cutting visibility to almost zero in the heavy traffic, and by the time we race down a long hill, teeth chattering, the icy wind sends us into a bar in the next town, only thirty kilometers from our morning mud, for hot coffee and directions to the nearest hotel. Finding that a room will cost three days' allowance, however, we grimly continue on through the rain in silence, ending up in the long wet grass of another abandoned house.

In the morning, a villager who brings his small horse to graze in the abandoned fields wants to know why we didn't sleep inside the dry house. Looking at each other, we shrug. "Because it doesn't belong to us," I say.

We're not happy campers. Tired, muddy, cold and smelly, we're angry at the weather, angry at ourselves and each other for allowing the weather to get to us, for not choosing a different route, for not being more cheerful, for not finding dry places to sleep, for not being able to afford a hotel. A snatch of morning sun postpones the inevitable. Each already brittle with hairline cracks from the last three days, we move about the bikes in silence, miserable, but neither will admit it. Let the other guy crumble. On top of everything else, the chain ring on my bike is bent. "Go!" Clarke shouts mid-morning after I'd waited for him to adjust a pack, then pedals ahead out of sight without looking back.

"Thanks for caring about my bike," I say later, finally catching up at an intersection. "If I'd broken down again, you and the tools were conveniently somewhere else."

"Maybe it's time you took care of your own bike, Susan."

"Fine. Give me the tools, then, or maybe we should buy a second set. We certainly wouldn't want to help each other on this trip." Clarke pedals off without answering.

Later, we stand at a place on the map that indicates the presence of a town, but there isn't one. "How far to the next mythical town, Clarke?"

"Not counting the one we're supposed to be in, I guess about twenty kilometers."

"Forget it. Let's put up the tent before it rains for a change. We'll survive with bread and yogurt."

"Come on, Susan, towns don't disappear. It must be around the corner." This time, I pedal off without answering, churning up the road wrapped in self-pity. Fifteen minutes later, I stop at the top of a hill for water. Clarke isn't behind me. I wait. And wait. Finally, far behind me around a long curve, I spot him, riding fast, closing the distance between us like a mortar shell. "Why the hell didn't you wait for me back there?" he screams. "I was trying to get directions from the highway police."

"I didn't know you'd stopped. Besides, this morning you yelled at me when I waited for you."

We miss the town completely, pitching camp in an open field with no shelter or permission. After a silent dinner, we crawl into our sleeping bags without a word. The next morning, still angry and frustrated, we pack in silence after I try with no success to start a conversation. After three hours of difficult cycling in cold wind, my stomach in a knot, I insist on a real toilet and hot coffee. Clarke doesn't want to spend the money, but I don't care. After silently huddling in misery around our hot cups, we leave the restaurant. "Fine, Clarke," I say, pulling my bike away from the wall, "don't speak to me for the rest of the trip."

Clarke straddles his bicycle. "I thought I'd lost you yesterday, Susan, that maybe you'd been run over or kidnapped. I love you. I was afraid, and afraid to admit how much you mean to me."

I look into his sad eyes, at his scraggly hair and dirty face. Finally, I say simply, "I love you too, Clarke. Let's agree to keep each other in sight from now on, no matter what."

Even with a pit stop for a flat tire, we pedal a hundred and eighteen kilometers that day, almost seventy-five miles, arriving in Albacete before dinner. "Let's get a hotel," Clarke suggests, "wash off the week's mud and go out to dinner."

"We deserve to relax, clean up and concentrate on each other for a change."

It takes three hours to find an affordable hotel that will allow the bikes inside but only a moment to take over both bathrooms on our floor, stripping off smelly, muddy clothes to stand gratefully under the drippy hot showers. Back in our room, we look from our muddy packs to each other. "Hot water instead of a cold river is irresistible, Clarke. Let's do laundry."

It's midnight before all of our clothes are clean and strung dripping from bungee cords and over radiators and closet doors. Clarke cooks omelettes on the camp stove and I wash dishes in the bathroom sink down the hall. At one o'clock, we stumble into our narrow twin beds and fall asleep instantly. So much for our romantic evening.

The bicycles have spent the night downstairs, chained to the jukebox of the restaurant beneath the little *pensione*. We extricate them in the morning after gathering up our wet laundry and drying the water on the floor with our damp towels, then start off into a hot, sunny day. Clarke wears dry his clothes, changing from one pair of shorts to the other as soon as the pair he's wearing is dry. "Wet

Spandex chafes my legs," I grumble after an hour on the road. "Can I wear your dry pair?" Clarke reluctantly gives me the cotton shorts he's just taken off, and my damp ones go with the rest of my wet clothes into a plastic bag–there's too much to hang on my bike.

The scenery is sparse and barren, the lush green and white of Andalucía muted to brown and gray. Suddenly, in the afternoon, the flat road plunges into a surprise canyon full of light and shadow. At the bottom, a river twists and turns and the road falls to meet it in great shuddering gasps. After all the rain and misery of the last few days, we wish we could stay forever in the beautiful, bright canyon. Apple trees line the river with delicate blooms, and ducks fly up the clear, blue waters that reflect the sky and the sun in sparkling light. We camp at the bottom of the gorge, and I string my wet clothes in the fruit trees while an old man shows Clarke where to find wild asparagus.

As dusk deepens the beauty of the canyon into shadow, I find great peace in being exactly where I am, with my husband, our bicycles and this canyon. But what a journey–each day has been fashioned from exuberance, frustration, sharing, pettiness, trust and self doubt, all in an abundance that makes the highs, like now, incredibly high, and the lows, like yesterday, painfully low. Our moments of bliss are of such purity and strength that we can't catch our breaths; we're amazed at the magnificence of the world and our lives. During the bad times, we choke on our separateness and our foolishness, feeling cut off from life.

"My clothes are almost dry," I announce, rummaging through the apple blossoms to test my socks for dampness. "I think I'll leave them out tonight; it doesn't look like rain for a change."

After dinner, we curl up in our sleeping bags, peaceful and philosophical. I sigh. "We were so concerned about the mechanics of the trip last night that we used our one night in a hotel to do laundry instead of enjoying each other's company. I don't know why we even bother to make promises to ourselves."

Clarke waits several moments before answering. "We're together every minute, Susan. How could we possibly be closer?"

"Maybe you're right. If I'd really wanted to have a romantic evening last night, I wouldn't have suggested laundry."

"Mmm," Clarke murmurs, falling asleep.

I lie awake. Although my mind understands Clarke's point, my heart feels that we're building a wall between us. We're so vulnerable on this trip–to weather, to traffic, to strangers—that maybe, out of self-protection, we're refusing to be vulnerable to each other anymore. As the days go by, I feel like I understand Clarke less and less. We're together, but only on the surface. Crawling out of the tent, I walk a bit, unable to sleep, worried. The moon etches the canyon in a jigsaw of silver edges, dark shadows of rock and tree climbing up the sheer walls in patches and designs like ancient runes. Sadness fills me as I go back to my sleeping bag in the tiny tent.

"Wake up, Susan." Clarke pops his head into the tent early the next morning. "The canyon is full of mist and your laundry is soaked. If we get an early start and the weather's nice, maybe you can dry your clothes at lunch."

As we push the bikes up the steep embankment to the road, I turn to Clarke. "I was awake for a long time last night. I think we're both full of it." I can't see Clarke's eyes behind his sunglasses, and he doesn't respond.

The canyon is full of old cave dwellings high on its walls, and we stop two old men to ask about a castle that stands on top of the cliff. It's Moorish, 1500 years old, the men tell us proudly. Under the castle, in the rock walls, white curtains blow in the fresh breeze from homes cut into sheer cliffs accessible only from inside the town. The men say that we're the first Americans they've seen in their canyon; they seem anxious to tell their friends of the discovery and hurry back down the road toward town.

Around the next bend, Alcala del Jucar appears as if dropped from the sky, full of people and Sunday morning bustle. In the square, we meet a Spanish lawyer who speaks English and ask him about Spanish laws. He explains that it's legal to camp anywhere in Spain as long as we don't kill any animals—after centuries of hunting, so little wild game is left in Europe that private property owners' hunting privileges are viciously protected.

"See those two women coming over the bridge?" he asks then. "The one in the black cape is American. I will introduce you." We speak with the pretty young woman in English, our common language, and she translates to her Spanish friend in French, their common language. Both are studying French in Grenoble. While we enjoy talking with these bright women, we feel the frustration of translations and pedal out of the canyon deep in our own thoughts.

We never argue going downhill. But on the steep road up the south wall of the paradise canyon, we find ourselves unable to handle the heat that we've prayed for, the fatigue from the difficult cycling, and our own European inadequacies. Clarke badly mispronounces a Spanish word and blows up when I correct him. Pulling off the road to argue, we combine our battle with lunch and a bungee cord clothesline strung around an abandoned truck. "What's your problem, Clarke? You asked me to help you with Spanish, then you get mad when I do."

"It was your sarcastic question, 'What word was that?'"

"I don't think your Spanish is the issue here," I say, refusing to be drawn into another senseless argument when something bigger is brewing. "Look, Clarke, I've always been independent, able to function quite well, thank you very much, on my own. On this trip, I can't, at least not physically. I need you—to carry equipment, to cheer me on, to do more than your share of the work. I feel vulnerable to you, and it's very uncomfortable. Maybe I'm building a wall between us for self-protection."

"Susan, you're doing great. You've cycled some very difficult terrain, about fifteen hundred kilometers so far. It's easy for me to ride all day and then cook at night."

"Thanks, but even if I were Wonder Woman, I couldn't take this trip alone. Logistically and emotionally, I rely on you, and this is a first for me. Jeepers, you've got the tent and I've got the food—we can't split up!" I pause. "So what's eating you, Clarke?"

He peels the wrapper off a chocolate bar before answering. "I feel manipulated by your not being able to do as much as I can, I guess. Rather than be myself, I end up worrying about you. And I'm frustrated by my lack of Spanish. I really enjoyed meeting those people back in Alcala, but I couldn't understand any of their Spanish. I was jealous of how much better you related to them."

Identifying possible reasons behind our recent defensiveness feels like a step toward mending our differences, and gathering up my sun-dried clothes off the rusty truck, we continue up the hot, winding canyon road in better spirits. "How about dinner out tonight?" we ask each other later. "Next town," we decide.

But Villatoya offers no café, just a lazy Sunday afternoon for serious dominoes players in a crowded bar. Pitching camp in the evening shadows outside of town, we watch dark storm clouds move south toward Valencia. We've learned our lesson; now there's always an extra meal of something at the bottom of my pannier. As we cook rice and lentils, a determined scorpion, no doubt displaced from its home by our tent, invites itself to dinner. Like the bumblebee, it finds itself in another territory, riding a small stick like a witch's broom.

We literally follow our noses to a bakery the next day, devouring a twelve-pack of cakes outside the door while visiting with a Spaniard who wants to know if Americans are all like the people in the television show *Dallas*. "No," we deny emphatically, "they are like us." But we know this isn't true either.

The rain begins again just as we crest a small pass. As we pedal past a cheering road crew, Clarke turns to wave and then points toward the sky. A green and gray cloud churns violently toward us. "Go!" he screams over the wind and rain, fear in his voice. The cloud catches up with us quickly; the sky turns yellow and the rain turns to hail. Lightning flashes and thunder rolls over us in deafening waves. Flash! Boom! We're definitely the highest objects on the horizon. "Pedal faster!" Clarke shouts from in front.

"I'm pedaling as fast as I can," I call ahead, falling behind.

Clarke points to a tiny stone building at the edge of a field. "Get off the road!" A bolt of lightning strikes, much too close, as we scramble our bikes through the mud into the rock hut. "We really have problems now," Clarke says as we enter the doorway with the wind and slanting rain. "These rocks are a great ground for lightning–but it's either stay here or get run over on the road. Nobody can see us out there."

The violent wind enters through the doorway of the smelly hut, instantly freezing our wet skin, then swirls in the dirt and shoots up through the open chimney. My bare legs are numb from the sharp hailstones. We shiver uncontrollably. "We can't afford to lose our body heat," Clarke worries, pacing back and forth in front of the doorway. He sticks his head outside. "I think the lightning's slacked off. Let's go before we freeze."

"Fine with me. This place seems to be the local outhouse."

The storm drenches the road with rivers and, near Requena, an inch of hail. We hurry to reach a tiny market before *siesta* after discovering that it's a local holiday and the stores will be closed for the rest of the day. After finding only macaroni and tomato sauce, we stop in a restaurant for hot chocolate, wrapping our blue fingers around the heavy cups, soaked to the bone. What a way to travel–the mood swings, the weather, the logistics to get a meal and keep moving!

The day closes under blue skies with our tent on the porch of yet another abandoned house after ninety kilometers that include a frustrating ten-kilometer backtrack after a missed turn. Two more days to Castellón and replenished travelers' checks.

The American Express office in Castellón doesn't sell travelers' checks, and we're shunted back and forth between their office and two banks, unable to arrange for funds. We'll have to go to Barcelona, three hundred kilometers north. "That's three hours for most people," I grumble, "but for us, it's almost a week."

After thirty kilometers along the crowded coast, we decide to head back to the quiet mountains. "I'd rather not take a shortcut just because of money," Clarke declares.

Pedaling toward the next road into the hills, we meet two bicyclists from Utah heading south along the coast to Portugal and suggest that they go inland until realizing that the pair has no camping equipment. "I'm glad we have a tent," I say after they pedal off toward their next beachfront hotel. "Lots of the little villages don't have hotels, but we can go anywhere we want as long as we can find food."

Although not all of the villages have markets, they all have at least one bar. And none except for those on the main routes have service stations—although they'd be two centuries out of place, we'd appreciate the restrooms. Regardless of the inconveniences, we love the mountain villages—they're more genuine, more Spanish, quiet, not so mixed up with the flood of international tourists and fast food restaurants, unfettered by the coastal shenanigans.

We ache for a bath but can't find a river. Finally, in the afternoon, we hide behind our tent's rain fly tied to a tree, strip, and pour water from our bike bottles over each other. As we pedal off, Clarke hears a grinding in his bike's bottom bracket but is able to tighten up the wobbly crank with a wrench.

He's been looking at trash for some days now. After spotting a brown-and-red paper sack by the side of the road, Clarke sifts through the rubble and produces enough material to fashion a large "U.S.A." sign for his rear pack, then pedals down the road wondering aloud whether Europeans will recognize the abbreviation. After all, in Spain, America is called *"Estados Unidos."*

The next day is sunny and we pedal toward Tortosa, considering lunch. The air is clean and fresh, the cycling easy. It's a nice change from rain and mud and mountains. I look down at the road in front of me. It's full of chicken feet, scattered like skinny stars all over the pavement. No chickens—just feet, bloody at the ends. Where are their chickens? I can't bear to stop, to put my feet down with the other feet; I ride through, cringing.

We move inland along the river Ebro. Suddenly, Clarke's bike begins to grind its teeth again. Clarke sounds no better when he makes the preliminary diagnosis. "The bearing is shot, Susan. We're thirty kilometers from a town of any size, and it's Sunday. Damn."

The tiny village of Rasquera is eight kilometers up a steep pass. It's Sunday there also, but at least it's in the direction of Barcelona. "I'll have to walk," Clarke grumbles.

"I'll walk with you," I offer, "but first come look at this view." Tiny houses are scattered at the bottom of the hills along the riverbank, their small garden patches a quilt of color, the tranquil scene mental miles from a broken down bike in the middle of nowhere.

"No, thanks. All I care about is getting my bicycle fixed," Clarke replies, then crabs all the way up the pass about inferior bearings and how silly he looks pushing a fully-laden bicycle that he's perfectly capable of pedaling. By Rasquera, he's beside himself.

"What can I do to help, Clarke?"

He glares at me. "Find a mechanic who's open on Sunday," he snaps, full of sarcasm.

I pedal away, on a mission, and ten minutes later, return with a goatherd, triumphant. "Ask and ye shall receive," I say, smug. "This man says that there's a mechanic working in his shop just down the hill."

Clarke looks at the goatherd, who nods excitedly. "Nobody works on Sunday in Spain," Clarke growls, "but let's go see."

Sure enough, this man is working. The bottom bracket on Clarke's bike is cracked and two sets of bearings are deformed, but the machine shop owner makes two trips into the village to a friend's for the right-sized ball bearings and loans Clarke the tools for a temporary repair, accepting only two hundred *pesetas*, less than two dollars, to cover the cost of the parts.

Although Clarke installs the low-gear chain ring ninety degrees out of position, there's only one more pass between us and the beach and hopefully a bicycle shop. Gray fog breaks apart at the edge of the coast, revealing the busy highway to Barcelona. "If only my bottom bracket doesn't turn to gravel before I can get it repaired," Clarke frets.

We have two packs of dirty clothes, and with no clean rivers available near the beach resorts, look for a self-service laundromat. By the time we find one, it's mid-day *siesta*, but the owner ushers us in with greetings in English and assures us that we can do our laundry during lunch. His two young sons help us unload the bikes and start the machines. "No, no, no," Carlos says as we sit down. "Please, come home with me." Although it's our first chance to have real Spanish home cooking, we discover as Carlos and his sons escort us through the streets that they've decided on a special American treat for us—hamburgers.

Carlos and his British wife lived in America for several years, and he enjoys speaking his excellent English as much as we enjoy conversing in our own language. At his crowded apartment, Carlos offers showers and shampoos and his sons scramble to bring milk and juice and cookies, filling our pockets with tea for our journey.

During our meal, Carlos speaks with concern about his country. "My government has announced a moratorium on building on the coastline after next year," he explains, "which is why there's so much construction underway. Much of the new construction is inferior, without building permits and sometimes even on land owned by absentee owners or the military. Just last week, the Army ordered a new apartment building torn down because it was on their land."

The only unfamiliar thing about lunch is *avas*, giant string beans with a mild taste. Other than that, we could be in America talking politics.

Carlos continues. "We have the World's Fair coming up, then the Summer Olympics. The Spanish believe that when the world discovers our country, Spain will flourish forever. But these preparations are very expensive for my country and its people. Our assets are liabilities in many ways. For example, rental costs are so high that no one can afford a place to live. Owners can get more in day rentals from northern Europeans in two months than Spaniards can pay in a year based on our wages and taxes. It's crazy.

"Now that we're a democracy and part of the European Common Market," he continues, "the country is euphoric. But it isn't based on anything. The taxes and red tape are terrible. Do you know how much a washing machine costs in Spain? Three thousand dollars! And because prices are so high and wages so low, the people, they are desperate. We have much crime in Spain. The court system is so crowded that people don't even care if they get caught because it takes so long to get sentenced."

"America has many problems also, Carlos," I say. "Are drugs a problem here?"

"Of course. Our people cannot cope with their new freedom. They want to try everything. To pay for it, they steal because most of us are still poor. And freedom to many Spaniards includes freedom to take what they want. It's not nearly so crazy in America. Here, all I do is fill out forms and pay taxes."

Outside a suburb of Tarragona that night, my heart travels back in time. "Why are you so quiet?" Clarke asks as he unpacks the skillet.

"My father died a year ago tomorrow."

Clarke looks up and touches my cheek. "I'll fix dinner if you like." While Clarke cooks, I remember that painful experience. Mother had died three years earlier. "Instead of mourning your father's death tomorrow," Clarke interrupts my thoughts, "why don't you celebrate his life?" Death makes Clarke nervous.

"I celebrate my father's life every day, but I also choose not to run away from the sadness." When Daddy had stopped breathing, the nurses looked at me. "Do you want us to do anything?" the head nurse asked gently. We knew it was time.

Shaking my head, I held tightly to Daddy's toes at the bottom of his hospital bed. "Just be with him," I whispered, choking on my own tears, shaking. I wasn't able to tell the exact moment of his death, but I was certain that he knew I was there. It was enough. "Goodbye, Daddy. I love you," I said in my heart where I knew he would hear it. "Go take care of Mother. She misses you."

Now, in my sleeping bag, I cry softly, remembering. Just before falling asleep, I ask my heart to let in both Mother and Daddy that night. In the dark silence, a noise fills my ears, white noise, the sound of a continuous ocean wave. And then it stops. Clarke wakes up with a start. "What was that?" he says. "I saw a red light."

"You must have dreamed it," I whisper. "Go back to sleep."

In the morning, I'm still unusually quiet, and Clarke and I fuss over nothing. I think he's insensitive to my grief; he thinks I should live for the present. He pedals off, and I wait for him to return while he waits for me to follow. Finally, I follow and he returns, and we meet half way. We pedal to Tarragona, where we buy a new bearing at a bike shop, but they have no tools with which to install it.

Late in the afternoon I suggest that we have a drink to toast Daddy's life. Ambling into a small liquor store, we decide on a quart of eleven-percent beer. The clerk wants to hear all about our trip, telling us again and again that she's too old to do such a thing, that even bicycling the few blocks to the beach is exhausting. "I'm forty-one," she confides in explanation.

"I'm forty-two," I admit, pocketing our change. When we leave the store, the woman is still standing at the open cash register, open-mouthed.

Pedaling toward a grove of trees, we drink our beer after supper. There's no white noise that night, no red lights. We never speak of either.

Outside a food market in Sitges, a woman approaches excitedly. "I overheard you speak English. I'm an American from California." She's been teaching psychology in Amsterdam, now on holiday in Spain before returning home.

Moments later, we're joined by a man from Maine who spent the last three years in Saudi Arabia. This city is the only one he'll visit in Spain, he explains. "When you've seen one city, you've seen them all, and I think they all stink."

"This city is nothing like the towns and villages we've seen the last few weeks," I tell him. "They're all different and wonderful." The unhappy man walks away, uninterested in further conversation.

We're amazed when yet another American joins our group on the sidewalk. "I'm staying with British friends," he explains with a Texas accent. "They told me that they gave you directions to the market, so I came to find you."

Gathered in a happy cluster in front of the vegetable market, we talk about Spain and America until a woman calls out in Spanish from an upstairs window that she's washing her shutters and is afraid we'll get wet. "It was great to speak English," Clarke says as we finish putting our groceries away after our countrymen disperse.

"It sounded weird," I reply.

Three hundred feet above the heaving sea, a fifteen-kilometer ribbon of road clings to the face of a tall, gray cliff. Marked on the map as both scenic and dangerous, it's definitely no place for bicycles, particularly on a windy day with heavy traffic—the road so narrow that the white lines marking its edge are painted on one side under the occasional guardrails and on the other, on the rock wall itself.

We can't waver even an inch from our bicycle-tire-wide corridor—a tiny jig to the right will plummet us into the sea hundreds of feet below, and the smallest jog to the left will send us into the long line of traffic that just squeezes past. I refuse to look over the edge or at the traffic, my eyes never wavering from the three-inch ribbon of asphalt in front of me. Once, Clarke is forced into the guardrail as two vehicles pass each other going opposite directions. His packs catch the concrete; he wavers but doesn't fall.

It starts to rain. Each time we turn a corner, strong wind sucks us this way and that, toward the edge of the cliff or into the heavy traffic. Three times, I miscalculate the wind shift and veer into the traffic lane; three times, I'm able to catch myself just before falling into a vehicle. And all three times, I'm afraid to get back on my bike. "Go, Susan!" Clarke calls back to me. "You're holding up traffic."

The road is now so narrow that even autos aren't able to pass our bicycles if there's an oncoming car. "This is insane, Clarke!" The scenery is beautiful, but I'm not about to admire it as I struggle with the wind and rain. And there's no place to stop. If this were my first day of bicycling, I decide, I'd be on the next plane home. Clarke is far ahead now, fighting his way off the road as fast as possible; I trail behind, slowed to a crawl by my fear. If walking wouldn't take up more room on the highway, I'd push my bicycle every step. When the road widens on the other side, I almost kiss the wet ground.

In the afternoon, our problems grow from narrow to wide with a vengeance. Riding into Barcelona is like bicycling on the rush-hour freeways of Los Angeles. We arrive on an eight-lane divided highway that converges with a two-laner to the right, and need to cross both lanes of speeding traffic to seek the safety of the right shoulder. Stopping at the point of intersection, we look over our shoulders at waves of cars approaching at a hundred kilometers an hour. Clarke puts out his right arm, motioning to the traffic to yield. No one does. So he starts pedaling, pulling into the fast lane, motioning again, frantically, for the cars to give way. This time, they do and I follow closely, grimly waiting to be hit.

By the time we get into the city, we've repeated this traffic dance several times and have learned that as long as we clearly signal our intentions and then act immediately, drivers will make room. If we hesitate, even for an instant, we're sure to be human Frisbees.

We reach the American Express office at four o'clock, exhausted by sixty kilometers of our most difficult cycling. Barcelona is incredibly beautiful, but at this late hour, the challenge is just to get in, get money, and get out in time to find a place to stay before dark.

With six weeks of travelers' checks in our pockets, we hit the streets during rush hour and get lost trying to find a way out on the smaller roads. Finally, a middle-aged cyclist comes to our rescue. "Follow me," he says in Spanish and zips off on his lightweight ten-speed. Of course, I never zip, especially with seventy-five pound packs and after eight hours of physically- and mentally-draining bicycling. But zip we do, over and under and around and through and back and forth, following roads and streets and underpasses and overpasses, turning right from left-hand lanes, swerving in and out of traffic with hand signals that seem merely to beg for forgiveness.

Clarke struggles to stay halfway between our escort and me, keeping us both in sight while I try to decide whether to keep pedaling or just to lie down and die in the streets, knees screaming in pain. Finally, the Spaniard stops at the edge of the great city, miles out of his way, and wishes us a safe trip. "He wasn't even out of breath!" I exclaim, gasping for air.

"Look, the Pyrénées!" Clarke points north. "On the other side is France."

"Not tonight," I recoil, eyeing the snow-capped peaks with horror. It's seven o'clock and dusk, and we're in a heavily industrial area. Finally, after bumping through a small village with rough cobblestone streets, we pitch our tent in total darkness behind a smelly factory after ninety kilometers, over fifty-five miles.

The next day, we pedal back to Cardedeu to buy a wrench, but the hardware store doesn't have the correct size. At the bicycle shop, the owner brings out every wrench he has, but none fits. Then the man who owns the tobacco shop next door takes Clarke to every mechanic in town until they find the right-sized tool at a tiny custom racing shop. While Clarke fixes his bike on the sidewalk, I shop for food and visit with the bike shop owner, who pulls out his maps to show me the easiest route through the Pyrénées. The little town seems to embrace us, as had Rasquera. "It's amazing what happens when we ask for help, isn't it, Clarke?" I say later.

"Uh-huh. The bike shop people warned me never to leave our bikes unlocked outside a store like we always do, but when we're trusting, the world seems to be trustworthy, doesn't it? I wonder what it would be like, though, to come outside of a shop someday and have everything gone."

"Don't even consider it," I shudder. "That's a lesson I can do without."

I go into a large, crowded supermarket one day to buy food. Instead of a self-service produce section, this store has a clerk who serves customers one at a time. "*Quarto kilometer fresas*," I say when it's my turn.

"*¿Que?*" asks the clerk.

"*Quarto kilometer fresas*," I say louder.

The clerk shakes her head, and the other shoppers snicker and talk all at once. Finally, one takes my arm and says, "*¿Quarto kilo fresas?*" Mortified, I nod, snatch my bag of strawberries and squirm off to the cheese counter, careful to phrase my order perfectly.

"Hey, Clarke!" I holler, emerging from the store, "I just tried to buy a quarter mile of strawberries!"

I suggest a shortcut through the mountains; the road is less than desirable and Clarke worries about the bikes on the gravel road. "For heaven's sake, our mountain bikes are made for rough terrain," I say, feeling guilty but determined to let him fuss by himself. The scenery is worth the extra work. The rustle of new leaves fills the air and tiny breezes blow fresh and fragrant.

We sleep in the woods that night but get a late start the next morning because Clarke has a flat tire. "It's from the rotten road you chose," Clarke points out, vindicated.

South of La Jonquera, rain clouds seriously threaten—we hear thunder and fight extremely cold headwinds all morning. Because of our sparse budget, we've agreed to only one restaurant meal per country; here we are on the Spanish/French border and have had only a snack in a Seville *cantina* the first week of our trip. At a small truck stop, we order veal, fresh string beans and salad, with baskets of hot bread, and wine. Two small dogs, black and white terriers, roam through the restaurant at will, barking and begging snacks. It's nice to see animals unchained.

In Spain, all the dogs seem to be watchdogs. Even in blistering heat, torrential rain and soggy mud, the mostly German shepherds live hard lives chained to dog houses or oil drums, barking at anything that comes near, doing what's asked of them, no matter what. Until today, we never once saw anyone acknowledge a dog with a word or a pet; we, of course, speak to them all in English, Spanish or, finally, in dog. "With animals, we don't need to know how to speak Spanish, Susan. With dogs, all we need to say is 'woof'—Spanish dogs can understand French dogs, Italian hounds can communicate with Austrian mutts. People have a lesson to learn from the animals about universal language, don't they?"

"I've always thought that animals were more evolved than humans," I declare.

It's our last day in Spain, April 16th. Tucked in the tent that night, I look back while Clarke looks forward, studying a French dictionary. It's his turn to be in charge of language. Now that we've gotten pretty good at communicating in Spanish, we're headed where we can't say a word. But isn't this what the trip is about, I ask myself, climbing again and again out of our comfort zones, as they say?

The air is cooler, and the Pyrénées beckon. Our first mail packet from America has been sent to Perpignan, just over the border, and we hunger for the first news of our families and friends. We've pedaled over 2300 kilometers, almost 1400 miles. While I'm thinner and stronger, my knees still hurt every day, often keeping me awake most of the night, and I still have trouble keeping up with Clarke because as I get better, so does he; but we're pedaling more than our original commitment, thirty-five or forty miles a day over rugged terrain, with a record of seventy-five miles.

Crawling into my sleeping bag, I stuff a small pillow under my aching knees, crossing my arms behind my head. Goat and sheep bells ring in the distance, and I picture the animals dancing through the fields to music that will forever remind me of this beautiful country. "Spain may need some tempering for its own sake," I say, thinking of its coastal growing pains, "but there's a joy for life here that's irresistible."

"*Oui, madame,*" Clarke agrees, caught between yesterday and tomorrow.

As darkness ends Clarke's study session, I think about how challenging our relationship has been over the last two months. Neither of us can run away from our problems—because we do the same things over and over, together, all of our issues just keep showing up, day after day. When we're able to let go of our stubbornness, we grow, and painful as it is sometimes, it also feels like the most beautiful freedom in the world. "*Buenos noches*, Clarke," I say, snuggling deep in my bag.

"*Bonne nuit*, Susan."

Chapter 5

F RANCE. To CLARKE, ALTHOUGH it's his family history and the epitome of romance and art, it's also just another place created by man out of a perverse need for boundaries and ownership. Clarke believes in one world without borders; I like the diversity of custom. But France looks the same as Spain as we cross the Pyrénées on a windy, rainy day.

To me, France means that I can no longer communicate. Because Clarke once listened to a few French language tapes, he's in charge of communication. I feel helpless. "I'll handle the next two countries, England and Scotland," I tease, "then you can learn Danish."

"Gee, thanks." Clarke digs into a pack for his passport.

"Anglais?" one of the border guards asks.

"American," he replies. The officer looks surprised. The Spaniards had guessed that we were French; now the French think we're English.

We hope to camp wild in France, as we did in Spain—a hiding place in the woods, a national park or an abandoned house—but as we near Perpignan, the protecting forests have been cleared for grapes. With no place to hide, we'll have to ask in French to sleep in someone's garden.

Our first mission is to pick up the mail that my sister has sent in care of general delivery to Perpignan. Leaving the bikes to fend for themselves in the rain, Clarke and I stand dripping in front of the information desk at the Credit Agricole Bank, asking for directions as men in business suits and women in smart dresses and high heels detour around us. A smiling secretary listens to Clarke's stumbling request, visibly relieved that his question is posed in her own language, and with great enthusiasm offers a three-minute description of the complicated route to the central post office. Clarke smiles and thanks her, then we escape out the door trailing water across the carpet. "Good for you," I congratulate him. "She thought you could understand French. Did you?" Clarke eyes the heavens and shakes his head. "Frustrating, isn't it?" I say smugly.

We locate the central post office after asking directions from a group of high school girls who offer ice cream along with advice, two women who walk arm-in-arm in the old part of town, and a man who stands right outside the post office building, as it turns out, but is too occupied with police searching his car to point us toward the door.

While Clarke goes in to collect our letters, I watch the bikes and watch people watching me. Leaning against the front of the imposing building, one foot braced against the stone wall behind me, I realize that I haven't showered since Carlos's two days before Barcelona and my frayed and grayed t-shirt no longer looks clean even when it is. My legs and arms collect shivers in the wind and leftover drizzle as chic citizens walk briskly down the sidewalk, skirting me and my two overburdened bicycle buddies with doubletakes and an occasional thumbs up.

When Clarke returns, he's empty-handed. "Let's camp nearby and check again tomorrow afternoon," he suggests, seeing my disappointment. "There's a beach a few kilometers from the city—maybe there aren't as many vineyards near the water."

Pedaling out of Perpignan along with all the other commuters, we balance precariously between the wind and the edge of the road as cars rush by in a steady stream. Although we find two large farms, no one is home to ask for permission to camp. Finally, we spot a small orchard and hide among the trees. As always, we leave behind no trace of our occupation of the small piece of land.

The Pyrénées are sharply outlined against the sky the next day as strong wind clears the air. Back in Perpignan, umbrellas mushroom in the sidewalk cafés, tempting us to try the fabled French cuisine, but instead we make sandwiches on a park bench and drink Spanish wine left over from a five-liter bottle that we bought before crossing the border.

Back at the post office, there's still no mail from American friends and family, and lonely beyond words, we pedal to the tourist office for information on routes to Paris. We're told that it's forbidden to camp wild in France, even on private property with permission from the owners. "How about a side trip into the mountains for a few days?" Clarke suggests. "Find some safe camping, see some countryside, then check back one more time for our mail."

"I'm certainly not ready to forego letters to start toward Paris," I agree, drawing a circle on the map. "What about this route? Maybe we can lose the wind."

The steady northwesterly that accompanies us out of Perpignan almost undoes us; we pedal only twenty-three kilometers in four hours. The wind comes from the left. Every truck that passes sends the bikes skittering, first from blocking the wind we've been leaning into and then from sucking us back into the slipstream. Inevitably, there's another vehicle behind each truck, ready to clip our swerving rear ends. "This is as bad as the wind on that pass north of Sitges," Clarke yells back to me.

"I should have found a restroom in Perpignan."

"There's a bush over there by the railroad track."

It's a quick job. The minute I'm bare, Clarke shouts that a train is coming and I jump out of the rosy foliage still tugging up my pants, hoping I've extricated all of the thorns from my rear end. "I guarantee I'll reincarnate next time as a man," I growl.

The markets aren't yet open after mid-day *siesta* in the little village of Estagel, but the town fountain offers five old Frenchmen holding court in the sunshine. Clarke jumps into their midst with his sprinkling of French, determined to learn more. Soon I leap into the fray with my Spanish after hearing that one of the men lived in Spain for a few years. *"Pomelo,"* I pronounce in Spanish.

"Pamplemousse," translates one of the old men into French.

"Grapefruit," Clarke says in English. The old men try to repeat the English word with missing teeth and great enthusiasm. By the time the food market opens, we've learned the French names for all of the fruits and vegetables we usually buy and the old men proudly guard our bicycles while we go into the store.

Although the next day is breezy, it's sunny and full of springtime; we pedal north to the Chateau de Quéribus, an eleventh-century mountaintop fortress, climbing 2000 feet by noon and finishing off the ascent with a kilometer-long seventeen percent grade to the castle. Neither of us can pedal at the end; we can hardly push the bikes on foot. On top, seen through crumbling wall slits, the Pyrénées edge out like fangs in the distance, drooling small streams to meet the fertile valleys of the largest wine-producing region in France.

A Dutch couple mounts the endless stairs to the ruins. "I'll bet that steep hill cost you both a chain," says the man as we pack up the remains of our lunch.

"Actually, no," Clarke replies. "We have eighteen- and twenty-one-speed bikes that are made for this stuff."

"No matter how many speeds you have," the man responds, shaking his head, "you still have to pedal. Bravo!"

Getting up the mountain has been almost impossible, but going down is even worse. No matter how hard I squeeze my front and back brakes, I can't slow down and race faster and faster down the narrow, winding road. My hands cramp, and by the time the road levels off, my fingers are gnarled into claws, stuck; and I wonder again if there's a good chance that one or both of us might not survive this little vacation.

We pedal up and down the hillsides in hot sun through tiny villages and farms, spotting a small stream late in the day. "Time for a bath and laundry," I announce, recalling our perfect river bath in the mountains of Andalucía. Soon, hot sun twinkles off tiny waves that rush past our swollen feet as we wash our clothes and string them into the trees. With our tent hidden in the bushes and the bicycles stripped for camp, we pedal to Padern in search of food. Without packs, we can barely control the bikes. "Yahoo!" I scream, racing as fast as I can, weaving back and forth across the road, Clarke close behind.

A light dinner of bread and fruit salad cools us off even more and we crawl into bed under a full moon in a beautiful clear sky. Lying in our sleeping bags, not touching, we get involved in another long discussion about our marriage. "I don't even know what a relationship is," Clarke says finally. "We're just two individuals doing whatever we do, acting however we act. Blaming problems on our relationship is irresponsible. I feel close to you. If you don't feel intimate enough, then what are you doing about it?"

"I'm not talking about sex, Clarke. Our communication is zilch except for what we need to say to get from one place to another. We hardly touch, even in friendship. To answer to your question, I'm past the point of trying to initiate lovemaking. Every time I do, you turn me down. You tell me to quit worrying all the time about being dirty," I continue, "yet you don't come near me even when I'm clean." When he still doesn't answer, I begin to cry. "All I've ever wanted is an open, honest, intimate relationship with one man for the rest of my life," I sob. "Why can't I have it?"

Clarke looks at me for a long few seconds, then reluctantly gathers me into his arms. Moonlight streams through the little tent window and I see that Clarke's eyes are filled with tears. We sleep huddled together, confused and frustrated.

In the morning, I crawl out of the tent as the rising sun admires its buttery face in the mirror of the little stream next to our tent. The grass is cool and wet under my knees, and early morning breezes dress my nakedness with goosebumps. Physically rested, I'm emotionally exhausted, empty and alone and lost, overwhelmed by the senselessness of the growing wall between Clarke and me, somehow unable or unwilling to make it right.

After a quiet meal of bread and yogurt, we ride our damp laundry back into Padern, a small village of friendly people who send us to the local wine cooperative. For less than five dollars, our five-liter jug is filled with rosé and we strap it sloshing in front of Clarke's handlebars.

Broken clouds make puzzle patterns across the countryside as our heads dance with wine after lunch. On a tiny road near Vingrau, all the way down a small pass, the air fills with our singing and make-believe chicken and tire-squealing noises as, half looped, legs held straight out on either side of our bikes, we meet each corner like out-of-control children, pretending that everything between us is fine.

The ride back to Perpignan the next day is a love/hate relationship with the wind. Along a long stretch of deserted road, we pick up a strong tailwind that shoots us along like silent arrows, unable to hear or see or feel the wind, or even to hear our own tires on the smooth new asphalt. Then a ninety-degree turn brings us up short, and the strong winds are so loud that we're unable to communicate without screaming. We feel as if we've each added fifty pounds to our panniers; the wind pushes us down onto our hard saddles until our rear ends ache, and we strain to push down our pedals just to move forward.

After riding to the Perpignan post office for the third time through heavy traffic, we're disappointed yet again. We'll have to leave without our mail. Clarke goes back inside to arrange to have the packet forwarded to St. Flour, part way to Paris, while I huddle outside with the bikes. Anticipating a fat mail packet, I haven't written home for two weeks and feel every inch of the thousands of miles we are from friends and families. Hunched on the curb, I fight tears.

We hope to enjoy an afternoon swim at the beach but find ourselves pedaling our chubby mountain bikes against a fifty-kilometer-an-hour headwind, managing only seven kilometers in two hours. That night, and the next and the next, as we strip off our shorts and t-shirts to lie naked in our sleeping bags, the wind calms outside the tent, then rises again with the day's sun; in desperation, we consider sleeping during the day and bicycling at night to escape it.

Lunches are eaten on the sunny sides of windbreaks, French baguettes slathered with vinaigrette, sliced veggies and cheese. Yogurt is plentiful, an inexpensive mainstay of our diet, and we always add fresh fruit and a chocolate bar to get us through the afternoon. Every three or four days, we buy a gallon of wine. Although people often pass as we eat our makeshift picnics, they never say more than *"bon appétit"*–eating is apparently very serious business in France, not to be disturbed.

Once back on the road, we're always rejoined by the wind, which always blows in the opposite direction. It seems a permanent fixture in our lives; whenever we change direction, the wind shifts also, staying in our faces. Our frustration grows. One Sunday morning in Narbonne, we sit on a curb outside of a busy *pâtisserie*, eating chocolate creme pastries. "Which direction, Susan?"

"Let me see the map." When it isn't raining, the Michelin is strapped to the plastic wine jug in front of Clarke's handlebars. "I don't like these national highways," I announce. "They're too narrow and crowded. Let's go north and avoid Béziers." We always debate whether to choose the small routes and tiny villages over the wonderful architecture of the cities on the main highways.

The countryside is charming. Manor houses with intricate rooflines peep over the treetops and bedding spills from second story windows in great puffs, petunias and daisies crowding the window boxes. For miles and miles, the narrow roads are framed with tall plane trees that survived the wars and man's penchant to widen his roadways. It's our seventh day in France, and already we're in love with the country.

As we stop at a quiet intersection in Capestang, an old man approaches, offering directions and water. It takes only a moment to determine that Spanish is our best common language, and I follow him across the road to fill our water bottles while Clarke looks after the bicycles. The old man introduces me to his wife, who speaks only French, then disappears into his house. I, of course, understand nothing of what she's saying, but finally follow her to an old water wheel to refill our bottles as her husband trundles back with a jug of bottled water. By the time I return, Clarke is irritable, uninterested in my happy story of the ancient water wheel, anxious to move on. "Look at that church. Over there," I point to a towering Gothic point among the modest surroundings of the small village. "Let's go see it." Clarke doesn't respond.

We stop for lunch at an old iron bridge that arches over a small canal filled with boats. The road across the bridge leads back to town, toward the church, and dense trees partially shade the rare day of full sun and quiet wind. "I'd like to visit the church," I say again after we eat.

Ignoring me, Clarke zips the mustard and vinaigrette into one of his packs. "Susan, it's downhill to the church but uphill back here," he growls finally. "Don't you care about your damn knees?"

"We go up and down hills all day, Clarke. I'll be fine." He looks at me in disbelief. Accepting defeat, I swing onto my bike, and after a few kilometers, hear the ringing bells of Sunday Mass. Why do we always do what Clarke wants? "I was willing to ride back up the hill after seeing the church," I hiss, catching up, "Why weren't you?"

"So what is it exactly that you want, Susan?"

"To see Europe, Clarke." He ignores me. "Forget it!"

I've chosen the route for the day with Clarke's concurrence, but in Lignan, he directs me to turn east instead of north as planned. Gritting my teeth, I say nothing and cycle on in frosty silence. At the next intersection, he asks, "Which way do you want to go?"

"I don't even know where we're going, now that you've changed the whole route."

My simmer begins to bubble as we wind up a steep grade into Corneilhan. Clarke pauses to take a photograph of an unusual churchyard, as usual stopping whenever he wants. One of my duties on the trip is to record in my daily log the place and number of each photo. "What number is that?" I ask grimly.

"Don't get so excited," he answers, leisurely setting his aperture, framing the photo just right.

I'm totally exasperated. "Why do you have to dictate every single move I make, Clarke?"

He ignores me, then we pedal out of town lobbing verbal shells back and forth until we pass three women with baby carriages. *"Bonjour,"* we say brightly, and when the women are out of earshot, fire off a few more rounds.

"The picture was number three on this roll," Clarke says finally.

"I suppose you want me to stop this minute to write it down."

Without answering, he pedals ahead and then stops abruptly, shoving his bicycle into a ditch. Picking up a rock, he heaves it into the wheat field. "Do you have any idea what it's like to put up with you, Susan?"

"Or with you?" I yell as he rescues his bike and pedals up the road. Sitting in the grass at the edge of the ditch, I refuse to follow and hope he won't come back. He doesn't. A gentle spring breeze moves the meadow grass, the rolling hills softening into purples and pale blues in the late afternoon sunshine. After ten minutes, I continue on. Clarke will be long gone by now, I think, but there he is, up ahead, waiting. "He knew I'd follow," I growl to myself, pedaling furiously to the top of the hill.

"You've been whining all day," Clarke starts in.

"And you've been a dictator!"

He rams my bike twice, knocking it over. I explode, now at full boil, spilling scalding venom everywhere. Nobody hurts my bicycle! I lunge for Clarke and we clutch, wrestling back and forth across the deserted road. Clarke has my face in a death grip and my sunglasses dig into my eyes. I can't get loose. "Stop! My contact lenses!" I scream, wresting myself away as my sunglasses fall to the ground, cracking the lenses.

"You never looked good in those stupid sunglasses anyway." Clarke is smug.

"You self-righteous jerk," I shout. "That was physical abuse. I won't live with someone who treats me like that," I announce with total conviction.

"If you want to even up the score, then give me your best shot." Clarke jabs his chest with a thumb. I give him my best shot. It's a pretty good one. Charging like an enraged mother protecting her young, I slam my fist into his ribs. Staggering two steps backward, he stares at me, wide-eyed, hand covering his chest. "I think you broke something, Susan."

"Good! If the nearest airport weren't so far away, I'd be on the next plane home. I don't even want to be in the same country as you, let alone on the same road!"

For a moment, we're quiet as we stand two feet apart on the dusty road, glaring at each other, panting. Then Clarke speaks. "I request twenty-four hours of silence tomorrow."

"Goody for you. Anything to escape dealing with our problems, eh? You can have your damn silence, but let's start it now." Pulling my bike from the ditch, I adjust my bulky packs and then discover a flat tire. "Thanks for ruining the tire, Clarke. Since you have all the tools, help me fix it."

Once again, I realize how much I depend on him. I really wanted to leave, but how could I? Clarke even has all the travelers' checks.

Stuck together by circumstance rather than choice, we pedal on, the unfamiliar road signs reminding us not only of how far we are from home, but now, from each other. Rain threatens as Clarke nods to indicate that it's time to camp and we build our tent for the fifty-seventh time since leaving America, for the first time in total silence.

By the time supper is ready, the weather has turned cold and my legs are covered with goosebumps. Noticing, Clarke hands me my sweats and I cry. Dipping strawberries in chocolate pudding, I feed them to him, one by one. His eyes fill with tears also, and we hold each other without a word, miserable.

The next day, we gesture and point through the markets and our route is decided with hand signals. When I see a service station in the distance, I race ahead to gesture a stop to top off my front tire. Pedaling through a tiny village, we greet everyone with just a wave, then the road curves through tall trees and bursts into sunshine. We hug at lunch, still silent, and late in the day, stopping for a break, I extend a chocolate bar to Clarke and he pours wine for us both. We end the day's ride and our silence next to a beautiful stand of thick trees, kissing gently across the bicycles. I'm exhausted.

It rains hard all night and into the morning. Finally, still inside our tent, we eat bread crusts and yogurt for breakfast–the eggs are outside in the rain along with our dirty plates from dinner. By eleven, the rain diminishes, so we rescue and wash the dishes, run for the eggs, and have a noontime brunch of mushroom and cheese omelettes, fried potatoes and wine.

In Gignac, we wait for an hour in the cold rain for a market to open, but near Aniane, the gray mist has a hint of yellow as low sun breaks through the clouds; when the road seems to disappear, we ask directions to St. Martin as it begins to rain again. "Why there?" the Frenchman asks in careful English, huddling under a large umbrella. "No, no, you must stay here," he insists, incredulous that we plan to continue bicycling in the heavy rain. "There's a school on this road that takes overnight campers."

With no chance of a dry night, we decide to at least inquire at the school, pedaling to a group of low stone buildings obscured by the heavy rain. Class is in session in the main lodge, but the director offers a room for two in an empty dorm, with hot water and breakfast, for seventy-six *francs*, less than thirteen dollars. "Or," he says with a shrug, "you can put up your tent in the rain for thirty *francs*. It is up to you." Dry and clean and warm win out, hands down, no contest, once we feel the warmth of the main building and smell baking French bread in the adjoining kitchen. Electricity to recharge the computer will be a special bonus; it's been almost a month since our last power and roof.

Although we no longer mind doing dishes in minute quantities of cold water from our bike bottles, or bathing in rivers or not at all, or not being able to lie full length in our small tent to keep the sleeping bags dry when it rains, we enjoy the extravagant evening of hot showers under a hand-held nozzle in a stall without an enclosure and a double batch of pancakes with jam. "I can actually take out my contact lenses with clean hands tonight," I say, "and go to the bathroom without squatting in wet bushes in the rain." Wrapped in my warm pink sweats, I happily type on the computer that sits on a chair next to one of the twin beds, damp curls falling over my shoulders. "If it stops raining in the morning, I'll wash our clothes in that laundry area in the yard rather than waiting to find a river without too much mud."

Clarke spreads the map on his bed, studying a shorter route to Montpellier. "What do you miss the most?" he asks, communicative for a change.

"Washers and dryers," I respond, caught in my thought of the moment before.

"How about peanut butter?"

"Fresh, cold milk!"

"And being able to read the labels and package directions at the grocery store." Clarke thinks of a serious one, as he's severely allergic to fish and nuts of every kind.

"Music."

Clarke smiles. "But we have the songs of birds and crickets every evening."

"True, and everything we need is in reach. We can have breakfast in bed – or in bag, rather – without even getting up. We can even get dressed before we get up."

"No rent, gasoline or telephone bills."

"And we have each other, Clarke, like it or not, every minute. It's miserably hard sometimes, but the rewards are immense. I'm really glad we did this."

"Me too, Susan." Clarke returns to his map under the overhead light that lengthens our day while I squint at the computer screen. I can type in almost any position by now and begin writing about how France is different from Spain.

Vineyards have replaced the herds of sheep and goats that graced the Andalucían hills, but the countryside is cleaner, I write. The terrain is flatter here, to this point anyway, and the French bring new meaning to the term *petite route*—we've found ourselves on several roads so tiny that they're like private bicycle paths meandering from one village to the next. And, while we saw some beautiful flowers in Spain, the French seem to fill their lives with blossoms, and with white lace curtains. Dogs aren't chained in this country and we rarely hear them bark; in Spain, dogs barking all night was routine. But we see fewer chickens now, and miss their morning wake-up calls.

We sleep well, waking every now and then to discover that it's raining hard, then fall back asleep, warm and dry and grateful. In the morning, we're ushered through the children's dining room to a smaller room with two tables set with silverware and bowls for coffee or chocolate. As the students collect in the next room, we feel left out as we listen to their musical French without understanding a word.

After breakfast of fresh hot bread, butter, homemade jam and hot chocolate, the youngsters return their cloth napkins to an antique sideboard in the room where we finish our last crusts of bread. Some throw theirs on the pile from half way across the room, bolting out of the door with a sideways look at us; others fold their napkins neatly, placing them carefully in a stack on a corner of the sideboard. One Asian boy folds his into perfect quarters and then, in a rush, throws it at the stack and runs from the room. Another pulls his through a silver napkin ring.

The rain is still heavy when we leave. "Does it hurt, Clarke?"

"What?" he asks.

"Where I hit you. You made a face when you lifted the computer pack this morning."

"I can still feel it, but it's okay."

We ride up into the woods and wind, inching up the crooked road toward Arles. Montpellier is mopping up after a record flood when we pedal through, heading south to the Mediterranean with a strong tailwind as the beach road narrows to two lanes for construction. After hiding from the wind in a bus shelter for lunch, we pull back onto the busy highway. My bike is stuck. "Stop! Clarke, stop!"

He looks back. "Get the hell off the road!" he screams.

"I can't!" Clarke shoves his bike up against a road grader with a grunt and runs back to grab mine. "The tires won't rotate," I try to explain. "The lower hook of the food pack is caught in my front axle."

"Move!" He flings the bike up and over a detour sign with a grimace.

"I thought you were all right," I say as he reshapes my pack hook with pliers.

"I'm a little sore."

Strong wind is always hard, but this stretch of road is impossible. As we cross a narrow isthmus, major fear adds to the sore knees and ribs and hard work of cycling in wind. Traffic is heavy and fast, and we're blown back and forth continuously. I fall twice—luckily into the ditch instead of into the traffic. Clarke manages to stay upright but seems as frightened and frustrated as I. The experience gets old very fast, and lasts for hours. "Let's head back into the mountains," Clarke decides when I fall again. "Maybe we're just not made to enjoy the beach."

Flooding rains have made camping here impossible and we turn inland, searching the countryside for protection, for a house or a farm. What we find is a *chateau*, an inhabited castle, complete with a long bell-pull at the side door. "We can't stay here," Clarke groans. "Why on earth would the owner of a castle allow a tent on his precious property?"

"Why not?" I reply. "I'm sure he has space."

"My French isn't good enough," Clarke finally admits. Like a typical artist, Clarke professes disdain of wealth and power, yet seems intimidated when confronted with them.

"I don't think we have a lot of choice, Clarke. It's almost dark. The guy is just a human being, for heaven's sake." As I decide which door might conceal the lord of the manor, a stately old gentleman emerges from one. *"Bonjour. Nous sommes Americains,"* I begin, the sum total of my French. Feeling stupid, I hiss at Clarke, "How do I tell him I don't speak French?"

"I don't speak American," the gentleman interrupts with a smile, "but I do speak English."

"It sounds to me like you speak British," I smile back, then ask in my best American if we can camp on the grounds for one night.

"It is forbidden to camp wild in France, you know," the man responds, "especially at an historical monument like this. This *chateau* has been in my family since the tenth century, and I must follow very strict rules in order to keep it."

Clarke turns to leave, perhaps sorry for once to be proved right; but I hang on, unwilling to let go of a safe place to sleep with no other in sight, explaining about our journey while I look into the man's eyes and try to feel his warm heart. The *chateau* owner looks from one to the other of us, no doubt seeing two very tired travelers. "Perhaps if it is only for one night, the authorities may not mind too much. Let me ask my wife." Clarke and I mentally cross our fingers. The man returns with a smile, his arms open wide. "You are welcome here," he says with twinkling eyes. "French laws are made not to be respected, eh?"

As he ushers us to a rose garden next to the tennis court, complete with a whitewashed stone wall for a windbreak, fresh water, a barbecue grill, chickens and a fountain full of goldfish, his wife appears, slim and graceful in a wool sweater and skirt, hands full of eggs. "Our chickens only lay lots of eggs when we don't have a cook," she tells us. "Please, take them."

After dinner, I can't resist one jab at Clarke. "So. Rich people are arrogant jerks, eh?"

"Oh, shut up," he replies, smiling.

Between marshy rice fields, on a deserted road too narrow for a bicycle to squeeze past a small car, I notice tiny spots of white light glittering in my vision and my stomach begins to churn—the beginning of a migraine headache. Soon, I can barely make out the road behind the sparkles of blinding light through my cracked yellow sunglasses and stop to dig out my medicine. "If this gets any worse, Clarke, I'm out of commission for a whole day. We'd better get to someplace where we can stay if we have to because I don't relish lying in a wet rice paddy for twenty-four hours." A few minutes later, my vision clears just a little and I pedal into Arles around shiny points of light, dizzy from the strong medication.

Leaning back on a park bench as the "so-la" music of police car sirens pass along the street, I close my eyes while Clarke enjoys French wine from the plastic jug, chocolate croissants, and our first newspaper in ten weeks. He watches the busy French as they chatter in the doorways of the tiny shops. "Even the air is filled with the French passion for life," he says finally. "Why can't we participate more?"

I try to concentrate on him instead of my headache. "Our most profound conversations so far do seem to be with grocers."

As we turn north toward Paris via St. Flour and our mail, I feel a tug from Italy, only four days to the east, a country I've longed to visit for twenty years, and wonder if we'll get there by the end of the trip.

A dirt road and a little stand of trees afford us shelter for the night. Strands of migraine still cling to my head, and Clarke's chest, he finally admits, hurts so much that it's been interfering with his sleep. "Maybe I broke your rib," I venture, full of remorse.

"Maybe," Clarke says. "Would you help lift my bike and the computer pack for a few days?"

"Sure. I could use a little penance."

An early start beats the wind to Beaucaire, but as we cross the river into the city, my vision blurs again with another migraine. "This is ridiculous," I announce, swallowing two pills. We sit on the sunny steps that lead down to the river, and closing my eyes, I imagine emptying myself of worry and fear and exhaustion, then inhale deeply, filling my mind with joy and adventure and happiness. The headache disappears, and we pedal toward Nîmes.

Choosing another tiny path west, we jog around orchards intersected by intercity train tracks and pick up the wind again, which turns the trees into dancers, their leaves rustling like skirts as they pirouette in shadows across the country road. Arriving in Nîmes for lunch, we share a city park plaza with the local winos, drinking from plastic while the winos drink from glass; all of us are homeless, sleep where we can and share conversation with all who pass.

A nasty sidewall bubble has developed in my rear tire, and while Clarke buys a replacement, I wait outside with the bikes. A car pulls alongside. "Are you English?" the driver asks in a British accent.

"American," I smile. "On bikes for a year."

"Well, I'll be damned!" the man exclaims, driving off with a wave as the light changes.

A hundred yards from the mainline tracks, we struggle the tent down into thick grass as high wind caves in its sides, then I fling myself inside with the packs adding ballast while Clarke attaches the tent to a nearby tree. "If the wind gets us, it'll have to take the tree also," he announces, then scurries inside for onion soup and most of a baguette of fresh bread. All night, the rumble of the freight trains competes with the wind to keep us awake. Once, Clarke opens the tent flap to reveal a fluorescent orange-dotted caterpillar passenger train rumbling past, and I wish we were on it, if only for a day's break from the wind.

The next day is worse, and we fight cold and wind for hours until we begin to accept that there's nothing we can do but endure; when the map indicates sheltering canyons and forests near Anduze, however, we're overwhelmed with relief. The steep walls of the magnificent canyon leave little ground on which to build even a tent, but across the river we finally spot two houses off a small road leading from a narrow bridge. Following the path, we look for a place to tuck our nylon house into the trees, stopping with the road at a sign near a large stone house in a tiny meadow. A woman greets us, smiling as she wipes her large hands on a flowered apron while Clarke assembles a question, realizing suddenly that this is a family-run campground. A tent trailer already nestles in the orchard. "Uh, this is camping area?" Clarke asks the woman in French.

"*Oui, monsieur, madame,*" the woman responds brightly.

"How much?" Clarke asks.

"*Vingt-cinq francs,*" she replies. Four dollars. The woman waits as we discuss in English our awkward discovery of a campground where we'd hoped to slip in among the trees. "One moment," she says, and hurries to retrieve a granddaughter.

"Hello," the girl says shyly in English. "I am Angelique. Is the price too expensive?"

"*Oui,*" I answer.

Angelique confers with her grandmother, then makes a counter offer. "Would twenty *francs* be okay?"

Anything more than nothing is too expensive, but we're embarrassed to decline the offer of this warm Frenchwoman. A large black dog romps playfully through the yard and a burro is parked in a barn outside the ancient stone house. Chickens rummage in the road. Seeing the eagerness in the two faces, we say together, "Yes, thank you, *merci beaucoup.*"

Drained from eating almost nothing for two days because of my headaches, by nine o'clock I'm tucked inside the tent while Clarke goes inside the house to practice his French and English with Angelique. She tells him that it's the dream of all French schoolchildren to visit America.

"Susan, wake up! Look at the sky!" Clarke calls early the next morning. "It's clear for the first time in two weeks!"

I stick my head out of the tent. Sure enough, there is a sky in France, cloudless blue above the canyon, the early sun sparking off the churning river below the green meadow that we share with the other camper. On hands and knees at the tent entrance, I breathe in the cold, dry air and feel the sun on my face. It soaks clear through to my bones—this is a day to bicycle! "Move 'em on out," I chirp, a new person, then prepare a quick meal of bread and butter and jam.

After breakfast, I pass the other campsite, searching for a trash barrel. Suddenly, Beethoven's Ninth Symphony bursts from the German tent trailer and I'm lost with the orchestra in this glorious Sunday morning, overwhelmed by the beautiful music in this peaceful French river canyon. Entranced, I cry with both joy and sorrow—joy at the beauty of the music and the surroundings and the wonder of our journey, and sorrow that classical music is not now part of my life. Here, our music is the birds and the rivers, the wind in the trees, and goat and sheep bells; but listening to a symphony is something I miss desperately, and suddenly I'm devastatingly homesick.

As I stand in the orchard, transfixed by the music and my overwhelming feelings, I realize that I can't tell the difference between the joy and the sorrow. They both feel the same. Maybe there is no such thing, I think, as good and bad—wind is just wind, hills are just hills, sun and river are just sun and river. We pedal from the meadow and the stone farmhouse accompanied by Beethoven and the braying of Angelique's little burro, and for once I'm able to experience each moment of the day without judgment or labels.

"Fuzzy on the road!" Clarke calls as he swerves to avoid a big furry caterpillar. I assume as I swerve also that the little fellow may not make it to the other side; even if he does, the grass across the highway is just the same as the grass from which he's just emerged. I chuckle. Most people probably think that Clarke and I are just like the caterpillar, risking life and limb just to see what folks are like on the other side of the ocean. And as we go back and forth across the highways, we see the same wants and needs reflected in the faces of people everywhere—just the tapestry of the background changes, which makes the journey interesting. *Bon voyage,* I wish the caterpillar.

Protected from the wind, the road follows the crystal clean river up into the mountains, weaving magic with its stunning beauty. We pedal slowly, memorizing every kilometer. Each turn is a picture. Old stone *chateaus* and farms nestle into the woods along the river punctuated by clear, cold waterfalls tumbling one after the other among the rocks, and the dazzling blue sky frames flowering fruit trees and ancient pines. Rainbows of bright tulips and iris cascade down the hillsides.

At two, we stop for lunch and letter-writing at the little village of St. André de Valborgne, our backs against a sunny wall next to the river full of fish. After a fill-up of clean, cold water from gargoyle faucets at the village fountain and a wave and a kiss off the fingertips to an old man who hangs over his flowery balcony to greet us, we pedal up a 1000-meter pass, cheered on by the drivers as they overtake us from either direction. On top of the mountain, we wash our hair in a cold waterfall, then ride through a long one-lane tunnel, emerging on the other side in a deep forest for a cold, windy ride along the river, which has changed direction to flow with us to Rousses.

How wonderful it had been to get out of the wind in the canyon, I think—as if by our finally accepting it, the wind no longer needed to prove its existence. Now I relax into it, knowing that it needs to blow just as I need to travel. And so what if we're going opposite directions?

Chapter 6

A MAP OF FRANCE LOOKS like shattered safety glass. It's hard to choose which tiny road will be the best, the most beautiful, the most fun. They're all wonderful. Winding our way into Florac, we realize that because we're on bikes, we enjoyed the scenic river canyon a full day; by car, the trip would have taken half an hour. Now, the canyon opens up to the growing river that spreads wide and falls gently across a small dam in glistening sheets with a soft melody that harmonizes with the quiet hum of our bicycle tires. Shadows hang on the morning, playing among the stone shapes of each tiny village; an early mist curls through the moss-covered houses and garden walls like the gentle touch of an old lady. Soon, the river gives way to lowlands of flowering meadows that, frosted with dew, wait for the sun that finally meets us at Florac.

I lust after a bottle of Rothschild Bordeaux in a small market; at five dollars, it's cheap by American standards but still ten times more expensive than what we buy at wine cooperatives along the way. "Couldn't we splurge, Clarke, just this once?" He continues down the aisle looking for yogurt. "Maybe we can ship a case home before we leave," I suggest, talking to myself and the bottle.

After lunch, we follow a tiny road up a steep pass. Switchbacks pile onto each other like stairs, and we stop for breaks every quarter-kilometer. The stone houses and farms below look like matchboxes scattered across a wide green carpet, and the sun is high and hot. "I'm glad it's just May," Clarke gulps warm water from his last bottle as waves of heat reflect from the pavement. At the top of the pass, a strong wind surprises us around a north corner, cooling us quickly. Enjoy your trip, I say in my mind to the wind, letting it push against me without complaint.

As slowly as we move on bicycles, we're constantly amazed at how quickly the countryside and the conditions change. Today, we've pedaled from river canyon to broad, flowering meadows, then to a steep, barren pass, and now to a wide plateau. We've been cold and hot and now cool again. Soon, the landscape turns another page, to a deep forest of tall pines that plunge with us down the other side of the staircase mountain in a tumbling green fall into the gorge below.

On the other side of Mende, a charming old town, the road zigzags and then disappears over a hill. "We need water," I remind Clarke, who's somewhere else in his mind.

"Up ahead," he responds absently, then leads the way past house after house without stopping. Soon we're working a major hill outside of town. "Wait here," he decides finally. "I'll go back."

Pulling my bicycle as far off the busy highway as possible, I sit on a rock up the steep embankment, knowing that if someone stops to help, I can't explain to anyone but an Englishman or a Spaniard that I'm just resting. Twenty minutes later, Clarke returns with water after convincing a guard dog at the end of a long, steep driveway that he isn't a burglar.

We pedal an hour longer than we want, unable to find a level spot for the tent in the steep forests, then duck out of sight over an embankment at the edge of the road. "If a drunk driver misjudges this turn by a foot, Clarke, we'll be memories. Why didn't you ask to stay in some farmer's field tonight, or for water in town? You're in charge of French, yet I'm the one who asked at the *chateau*." My words feel empty, devoid of substance, and I consider the real question. "What are you afraid of?" I ask softly.

Clarke allows himself to be honest instead of defensive. "It's hard for me to ask for help," he says finally. "And if I do it in a foreign language and I'm not understood, I feel stupid on top of feeling needy."

"If a Frenchman knocked on your door to ask for water or to camp for the night, would you think he's stupid if he speaks poor English?"

"Of course not," Clarke answers immediately, then hesitates. "I don't like the take-what-we-can-find camping plan much anymore either, Susan. If we want to meet people, to be a part of Europe, hiding every night doesn't get us closer." For once, I just listen. "I'll ask tomorrow if we can camp in someone's yard."

In the morning, we choose a meandering road that follows the hills and valleys. Patches of snow frost the top of a 1200-meter pass, and farther back into the rolling woods, the road becomes our private path between stone houses topped with mossy slate roofs, bright flowers adding color like exclamation marks. The tiny villages are held together by a delivery truck that delivers produce, meat and gossip from the city.

A surprise roadside picnic table of marble overlooks a long meadow, and we take advantage of our first-ever opportunity to have a flat place to prepare lunch. A rivulet feeds the tall grasses below, and the sound of the cowbells floating up in the warm breeze is as beautiful as any church bell.

"If I can get to the river again," I declare in the afternoon, "I'm taking a bath." All morning, we've followed the river, but now that I want to use it, it zigs while the road zags and the map shows only one more spot where they intersect. It turns out to be in plain view of the little highway, barren of trees, but after only a second's hesitation, I strip from the waist down, soap and rinse and then start on my hair as the sun dries my rear. As I bend over to gather more rinse water, a small truck rattles by and the driver honks, waving happily.

"You just mooned your first Frenchman," Clarke laughs. I hesitate only a moment, then pull off my t-shirt to scoop water over my breasts.

Although Clarke has promised to ask permission to camp, we find no houses that night and camp outside St. Chély d'Apcher in a thick forest of moss. Instead of being relieved, he's disappointed, eager to make a change in his life. As we settle in the deep moss, we listen to news brought by the cuckoo bird that seems to have followed us from Spain. We hope to reach St. Flour and mail from home the next day.

The closer we get to St. Flour the next afternoon, the faster we pedal, thundering into town like the Pony Express. Tumbling out the door of a bike shop near the edge of town, a young man gazes longingly as we pass, pedaling furiously, one after the other. "Now where?" I wonder at the first traffic light, eyes shaded from the late sun by a hand as I look for signs to the post office. The city is built in two parts. The new part, where we are, spreads out from the base of a steep cliff; the old part is crouched on the top of the cliff like a hat on a straight face.

"Better hope this is the main post office, Susan." Clarke looks at my swollen knees and points to a sign that directs us two blocks to the right. It isn't, of course. Lured by the thought of news from home, however, we churn up the steep cliff toward the high village. Bumper-to-bumper cars squeeze past as we crawl up the side of the bluff, walking and riding and walking again. The road turns back on itself only once, and as we crowd the edge of the switchback, we look down on the narrow street far below.

"There'd better be mail up here," I grumble, wiping sweat from my face with the back of my glove, knees exploding with firecracker pain as we creep up the steep hill in the blazing sun, barely moving.

"Come on, Susan," Clarke encourages tiredly, "it's almost five o'clock."

We inch to the top. After a long drink, I pour the remains of my water bottle over my head and slump to the curb to wait with the bikes while Clarke retrieves our mail from the French postal system. Absently, I rub my knees and comb my dripping hair with my fingers, fluffing it into curls while I guess whose letters will be included in our packet. Knees and fatigue forgotten, I mentally open letter after letter full of news. But Clarke returns empty-handed. "Maybe Jill never sent a packet," I groan, feeling deserted by everyone.

"Do you want to call?"

"Yes!" Abandoning the bikes to look after themselves, we stuff into an international phone booth inside the post office and direct dial America. "Did you send mail?" I ask my sister without even a greeting.

"Lots of it. Tell Clarke there was a letter from his son."

"Well, it never arrived. Thanksweloveyoubye!" Although I'm thrilled to know that our friends cared enough to write, it's not enough.

"Maybe I can get someone to help me call the post office at Perpignan," Clarke says. Muttering to myself, I go outside to sit on the curb and complain to the bicycles about no mail for the fourth time.

Clarke doesn't return for a long time. When he finally does, he looks guilty, and smitten. Uh-oh, I think. "Who is she?" I ask.

"Huh? What?" he answers, totally distracted.

"The mail, Clarke! Did you arrange anything?"

He shakes himself. "Of course!" He sounds irritated that I interrupted his thoughts. "The postmistress wants me to call her in a week and will forward all of our mail to wherever we are."

"Postmistress, is it?" I tease. "Well, I hope you consummate your relationship—by getting our letters!"

By the time we leave the post office, it's six o'clock and there's no place to stay on top of the crowded bluff. We need food. Riding through the beautiful old high city, we look for a market and a place to buy sunglasses—I'm tired of looking at the world through cracks that remind me of our earlier tussle and Clarke's sore ribs. As we round a corner, I spot a black-and-white Siberian husky walking its master on a long leash past the bakery. "Annie!" I shriek, craning my neck to see my own dog's look-alike. We find food but no affordable sunglasses and rewind our route out of the maze of crowded streets. "There she is again!" I whoop as the fluffy black-and-white tail disappears through a doorway, and I pretend that Annie herself has shown up to say hello for our friends and families.

The road out of St. Flour collects long shadows. Clarke leads, repeating aloud French phrases with which to ask for a campsite. A small road off the highway ends at a stone house, and Clarke rattles the screen door with his knock. *"Bonjour, madame,"* he says to the woman who answers. *"Nous sommes Americains...nous sommes...en velo en Europe...pour une année."* I encourage him silently, wishing I could fill his awkward pauses. *"Est possible...pour camping une nuit...s'il vous plait?"*

"Where would you like to camp?" the woman asks in French after wrestling Clarke's request into a semblance of her own language.

"Anywhere," he replies eagerly.

The woman lifts a two-year-old to her shoulder and leads the way to a flat space on a hill above the house. *"C'est bien?"*

"Oui, oui. Merci beaucoup," we answer, then remember to introduce ourselves.

I can't sleep that night because of the pain in my knees. Usually, I push a small pillow beneath them and eventually fall asleep; but the hills of the past few days have finally caught up with me and I toss and turn, unable to get comfortable enough even to rest. Finally, at two o'clock, Clarke says sleepily, "What are you going to do about them, Susan?"

We talk about my taking more anti-inflammatory medication on difficult days, cycling fewer miles, making changes in our diet, taking longer breaks and aspirin before bedtime – anything we can think of that might alleviate the pain and swelling. After agreeing on a late start in the morning, we fall asleep about four. "I can use some extra time to clean and adjust the bikes," Clarke had assured me, "and I need to write home for a new bottom bracket and headset."

I wake up when the heat in the tent becomes unbearable, finding Clarke with his bicycle in pieces. As I prepare a pasta salad for lunch, the bells from the cathedral in St. Flour ring through the clean air, their clear, deep, resounding chimes reverberating through the whole valley, breaking the pastoral silence with throaty echoes that flood the newly-plowed fields. Across the valley, the church at Mentières answers with light grace the dignity of the larger bells from St. Flour. Clarke and I hug, surrounded by the music of centuries, and I imagine our family and friends standing in a circle around us just the way they did during our wedding celebration in the Colorado meadow.

Before leaving, we return to the house for water. The whole family helps fill the plastic bottles. *"Merci pour camping ici,"* Clarke tells them. *"C'est très beau."*

The oldest boy studies an English language textbook at the kitchen table. "Goodbye," he says shyly but seems afraid to go beyond what he knows for sure. We understand.

At the small village of St. Anastasie, we knock at a tiny market. A slender man with white hair smiles and gestures us in with a gallant wave. *"Bonjour, monsieur, madame,"* he greets us with warmth.

Shelves climb to the ceiling, heavy with dusty cans of soup and vegetables and bags of sugar and flour. A small table by the window is cluttered with boxes of cookies and crackers, and a tiny cooler holds a small selection of meats and cheeses. A doorway leads to the kitchen, where the shopkeeper's tiny wife presides over an ancient stove. We look for what we need: bread, fruit, fresh vegetables, yogurt. But we need nothing of what we find. Clarke looks at the expectant proprietor. *"Yogourt, s'il vous plait?"*

The man's face reflects disappointment, then inspiration. Holding up an index finger, he hurries to his adjoining home and returns with four cartons of unflavored yogurt from his own refrigerator and a smile of triumph.

That night, unable to locate a house or farm at which to ask permission to camp, we sleep in a quiet pine forest off a logging road. For the first time, we pull only what we need off the bikes and enjoy the new roominess of our tent and the ease with which we pack in the morning. After an early start, we're rewarded with a long and gradual descent through cool forests and meadows strewn with lambs to Marcenat, where we stop on a sunny bench outside a tiny *pâtisserie* for flaky pastries filled with sweet chocolate, then have seconds and consider thirds before reluctantly winding past the old stone church at the edge of town.

Clarke pedals up ahead in the sunshine. I'm engrossed in the perfect weather and the bright flowers that fill every garden and window box. Our late start of the day before has rested my knees and I feel refreshed, fit, and ready to ride a full day. The small houses give way to meadowland and it feels as if I can see forever in the clear air. Suddenly, my eyes are wrenched right, to the east, where a jagged line of snow-covered mountains glows purple in the distance, engulfing my senses totally. I can see them, oh yes; but it feels like I can also hear and feel and taste and smell them—every valley and canyon and mountaintop and forest, every stream and rock and curving slope. Most of all, I feel their spirit—their beauty and their power—with my own spirit. For the first time in my life, I feel totally comfortable with nature—part of and at peace with its forces.

We've finally adjusted our mental schedules to the *siestas* that plagued us in Spain, and in Bort les Orgues, write postcards and letters until the post office opens late in the afternoon. It's a nice break; we even indulge in a beer at a sidewalk café, our first in France.

A 220-meter climb out of town encourages us to seek shelter for the night at the next town, St. Victour. Around and around we pedal between farms, searching for the village. Finally, an old woman tells us that we're indeed in St. Victour, but we need a market as well as water and a flat place to camp. We never find another town or a market, but settle instead in a small meadow; as we wait for the owner to appear so that we can ask permission to camp, I burrow into my food pack for rice and lentils. By dark, no one comes along, so we homestead.

The morning is cool, and we're anxious to get on the road to warm up and to find food for breakfast. As we cinch the tent to Clarke's bike, we turn at the sound of a bell to see cows moving like slow brown lava through an open meadow gate. When the molten mass catches sight of us, they stop, startled, and stare, apparently afraid to move closer for introductions. "Oops," Clarke laughs. "Time to go."

"Excuse me, girls," I say as we push our heavy bikes through the deep grass toward the cows. The brown sea parts to reveal a farmer at the gate, watching us curiously.

"*Bonjour!*" Clarke greets him, passing nonchalantly through the fence.

I think we should say more, but don't know how. "Um, *bonjour, monsieur.*" I gesture back into the meadow, where the cows spread out to graze. "*Tente,*" I say, tenting the tips of my fingers together. The man looks at me. "*Dormir,*" I continue, cocking my head to the right over my pressed-together hands in the international gesture for sleep. "*Merci, monsieur.*" The man nods, shutting the gate behind us.

It's Saturday, and after discovering that Monday is a holiday, the forty-fourth anniversary of the end of World War II in Europe, we pedal into Meymac to shop for three days' food, a difficult task with our limited pack space. The lovely town is built on a hill, and we can either turn up or down when we arrive. Out is up, so we turn up and find a wonderful vegetable market where we buy all the small, light veggies we can stow. Pedaling to the top of the hill, we find nowhere to buy staples so coast back down the hill past the vegetable market and the road we took into town, to the bottom of the village. Instead of a market, we find signs to the *centre ville* off to the left, and grind back up to the top of the village to another market. "Let's make Monday our restaurant day in France," I suggest as we stuff my food pack to overflowing and tie five long loaves of crusty bread on top of the computer pack behind Clarke.

At the top of the hill for the second time, we eat lunch on a shady bench. Looking up from my veggie sandwich, I spot a man wearing a tie. "He's going to a wedding," I observe as he drives past.

"How do you know?"

"He's the first Frenchman I've seen wearing a tie outside a city."

Sure enough, as we pedal through Pérols south of Vézère, the bride and groom stand outside the church in the sunshine, hugging and kissing friends and relatives. White lace bows decorate auto antennas up and down the street, and a car hood blooms with a huge bouquet of pink and white roses and carnations. Clarke and I wave our congratulations; the newlyweds and their guests wave back happily.

In contrast, at the other end of town, an old man sleeps curled on a wooden bench in front of a market, a thin jacket pulled tightly across his chest above wrinkled brown pants, his dark leather face firm and strong under a cap pulled down over his eyes.

We wind up and down through pine forests at the edge of the mountains. Tomorrow the roads flatten. Except for small nibbles at the beach, we've been bicycling in the mountains for over two and a half months. "Won't northern England be our next real hills?" I ask.

"I'll bet your knees are happy," Clarke says over his shoulder.

I don't answer, imagining what it will feel like to sail along the flat plains with ease. No more aching knees and sleepless nights, I hope; no more agonizing grades in the hot sun with four breaks per kilometer. Yet I'm a Colorado mountain girl–I'll miss their beauty, their clear air, their people, our screaming freefalls down long cool passes and secluded baths in crystal mountain streams. No longer will we find safe campsites tucked in the forests—instead, I picture wheat fields as far as the eye can see. "Where will we ever find places to pee?" I ask.

In spite of its English pronunciation, Bugeat is a pretty little town with glass porches and awnings. The bottom bracket on Clarke's bike starts making horrible noises, and as we pull over to investigate, the entire town erupts in music from a public address system strung the entire length of the village. We ride out of town on a song, from one speaker to another.

Out of Bugeat, it's up and down to Lacelle, where we expect a fifteen-kilometer downhill stretch because the map shows a three-hundred-meter drop in elevation. We've pedaled sixty mountain kilometers already and look forward to the long descent to finish our day. Deciding who will lead the plunge, we round the next corner and gaze at the first dip of a roller coaster—from the bottom. "Well, rats, Susan."

"Well, rats, Clarke."

"Do you want to take this hill today or tomorrow?"

"No and no. Actually," I decide after a pause, "I'd rather get it out of the way."

"Not bad for an old lady," Clarke smiles as I crest the hill without a break.

"Leave it to me to get my mountain legs on our last day in the mountains."

After no one answers at the house we've chosen at the edge of a field, we build our cloth bedroom on an unused road between two wide meadows. Clarke is concerned about the noise he heard earlier under his feet, worried that his freewheel is breaking down. After working on his own bike, he gives mine a tune-up and adjusts my ongoing shift problem. "Although I still think the problem is the shifty operator," he insists.

Ignoring him, I organize our dinner of fried eggplant with tomato sauce, fresh bread and chocolate pudding, then reorganize the food supplies: thirteen containers of yogurt and pudding, cheese, onions, tomatoes, rice, three kinds of pasta, lentils, soup mix, bouillon cubes, sugar, tea, carrots, green peppers, chocolate bars and mushrooms. Clarke carries the overflow: ketchup, mustard, vinaigrette, flour, seasonings, oil, salt (lots of it—the smallest amount we'd been able to buy was two pounds), and five liters of wine.

As the eggplant fries, I think about my relationship with Clarke, which is improving with the weather. Finally, neither of us needs to be right all the time or to control the other. It isn't an effort either; we do it with joy. Now, every meal is a picnic, every night a new home in a meadow or forest or orchard, and we take pleasure in our surroundings and in each other. But the weather has been nice for a week, the scenery glorious, the traffic nonexistent. How will we manage when the rains come again, and the wind?

On Sunday, Clarke breaks down on a steep hill north of Eymoutiers. Pulling off the road, Clarke starts dismantling his lower bracket but can't loosen the bearing without a proper wrench. "It's almost noon, Clarke. If we coast back down to town, maybe we can find an open bike shop. In another hour, everything will be closed until Tuesday because of the holiday."

Always one to do it himself, Clarke agrees reluctantly and we coast back into Eymoutiers. Both bike shops are already closed, but we find an open auto garage, where Clarke sketches his problem on a scrap of paper and the correct tools are offered along with advice and commiseration. We're back on the road by lunch.

That night, we settle in another field. "Where do you think the tent should go?" Clarke asks, although I know he has a spot in mind.

"This looks flat to me," I say, drawing my toe in a circle where I stand.

"This side looks a little high, doesn't it?"

"Not to me."

"This spot is good over here, Susan. It's a little higher right here, but our heads can go there. Side to side is no problem."

"Okay," I sigh. We go through this every night.

Feeding the flexible tent poles through the guides and then into three toe pockets, I stabilize the fabric while Clarke bends the poles into the other three pockets. Then he unloads the bikes while I set up housekeeping inside the tent. Clarke is pulling packs off my bike. "You think it will rain, Susan?"

"No, but I want my packs in here anyway, plus the computer. I may actually change clothes tomorrow." Arranging my panniers neatly on one side of the tent, I watch Clarke tear his apart in preparation for the evening meal.

We're chopping vegetables when we hear someone in the meadow on the other side of the trees. "Sssh!" Clarke touches his lips with a finger. It's too late to ask for permission, too late to run the risk of refusal. We may or may not have been seen; the visitor leaves.

"What would we do if someone makes us leave their property after dark?" I whisper.

"Don't even think about it."

I've been thinking a lot about Italy lately, mentally calculating how long it will take to get there based on our current rate of progress and vague plans. "We've been gone almost three months already, Clarke," I say at dinner. "If we spend another in France, and one each in England, Scotland and Denmark and two weeks each in the little countries of Belgium and Holland"—I'm counting on my fingers as I name each country—"and two months in Germany, say, and a month in Austria—I know it's little but it's also the Alps—then that brings us to Italy in the last month of our trip."

"So?"

"Money. If we run short and have to go home early, you'll have seen France, the country you most wanted to see, but I'll miss Italy. Even though I adore France, Italy has been number one on my wish list since I took Italian in college."

"Are you suggesting we turn back?"

I hesitate. "No, I guess not, but I just want to go on record that I'll be really upset if we don't get there."

"Because it's your money paying for the trip?"

"Because I want to see Italy, Clarke. But yes, that would make it harder for me to accept." I feel childish, but it's true. "If we could agree to take a train to Italy if we're short of time or to find work along the way if we're short of money, I'd feel much better."

"I'll consider it."

In the middle of the night, I wake with my nose smashed into Clarke's armpit. Jabbing him with my elbow, I roll him back up the hill. "Nice flat spot you picked."

At eleven-thirty the next morning, we pedal into le Grand Bourg, hoping to find an open market for yogurt and juice. Barricades block regular parking areas around the central plaza. "I'll bet they're having a parade today," I exclaim. "I'd love to celebrate the end of the Second World War."

"We're here to shop for food. Let's do one thing at a time."

Inside a tiny market, several women chat with the clerk. "*Où se trouve le jus d'orange?*" Clarke asks after a quick tour up and down the aisles.

The clerk points to a shelf on the back wall. "*Anglais?*" she asks.

"*Non, madame, nous sommes Americains.*"

A very old woman touches his arm and points to her ample bosom. "*Francaise,*" she boasts. She holds up five fingers and then two, indicating, we guess, the number of years she's lived in France rather than her age. Clarke nods and asks where she was born. "*Yugoslavia,*" she responds sadly and then finds words that we understand about how much VE Day means to her.

"*Vive la France!*" Clarke and I give her a thumbs up and a smile, and she claps her hands with tears in her eyes.

"Please, can't we stay for the parade?" I beg outside the store, struck by how alive the war still is to these people, wishing to recognize the extra sacrifice of this country by celebrating its end with them.

"No. Every time we stop, our muscles cool down. Besides, how can I in good conscience celebrate an ending to something that shouldn't have begun in the first place?"

As we pedal out of town, I feel cheated but know that if staying had meant that much to me, I should have insisted. At noon, I share my own silent minute with the farm animals, wondering if anyone took much notice of the lives of animals lost to human aggression.

We cross a small stream on a stone bridge. The air is hot and still. "Stop!" Clarke calls back, dismounting. "If we're eating out tonight, let's clean up." Pulling smelly clothes out of his panniers, he heads down the embankment, weaving through the dense underbrush while I grab our towel and my own bag of laundry.

Peeling off our shorts in the six-foot culvert, we shiver in the cold water as we bathe and wash clothes, stretching t-shirts and socks around the brush. Mud oozes between our toes as we slip and slide, dropping things in the water, running to retrieve our laundry before it disappears under the tangled bushes. Cool and refreshed, I tie a pair of underpants in a bow on my rear pack. "Do you think anyone guessed we were down there, Clarke?"

"Of course," Clarke laughs as he attaches a wet sock to a side pannier. "They knew that you were naked."

"You're all talk, buddy."

The bikes are saddled with laundry but Clarke's bike isn't ready to leave. "That figures," he grouses. "I get all cleaned up to go out to dinner, but first I have to fix a flat."

We pedal into St. Sulpice-les-Feuilles. "I'm not hungry yet, Clarke. Let's go on." I want to be properly starving to fully appreciate my only French restaurant.

After twenty more kilometers, we're properly starving but find only a small bar at Lussac-les-Eglises. "The next town big enough for a restaurant is another twenty kilometers," Clarke announces after studying the map. "Can you ride a hundred today?"

"I'll have to. My stomach has its little heart set on *coq au vin* and mushrooms. Besides, we don't have anything to eat but lentil beans."

The late afternoon light softens the rolling countryside with long, smoky shadows. Sheep are strewn about the meadows like cotton balls with noses and ears, and the setting sun glittering in the leaves paints the landscape with its own impressionism. My stomach pleads for courage from my knees, spurring them on with French food fantasies. "I'll bet you'd ride two hundred kilometers to sit in a chair for a meal," Clarke says, shaking his head.

We arrive in la Trimouille after eleven hours on the road. "Our bath did a lot of good," I say, pulling at my sweaty t-shirt.

"It's getting dark already. Where will we sleep tonight?"

"Who cares? On the floor of the restaurant if we have to. Let's eat!"

So. We set off to find the perfect French restaurant – a few tables set with snowy white tablecloths, flowers and flickering candles, a handwritten menu with mouth-watering delicacies, a dusty wine cellar of precious Bordeaux. Pedaling down the main street, we look right and left. No restaurant, just one small bar. Then we pedal to the top of the village. Nothing. Then we coast down to the river, but all we find is ourselves, back where we started, and a second small bar below the Hotel du Nord.

Soft yellow lights appear in second story windows over the shops, and the cobblestone streets are deserted under the pale light of old lampposts. Standing silently on the corner, tired and hungry, we have no place to stay, no idea what to do next, no words to express our frustration. Gentle laughter escapes from the bar below the hotel as the door opens to release a Frenchman who walks alone up the hill, the solitary sound of his footsteps echoing our disappointment. "Want to drown your sorrows in a beer?" Clarke asks finally.

Leaning the bikes against the building to look after each other, we enter the tiny room. From behind the long bar, the white-aproned bartender wipes the counter with a damp cloth, detouring around his last customer, who holds a glass of milky liquor between his hands. "*Bonsoir, messieurs,*" Clarke greets both men, then tries to ask in French, without much hope, if we can get something to eat.

A woman emerges from a back room. "*Oui, monsieur,*" she affirms politely and then walks through a door. Delighted, I follow, expecting to be shown to a table. Instead, I find myself in a tiny back room full of serving trays. Embarrassed, I retreat back to the bar.

"*Non, non, non, madame,*" the customer chuckles, turning toward me with an open smile blossoming under unruly dark hair. He points toward an accordion partition across the side of the room.

"Through here?" I ask in English. The man continues to point. Sure enough, behind the partition are half a dozen tables covered with white cloths and candles. "Clarke! A real restaurant! Real food!" I whisper excitedly. Only one table is occupied, by a couple sharing a quiet glass of wine, their dog tied to a chair leg under the man's feet; as we slip into the next table, the Frenchman nods, politely tugging the dog farther under his chair.

"*Le menu, s'il vous plaît?*" Clarke asks the young man who greets us. The boy looks confused and calls to his look-alike sister. "*Le menu, s'il vous plaît?*" Clarke repeats hopefully. The boy and girl look at each other in confusion, then leave the room and return with the customer from the bar as Clarke thumbs through his phrase book to find another way to ask for a menu. "*S'il vous plaît, le menu?*" he tries again.

The man responds with a long unintelligible explanation—of something—then stands back, pleased to be of service. Clarke looks at me for help; I shrug. Then everyone else shrugs and the girl disappears into another room. *Dear Friends*, I begin another mental postcard, *we've been in France for three weeks but are on the verge of starvation because we're not smart enough to ask for a menu.*

Before I can wonder what will happen to our bicycles if we starve to death in a restaurant, the girl returns with a plate of hardboiled eggs and sliced tomatoes in a vinaigrette dressing, a huge bowl of what looks like minced meat, and a basket of fresh crusty bread. "Maybe there's no menu here," Clarke guesses, "and she's showing us dinner." He nods approval.

"But what about your allergies? How do you say 'fish' in French?" My lack of French is proving to be more than frustrating, and before Clarke can look up the word, I pantomime the motion of a swimming fish.

"*Poisson!*" says the girl, eyes alight with understanding. "*Non, madame, non poisson!*"

"*Très bien, mademoiselle, merci,*" I thank her profusely, and there are smiles all around, including at the next table.

Clarke orders a bottle of chilled white wine, certain of his pronunciation after three weeks of buying French wines at the cooperatives. Raising our glasses in a toast, we serve each other hardboiled eggs and sliced tomatoes. "This dressing is delicious!" I exclaim, wiping up the last of the vinaigrette with a piece of bread. "How do we eat this?" I ask, hungrily eyeing the minced meat.

"Beats me." Clarke spoons a large chunk onto his plate. A forkful disappears into his mouth, followed by a big chunk of bread. "Wait'll you taste it!"

I stab a bite of the delicately spiced meat. "Whatever it is, it's heaven!" I exclaim, munching contentedly.

We eat in silence, looking up from time to time to smile at each other and the proprietress as she walks back and forth to check on her four customers. Our bread disappears and she brings more, hesitating for a moment to observe our feeding frenzy as I look over Clarke's shoulder at the other diners, who delicately spread small pieces of bread with tiny bits of the *paté*. Our bowl has only one bite left in the bottom. As the proprietress returns with yet another basket of hot bread, I daintily spread a tiny portion of the *paté* on a small crust and pop it into my mouth. The woman, eyes twinkling, tips the bowl toward Clarke to ask if he wants to finish the last crumb. "*Non, merci,*" he says in a stoic gesture of moderation.

Then comes the main course – tender veal and fresh green beans lightly seasoned with garlic. With more fresh bread and wine, it's better than all of our food fantasies, and is followed by Brie, camembert and Swiss cheeses and an apple tart. Stuffed and happy, we groan with pleasure. The bill, handwritten in careful calligraphy, is a hundred and forty *francs*, twenty-three dollars, including wine. "Let's have an after-dinner drink," Clarke suggests, not wanting the evening to end. Waddling through the partition to the bar, we nod to the man and woman at the next table, who are just beginning their main course. "*Deux Grand Marniers,*" Clarke says to the bartender after paying the dinner tab.

"Which way are you traveling?" asks the bartender in French, joining us in a toast to our wonderful meal.

"I'll get our map," Clarke replies. While the roomful of customers discusses the best route to Paris, Clarke circles the favorite towns, and in the embrace of French liquor and the villagers of la Trimouille, we lurch out in the black evening to camp in the town park. Over the bridge, past the swing set, under the keep of a tall tree, we fumble together our tent and usher out the last mosquito as the cuckoo bird from Spain calls high above from an outstretched branch.

Early sun makes a picture of the glassy river the next morning. The river's thin orange bank splits the white face of an old mill into twins, and shrubs of fluorescent green are background for the bursting spring yellow along the water. Standing on this floating canvas are young elder trees, all tied at the top like field broccoli, coppery tree trunks mirrored to look like the outstretched legs of Alaskan King Crab.

The small road out of town is a horse cart wide. Side by side, we pedal on our own silent bicycle path, enjoying the cotton ball lambs in the morning sun.

Chapter 7

THE FARTHER WE TRAVEL north, the more elaborate the bells. In Spain, they were the tiny brass wind chimes of the sheep and goats and then the simple village churches ringing the hour. Now, in Le Blanc, the church bells play an entire song, deep and harmonious.

At Chatellerault, a lively mix of old and new architecture and fashion, I find replacement sunglasses and now see the world without cracks. My old yellow lenses made the world appear greener and brighter than it was; these don't distort color, and I'm mildly disappointed that spring isn't as far along as I pretended it to be.

Roller coaster hills pull us gasping into St. Gervais for water, and I'm led into the men's room by the mayor himself. After Clarke hurries to join us, the man asks about our trip in French and, proudly, a little English. We chat next to the smelly urinals as rain clouds crowd the horizon outside, then pedal down the pretty road under darkening shadows. Eager to ask permission to camp in someone's garden, we turn down a tiny road. As we pedal away from the main highway, I have a strong sense that we aren't safe. The air feels wrong somehow, the light in the sky forecasting more than just rain. The rundown farms don't feel poor – they feel sick, or dangerous. "This doesn't feel right, Clarke."

He snaps his head around. "You feel it too? Let's get out of here." Glancing back to make sure that nothing follows us, we pedal fast out of the area.

Near Jaulnay, a beautiful manor house complete with a large garden and fenced courtyard seems to reach out and grab me. "How about here?" I call ahead to Clarke as he peers through the courtyard at the magnificent home. The place is perfect; the garden is roomy, rain is threatening, and we're both tired. But if we ask to stay here,

Clarke will have to expose his meager language skills to people of means. One thing about this trip—if we have issues about anything, we have ample opportunities to face them.

"I'll give it a try," he says reluctantly, then consults his pocket French dictionary. As we pull into the courtyard, a white car with a woman and a young girl inside follows us. Clarke introduces us in French.

"You may speak English if you like," the woman says gently in perfect English.

"*S'il vous plait*," Clarke continues in halting French, "let me try to speak your language."

"*Très bien*," the woman smiles. A man and two young boys come outside, and the whole family escorts us to a soft bed of thick grass next to a row of tall trees and flowering hedges. The woman, a teacher at her daughter's school, allows the children to help put up our tent; and David, Matthew and Mary help us with their language as we describe our trip in gestures and limited French. No sooner have we started our meal than the boys appear with their own bicycles; we let them take turns riding my bike, then Clarke rides with them until dark as I show Mary the inside of the tent, which we call the *petite chateau*.

"When someone spoke English to me in Spain," I say to Clarke later, "I was delighted. Good for you to continue in French, particularly with someone wealthy."

"Thanks for the nudge."

The *chateau* at Chinon, where Joan of Arc recognized Charles VII hidden among his courtiers and inspired him to reconquer his kingdom, dominates the city from a high bluff across the Loire. There are few visitors except for schoolchildren, so we let the bikes guard themselves while we wander about the castle, checking from the high stone walls every now and then to make sure that they haven't rolled away.

When we see that they've been joined by two shiny ten-speeds with brand new panniers, it doesn't take long to identify their riders, in black padded bicycle shorts, among the other tourists. New Yorkers Eric and Mary are just beginning a two-week bicycle tour of the castles of the Loire complete with confirmed hotel reservations for each night and a detailed plan of their daily route and mileage. Our non-scheduled meanderings surprise them, and Clarke and I wonder what they'll do if bad weather or bicycle repairs interfere with their careful itinerary.

"Our bikes need a bath," Clarke remarks later as we pull them from their locks outside the famous gates, noting how much our panniers have faded compared to

Eric and Mary's new packs. In short order, we all get one, as the storm that has threatened for two days follows us up the Loire, and holed up next to a barn against the driving rain, we worry about our new friends' ability to reach their planned destination that night.

The *chateau* at Saumur is closing for the traditional two-hour lunch when we pedal up the next day in a depressing drizzle. Unwilling to stand in the rain until two o'clock, we admire it only from the outside; as we turn our bikes around in the parking lot, we're spotted by a tall woman and a white-haired man walking from the castle. In crisp English, the woman explains that she and her friend are from Frankfurt and that she traveled in Asia by motorcycle many years ago. Anxious to compare travel stories, Christa invites us to join them the next day in Angers, giving us their address in Germany along with a great deal of stern advice not to camp alone in the woods, insisting that we take her small can of mace, amazed that we've been in Europe almost three months without being robbed.

Because of rain and headwinds, we decide against Angers, and pedal east through the Loire Valley. The cycling is blessedly flat, a delightful change for my knees. Nor far from Saumur, we follow a tiny road that turns out to be a dead end. Coming back, we spot two men standing by a car, perhaps Moroccans. As usual, we greet them with waves and a friendly, "*bonjour, messieurs!*" They shout angrily in reply. Uneasy, we hurry along the dirt road back toward the main highway.

Suddenly, a car pulls alongside us, then cuts in front of Clarke, forcing us to stop. The two men have followed us. The passenger yells at Clarke, looking not at him, but at me, and at our heavy packs. Transported back to Morocco, I wish that I hadn't stuck Christa's mace deep in a rear pannier, and scanning the area for help, I see that we're still well away from the main road with no houses or farms to which we might run.

Two more cars, one right after the other, pull in behind us on the little dirt road, trapping us completely. Looking at Clarke, I'm sure the trip is over.

Our rescue happens in seconds. The driver of the last car blasts his horn. The first driver glares in his rear view mirror and shakes his fist out the window while his companion continues to threaten Clarke. Then the middle driver honks, revving his engine angrily. After a moment of indecision, the first man drives off in a spray of dirt, shouting curses out his window, followed by the other two cars.

"Get back to the main road!" Clarke yells as he pedals away from the cars, finding a shortcut up a ravine to the main highway just as the first car doubles back, moving slowly as if searching for us among the trees. They pass below us, unable to follow our path up the ravine.

Too frightened to speak, I dig out the mace and jam it into my jacket pocket, then pedal down the highway, shaking, scanning every passing car for our assailants. "What do you think they really wanted, Clarke?" I ask when I can talk.

"I'm glad we didn't find out."

Depressed and nervous, we spend the rest of the day crisscrossing through the countryside in a circuitous route in case the men are still looking for us. France seems different now, gray and lonely and cold. Is this how we'll feel from now on?

Later, we call the St. Flour post office, and although Clarke enjoys the lovely voice of his postmistress, it isn't enough to lift his spirits. No mail has arrived from America. Slowly, we cycle against strong winds and drizzle, wondering what would have happened to our trip if we'd been robbed. After all, we carry everything on our backs, or our bikes' backs anyway, including our plane tickets home.

Hearing a noise behind us, I turn quickly, heart thumping. A young boy on a bicycle moves up to ride alongside me, anxious to know who we are and where we're going, cheering us immediately. At an intersection, an old couple comes out of their farmhouse to visit, and we soon begin to push away the memory of the two men.

But we don't push it far enough. That evening, Clarke asks an old woman if we can camp in her garden; frightened, she gives us directions to the nearest campground, plainly wanting us to leave quickly. "When we feel something, Clarke, the whole world seems to feel it around us."

"Yeah. Well, we'd better shake it off if we expect to find a place to stay tonight."

"After what that German woman told us about how dangerous it is to sleep in the forest, I'm not in the mood to push our luck any farther today."

We find an old flour mill at the end of a long lane. A fashionable young woman answers the door, and although her English is excellent, Clarke again insists on speaking French. Gwendoline lives in Paris, she explains, but is spending the weekend with her mother and her sister's family. We're welcome to ask her mother for permission to camp when she returns home in a few minutes.

Albane welcomes us with no hesitation, and we put up our tent behind the old mill house. After our dinner, the family invites us into the house for drinks, and we visit over Bordeaux and cognac about travel and language. Albane, an attractive widow, is open and lively, very happy with her life in the French countryside after living for many years in Paris. "As long as my children and grandchildren visit often," she says, smiling, "I love it here." As we leave, she expresses regret that we didn't arrive early enough for her to prepare enough food for us to share a meal with her family after her oldest daughter arrives from Paris at midnight.

In the morning, we meet Albane's other daughter. "This will not happen to you again in France," she explains. "My mother is not a typical Frenchwoman. She is open and outgoing—but most French, they are private and reserved. You will not be entertained in another French home like this."

"Then what a nice way to forget about those men on the road," I tell Clarke as we pedal back to the small highway.

Another special treat comes our way at noon when we discover a small park with a restroom offering hot water. It's a first, and we hurry to wash our hair before anyone can stop us, then set up our picnic lunch on a real table among several other French families.

In the afternoon, we pedal through Tours, stopping in a tiny village east of Dierre for the night. Olivier and Sylvie are renovating an old wine *cave* for their home, living in the house next door while they work. Of course we can sleep in their garden, they say, giving us a tour of their house-to-be. After dinner, they invite us in for coffee and cognac. Sylvie speaks no English and I no French, but Olivier and Clarke understand enough of each other's languages to make conversation. Olivier asks what we miss most. "Music," I answer immediately.

Insisting that we join them for coffee in the morning, Olivier produces a tape of "Love Me Tender" recorded by his brother's band, and the American song and the French couple's thoughtfulness bring tears to us both. "I thought the French were private and reserved and they don't entertain strangers in their homes," Clarke remarks as we pedal toward the famous *chateau* at Chenonceaux in the morning.

The castle is magnificent. Clarke stands for thirty minutes in front of an intricately carved fireplace. "This fireplace alone is a life's work," he says.

As we leave the grounds, Eric and Mary, the New York bicyclists we met at Chinon, walk up the path toward us. "Hello!" they shout. "We saw your bicycles outside."

"What a coincidence," Clarke remarks later, back on the highway. "We even went two different directions at Chinon."

But I'm not listening. Instead, I feel a voice deep inside insisting that we stop. "I know this is dumb," I say finally, "but if we don't stop right now something awful is going to happen."

Clarke decides that I'm serious. "Let's take a break over by that bus stop," he offers, then sits quietly while I wrestle with my feelings.

Finally, my discomfort lessens and feeling rather silly, I say, "I have no idea what that was all about, but I feel better now. Let's go." As I pedal down the road, I search the roadside and my intuition for clues, distracted. Although my premonition is no longer one of physical danger—perhaps because we followed my hunch—I still have the strong sense that something or someone is in control of my actions, or wants to be.

"I have a feeling too," Clarke says after awhile, "but it's not one of danger. It's more that we're going to meet someone."

"I hope they're friendly," I say, shivering as I remember our unpleasant encounter the day before.

At Bourre, we seek shelter for lunch at a deserted train station. Although we eat the last of our food and the next day is a holiday, we take our time. "We're not supposed to leave here yet," I announce finally.

"I know," Clarke responds, to my surprise.

To distract us from our unsettling thoughts, we talk about what it might have been like to live in Europe during the war, worrying each day about nearby bombs and battles, actually seeing the destruction that men wreak on each other instead of reading about it in newspapers thousands of miles away. After two hours, we both get cold at the same time and stand, knowing without a word that we're supposed to continue on. Late in the day, Clarke says, "Stop at the next farm, wherever it is." The next farm seems to be a big farmer's market, or a celebration of some kind, and as we weave through the crowds, one couple catches my eye for some reason and I greet them in passing. Clarke stops dead.

"Where are you going?" the man asks in perfect English.

I start to answer, then can't. The someone or something seemingly leading us has neglected to share with me the final plans for our destination. "We were thinking of seeing the *chateau* at Chambord on our way to Paris," I say tentatively, remembering yesterday's plan of a thousand years ago.

"Perfect," smiles the man. "Régine and I live thirty-five kilometers from here on the road to Chambord, which is only ten kilometers from our house. Will you stay with us tonight?"

"We'll be there in two hours," I respond, certain that this meeting is the one we've been waiting for all day.

"You realize, Susan," Clarke says as we pedal as fast as we can to reach Vineuil by seven o'clock, "that if we'd ridden at our normal pace today, we would have missed meeting these people."

"We certainly wouldn't have been able to tackle an extra thirty-five kilometers at the end of the day."

A car honks behind us an hour later. Régine sticks her head out of the passenger window. "See you for dinner!"

Gilles and Régine live in a refurbished sixteenth-century monastery complete with tunnels to the woods and to the chapel by the river. As soon as we arrive, our bicycles are tucked safely into the garage and we're escorted upstairs to a real bedroom with the first double bed we've seen since our arrival in Europe. "Would you enjoy a hot shower before dinner?" Régine asks, eyes sparkling. "Here are some fresh towels. Take your time and join us for drinks when it is convenient."

"How can we ever thank you for this?" Clarke begins, but she cuts him off.

"It is our pleasure."

As I stand under the hot steamy water, I can't remember my last shower—was it at Carlos's in Spain, kneeling in his tub, washing my hair in his hand-held nozzle? No, it was in Aniane, at the boarding school, where we washed under a hand-held shower without an enclosure. Whenever, this is fabulous—the water pours over my head, washing dirt and soap and grateful tears down my face. Wrapping myself in a clean white towel, I weigh myself; I've lost thirteen pounds.

Gilles is in the living room pouring Clarke a scotch and water when I join them. "I was an exchange student to California in high school," Gilles explains. "When I saw the 'U.S.A.' sign on the back of your bicycle, I had to visit with you."

"My husband loves Americans," says Régine, her hand on Gilles's shoulder.

During dinner, we try to explain what happened that day. "We had the strongest feeling that we were being led to meet someone," Clarke begins.

"We know," says Régine with a smile.

The conversation is in English; it's glorious to converse with Europeans about more than just bare necessities, and we speak in depth of our trip, our countries, our families. "Meeting your children makes me miss mine even more," Clarke comments after discussing school and foreign language study with their eighteen-year-old daughter.

"When did you last talk with your children?" Gilles inquires.

"Not since the day we left America, because of the time difference. When we're near telephones during the day, it's the middle of the night in California. And when my children would be home from school, we're tucked away in someone's field, miles from the nearest pay telephone."

"You must call them from here," Gilles says. "Our treat."

Clarke protests but Gilles is already dialing California. Clarke weeps to hear Jennifer's voice. Chris is out. "I miss you, Jenny. Tell Chris we'll find a way to call you both on May twenty-fifth, at six in the morning. Get up an hour early for school, okay?"

After breakfast the next morning, Régine offers the use of her washing machine for all of our clothes while their son bicycles with us to the castle at Chambord. Without our heavy packs, we race to the castle, amazed at its immensity. "It was built as a hunting lodge for the king," the young man explains.

"A hunting lodge with four hundred and forty rooms?" I'm aghast. "How could they ever find each other?"

Returning to the house, we find clean, dry clothes and lunch. We've been taken into this warm, loving family as if we belong, and we accept their generosity with gratitude. "Perhaps one summer we can trade homes, so that you can visit France again and we can visit America," Gilles suggests.

"As soon as we have a home to trade."

After photos all around, they kiss us on both cheeks and we hug them American-style. "Stay at the campground at Bois de Boulogne in Paris," Régine calls as we reluctantly pedal away from their house.

"It will be hard to sleep in someone's field tonight after such a wonderful evening," Clarke says after a few quiet kilometers.

"Especially since we still have no food, and today is a holiday."

"Ouch. And it's already five o'clock. But keep your eyes open, just in case. We seem to be well taken care of at the moment."

We pedal through the large city of Blois but the stores are closed. And then someone comes out the door of a tiny sweet shop in a nearby village. "Why aren't you closed today?" Clarke asks the owner.

"I will close tomorrow instead," he explains. We buy ice cream and tarts and bread—not a real meal, but enough to tide us over until morning.

Amazed that our recent experiences seem to be no accident, sad to lose the special family we just found, we keep to tiny roads two bicycles wide and pedal side by side until the tent posts on my bike catch on one of Clarke's side packs, spilling all of us in the ditch with me on the bottom. "Our first real accident, and it's with each other," I laugh. "Not a car in sight! Get off me, you guys."

The landscape is flat and rolling, miles and miles of cereal fields spread out under the blue sky like soft fur. Gliders float silently overhead, watching over us like quiet spirits. Near the village of Villemardy, near Vendome, Clarke points to a tower in the distance. "We'll stay there tonight," he declares.

"What is it?"

"I don't know."

Later, as we pedal past the tower in back of an old farm, I greet a woman across the road as another pedals toward us on an old bicycle. The cyclist stops as the first woman approaches, arms full of newspapers and fresh lettuce. The women speak no English, but full of encouragement from Gilles and Régine, Clarke bursts into a lively dialogue of gestures and a bit of French, explaining about us and our trip. Across the road, three heads pop over a fence, then join us in the dusty street—we must look like sparrows gathered around a bread crust, chirping and pecking and fluttering our wings.

Clarke asks if we can camp in someone's garden. The group looks confused, not understanding his request, debating at length the location of the nearest nice campground. I remember the woman outside of Saumur who tried to send us to a camping site away from her home. This time, I refuse to miss an opportunity to talk with these boisterous people. "*Non*," I insist, "*c'est possible dormir ici?*" Is it possible to sleep here, I try to say.

Just then, a car approaches and a young man and woman join the throng around us. The woman with her arms full of lettuce explains that the man is her son, a doctor who speaks a little English. He listens to our request and translates it to his mother, who responds in French, smiling broadly. "Of course you may sleep in my field, but you will have to share it with the sheep and geese and chickens." After we assure her that we would be delighted to sleep with her animals, Simone leads us across the road to the farm under the tower that Clarke predicted would be our home for the night. I look at him sideways, and he shrugs.

Simone's cat watches us put up our tent, sitting in the doorway like a sentinel while we dig into the bottom of the food packs for something or other to go with our bread and tarts. Clarke pulls an almost-empty package of macaroni out of my pack and rummages in his panniers for our tiny stove. "It seems too much of a coincidence that we're staying under a tower that you picked from a distance," I announce, "not even knowing if anyone lived nearby."

"After all that's happened to us the last few days, nothing surprises me," Clarke responds, pouring the dry macaroni into a pan of boiling water. "Tear me off a hunk of that bread, will you?" A head pops in the tent flap, followed by hands filled with ice cream bars and an invitation for coffee at the farmhouse.

Inside Simone's simple kitchen after dinner, a large table joins French friends with coffee and a bottle of *calvados*, homemade apple brandy. Smiles light up the room as we enter, and we're greeted like heroes, like Martians, like movie stars. Behind a cup of sweet, strong coffee and a tiny glass of *calvados*, I try to follow the conversation the best I can, allowing Clarke to do the talking and gesturing and sketching for us both.

Therese, Simone's bicycle friend, sings in a beautiful, pure voice. As everyone joins in the chorus, I join along, filled with deep, comfortable joy. Clarke reaches for my hand, and we hold tightly to each other, pressing each other's fingers.

As the strong brandy flows, so does the conversation. English is almost non-existent at the table, but the villagers who know not a word, unwilling to be left out of the conversation, use whatever means they have—gestures, words, pictures, volume, speed, arm-waving—to communicate. And I can understand them, I realize with a shock. So maybe I can be understood also. Jumping in with my own arms and legs, I discover instantly that language is only a barrier if I allow it to be. I laugh and joke and talk about America and our trip and our lives as if I can speak French; and Simone, Therese, Bernard, Didea, Hermonie, Monique, Christelle and Mathias understand me as if they can speak English.

At midnight, we leave the farmhouse with fresh eggs for breakfast and an invitation to use the bathroom next door before coffee at Simone's the next morning. We cross the yard holding hands. "I really got it tonight about communication, Clarke. Language is just intention—of the speaker to be understood and by the listener to understand. That's all. Those people weren't in the least intimidated by foreigners or by their not speaking English. They were just who they were, ready to share their whole hearts in whatever way they could. I shouldn't be intimidated, either." I come out of my self-imposed barriers like a flood, no longer willing to allow my inadequacies to be inadequacies. I can communicate with the French without French!

"Welcome to France," Clarke says softly. That night, France holds us in its arms like a cradle.

The best bathroom in the village must have been selected for our use the next morning—tub, sink, toilet and bidet all in lavender, scrubbed clean, with fresh, fluffy towels. We don't bathe; after showering at Gilles and Régine's two days earlier, it seems wasteful compared to river baths every two weeks.

Coffee includes bread and homemade jam and honey from the family bees. As we pack our bikes, the townspeople gather, pressing our hands full of eggs and apples for our trip. After all the times we've packed, automatically and efficiently, this morning I can't even remember how to dismantle our tent. The loving audience flusters me, but I'm so happy that I could dance on the sunlight. We take pictures and hug and kiss everyone, and then kiss them again. There are tears all around. Simone and I walk across the lawn, arms entwined, not knowing how to say what we feel. We kiss again, and hold each other.

Clarke leads when we pedal away, and we wave to Simone and her friends across the garden wall until they're out of sight. Then I dissolve into tears, astounded by the overwhelming love shown us by the village people and by the lesson I learned about communicating with love instead of language. Sad as I am to leave Simone and her friends, I realize that it doesn't really matter that I will never see them again, because as a part of me, they're in my heart forever, wherever I go.

Clarke gets his own lesson about inadequacies not being inadequacies that evening. Because of our late start from Simone's and a leisurely tour of the church at Vendome, we decide to ride only sixty kilometers. In the afternoon, as we stop at an intersection to check the map, a gray Citroën passes, its occupants waving. It stops briefly up ahead, then goes on.

We continue down the road as planned. As my odometer turns 60.1 kilometers, I notice a handsome man at the gate of a large, wooded yard. When I stop, the Frenchman promptly invites us for a cold drink, and as he opens the ornate gates, the gray Citroën that passed us earlier is parked in the drive. André has been waiting for us, he admits, and fetches his family and a wicker basket of beer, wine and sparkling water.

On the patio of the beautiful country home deep in the woods, we meet André's family. His daughter Caroline is studying English and German in school and wants to be a translator; his wife Francoise speaks English quite well also; André's English improves with every sentence. Little Marie, too young to study foreign languages, tries to look interested; Clarke and I know how she feels and do our best to use French words when we can.

This is a perfect place to spend the night–large green lawns flat and protected from the wind by towering trees and a family who's already expressed kind hospitality toward us. In France, Clarke has always been the one to ask for permission to camp, but he seems not in the least inclined to pose the question. We usually consult each other before asking at a house or farm, but there's no opportunity now. "Would you mind if we put our tent in your garden tonight?" I ask André.

Clarke frowns as if I've committed an unpardonable sin. "Of course, you are welcome to stay here," André says. "And please join us for dinner. Would you like a shower first?"

In our long cotton pants–as dressy as we can get–we begin the meal on the patio with *paté* and chilled champagne, then go inside for dinner. The house is magnificent, filled with original art, fine furniture and antiques, china, silver and fresh flowers. Dinner is superb, beautifully served complete with fine Bordeaux and cognac; the family is reserved, well-bred and gracious. They have traveled only once outside of France, and according to Francoise, see no reason ever to do so again; our decision to leave our own country for a year must be unthinkable to her.

Clarke is unusually quiet during the meal. André, speaking better and better English as his self-consciousness is overcome by his desire to communicate, touches me immensely as he struggles to understand what we've learned, how we feel, who we are. Well after midnight, we leave André and Francoise's with a breakfast invitation. As we crawl into our sleeping bags, Clarke complains about the expensive wines and *patés* that we were served. "Spending money on such frivolous things is shallow and greedy. I should have told them that I don't eat this kind of food, that I believe it's wasteful to spend so much on delicacies when people are starving."

I'm relieved that Clarke kept his comments to himself. In contrast to Clarke's discomfort around money, I'd been perfectly comfortable being kidnapped by this affluent family. While never truly rich, as a successful stockbroker before moving to the Colorado mountains, I'd been surrounded by money for years and have many friends with real wealth. To me, money has nothing to do with what a person is inside, and believing that someone is less of a person because of success is as unjust as believing that someone is less of a person because of poverty.

After breakfast the next morning, we pedal a few kilometers down the road in silence, then I stop. "We all have shells," I begin, "nationality, religion, money or occupation. But inside those shells, whether they're white or brown or porcelain, are human beings just like you. Shutting someone out of your life because of money–too much or not enough–denies their humanity, which transcends materialism. That's not like you, Clarke. Your unwillingness to allow yourself to go inside André's success is no different than his wife's unwillingness to discover lands and people outside of France."

"It just seems so unfair that a few people in the world have all the wealth while others are starving."

"Maybe, but look at all the people who earn their own livelihood by providing things that wealthy people buy. And the more money people have, the more they have to give."

Our next kidnapping happens only hours after we leave André's. Clarke is leading, pedaling through a small village, when a man runs out in the dusty road and stares after Clarke, hands on his hips in amazement, planting himself, legs spread, mouth open, in the middle of the street. *"Bonjour, monsieur,"* I call, swerving to avoid running over him.

"Okay, *adios!*" the Frenchman replies.

Catching up with Clarke, who missed the whole exchange, I say, "A man just chased you into the street and yelled 'okay, goodbye' to me in Spanish."

Just then a black car rolls past, traveling in front of us at a bicycle's pace, turning left on the road we plan to take out of town. Once, it stops as if to wait for us, but as we approach the car creeps ahead again. Finally, it turns onto a dirt road, and Clarke and I continue on our way. "I wonder what that was all about," Clarke says as I glance back. The black car is stopped on the dirt road, the driver frantically motioning us to come back. It's the same man who ran into the street behind Clarke.

"Let's go back," I suggest. "I'm curious." As we turn around, the Frenchman leads us slowly in his car down the dirt side road into the woods, to a tiny shack by a small river. Here's where we get robbed, I think, having second thoughts as I remember the angry men who chased us near Saumur.

Getting stiffly out of his car, the man puts out a strong, gnarled peasant's hand to each of us, motioning us to follow him into the shack. Inside are a dusty table and two chairs; a small cabinet hangs on the tarpaper wall. Still silent, the man gestures for us to sit and pulls from the cupboard a bottle of red wine and three sticky glasses. From a corner, he brings up a wooden crate and sits down with the same dignity as if he were presiding at a banquet. Ceremoniously, he opens the bottle of wine, filling the three glasses, raising his in a toast. "*Salut*," he says, his first word, and we respond. He pours again, holds up his glass in a toast, drinks, and then tries to explain, searching the graffiti on the shack's walls for words.

"Wait," I say, holding up a hand, "*dictionnaire*," then bound off to get our French/English dictionary.

We piece together this story: the Frenchman was a pilot in World War II, and when his plane crashed over Great Britain, the English pulled him from the wreckage. Seeing Clarke's "U.S.A." sign, the man must have thought that this was a chance to repay the kindness our English cousins had lavished on him almost fifty years earlier.

He tries to explain about the shack, using simple words. I understand immediately that this is his hiding place, the place where he can enjoy a bottle of wine and quiet without being bothered. "*C'est cachette*," I suggest after looking in the dictionary for just the right word.

"*Oui, madame, oui!*" he exclaims, eyes shining. "*C'est cachette!*" This special place is ours, he explains, to enjoy for as long as we want. He points to a small rowboat tied to a willow; the water is clear, the grasses along the bank barely moving in the invisible current, the sun bright in welcome. With another nod and handshake and a rusty tin of sardines from the tiny cupboard for our lunch, the Frenchman leaves the wine on the table and drives slowly back up the road toward his village.

"We really need to move on," Clarke says, "but would you like to catch up on your journal first?" Would I? We've experienced so much over the last four days that I haven't had time to write and am afraid that if I don't record it soon, I'll never believe it happened. Setting up the computer on a tree stump, I crouch on a log in the sunshine to write of Gilles and Régine, Simone, André, and this man who never told us his name. Clarke crawls into the rowboat, unties the line, and floats slowly down the stream, his brown face drenched in sunlight. Two hours later, he's beside me. "Are you finished?"

I hold up my left hand and continue typing with my right. "Twenty more minutes," I say.

Late in the afternoon, we pedal through a small village but find no place where we feel we can ask to camp. Perhaps after the last few days, we're waiting for someone to invite us. Usually, when we're ready to stop, we ride until something about a house or farm catches our eye, something that feels right. If we both agree, we ask to camp. If we both don't feel welcome, we continue on until we do. Sure, we look for flat spots for the tent and shelter from the wind or rain if necessary, but mostly we just respond to our intuition.

We're back on the main road to Chartes. As we pass a long road to a small farm, I hear church bells in the distance. They feel like a signal. "This is it," I say.

Pedaling up the road, we find an old man bent over a vegetable garden. He smiles at our request. "One moment while I ask my son and daughter-in-law, who also live here," he says in French, then walks slowly through the yard to a clean white house. Jean Paul returns in moments with his son and a suggestion to put our tent on a grassy spot next to his vegetables, then continues weeding while we build our tent.

As we unroll our sleeping mats, we discover Jean Paul outside the tent opening, two huge heads of butter lettuce in his strong, bent hands. "For your dinner," he says. We never buy lettuce because it wilts immediately. This is a real treat, gratefully accepted. "Come," he says to Clarke, leading him to a faucet to wash the greens. As I tear lettuce leaves into a plastic grocery bag, the old man appears again, this time with oil and homemade vinegar. Two minutes later, he arrives with salt and pepper. "Come," he says again to Clarke, then leads him into his house, where he cuts a large chunk of fresh bread for our meal. Dinner is wonderful, the simple, fresh salad and bread, compliments of a fine old Frenchman.

In the morning, Jean Paul's daughter-in-law invites us in for coffee. On the table inside her spotless kitchen are coffee cups and antique liqueur glasses with a bottle of the killer *calvados* in the middle; we feel like we're a special occasion. When it's time to leave, Elaine kisses us, teary-eyed, as eighty-eight-year-old Jean Paul proudly proclaims that he will wait for us to return next year. "We would like that very much," I say softly, wondering how many more lovely gardens this gentle man will be able to plant.

At the cathedral at Chartes, I finally see in person the stained-glass windows that I wrote about for a college art class—kaleidoscopes of deep blue and red that shatter the sun into thousands of glittering sparkles.

That afternoon, we hear village church bells strung like popcorn. Every hour, we find ourselves pedaling through another tiny town, listening to the bells ring four, then five, then six and seven o'clock.

In a deep, dark, beautiful forest, I stop to relieve myself behind a tree and am instantly covered with mosquitoes. "Let's not sleep here," I declare, vaulting onto my bicycle, a little black cloud of vampire insects in close pursuit. We pedal and pedal and pedal. Finally, near dark, we find a large horse farm at the edge of a forest south of Paris and receive permission to sleep on the lawn next to a lush pasture of graceful horses.

In the morning, as the owner shows us his horses, which he breeds and trains for surrey racing, I notice that Clarke seems totally at ease in spite of the fact that the man is obviously wealthy. Clarke is treating him like a person instead of a checkbook, I realize happily.

Chapter 8

I've been to Paris before. Because it's the place Clarke most wants to see, I take it upon myself to make sure that he sees it. The first morning, trusting our tent to guard most of our belongings at the campground at the edge of Paris, we find an outdoor market for strawberries and tomatoes and onions, and a *boulangerie* for still-warm bread. At a tiny liquor store, the owner carefully helps us choose just the right white Bordeaux for lunch as a little bird flies in through the door and perches chirping on the cash register. "He comes in every day to visit," the man tells us with a proud smile.

Clarke is silent as we walk our bicycles under the Eiffel Tower. "The whole thing looks like it's made of wire," he says finally.

"How did they know how to engineer this a hundred years ago?" I wonder. Determined to be a good tour guide, I bury my nose in a guidebook. "It weighs seven thousand tons and took two-and-a-half million rivets. Although it's almost a thousand feet tall, it's never swayed more than four-and-a-half inches at the top in the highest winds."

Clarke doesn't care about the trivia; he doesn't need the details to appreciate the magnificence of this once-controversial monument. As we eat lunch in the formal garden at the base, he's torn between gazing at the tower and at the women sunbathers strewn like flowers around the grass. "Let's ride down the Champs-Élysées," I suggest after we stretch out for our own bit of sun.

"You're the guide," Clarke responds. He doesn't seem to care where we are as long as he's in the city of his dreams.

Without our heavy packs, we dart in and out of traffic like Parisian road racers. I shout the names of the buildings and monuments as we streak past, and at the Louvre, circle back for a dash to the Arc de Triomphe, the famous arch which sits like a hole in a phonograph record in the center of twelve streets that spike out from its edge like the rays of the sun. "Where are you going?" I yell as Clarke pedals like an old-fashioned phonograph needle onto the outer edge of the asphalt disk.

"To the middle!" he calls back, holding out his left arm to signal his intention to cross through the jumble of speeding cars. I follow, cringing.

There are no traffic lanes around the arch—just cars and more cars, cutting in and out and across each other as they merge on, or off, to and from the twelve feeder streets. Around and around we go, dodging through vehicles that give us just enough room to slip through, until we reach the arch in the middle. "Over my dead body will I bicycle back out of here," I announce, afraid that my words will come true.

Ignoring me, Clarke examines the sculptures along the faces of the arch as I watch the swarm of traffic flowing around our island of safety. "Ready?" he says, jumping back on his bike.

"See you in my next life," I sigh. Swimming with the rest of the traffic, we flow through row after row of cars until we reach the edge and spin off on a sunray street. After that, riding through Paris is easy—well, easier.

We stay in the city five days. After three months of discovery, of every single thing being new every minute—every mile, every person, every campsite—Paris for me isn't nearly as special as my first visit half a dozen years earlier and I feel a bit let down by the City of Light, perhaps because I'm trying so hard to be Clarke's tour guide that I forget to experience it myself.

Paris isn't all secondhand for me. Although the Louvre still feels dark and crowded and overwhelming, the new Musée d'Orsay is magnificent, in itself a work of art. Riding bicycles every day into the city through the Arc de Triomphe is an adventure—and a terrific mode of transportation. I feel safer on bicycle in Paris than I ever did on foot or in a car.

The highlight of Paris is a friend of a friend. After we settle in to the nine-dollar-a-day campground on the Seine, I telephone Marie Claire, a Parisian I met once at an American dinner party, inviting her to meet us for coffee. "No, that is not enough," she declares in beautiful English. "We must share a meal together."

I balk. "Our entertainment budget doesn't allow for restaurants, Marie Claire, and we only have a pair of cotton pants each—hardly the clothes for Parisian dining."

"Let me take you to dinner. We will go somewhere simple, and you may dress however you wish. I will not take no for an answer."

Arriving at our campground the next night dressed in a simple cotton dress and sandals, shiny blond hair curved neatly below her jaw, Marie Claire jumps out of her car to kiss us each on both cheeks. "Welcome to Paris!" she says in a musical voice. Driving through the city, she points out monuments and buildings with obvious love, and at the restaurant, immediately takes charge. "You must start with white asparagus," she announces. "It is only in season a very short time in France."

Our huge meal ends with chocolate mousse and cheese and fruit. All during dinner, we talk of our mutual friends, Marie Claire's lover, her new job as a magazine writer, our experiences, politics, and the differences between America and France. Marie Claire is open and honest about everything, as if we've been friends for years. "I must see you again before you leave Paris," she says at the end of the evening. "Let's drive the long way to your campground so that you can see more of the lights, and then I will prepare dinner for you in two days." She holds up her small hand. "Please, do not say no. I want you to meet my son."

This time, we don't protest. Sharing more time with Marie Claire will be our greatest pleasure. "Only if you promise to come visit us in Colorado," we say, and she agrees.

After returning to the campground, Clarke and I stop in the bar for a beer, too wound up to sleep, and talk to a couple from Germany until two o'clock in the morning. Horst and Marissa invite us to drive with them to the *chateau* at Chantilly the next day. "We will go there in the morning, and then to the Palace of Versailles in the afternoon. Meet us at our car for breakfast at eight; going with us will save you a great deal of bicycling," Horst announces.

As instructed, we arrive on time for coffee and bread and fruit and cheese at the Germans' campsite, then pile into the back of their old Mercedes for the trip to Chantilly. After trundling along at twenty kilometers an hour for months, hurtling down the highway at a hundred and fifty kilometers an hour—almost ninety-five miles an hour—is terrifying, and Clarke and I are off-pace most of the day. We're used to moving at our own slow speed with no itinerary. Now, all of a sudden, we're being organized by these kind Germans and must please four people instead of two. By the time we leave Chantilly, Clarke and I are too tired and tense to go to Versailles; we feel like we've spent the entire morning meeting people at correct places at precise times. "Horst, if you don't mind, will you drop us off at the campground on your way to Versailles?" Clarke leans forward from the back seat as we near Paris.

"Suit yourselves," Horst says, clearly disturbed at the change of plans.

"I'm sorry if we're inconveniencing you."

"It is not to be helped." He drives in silence the rest of the way to the campground, where Clarke and I head to the tent for a nap after more apologies to our German hosts.

"What's the matter?" Clarke asks as we cook our simple meal on the camp stove that evening.

"I'm sick to death of bike shorts. Is it okay with you if I buy a dress tomorrow to wear to Marie Claire's? Can we afford it?"

"Of course we can't afford it, but buy one if you want. We're spending your money—you don't need my permission."

I had planned to purchase a simple flowered skirt in Morocco or Spain, but didn't take time to shop. And now that we're having meals in people's homes, I desperately want something to wear besides bicycle shorts or my baggy cotton pants, wanting to look female and to show off the results of my marathon exercise program.

The next day, we mix sightseeing with shopping. On the Left Bank, I poke my head into a few stores but feel rushed with Clarke waiting outside with the bicycles. Finally, in the afternoon, he says, "I thought you wanted a new dress."

"You hate shopping."

"Don't make it my fault that you don't get something."

"Wait here, then." Spotting a pretty flowered dress in the window of a little boutique, I hurry inside to try it on. With its low neckline and split ruffly skirt, I feel like a Barbie doll after three months of Spandex bicycle shorts, but decide that I definitely look feminine. "Now I need shoes," I say, returning to the sidewalk.

Clarke sighs. "It's time to go back and clean up."

"I'll look on the way." Although we pedal past several shoe stores, the cheapest pair is a hundred dollars. "I'll wear my bicycle sandals tonight," I decide, disappointed.

I shower and slip on my sexy new dress, then my thick-soled blue rubber thongs. The combination is horrible. To make matters worse, when Marie Claire picks us up, she's considerately wearing the same simple dress that she wore out to dinner. I feel like an idiot—a silly-looking one at that—and all across Paris to Marie Claire's apartment, riding next to her in the front seat, I fiddle with my dress, pulling up the neckline and holding together the slit skirt, wondering if I can cut off my clumpety feet without her noticing. Or my head. "We went shopping today," I tell Marie Claire finally, "but ran out of time before I could buy shoes." Oh, Susan, what have you done—you can't afford to buy your own dinner two nights ago, but now you can afford a Paris dress?

Marie Claire's spacious apartment is full of antiques and art and mementos of her world travels. "I bought you a present, Clarke," she smiles, gesturing gracefully to a small packet on the coffee table.

Inside the pretty package are three small jars of the French equivalent of peanut butter. "I found this at my favorite gourmet store," she explains. "You mentioned that you miss this delicacy in Europe. May Jerome and I taste it? Jerome," she calls in French, "come and meet Suzanne and Clarke."

Jerome speaks shyly to his mother as she brings bits of crusty French bread from the kitchen to spread with the French peanut *paté*. "Oh dear," Marie Claire says after a nibble. "Do Americans really like this?"

"Yup," answers Clarke, munching happily.

"It is quite different. Well," she continues, "because I had a difficult day and it is very warm, I hope you don't mind that I have prepared a simple cold meal. And I need to make it an early night, as I have a little headache. Shall we eat?"

"Of course," I say, hiding my rubber sandals under the coffee table, "but I wish you'd canceled dinner if you don't feel well."

"Don't be silly. Did you bring your laundry as I asked? Let's put it in the machine before dinner so that your clothes can begin to dry while we eat—I am sorry, but I have no clothes dryer. We will hang them over the bathtub."

"Just having a machine wash our clothes in hot water is a treat."

On the way into the dining room, Clarke admires a signed Renoir lithograph. "Do you like it?" Marie Claire asks. "Then take it."

"Excuse me?"

"I will loan it to you for a year."

Clarke's mouth drops open. "I could never take responsibility for such a treasure." He shakes his head in wonder. "But thank you, thank you very much."

Dinner is elegant cold chicken, artistically prepared, but I feel so self-conscious next to this charming Frenchwoman that I can't enjoy my meal. Wearing the simple dress again, Marie Claire shows more class than I can ever possess, I decide, no matter what I wear. It's not my finest moment, particularly after my lecture to Clarke about people not being worth more or less because of what they have. Clarke pours wine into his water glass—already embarrassed at my own social inadequacies, I correct him, then want to bite off my tongue. "In France," Marie Claire says graciously, "men can use whatever glass they want."

"Of course," I say in a tiny voice, peeking under the lace tablecloth to see if there's room for me to crawl underneath. *Dear Amy Vanderbilt*, I write in my mind, then can't bear to go on.

The phone rings. While Marie Claire answers, Clarke and I speak in French and English with Jerome, who knows quite a few English words. "Do you mind very much if I take you home now?" Marie Claire asks when she returns to the table. "My headache is getting worse and I must get up early in the morning." Gathering our clean clothes, unable to convince her to let us take a cab, we kiss Jerome and pile into Marie Claire's car with a book about northern France that she insists we take.

"Boy, do I have a lot to learn," I say to Clarke as we drape wet laundry over our packs in the tent. "You never said how I looked tonight. Do you like my new dress?"

"I'm waiting to see the whole outfit," he replies as I put away my rubber bicycle sandals and struggle the frilly dress into my pack. My humiliation is complete.

We leave Paris on May 25th. After five days of riding naked bicycles, it's all we can do to keep from wobbling our fat bikes into the heavy traffic along the Seine, and by the time we pedal uphill to Versailles, we're exhausted in spite of our bicycling at least thirty kilometers every day in Paris. "Today is the day I told Jennifer we'd call," Clarke reminds me as we pass the palace looking for lunch.

Sharing bread and cheese on a park bench, we meet three Americans attending a month-long art seminar in France. One of the women has children at home. "Don't you miss your kids?" she asks Clarke after learning that we've been in Europe since February.

"Of course. Susan and I were just talking the other day, though, and in a way are glad they decided not to ride with us this summer. It's really hard work, and we don't think teenagers would get much out of a trip like this. It probably wouldn't be worth the work for them."

We hurry to dial America. "I hope they haven't forgotten our call," Clarke says, excited, then hears his son's voice for the first time in three months.

"I haven't been able to get a summer job after all," Chris moans. "Now I've missed Europe and probably won't be able to buy a car."

"Something will turn up if you keep trying, Chris. School isn't even out yet."

"I'm in a school play, Dad," is Jennifer's news.

Clarke hangs up the phone slowly. "I really miss them. Chris sounds really unhappy and here I am, thousands of miles away, unable to help. Do you mind if I call again in a week or two?"

"Of course not. Now let's call Jill. I sent her a postcard that we'd call her today also."

"Great news!" my sister says when she answers the phone. "Kelly and Megan are coming to bicycle with you for the summer! They'll arrive in London on June sixth. Isn't that wonderful?" Clarke tells me later that from outside the phone booth, all he heard was buzzing from the American side of the conversation and then silence; I'm caught speechless.

"Are you sure?" I say finally, remembering what we just told the art students about this being a difficult trip for teenagers; now my sixteen-year-old niece and her best friend want to join us. My mind races. We've just gotten our own act together to ask for two to sleep in people's gardens. Will anyone allow four? Surely, no one will have enough food to share with us all; will we have to give up our wonderful dinner and breakfast conversations now that we finally know how to communicate? I look pleadingly at Clarke. "How far can they ride, Jill?" I ask.

"Eight miles," she answers proudly. Poor Clarke—now that I finally can bicycle fifty miles a day, he'll have to start all over with two teenaged girls who aren't even his own children.

"Tell them they'll have to ride at least thirty miles by the time they arrive. Listen, Clarke and I were just saying that we don't think Chris and Jennifer would enjoy this trip. I don't think Kelly will either. We sleep on the ground every night and wash our clothes and ourselves in rivers or not at all. It's really hard work."

"If you don't want them to come..." Jill sounds crushed. "Look, send them home any time you want, and I'll tell them they can leave if they don't like it. Do you want time to think about this? I thought you'd be really excited—but they shouldn't come if you don't want them."

I'm remembering our day at Chantilly with the Germans. "It's hard for the two of us to function well together, let alone four. Let's all think about this—we'll call tomorrow."

"Okay," she says sadly.

"I love you, Jill," I remember to say after she hangs up. "Now what do we do, Clarke?"

"Don't think about it now. Let's go see the palace." But we see only the gardens. Overdosed on sightseeing in Paris, we don't have the energy to take another tour. Besides, my mind is busy with my niece and her friend. Kelly hates sports of every kind, has waist-length blond hair and skin so fair that she blisters from even a couple of hours in the sun—how can the poor kid possibly live outside for ten weeks? If the girls can only ride eight miles a day, will we ever get where we want to go before the end of the summer—up through England and Scotland, then over to Denmark, down into Belgium and Holland and through Germany and Austria?

We pedal northeast out of Versailles. Finally, I let my heart decide. "This trip is an experience of a lifetime, Clarke. Kelly and Megan won't get out of it what we do—but they'll get exactly what they need and so will we. I'm ready for them to come. How about you?"

"It'll be a challenge, but isn't everything that's worthwhile?"

In Bazemont, we stay at the home of a family whose daughter is going to England the next day. They want us to help her practice English, so we skip dinner and sit on their terrace and drink coffee and brandy and teach her simple English phrases until midnight.

That night, I lie awake chasing mosquitoes around the tent, deciding what Kelly and Megan should bring to Europe. Clarke and I are packed to the gills and can't carry more, but at least the girls won't need tools or cooking equipment. The first thing out of my mouth in the morning is, "Do you think Kelly and Megan can get by with two panniers each instead of four?"

"Did you get any sleep at all last night?"

"Well, no. But I have to call Jill today and it's my only chance to tell her what to do to get them ready," I justify myself.

I call Jill in the afternoon. "Send them on!"

"Are you sure?" Her voice is filled with relief. "Kelly was afraid you wouldn't let her come."

"Tell her that I went temporarily brain dead. But tell them both that this is no vacation, that they'll learn more than they ever want about themselves. We're game if they are."

"Thank God!"

"Just make sure they know that they'll have to carry everything they bring and that they'll need to leave room in their packs for food. We don't have an inch of extra space."

"I can't wait to tell Kelly when she comes home from school."

"We'd love it if they'll bring us peanut butter and M&M's, and we'll need a twelve-inch folding skillet to cook for us all."

"Feel better?" Clarke asks as I hang up the phone.

"I hope so."

Near Giverny, home of Claude Monet, we can see impressionism all around: the air is full of moisture that flecks the sunshine with sparkles of light, and along the Seine leading northeast toward Rouen, the soft landscape is brushed in pale shades of blue and green. Overjoyed to be back on our little roads after the chaos of Paris, we pedal seventy kilometers. Now, all of a sudden, we have a date in London in less than two weeks and want to cover some ground while we can—soon enough, we'll have to cut back for Kelly and Megan. "I'm beat," I say finally. "After worrying all night about the girls and feeling out of condition after Paris, I need a good night's rest."

"Let's sleep in the forest so that we can go to bed right after dinner," Clarke agrees. But as we turn up a dirt road into the woods, we realize that we're out of water. "I've gotten so used to filling up at people's homes that I never gave it a thought at the last village. Guess we'll have to find a farm after all."

And there in front of us, once back on the main road, is a beautiful farm that I know is right. But no one is home. "Let's wait for a few minutes to see if someone comes back."

"It feels perfect to me too."

We stand by the fence and wait, sure that someone will return. Within minutes, a man arrives who looks more American than French, complete with a beer belly over his belt. He escorts us up a long road to a hunting lodge away from the farm. "It will be quiet here," he says in French, "and there is water in back."

"We get our quiet after all," Clarke says after the man leaves.

"And a place to hang our wet laundry from Paris. I can wash out my pack where the chocolate pudding exploded yesterday."

After a quick dinner of onion soup, we're both asleep by nine o'clock and stay that way for twelve hours. As we pack in the morning, a little girl comes up from the farm with her collie Lassie and a flower for us.

Lunch is peanut butter and honey sandwiches, compliments of Marie Claire, and afterwards I meet three burros that nuzzle me and my food pack until I give them fresh French bread, refusing to share our precious peanut *paté*.

Along the Seine near Rouen, where Joan of Arc was burned alive, Clarke and I inhale the fragrances and colors of the flower gardens at every house. Explosions of bright flowers churn and curl around the neat white homes like ruffles, and in the side yards, vegetable gardens are striped with perfect rows of veggies dressed in military greens.

"I wonder how Kelly and Megan will adjust to sleeping on the ground and giving up fast food all summer?" I ask myself more than Clarke. "They may be bicycling only eight miles a day now, but I bet that by the end of the summer they'll be riding rings around us both." It will be hard for Clarke to be patient about the cycling, I think, but I'll finally learn how it feels to want to pedal farther than my companions, at least for awhile.

We're in Normandy. Full of stately mansions, pastures of sleek horses, sunshine and rolling hills, it feels old to us, and we sense that we're getting close to England. After sixty kilometers of beautiful scenery and difficult cycling, I'm ready to stop for the night. "Let's ride awhile longer to cool down," Clarke suggests. "We'll get water at the next farm." He's leading but passes the next farm, and the next, then pedals to and through the next town, and the next.

"I thought you were going to stop miles ago, Clarke." We're riding through a tiny village past a house where two young boys play in a grassy yard. Stopping, Clarke asks for water, and the older boy runs inside to get his mother.

"Please," she says in French, "come in for a cold drink." Filling our bike bottles with water and, for the first time, ice, she insists that we have a glass of cold fruit juice as her husband and children crowd around the kitchen table to ask about our trip and then invite us for dinner.

"No, I am sorry, but we need to ride farther," Clarke says for some reason, although it's obvious that this young family would love to share their evening with us and I'd been ready to stop two hours earlier.

"Well, then take a box of juice with you," the husband says, disappointed.

We turn to wave at the family lined up on their lawn as we pedal off. "Why did you say we couldn't stay for dinner?" I ask.

"I don't know." Later, as I wonder if Clarke plans to bicycle all night, he spots a grove of trees up ahead. "Let's ask there," he points. By now, I'll ask anywhere.

A woman ushers us to a pasture with long wet grass, then leads me to a room with a toilet that adjoins the house. "I will leave this open for you," she says in French, then returns to her home.

Clarke and I visit with the cows that evening, lonely without human companionship. "I wish we'd had dinner with that family," he says finally. "I'm tempted to ride back tomorrow."

"We did what we did, Clarke. Let's just go on."

Cows wake me up in the morning. "They sound like they're all in a row," I decide, poking my head out of the tent. Sure enough, a dozen curious cows stand in single file against the fence, looking at me. As we pack the bikes, which lean against the fence, the cows nibble at our panniers, slobbering wet grass all over the canvas.

The day brings cold wind and threatening rain. Late in the afternoon, we choose a farm built around all four sides of a large yard, hoping that the owners will let us put our tent inside the walls away from the wind. As we ride in, I hear a bark and see a white streak, then feel a chunk disappear from the back of my knee. The fluffy white dog stands next to my foot, staring up at me in confusion as I hold out my hand instead of running away. Finally, he wags his tail and sniffs my fingers in apology as his owners come into the yard. We aren't allowed to stay inside the walls because of the dog, but the woman cleans my wound and her husband escorts us to an open pasture down the road after we promise not to build a fire near their harvested hay.

"I finally have strong, tan legs," I say to Clarke after dinner, "but look at them! This gash is the dog bite, of course," I crane my head around to see the bloody scab forming at the back of my knee. "And here's where my bike fell on me a couple of weeks ago." I point to a deep scrape at the top of my right ankle. "And I still have marks from where I fell in that chicken yard in Spain." My left knee and calf are still red with sandy burns. Clarke glances over, uninterested, as the disfigurement of his legs happened only early on, when grease from his chain ring made black tooth marks on his calves when he stopped to rest.

As we move north, we're filled with regrets about leaving France, where we learned about communication by intention and about asking for help. "I'd live in France in a minute," I say.

"Me too. Maybe we can just do that some day."

That night, we stop at a small cluster of well-kept homes. No one is home at the first door we try. "How about the next one on the left?" Clarke suggests. It has level grass up to the forest, and a small pond.

Jo and Pierre invite us for drinks on the patio. And then for dinner. Jo eats a hard-boiled egg so that Pierre and Clarke and I can eat the meal that she prepared for herself and Pierre, insisting that she would rather go without than miss our company. Even though their English is only slightly better than our French, we become friends immediately and drink coffee inside until midnight. Jo and Pierre's house is a tangle of comfortable furniture, with photos and art crookedly lining the walls and gallery. In its very untidiness, we feel immediately welcome as we curl into chairs in the living room. We can tell that people are more important to Jo and Pierre than things. As we kiss each other goodnight, Clarke asks permission to stay in the morning long enough to sketch their house, which they built themselves a few years earlier. "If you stay until lunch," they agree, "so that we can see you one more time. We both work in the city."

In the morning, I make pasta salad for lunch while Clarke draws. Shortly after noon, Jo and Pierre tumble out of their car with baskets of groceries. "But I already prepared our meal," I protest.

We eat the pasta as an appetizer with melons, then have a tender roast which turns out to be horse, green beans seasoned with garlic, bread, cheese and wine. Jo and Pierre rave about Clarke's drawing and make us agree to return on our way back from England. It's a promise we're happy to make. In town, as we pedal down the main street, Jo emerges from a store, calling our names excitedly. "*S'il vous plait, cheries*, please stay longer!" Jo says in French. We're tempted beyond words but pedal on, sad, yet knowing that our lives are full wherever we are.

"Let's stay at the house with the pretty daisies," I suggest that evening, and we knock on the door to greet a cautious, white-haired man who lets us camp only after we promise not to build a fire. Even so, he brings us a bucket of water, just in case. The house is spotless, the gardens perfect. Baby chicks run through the field next to the house, and when we leave in the morning, we make sure that the grass is fluffed where we put up our tent.

It's our last day in France. As in Spain, we're sorry to leave this country of warm people and beautiful flowers and fine wines, but we're excited to discover England, to find out what it will be like to communicate with strangers in our own language again, to be able to share more than just the basics.

Stopping in Frethun just outside of Calais, where we'll take a ferry across to Dover the next morning, we knock on the door of a large white house. A head appears out of an upstairs window, and Clarke asks it in French if we can camp in the garden. "Just a moment, I'll be down as soon as I put the baby to bed," the young woman responds in English. Christine offers not only her yard but also cold drinks in the living room. "I learned to speak a little English when I worked for the ferry company," she explains. "My husband, who is an engineer, has much better English."

When Armel arrives with the older children, he takes us to see the Eurotunnel construction site nearby. "Many English people are opposed to connecting England and France with a tunnel," he says. "Prices are less in France and the English are afraid that too much money will leave their country. Already they shop in Calais on weekends, but now they are buying houses and land here, and the real estate market in England is dropping." Anything that will bring countries closer together sounds fine with us, and we marvel at the plans to burrow under the English Channel.

We arrive back at the house in time to be included for drinks at the neighbors', then Christine insists that we join her family for dinner and breakfast. Early in the morning, we share coffee and sunshine on a patio surrounded by roses. "We will miss France, and the French, and French food," I say. "These croissants are fabulous."

"I went to my favorite bakery very early to get them for you," Christine says, passing cherry preserves, sweet butter and rich, dark coffee. "Please, if you return from England across the Channel, come back to our home."

In Calais, we pass the famous *Burghers of Calais* sculpture by Rodin and then pedal onto the ferry for England. Much as we love France, we're ready for Great Britain, for Kelly and Megan, for the white cliffs of Dover, for our own language. It's June 3rd. Over the last seven weeks in France, we've bicycled more than 2500 kilometers; for the whole trip, almost 5000 kilometers or 3000 miles. We've been away from home sixteen weeks.

Chapter 9

Lashed to the ferry's hold with ropes, our bicycles look like mosquitoes next to the transport trucks as the ship creaks across the English Channel and Clarke and I roam the upper decks watching seagulls float above the frothy wake. As we near the chalky cliffs of Dover, clouds crowd the sky and push away its blue with gray. The ferry finds its berth with rattles and clangs; Clarke and I wait with the bikes as drivers stream onto the lower decks to reclaim their vehicles and the boat reverses its engines to nose gently to its ramp.

A uniformed worker motions us forward as the huge trucks start their engines, diesel fumes filling the air. "You first, mates," he hollers. Over my shoulder, a huge transport truck belches black smoke above its cab, front bumper nudging my rear tire. Racing up the ramp, we're followed by dozens of vehicles whose drivers honk and wave, careful to give us a wide berth as we're directed to the front of the line.

"Welcome to England," the Customs agent says from her glass booth as she checks our passports. "How long will you be staying?"

"We don't know," Clarke answers.

"What cities will you be visiting?"

"We have no idea."

"What address will be your home base while you're here?"

"We don't have one," I respond, glad to communicate in a familiar language. The agent looks over our bicycles and packs, then wishes us a pleasant visit to her country. "I guess they figure that if we do anything illegal, it won't be hard to catch us," I laugh, pedaling away.

"We certainly can't steal anything very big."

"Wrong, Clarke. I'm going for a refrigerator if I go for anything."

The streets are wet and it begins to rain as we pedal into Dover to look for a road map. We've been using small-scale Michelins, easy to read and accurate, but the company doesn't make maps for Great Britain. On the ordnance surveys, English roads look like a plate of spaghetti dotted with quaint villages like tiny mushrooms. "Oh boy, this'll be fun," groans Clarke, our official navigator since Spain, when we'd argued about who was the best with maps. "I make maps for a living," Clarke had insisted at the time.

"That doesn't mean I can't read them just as well," I retorted, confident of my ability to get us from one place to the next. Then I realized that it didn't matter what route we chose or how long it took to get where we were going. And trying to pedal and read a map at the same time isn't that easy. "I'd rather watch the scenery," I decided after we'd both proved our competence. Clarke had been an excellent guide, choosing routes along the railroad tracks and streams for milder grades, finding tiny roads that wound through ancient villages without traffic.

Now, looking over his shoulder at the new map of this section of England, I'm glad he's in charge. "Which strand of spaghetti do you want to follow out of here?" I ask.

"Let me find an end first."

Bent over the map outside the bookstore, we're tracing with our fingers a pattern backward from Gatwick Airport to Dover when another bicyclist rides up. "Hello!" we flag him down. "Where are you from?"

"California," he replies, shaking rain from his jacket as he scrunches in with us under the eaves. "I've ridden down from London but haven't decided where to go next."

"We've just come from France," I tell him. "The people there are fabulous."

"You must speak French."

Clarke and I laugh. "Barely," I reply, "but a new family every night let us camp on their property."

"You didn't stay in campgrounds or hotels?"

"Nope," Clarke says. "Couldn't afford it."

"Maybe I should try that. I'm not having a very good time by myself." After a short pause, he adds, "Actually, I was thinking of going home."

"Don't," Clarke and I respond together.

Fumbling our way out of Dover in the drizzle, we get lost. "Left, Clarke, left! Stay to the left!" I yell a zillion times. Traffic is heavy, and Clarke is so busy trying to understand the map that he keeps wandering toward the right side of the road. The roundabouts, or traffic circles, confuse us both because the lane we need to be in for our spin-off onto another road is the fast lane, and we weave and wobble uncertainly from the right side of the lanes to the left and from one lane to another.

England appears as different from France as night and day. Most striking, we can understand the signs, read the headlines in the newsstands, and communicate fully with anyone. But the white lace curtains are gone from the windows and everyone seems busy and hurried, flushed cheeks red as apples as the Brits scurry through the streets or careen madly through the crowded roundabouts in tiny cars. With lots of people in little space, English traffic is horrendous for bicyclists, notwithstanding the added confusion of riding on the left, and we miss our bicycle paths for two winding through the quiet countryside. Pedaling through the drizzle with mixed emotions, we're glad to be communicative again but sorry to leave the hospitality and peace of France.

As Americans, we're no longer a novelty and begin to feel silly greeting people we pass on the road. Suddenly, we're so-what visitors. In France and Spain and Morocco, we greeted everyone with *bonjour* or *hola* or *salaam*—a hello in England seems ridiculous for some reason.

At the farm of a single mother, we receive permission to camp, and anxious to communicate in our own language, return to the house after dinner to share tea with the woman and one of her daughters until bedtime.

Early the next morning, we leave a thank-you note on the door and make our way west on roads that seem more like a grid system than highways from one town to another. Unnamed or unnumbered on the map or in reality, they're difficult to follow and we find ourselves asking directions at every turn where we can find someone to ask. "Hello!" I call to a man washing a car in his driveway. "We're lost."

"You sound lost," he replies, referring no doubt to my American accent. "I'll give you directions if you'll join me and my wife for tea. It's going to rain, you know."

George and Eileen feel like instant friends—just add water—from the moment we arrive in their front yard. As Eileen passes her cookie tin and fills our cups with steaming tea, we share stories in a frenzy of British barbed witticism. Retrieving a stack of maps from a cupboard, George gives us a lengthy explanation of how to find our next destination. "You must go through Canterbury. You're in Shepherdswell now, in case you don't know," he smiles. We don't. "Go on straight to Woolage Green and then either right then left to Womenswold or left, right, left to Womenswold. Then right and another right with an immediate left to Aylesham."

"We'll keep asking," we assure George. "And thank you both for the tea. It's a bit cold and damp outside today."

"Oh, you can't leave now," Eileen announces as if she planned it that way. "Look at the rain." Indeed. And there's no place we'd rather be. Her sense of humor reminds us both of my sister, and we could listen to her laughter forever. "We insist you stay for lunch," she declares.

"You just want to make more fun of our accents," I say.

As cold rain washes the street outside, we gather around pork and mushy peas, then ask one more favor as we leave. "May we refill our water bottles?"

"Here, let me," George offers. And then looks inside them. "No, no, this won't do. Won't do at all. Eileen," and trails back inside to confer with his wife.

"They're positively green inside," Eileen exclaims. "What did you do to them?" We look inside the bottles. They're covered with slimy green mold. "I'll have them clean in a jiffy," Eileen promises, but no amount of hot water and soap and bottlebrushes will remove the mold. "Maybe baking soda. Let them soak a bit," Eileen suggests as she plops in a chair to tell another hilarious story.

Finally, after solving all the world's problems, we leave this wonderfully funny couple with marginally-less-green water bottles. "If you come back this way, please come see us," they say.

"If we can find you," Clarke promises as we mount up.

"We may be back for dinner," I add, "if we can't find our way out of town."

Six kilometers later, we're lost again. A pretty woman stands on a grassy town square. "Is this the way to Womenswold?" Clarke asks.

"Turn left," she smiles. "But first, come home with me for tea."

Clarke and I look at each other. At this rate, we'll never get to London to meet Kelly and Megan. Or to Womenswold. But our visit with George and Eileen was so wonderful that we can't resist— besides, English tea is well worth stopping for on a cold, wet day.

Following the woman across the green to a remodeled church where she lives with her artist husband and two daughters, our tea turns into dinner, then we spend the night on Richard and Alison's living room couch. "Next time," I say in the morning as we hug, "think twice before inviting anyone to tea!"

"When in doubt, turn left!" Alison calls as we pedal off under an overcast sky.

We're instantly lost again and suddenly don't care–after all, we decide, the trip isn't about the scenery or the cycling; it's about the people. Where we are doesn't matter.

All day, we bump around the little roads like pinballs, reaching Canterbury almost by chance in the afternoon. "Let's get a Michelin guide for London while we're here," I suggest in the bookstore while Clarke searches in vain for decipherable maps.

"They cost too much."

"But they're full of interesting information, Clarke. Kelly and Megan will have a much better time in the city if they can read about some of the places they're seeing. So will you."

"I don't want my experience influenced by other people's perspectives."

"Not everyone feels the same way you do, Clarke."

"Then let Kelly and Megan buy a guide. You're already mothering them, and they haven't even left America." He glares at me sternly. "Remember what happened in Paris when you worried more about my sightseeing than your own?"

We don't even see Canterbury Cathedral, and our little tussle is one of only two memories I have of the city, aside from the bike shop that didn't have the parts Clarke needed. The other is born after I flounce out of the bookstore to wait with the bikes, which lean against the old stone building. A tiny old lady trots up, eyes burning with anger, white hair floating around her head like electrified fuzz. "Are those your bicycles, young lady?" She points with a crooked finger.

"Yes, ma'am."

"Well, they're in the way of the pigeon food I scattered. How dare you!" The lady is more than indignant; she's furious. Sure enough, half a dozen pigeons are hopping around our bicycle tires, happily pecking food from the ground and seemingly not the least inconvenienced by the presence of two metal pack mules. But I'm no match for this woman, and apologizing profusely, try to coax Clarke's bike away from the wall as he rounds the corner.

"What are you doing?" Clarke snaps. Moving his bike with its hundred-plus pounds of baggage is precarious duty, no matter who has it.

"Hush," I hiss, nodding toward the bristly woman. "It's standing in the pigeons' dinner."

We can't even get out of Canterbury without getting lost. Once, Clarke almost gets run over after cutting in front of a car in a roundabout. "Pay attention, Clarke!" I shout, my heart racing. "If you're getting off at the next road, stay on the left—don't get in the middle and then cut across all the other cars!"

"Leave me alone, Susan."

I stop on a corner to ask for help before Clarke gets squashed in the city traffic, but since I'm not sure what I'm asking for because Clarke has the map, I inquire of a handsome young man, "Where are we?"

"Canterbury," he replies, eyes dancing.

"Really," I respond, trying to match his wit, "is that in England?"

After only one wrong turn this time, we're headed the right direction in minutes. As we pedal out of town, it starts to rain—as it has every day in this country—and our moods are soon as sodden as our clothes, or vice versa. I can't get Clarke's near-accident out of my mind. Fat as it is with all of its packs, Clarke's bike looked awfully small in front of the swerving, honking car. I signal a stop. It's raining too hard to bicycle anyway. "Look, Clarke, I know it's hard to lead and keep track of the traffic and the map and riding on the left," I begin. "Won't you just discuss how to get through roundabouts so you won't get killed next time?"

"I already know how." We argue for half an hour, neither of us listening to the other, then pedal off, both grumbling, into the rain.

"How far did we ride yesterday?" Clarke asks later.

"Eleven kilometers," I answer sheepishly, "but we've gone almost seventy so far today." Why do I feel guilty for the short day, I wonder—I had a wonderful time. Why should I have to want to ride a million miles a day just because Clarke does? In addition to still being snitty about the Michelin guide and the roundabout, now I'm sure that he's lost. "You're going the wrong way, Clarke."

"Fine. You find our way, then, since you know everything today."

I lead us to a dead end. "At least I admit when I'm wrong," I say sarcastically, referring for the umpteenth time to the roundabout. We continue in silence, wet and miserable.

Late in the afternoon, South of Maidstone, on Gravelly Bottom Road, we find a tidy house with a beautiful garden. The hard rain has finally stopped; we're down to drizzle and grateful for it. "Here?" Clarke asks.

"I don't care."

A man answers Clarke's knock, then hesitates at our request. "I don't know," he says. "You're strangers and all and we're a retired couple. You might frighten my wife." Curiosity keeps him on the front porch asking questions, however, and anxious to talk to anyone but each other, we're happy to answer. "Let me speak with Winnie," he says finally, then goes inside. Clarke and I wait in silence. "You can stay," the man says, returning to the porch with a smile.

We're putting up our tent when Ken comes back outside. "Winnie wants to know if you'd like a shower."

Tired, cold, rain-soaked and angry, it's just what I need. "I'll be right in," I say gratefully.

"No thanks," Clarke says sullenly, then continues after Ken leaves, "I'm hungry."

"So cook dinner while I shower. You don't need me for an audience."

"Hurry up, then."

Winnie answers the door. "We've already had supper," she says shyly, "but you're welcome to whatever we have, maybe some poached eggs and toast."

"That's very sweet of you, Winnie. I'll check with Clarke."

"I don't feel like eating with anyone," he says after I stick my nose into the tent with Winnie's invitation.

"I thought you were in a hurry to eat. Besides, we decided this morning that the whole point of this trip is meeting people." I go back to the house and lie. "Clarke's already started our dinner, but thank you anyway."

"Surely you'll come in for tea after you eat, won't you?" Winnie persists.

"Of course," I answer with more assurance than I feel. I'll go regardless, and make up another story if I have to.

"Why did you tell her we'd go in for tea?" Clarke grouses when I return from the hot shower, wet hair wrapped in our dirty towel.

"Because I want to go in for tea. And because their company is better than yours."

After dinner, sitting far apart on Ken and Winnie's couch, we hear on the BBC news of the Ayatollah Khomeni's death, of the Chinese students who were killed in Beijing, and of a huge gas explosion in Russia. "I think I liked it better when we weren't able to understand the news," Clarke observes.

Ken and Winnie are kind and warm in a very proper sort of British way. A bicycle racer in his youth, Ken wants to know all about our equipment and current difficulty in finding even small parts for the mountain bikes. Although we're grateful for the company, Clarke and I feel stiff and uncomfortable because of our unresolved differences, and by the time we get back to our tent, I'm too tired to discuss anything. "Why did you insist we spend the evening with two strangers instead of dealing with our own problems?" Clarke asks me.

"I don't know. Just let me be mad for the night." I turn my back to sleep.

If anything, things are worse in the morning. "I'll get the bikes, Clarke. You take down the tent." Usually, we do everything together.

As I open the big garage door, Ken comes out of the house. "Surely you're not leaving yet," he says, eyes huge. "I've called all the bicycle shops in Maidstone and think I've found the parts your husband needs. I'll drive you there. Please." And then timidly, "Winnie is already cooking breakfast."

We don't deserve this, I think, and Clarke probably won't accept it. But he has to. Breakfast is delightful, and although there's no communication between Clarke and me, Ken and Winnie make up for our lack. In Maidstone, we get our bike parts and a driving tour of the city. "Let me help you fix your bike," Ken says eagerly to Clarke. "Winnie and Susan can fix lunch." Clarke hesitates.

"It's raining," Winnie says to settle the issue, as if it hadn't been raining all week. After lunch, we head off into the storm again, marginally cheered by the generosity of this elderly couple.

That night, cold and wet from the all-afternoon dousing of English rain, we call a truce and camp at the dairy farm of a tall, angular woman who gives us a bottle of fresh milk. Rich and creamy, the cold milk makes us realize how much we miss refrigerated foods. We've been able to buy real milk only once, in a grocery store in Spain. We've forgotten what cold, firm yogurt tastes like; after a few hours in a bike pack, it's always warm and runny.

Tromping through the wet pasture grass, we search for a flat space for the tent and finally settle near a tree footed with a little less cow dung. Our packs are soaked. We try to cover those that we don't need with our tattered orange rain jackets, bringing the food, cooking gear and computer inside the tent. In the morning, it's still raining. "Why don't you stay here and write," Clarke suggests, "while I ride into town to buy more spokes. I seem to break one a day all of a sudden. Maybe I can even find a laundromat—this humidity makes these dirty clothes stink." In no mood to go out in the rain again, I agree happily.

Half an hour later, I hear a woman's voice outside the tent. "Hallo, are you in there?" I stick my head into the rain to see our hostess under an umbrella. "Your husband told me you were writing. Wouldn't you like to come inside the house?" Hunched over the computer to keep it dry, I hurry to keep up with Judy's long strides across the lumpy field covered with cow manure, feeling sorry for Clarke but glad to be without him for awhile.

I settle at a small desk in the warm dining room with hot tea laced liberally with milk and sugar. Although I'm behind on my writing, I remember easily each day and each experience—the people, the weather, the scenery, the cycling. Without other things on my mind, I can focus completely on the trip as it happens. Nothing, it seems, escapes my memory. I can even remember the names of everyone we meet, including the children, something I could never do before we left home. I write for four hours, oblivious to the rain from which I'm now sheltered, warm and dry. When have I last been able to be unaware of the current weather? "Will you have lunch with us?" Judy startles me out of my memories.

I look at my watch with a start. "Thank you," I answer, wondering where Clarke is, "but I really should pack up our gear."

"I wouldn't at the moment. Look outside." The rain is coming down so hard that I can't see the tent.

"Well, yes, you're right, of course. Just let me save my work," But when I push the "save" key, the screen goes black. All four hours' work is gone because I can't seem to get it into my head to save data every few minutes.

As I finish my meal with this well-educated couple whose children are at Oxford, Clarke arrives, cold, wet and frustrated. "Why haven't you packed up the tent, Susan?"

"Because I was writing, and waiting for it to stop raining." Then I continue in a very small voice, "but the computer malfunctioned and I lost everything."

"So you wasted the whole morning."

Not really, I say to myself, because I was warm and dry. "I have to write it all over again later, you know," I say to Clarke.

Judy comes into the room. "Please have some lunch, Clarke, and warm up." He hesitates, anxious to be on our way, but the lure of hot tea sits him at the large table as I play with Judy's new puppies and feel guilty for not slogging through the field earlier to pack. Kelly and Megan arrive in two days. Is that why we're so irritable? Whatever is troubling us, it's certainly creating mammoth tension between us. *Dear Kelly and Megan,* I begin a mental postcard, *you're entering the twilight zone. Proceed at your own risk.*

Clarke has bought himself a pair of waterproof rain pants for fifteen dollars, a day and a half's allowance. "Did you get me some?" I ask hopefully as we walk through the muddy field to our tent.

"Of course not. I'd never pick out clothes for you." Pulling down the tent, Clarke rolls it around its dripping rain fly as I tie the sleeping bags to the back of my bike while rain washes under my collar.

We leave Judy's at two o'clock, armed with another bottle of fresh, rich milk, but it isn't enough to raise our spirits. The closer we get to London, the harder it rains and the colder it gets. The traffic gets heavier and heavier. Trucks and cars, unable to pull out around our bicycles on the narrow roads, drench us with cold sheets of muddy water. With or without sunglasses, it's almost impossible to see—either our eyes or our sunglasses are full of rain. And all I need is for my contact lenses to wash out.

Clarke uses the last of our torn Zip-Loc bags for the map, stuffing it into his jacket pocket between consultations to keep it from disintegrating. Every now and then we pull under a tree to shield us from a new cloudburst, but the break is purely psychological; we've been soaked for hours. My legs are like ice cubes, and I resent Clarke's new warm and waterproofed legs. "I've had enough," I announce near East Grinstead.

Clarke looks at the sky. "Maybe we can get the tent up between storms."

Winding through a maze of spacious houses on large lots set deep in the woods, we spot a spectacular garden and immaculate lawn on either side of a long drive that beckons like an outstretched arm. A woman in her fifties opens the door of a large stone house after we swim up the driveway. "I have no idea how we found your house or how to get back to the highway," I begin, "but is it okay to put a tent in your garden tonight?"

The woman looks from one of us to the other, dripping hair plastered to our faces. "I certainly think so, but let me ask my mother."

The two women return to the door together. "You can sleep in our garden shed out of the rain," offers the daughter. Grabbing an umbrella, she leads us to the shed and moves a large bag of plant food to one side.

"You're just what the doctor ordered tonight," I tell her, pushing a wheelbarrow into a corner.

Jackie turns, looking hard at us. "You are a bit soppy, aren't you?"

Her mother trundles out under a big, black umbrella. "Listen, loves, my name is Win and you both look horrid. Come inside and take a nice hot shower, both of you." I stare at her, overcome with delight. "It would be very nice," she continues shyly, "if you would have some fish and chips with us. We could pop down to town and bring some back and open a bottle of wine. Our treat." She looks at us hopefully. "We don't get many visitors, you know. Do say yes."

The woman and her invitation are irresistible. "But you can't buy our dinner," Clarke says.

"Oh, go on, let me have some fun. Now do get your showers and then you can ride to town with Jackie for the food."

The greasy chicken and fish 'n chips wrapped in newspaper is a huge success, thanks to our two new friends, three bottles of German white wine, and conversation and laughter late into the night. The two divorcees' stories about men are hysterical. "Besides," laughs Jackie, "every time I bring home a date, he takes one look at this two-and-a-half acre garden and never comes back." She brings another bottle of wine to the table. "Oh, my God," she exclaims suddenly. "The foxes! Mum, we're late for the foxes!" Following their hurried steps to the kitchen, Clarke and I watch as Jackie and Win prepare fat quarter-sandwiches of dog food, trimming the crusts, and Jackie rushes the plate outside the back door. As soon as she's back inside, a red fox trots around the side of the garden shed, bushy tail streaming behind, pointed nose sniffing the air. Reassured after looking right and left, she bounds up to the plate and stuffs several sandwiches into her mouth, then hurries away, dropping one in her rush. "She takes them to her babies," Winnie whispers.

Earlier, I'd noticed a shopping list on the kitchen counter. Food for the animals—the foxes and cats and birds—headed the list; the people food list was much shorter, at the bottom, an afterthought.

Jackie and Win insist on our coming in for breakfast in the morning. "You're almost at Gatwick," Jackie announces. "Surely you can stay a bit longer. Can we help with any errands?"

"If we have plenty of time to get to the airport," Clarke says, "maybe you could tell me where to get a haircut." He hasn't had one in four months.

"I'll do better than that, love. I'll drive you over; I need to pick up some suet for the birds anyway, don't I, Mum?"

I'm honored to be in Winnie's loving presence while Jackie and Clarke drive into East Grinstead. Her wit and wisdom are delightful, and we chat like lifelong friends—which we are, as far as I'm concerned. "I'm so glad you came to our door," she confides. "To be honest, we don't have a lot of friends and rattle around in this house and garden a bit too much. I wish Jackie would get out more."

"How could anyone else's company be better than yours?" I say and mean it. The world will be smaller when Winnie is no longer in it.

She prepares an elegant lunch while Jackie takes Clarke and me to meet her brother. "When you come back on your return to the Continent," she says, "my brother and I will give you a barbecue so you can meet the rest of our daffy family."

"We'll plan on it," we agree immediately, unwilling to say goodbye forever to these astounding women.

Prolonging our departure long after lunch, we gather around the table with coffee and sherry, all of us finding every possible reason to delay. We manage to stay until five o'clock. Win refuses to come outside to say goodbye but finally walks us to the end of the drive. We all hug. "We never admit to being lonely," she says tearfully, "but your visit meant ever so much to us both."

"Then we'll be back, with two teenagers."

Chapter 10

"What if something happens to Kelly and Megan while they're here?" I ask as we pedal toward Gatwick.

"Quit worrying!"

Guessing how I might have felt at sixteen—flying into a foreign country for a summer, tackling Customs with a giant bicycle box, hoping to be met at the airport by someone who had to pedal from another country to meet me on time—I decide that they must be scared to death. But at least they don't have to worry about a foreign language. Yet.

We're cutting it close, time-wise, then find to our dismay that Gatwick has two terminals. We try the closest. "This should be the correct terminal," the woman at the information counter says briskly, "but I show no listing for a Northwest Air flight 844. What city did they embark from?"

"Denver, Colorado. But I don't know where the international part of their flight originated. Atlanta, maybe, or New York or Dallas."

"I'm sorry, ma'am. I have nothing coming from those cities at this time."

"Let's wait by Customs," Clarke suggests. "They'll have to go through sometime."

"Assuming they arrive today. Maybe we should call Jill."

"Stop fussing, Susan."

We wait by the Customs area. And wait. I fidget, reluctant to alarm my sister. We wait some more. Clarke fidgets at my fidgeting, then I return to the Northwest Air representative. "What flights do you have originating from anywhere in the U.S. today?"

"Only one this morning," she replies. "From Los Angeles via Minneapolis."

"Did it stop in Denver?"

"No."

It's time to tell my sister that we've already lost her daughter. Then two giant flat boxes roll toward us on a luggage cart. "They're here!" I shout. Sure enough, two familiar faces peek from behind the boxes at the sound of my shriek. Megan's hair is brown instead of blond and Kelly's is cut in a stylish bob below her ears. They look gorgeous—excited and happy and totally at ease. I fling myself at Kelly, relieved and delighted to see her dear face. "You both look wonderful!" I gush. "Kelly! I love your hair. Your first haircut—what did your father say? And Megan, why is yours brown?"

"He hated it," Kelly says as Megan replies,

"So my roots won't show this summer."

"Were you nervous going through Customs?" I ask. "Did you think we might not be here to meet you?"

"Of course not," Kelly says, blasé and sophisticated. Kelly flew alone to visit me when I lived in Dallas from the time she was five; come to think of it, I've never seen her afraid of anything.

"How far can you bicycle?" Clarke asks Megan.

"Twenty-five miles yesterday," she answers proudly.

"That's wonderful." I note the relief in Clarke's eyes. "You'll ride circles around us in no time."

Clarke puts together their bikes while Kelly and Megan unpack boxes and catch us up on news from home. "Your mail, madam," Kelly says in a British accent as I pounce on our first letters since leaving America. "Here's your peanut butter, Clarke." She extricates two four-pound cans from a box.

"Oh, my gosh, how will we carry all that?"

"That's your problem." She turns to me. "You wanted M&M's? Catch!"

Two huge bags fly through the air. "I'll carry them in my stomach," I laugh. "American candy is horrendously expensive here."

"Jill made you some of her world-famous brownies," Megan says, her head in a box.

"Those we won't share," Clarke says.

"No problem. We had a whole batch to ourselves before we left," Megan replies.

Bright and shiny as their new bicycles, the teenagers look glorious. Clarke and I look as ragged as our scratched and muddy bike buddies. "That's okay," I say, patting my bike, "these guys have lots to learn, don't they?" I turn to Kelly. "Did you sleep on the plane?"

"Nope. Or the night before, either. We were too excited."

"Great. Your first day of cycling is on the left side of the road, into London, and you're half-asleep. Sounds exactly like our rush hour ride through Paris at the first of our trip, come to think of it. You'll be fine, but pay attention. Your parents will be more than a bit upset, duckies, if you get run over your first day."

Clarke leads and I bring up the rear like a sheep dog herding lambs. Once away from the main highway, Kelly and Megan race ahead, stopping to take pictures around every corner, screaming and laughing and telling jokes in their best British accents. "Adrenaline does wonders," I say to Clarke, feeling old.

"We're not there yet."

"Hey, you guys, thanks for the sunshine," I call up ahead. "This is the first day it hasn't rained since we left France." To Clarke, I add, "They look like they could float to London," as Megan erupts into giggles at one of Kelly's witticisms. Kelly, with Jill's dry and zany sense of humor, reminds me how much I miss my sister.

Clarke is on the same wavelength. "I wish Chris and Jennifer had come also," he says softly.

"I know you do. So do I."

As the afternoon wears on, the difficult cycling and hot sun knocks the wind out of the teenaged sails, and the laughter and singing stop. Clarke is back in the lead, Megan close behind, grinding up the hills in high gear instead of shifting down for easier pedaling, determined to keep up, supple and shapely. Feeling frumpy, I pedal faster.

Behind Megan, Kelly lags as we climb another long, steep hill in the hot, muggy sun. "Take a break if you need to, Kelly," I call to her. "I do it all the time." She finally stops to rest, looking resentfully up ahead at Megan, who pedals like Mary Poppins, erect and perky, crowding Clarke and humming to herself. "We've already ridden twenty-five miles, Kelly, and you haven't slept in two days. You're doing great." I try to be reassuring.

She isn't listening. "I thought England was flat," she snarls.

"Nothing is flat. Trust me." Kelly and I are a lot alike, I think for the thousandth time since she was born. We always have to be best or we hate it.

Clarke and Megan wait up ahead. "Problems?" Clarke asks innocently.

"Slow down a little, would you?" I respond. "We're running out of gas back here." It seems to me that Clarke is riding faster than his normal pace. Either he's showing off for Megan or her crowding pushes him faster. Once, as Megan stands up on her pedals to climb a steep grade in high gear, I call ahead, "Gear down, Megan. You're working too hard."

She stops. "I can't shift when I'm pedaling," she apologizes.

"Try to anticipate your gear changes," I explain. "Shift before you start up a hill. It won't go in if you're putting pressure on the pedals."

"I like high gear better anyway," she announces, pedaling ahead to catch up with Clarke.

Kelly finally loses it on White Hill. Time and again, she has to rest and then has trouble starting on the steep grade. Furious, deep in her own frustration, she's unwilling to be encouraged by anyone. I lag behind, mentally cringing, waiting for her poor bike to be flung into the ditch. But Kelly presses on, teeth clenched, face red, expletives wafting behind like exhaust fumes.

Megan is tired too by the time we reach the outskirts of London. Naturally, it's rush hour. Clarke and I aren't used to riding through cities with four people, and we keep getting separated as we weave in and out of bus lanes. "You have to keep track of us, Clarke," I admonish him when we stop at a market for groceries. "If the rear end of this bike train misses a light, we have no idea where you're going. You've got the only map."

"Just keep up. It's too dangerous for me to turn around to count noses."

"We try, but four cyclists take awhile to get through a light in this traffic. Just keep track of Megan, will you, then she can worry about Kelly, and Kelly can watch for me."

Finally, tucked into the campground at the old Crystal Palace, we relax before dinner. As I voraciously read the mail, Clarke sticks his head into Kelly and Megan's tent. "It doesn't look like you have enough room to stretch out in there."

"It looked bigger in the catalogue."

"Do you have a sleeping mat, Megan?"

"Nope. But I sleep on the floor all the time at Kelly's. I'm fine."

"You guys bring anything to put your sleeping bags in when it rains?"

They look at each other. "No."

"Maybe we can dig up a couple of plastic trash bags until we find something better. Believe me, you won't want to sleep in soggy bags."

Cooking for four on a one-burner camp stove isn't easy, but having extra hands for cleanup makes up for the inconvenience. Crowded into our tent after dinner, we don't talk much. It's been a long day. "Look, guys," I say finally, "you rode thirty-five miles today, almost sixty kilometers. That's ten miles farther than you've ever ridden, with full packs and no sleep. You did great, no matter how hard it seemed, much better than I ever imagined. By far." Kelly flashes her big blue eyes toward the top of the tent and growls.

"Instead of bicycling, let's take the bus into London tomorrow," Clarke suggests to everyone's delight, and although we go to bed early, giggles burst from Kelly and Megan's tent well into the wee hours. "Well, how was your day?" Clarke asks, unable to sleep.

"I don't know. I never thought about it."

It feels strange to ride the double-decker bus into London and to walk instead of pedal. It seems to take forever to get from one place to another on foot, and my tennis shoes are so uncomfortable compared to my sturdy bike shoes that I get blisters immediately.

Kelly and Megan, wide-eyed and full of laughter, love the city, snapping photos as they whirl from one famous view to another—Westminster Abbey, Parliament, Big Ben, Trafalgar Square, Picadilly Circus, Soho—all the tourist sites. "Why are you each taking the same pictures?" I ask. "Your film will go twice as far if you just get double prints when you develop your photos."

After four months in Europe, Clarke is only into his seventh roll of film; a year-long adventure calls for an entirely different attitude about picture taking than a two-week vacation. So does a summer—when Kelly and Megan discover how much more expensive film is in Europe when they buy a roll in a London curio shop, their flood of photographs slows to a trickle.

We have an invitation for supper with Christine and Michael, the Londoners we stayed with in Spain who'd given us everything from a picnic table to a key to their house. "Let's take the subway and stop at St. Paul's on the way," I suggest. "It's a gorgeous cathedral with an interesting history—if I could recall it." I'm still grumpy about not having a Michelin guide to London.

Standing in the back of the church, the four of us stare at its incredible ceiling. Unlike most cathedrals, which seem dark and imposing, St. Paul's exudes size and light and delicate gold mosaic. "The crypt is really neat," I whisper to Kelly. "Christopher Wren is buried there, and Wellington and Nelson, I think. But we can't go down because it's Sunday."

At Christine and Michael's, Clarke's drawing of their Spanish house hangs in the living room. "Clarke did that?" Megan and Kelly ask together. Both are aspiring artists and musicians. "People with that much talent make me sick," Kelly adds, shaking her head.

During dinner, Clarke and I get Christine and Michael's advice on a route through England while Kelly and Megan make friends with their daughter Stasi. Afterwards, the girls ask if they can go to a disco and spend the night with Stasi. "I'll bring them into the city tomorrow," Michael offers. "We'll meet you at the Tower Bridge." After raiding Stasi's closet, the three young women head into the heart of London while the rest of us talk so long that Christine fixes sandwiches for a light supper before Clarke and I take the last train to the campground.

In the morning, Michael escorts us through the financial district and the old marketplace, then leaves us at the Tower of London, where we take a tour but keep losing Megan as she wanders about on her own. "She's always disappearing," Kelly complains. "She does that all the time at home."

"Well, I refuse to spend all day looking for her," I reply, exasperated. "Come on, let's see the crown jewels." I'm just as impressed as when I'd seen them on an earlier trip—530-carat diamonds do that, I guess, and crowns made of 3000 jewels. It makes no difference to me if they're replicas. "It's hard to grasp that all this history we read about is real," I say to Kelly, "that kings and queens and beheadings aren't just fairy tales. Can you imagine wearing armor weighing ninety-four pounds?"

We've decided to try American Express as a way to receive mail, but after dragging Kelly and Megan along to one of their offices, realize that teenagers have better things to do in London than follow us on our errands. "Would you guys like to take off on your own for awhile and meet us for dinner at eight?" Clarke asks them. As they dash off, I mention that I hope we'll all find our way back to Picadilly Circus. "Stop it, Susan. You're not their mother."

"We're still responsible for them. Megan's not even sixteen yet."

Later, Clarke and I share a glass of dark ale in a pub. We're still talking about Kelly and Megan. "It doesn't matter where I am, Susan, it's all wonderful. Let's let the girls choose our route this summer."

"What if they want to go somewhere we're not interested in?"

"Is there any place you wouldn't like to see?"

"Well no, but I don't like the idea of just following those two around. Why not work on developing a consensus, finding places we'll all like?"

"That's too complicated, Susan. Come on, you don't have to control everything."

"Well…" It might be good for me, but it doesn't feel right. "Okay, but if it doesn't work out…"

"Then it doesn't work out. Once we've agreed to this, we can't change our minds."

"Maybe that's what bothers me."

Kelly and Megan are taking pictures of each other at Picadilly Circus when we arrive. "You're late," Kelly says. "We're starved."

"After London, we'll be back to cooking our own dinners, ducks," I reply, grumpy. "Don't get spoiled."

We eat at a fast food place and talk about the upcoming summer. "If you could cycle anywhere," I ask Megan, testing the waters, "where would you go?"

"France!" I sigh—after seven weeks in France, I'm ready to see a different country.

"Germany!" says Kelly.

Clarke breaks in. "We've decided that you should choose our route." He looks at me sternly. "It doesn't matter to us where we are, does it, Susan?"

"I guess not," I say hesitantly, looking down at my sandwich, then take a deep breath. "You've got ten weeks. Where do you want to spend them?"

They decide on four weeks in England and Scotland, one week each in France, Belgium and Holland, and three weeks in Germany. "I know you've already been to France," Megan apologizes, "but I've taken five years of French and am dying to hear it spoken. I hope you don't mind."

"We loved France," Clarke tells her kindly while I absorb the fact that they haven't mentioned Denmark, a beautiful country I'd visited briefly before and looked forward to seeing at our new leisurely pace.

"Even just a day or two in France would be wonderful," Megan says, looking at my face.

"It's up to you and Kelly," Clarke says, sticking to his guns. "Whatever you two decide is fine with us. So. What would you like to see in England?"

"Stonehenge," they both say.

"Sherwood Forest," Kelly chooses.

"Where the Brontë sisters lived," Megan adds. "I loved Heathcliff in *Wuthering Heights*."

"The Cotswolds are beautiful," I venture, "and on our way to Stonehenge." In spite of our agreement, I can't totally let go of my destiny for ten weeks.

"To Stonehenge," Clarke rallies the troops in the morning. Off we pedal, with Clarke the head duck and me in the rear again. Bicycling seems more than twice as hard with four. Stringing out one by one on the narrow highways, we're more of a hazard to motorists, and while it's easy to communicate with the person just ahead or behind, for Clarke and me to talk is impossible. Megan, still in high gear, still tails Clarke, who still cycles faster than usual. Kelly, already better at changing gears, is still frustrated at herself for tiring.

When Megan has gear troubles, Kelly and Clarke pedal ahead while I help. Everything adjusted, we race off to find the others, but they're nowhere in sight. At a fork in the road, Megan asks, "Which way?"

"I have no idea. Clarke's got the map. Stop, I guess—they'll have to come back for us sometime." We wait for half an hour as my irritation grows, then turns to alarm—I haven't the foggiest idea where we are or the route Clarke has chosen to Stonehenge. But I say, "Don't worry, I have the food. They'll come back."

And they do, eventually, irritated themselves because they had to pedal uphill to retrieve us. "Where have you been?" Clarke asks.

"What happened to watching out for the person behind? You should have noticed when Megan disappeared, Kelly, at least at this turn. If someone really got lost, we'd never find each other."

"Hey, I was just glad to keep up with Clarke."

The day lasts much longer than we intend. About the time we finally decide to pack it in for the day—Clarke and I, that is; the girls were ready to quit earlier—we find ourselves in the middle of a military base. Eventually, we reach a little village and ask to camp at a large farm with pastures all around. We've wondered if it will be harder to get permission for four than two, but Mark and Sarah are happy to have us all.

"You guys pedaled eighty kilometers today, almost fifty miles," I announce at dinner. I always keep score. "Congratulations."

"I did awful," Kelly says.

"No, you didn't. I certainly didn't ride fifty miles on my second day in Spain. But then I'm old, of course," I add before she can.

"We're all tired," Clarke says. "Let's go to sleep early so we can get a good start in the morning."

He and I lie awake listening to the girls giggling until we can't stand it anymore. "Hey, you two, knock it off," I hiss, unwilling to endure a ten-week slumber party three feet from my head.

In the morning, Megan is up first, scrubbed and made up into her pretty self before Clarke crawls out of our tent, and the teenagers are ready to go first because the cooking gear has to be washed and packed after breakfast. "How about some help here?" Clarke asks Megan. "Go see if Mark and Sarah will let you fill our water bottles."

"Me?"

"Sure. Susan and I asked for a place to stay last night."

Megan looks stricken but walks off with Kelly, arms loaded with empty bike bottles. "They didn't mind at all," the girls report happily when they return, smug in their victory.

"Asking is much more interesting in a foreign language," I remind them. "Enjoy English while you can."

Although I'm more than relieved that Clarke and I got to London in time for the girls' plane, that Kelly and Megan arrived safely, that everyone can pedal more than eight miles a day and that the rain has finally stopped, I realize that I haven't thought about anything but Kelly and Megan since they arrived. I worry about their cycling, whether they're having a good time, whether they're learning anything useful. Clarke and I haven't talked about anything else. Am I having a good time? I haven't even thought about it. Clarke and I can't even communicate anymore, separated all day by the physical presence of the girls between us. "Let me ride behind Clarke for awhile," I say at our next rest break.

Megan drops way behind, and I wonder if it's because she isn't getting to show off by keeping up with Clarke or because she doesn't have Kelly on her tail, pushing her along. Here I am again, thinking about the girls, I chastise myself, forcing myself to think of something—anything—else.

England seems so much like America that I'm not putting myself out much, I decide. Lost in Kelly and Megan, I don't greet people I pass, and even the markets are just like at home. Who can get excited about a giant Safeway compared to a tiny *boulangerie* warm with the smell of fresh pastries? We've even found peanut butter here, now that we have two jars as big as oil drums.

"I'm ready to quit," Kelly says late in the afternoon, wilting over her handlebars.

"Megan, can you go farther?" Clarke asks.

"Sure," she responds, not overly enthusiastic.

"Susan?"

"Of course." I'm torn between sticking up for Kelly and not wanting to be outdone by Megan.

We pedal farther, and when Clarke is ready to stop near Stonehenge, he calls back to Megan, "Do you want to pick out a house?"

"That one," she says, choosing the closest.

We knock on the door. A woman drives up from the back of the house, on her way out of the driveway, rolling down her window just a crack. "May we put our tents in your garden for one night?" I inquire after as she brusquely asks what we want.

"No." Shutting her window, she drives away.

"Care to choose another house, ladies?" Clarke asks.

"That one." This time, Kelly points to the house next door.

The owner is outside on the back patio. "I'm sorry, but I have some very rare plants in my garden and this is a conservation area," he says as if that explains everything.

"Friendly little neighborhood, isn't it?" Clarke remarks as we pedal out of the driveway.

"Let's try this house across the road," I suggest. "It looks friendly, at least."

Leaving our bikes at the foot of the sidewalk, we struggle up to the door of the quaint little cottage, dirty, tired and dejected, and ask the elderly woman who answers our tentative knock if we can camp in her yard. "Yes, I think that would be all right," she says slowly, then hesitates. "But let me check with my husband." She returns in a moment. "Would you mind waiting outside for a few minutes? My son is on his way over anyway, and I'd like to make sure he thinks it's all right."

Puzzled, we walk back to the road. While we wait, the woman reappears carrying a tray with tea and milk and sugar, then her son arrives. After asking us a few questions, the young man smiles. "I'm sure it will be all right if you stay here," he says, then reports to his mother that we passed muster.

She escorts us to her backyard. "Your garden is lovely," I say to the tiny woman.

"It used to be much nicer. I—um, we—just can't keep up with it anymore," she explains. "We haven't had enough rain this summer."

In the morning, as I fill water bottles from the garden hose, she comes outside. "Yoo-hoo, dear, would you like some tea?"

Inside the bright kitchen, the woman confesses. "My name is Glad Peacock and I told you a lie. I have no husband—he died ten months ago." She struggles to hold back tears. "I made up that story about asking him if you could stay because I was frightened. There's been so much trouble here because of Stonehenge—during summer solstice, so many young people break into houses, destroy fields, and leave trash everywhere that we're all nervous. I didn't want you to think I live alone. I feel terribly guilty."

She's adorable. "You were smart to do that, ma'am," I reassure her. "But tell me, if you were frightened, why didn't you just send us away?" Like all of your other neighbors, I add to myself.

"You looked so nice, and the girls, they looked so tired."

The tea is ready. "I'll carry this out to the garden," I offer.

"Please, would you join me inside? My son takes very good care of me, but I'm quite lonely."

I go outside to get Clarke and the girls. "Where have you been?" Clarke grouses. I relay our hostess's invitation. "We'll get an awfully late start," he complains, then succumbs to this woman's hospitality just like the rest of us. When we leave, Mrs. Peacock has tears in her eyes as she thanks us for staying with her.

At Stonehenge, I offer to watch the bikes while the others walk down to the sacred circle of stones. For some reason, I was unimpressed with Stonehenge when

I saw it years ago and have little desire to see it again. As it turns out, none of the others are particularly intrigued with it either. Maybe it's the fence around it.

We turn north. "Nobody seems too excited about campers in these parts," Clarke says. "Let's put some miles behind us."

Although it's hot and hilly, scattered fields of red poppies cheer us with their bright beauty. Once, we stop to ask directions. "Are people nice to you in England?" the man asks after telling us where to turn.

"All except around Stonehenge, and we can't blame them for that," Clarke replies.

"Well, I'm Scottish, and if you think the British are nice, just wait until you get to Scotland."

I don't remember how the water fight starts, but it ends with all four of us squirting our entire supply onto each other as we weave and laugh our way down a small, quiet road. "If they're having a drought here, maybe we should conserve," Clarke says too late. It's the first time we haven't. Clarke and I can both bathe and wash our hair in a liter bottle from the bikes and the dishes are washed in a half-liter. We still don't wash fruits and vegetables. We refill our bottles at a farm with a huge, shaggy dog.

That night, when Kelly suggests stopping, Megan agrees. "Pick a place, then," Clarke says. I know that he wants to ride farther. Megan picks the first house we come to.

"No, I'm sorry, it isn't possible here," we're told.

"Maybe we're still too close to Stonehenge," I say, secretly wondering if it isn't because four people at the door are overwhelming. If so, it will be a long summer. I think of France, where we were turned down only once.

"Want to pick another place?" Clarke says to Megan.

"There, there and there," she points to the three nearest houses.

"You ask, then," Clarke demands.

"How stupid would it look for a teenager to ask for a place to stay for adults?" Megan sneers. "Get real, Clarke—you ask." We're refused at the first house.

"Come on, you guys, this feels all wrong," I say. "Let's go on."

"What difference will riding farther make, Susan?" Kelly snarls.

"I can't explain it. Just come on." As we leave, I'm tempted to ride back and ask the people at the last house why they said no. Was it Stonehenge or us?

Passing an old man on a bicycle, I signal a stop up ahead. The man catches up. "Are you going somewhere nice?" he asks.

"We're trying to find a backyard for our tents tonight," I reply.

"I'd love to have you," he flirts, "but I haven't a backyard. The next tavern on the left has some extra land across the road."

"A cold drink sounds good."

"Anything to stop," grouses Kelly.

We pull into the tavern parking lot as three people on their way inside complain about the old bicyclist, who apparently slowed them down on the road earlier. "I'm beginning to wonder about the people in this part of England," I say. "They sure seem grouchy." We are too.

Inside, we sip our drinks in silence and listen to everyone gripe about this and that. No one seems happy about anything. Clarke and I feel uncomfortable asking these people for help, but it isn't getting any earlier in the evening. "Does anyone know of a place where we can put our tents for the night?" we ask after explaining who we are to the bar in general.

One man suggests a campground several miles away. Kelly and Megan kick each other under the table, no doubt delighted that our choice was no better than theirs. Finally, one young woman says, "You can camp in my backyard across the street." She stands up. "My name is Gitte. I'm from Denmark. Come, I'll show you the way."

While Kelly and Megan wash their hair and dirty laundry with a watering can in Gitte and Tony's garden, Clarke and I return with Gitte to the tavern for another beer. That night, she leaves the back door open so that we have access to the bathroom, and in the morning shows us around the five-hundred-year-old thatched-roof farm while Kelly enjoys a real bath. "My legs were so hairy that I sounded like a cricket when they rubbed together in my sleeping bag last night," Kelly announces when she joins us for tea.

As we pack the bikes, Tony warns us that the road to Marlborough begins with a three-mile, ten percent grade. Kelly groans. "If we hadn't been able to stop here last night, I would have died." But the hill outside of town is easy–Tony was apparently teasing, pulling our bicycle legs.

Chapter 11

The Cotswolds are that quaint and cutesy part of England characterized by tiny limestone villages strung together by rock walls undulating up and down the hilly countryside, but it's so hot and humid that the air takes on a watery cast, shrouding the usually-beautiful scenery like the drab gray skirts of a charwoman. "I don't like these roads," Clarke complains. "They're too narrow."

"I love them," I defend the place I chose. "They're peaceful."

"But they don't go anywhere."

Kelly spits out another mouthful of bugs. "I'm hungry, but not this hungry!"

Bells fill the air with five o'clock chimes. "Listen," I say, hoping to lighten the mood. Kelly and Megan look at each other and gag theatrically.

"Be quiet, Susan," Clarke snaps. "We're all perfectly capable of noticing things on our own."

I'm crushed. All through Spain and France, Clarke and I commented on the things we saw and smelled and heard. Now, if I can't talk about our joint experience and don't want to talk about Kelly and Megan, should I sew my lips shut?

The girls want to quit for the day. "These hills are awful," Kelly complains.

"It's too hot," Megan adds.

"I'm not ready to quit," Clarke replies. "We hardly rode at all before noon. At this rate, we'll never get anywhere."

Kelly and Megan look at each other in disgust while I propose a compromise that makes no one happy. "Let's ride as far as Little Rissington, which will give us seventy kilometers for the day." It's too far for the girls and not far enough for Clarke.

I have no idea what I want to do—I'm too busy refereeing everyone else's opinions to form one of my own.

Around the back of a stone farm in Little Rissington, a tall, strong man sticks his head out the kitchen window. "Do you want water?" he asks. "Come around front." Inside, the house is all male—tall ceilings, game trophies, stone floors. We get our water and then ask if he has a place for our tents. He shakes his head, then apparently reconsiders. "I have a field down the road where no one will bother you."

The just-harvested field is so lumpy that we put our tents on the road that connects it to the next pasture, hoping to leave in the morning before being flattened by a tractor. After Clarke and I splash water over each other near the far side of the field, we cook dinner, then ask the girls as they do dishes what time they want to leave the next day. "Early," says Megan.

But Clarke and I are ready to go before Kelly and Megan are packed in the morning. "Can I help?" I ask.

"Let them do it," Clarke says. "They have to learn to be responsible."

"You asked them to help the other day when they were ready before we were," I remind him.

"That's different. Our cooking gear can't be packed until we've all eaten."

"Why does everything have to be the way Clarke wants it?" Kelly hisses as she straps their tent on her bike, finishing up in stony silence.

Bumping out of the field at nine, we pedal up and down the Cotswold hills to Burton-on-the-Water, a quaint but touristy village where we stop for meat pies. The disagreement from morning has carried into the day. "Come on, you guys," Clarke complains after the girls go back for seconds. "It's not even noon and you're already dragging your tails."

I seem to be the only one noticing the charming clusters of stone houses surrounded by hedges clipped into patterns. Although I remember the Cotswolds as flat, they definitely aren't. Up and down and down and up we cycle, circling through the tiny villages on circuitous roads, wishing we could cut through the fields. I lead through Lower Slaughter and then Upper Slaughter. "We've already been here," moans Megan. Sure enough, we're in Lower Slaughter again. "Let Clarke lead. I'm not pedaling up this hill again."

After helping me fix a flat, Clarke takes it upon himself to give Kelly and Megan a brief bicycle maintenance lesson. "Stop patronizing us," Megan interrupts. "I already know all about bikes."

"Then how come I have to fix everything that goes wrong with yours?" Clarke asks. "You don't even know how to shift properly."

We cycle a bit farther. In London, we agreed to alternate cooking and cleaning up. It's Kelly and Megan's turn to fix dinner, so I try to start a harmless conversation to clear the air. "What's for dinner tonight?" I ask.

"We haven't a clue," snaps Kelly, hot and tired. Megan's still furious at Clarke, who's pedaling fast, fuming himself. My stomach is knotted with tension—didn't I read somewhere that vacations were supposed to be fun?

Kelly and I have always gotten along. I understand her because we're a lot alike and I admire her wit and intelligence. Although she's always confided in me about school and clothes and boys, after this trip, I decide sadly, she'll probably never speak to me again. Signaling a stop, I pull over to the shady side of the road. "Okay, let's decide about dinner."

Kelly and Megan put their heads together and decide on tuna salad. "Do we have any mayonnaise?" Megan asks.

"I'll check." I get up to rummage through my food pack.

Clarke stops me. "Let her look, Susan. Megan, how do you expect to handle your own life if everyone else has to be responsible for you?"

"It's not my pack," Megan says, eyes flashing. "Can't you ever help, Clarke?"

"We're sick of being treated like children," Kelly says. "If this is the way it's going to be all summer, we'll just go off on our own!"

"Wrong!" I puff up my mother hen feathers. "We're here together, like it or not." Kelly glares at me while Megan stares at the ground.

"If you two want to be treated like adults," Clarke begins, "then quit expecting us to make all the decisions and do all the work. All you ever do is complain."

"All you ever do is lecture, Clarke," Megan retorts.

During my earlier trip to the Cotswolds, I'd stayed in seven-hundred-year-old monasteries and elegant manor houses. Now, instead of ordering dinner in the library of an old mansion and returning after a lavish meal for cognac and chocolates on a silver tray, I'm sleeping in a tent in a rocky field trying to creatively cook an egg and keep peace inside a squirmy bag of weasels. "That's enough, everybody," I declare. "Let's go on."

To top it off, my three companions aren't taken with the scenery at all, and I'd suggested it. Mostly, we see hills and fields; the quaint villages, while easily accessible by car, never seem to be on the road where we're going and everyone is tired of my detours up another steep hill just to see another limestone village with box hedges around the windows.

We pedal in silence for miles. Yet again, because of our late start and snitty argument, most of our bicycling occurs after lunch. Although my knees ache, I refuse to say anything—Kelly is having enough trouble for both of us although she insists on keeping up, no matter what. "If you need to, take a break," I tell her over and over. "I can always use one."

Eventually, she stops, panting, for about three seconds, then goes on. Snarling, she tries to downshift but her chain falls off. Furious, she yanks it back on, wipes her greasy hands on the roadside grass and grinds ahead, nose to tail with Megan. The scene replays all afternoon. "Why doesn't this happen to anyone else?" she spits, jerking her chain on again.

Late in the hot afternoon, we meet a long hill just past the turnoff to Moreton Morrell. It would be a great ski slope—we'd kill for snow and a chairlift. "No. Absolutely not," Kelly announces. "Over my dead body. Air mail me home. Now!"

"You're about three hundred kilometers from the nearest airport, luv," I say in a British accent not as good as the girls'.

Staring at the hill, she says to Clarke, "If I go up that thing, I'm through for the day." Her eyes strain toward the summit. "If I don't die first."

"How far have we ridden today?" Clarke asks me pointedly.

"About fifty kilometers, mostly this afternoon."

"I'd like to ride farther," he announces.

Kelly and Megan groan. I can go farther, I think, but why? The girls are beat; it's their trip too. It's time to take their side. "We're riding between thirty and fifty miles a day, which is much better than we thought we could do at first. We only asked for thirty miles a day, Clarke, not fifty. It's hot and humid and hilly, and Kelly and Megan haven't been bicycling for four months like we have. Why make them suffer just so we can go a little farther?" I feel like Pollyanna.

"Okay, Susan, but remember, Kelly, that you're the one who wants to spend three weeks in Germany. Are you prepared to give that up?"

"Sure." Anything to rest.

"Let's go, everybody," I say in a cheerleader voice that gags even me, "let's get this hill out of the way." It's hard but not terminal. Kelly and Megan do fine.

"There's a farm up ahead on the left." Hoping to avoid a mutiny, I choose the first farm I see. "Does this look okay to you, Clarke?"

"I suppose."

Clarke is extremely strong, and riding up steep roads with a hundred-plus pounds of equipment affects him about as much as pedaling to the corner store for milk. Oh, he has hard times, but his body is made for bicycling. Once in Spain, we met a group of young men bicycling the opposite direction over a rugged pass. They were on fast ten-speeds with light packs; Clarke watched them longingly, no doubt wishing that he could ride with people who would challenge him physically, push his limits farther. Instead, he gets me—and now two teenagers—and has to learn about patience while the rest of us learn about pushing our physical limits.

The woman who comes outside the large brick farmhouse has clear gray eyes and graying hair pulled up in a knot. Her bulky figure is wrapped in a simple cotton dress, but she's beautiful, a classy lady happily trapped in the body of a farmer's wife. "May I help you?" she asks, business-like, drying her strong hands on a colorful apron.

We make our request. The woman looks from Clarke to me, then to Kelly and Megan, her eyes cool with appraisal. Then they twinkle. "Yes, you may. And we have a bathroom alongside the house you may use. It has a sink and a loo." She notices Megan's dirty t-shirt. "I'm washing clothes—may I do some laundry for you?"

We settle our tents in the middle of a magnificent yard surrounded by flowers and hedges. Not a twig or a leaf mars the perfectly smooth lawn. After Kelly and Megan deliver their dirty clothes, they flop on the cool grass to enjoy the peace and quiet of non-pedaling while Clarke and I talk in our tent. "Remember how much trouble I had in Spain when we first started, Clarke? You always wanted to go farther than I could."

"Uh-huh."

"Well, I started asking to quit for the day before I really needed to so that I'd have something left in me when you pushed me farther. I almost always ended up quitting when I needed to anyway."

"Yeah?"

"After we agreed to let me decide when to quit, I felt lots better pushing myself, knowing that when I really needed to stop, I could. Let's let Kelly and Megan decide our stop time every night, no questions asked. Our start time too. We can't leave in the morning until they're ready anyway, and if they set the time, they may be more likely to honor it."

Clarke sighs. "Okay, let's try it."

"If it doesn't work out after a week or two, we can renegotiate." I'm still sorry that Clarke talked me into letting Kelly and Megan be in charge of our route. "Hey, ladies, I've got a proposal for you," I call out of the tent. This one they love.

Accompanied by three dogs happily running about her feet, our hostess comes across the grass with her hands full of fresh strawberries and eggs. "I just gathered these," Marge says, handing them over. Nestled in the carton with eleven brown eggs is a pale green one.

"I've never seen a green egg before," I exclaim.

Marge laughs. "It was laid by that lavender hen over there," she points, then explains that she tries to buy hens that lay interesting eggs. "They're more fun to gather."

After dinner, I knock on the door of the farmhouse. "My name is Susan," I say to the man who answers, "and my tent is in your garden."

"I'm Dick and yes, I noticed."

"I thought you had. We're rather an odd bunch of new foliage. Sorry to bother you, but I'm writing a book about our travels on a laptop computer. Would you mind if I plugged it in to recharge the batteries overnight?"

The large house is full of oriental rugs and comfortable furniture on polished hardwood floors. Marge emerges from the kitchen as I plug my computer into a hall outlet. "I'm fixing Dick some homemade bread and raspberry jam. Would you and your friends like to join us?"

I run outside to collect the troops. "Anybody up for homemade bread and jam?" I call toward Kelly and Megan's tent, but they're already sound asleep. Maybe if we can all get some rest, I think, we won't be so grouchy tomorrow.

After Clarke and I chat with Dick and Marge about this and that for an hour, Marge offers us showers. "Kelly and Megan will die when they hear what they've missed tonight," I say to Clarke as we take turns in the huge upstairs bathroom.

In the morning, we devour all twelve gift eggs with strawberries, juice and yogurt. As Kelly gathers her clean clothes from Marge, Megan comes to where we're cinching the last of the packs on our bicycles, yogurt cup in hand. "I don't care for this flavor yogurt," she says. "Would either of you like it?"

"No, thank you," I say, passing it to Clarke. "I'm full of brown and green eggs."

One bite later, Clarke's eyes get big. "I'm allergic to nuts!"

I snatch the container from his hand. "'Brazil nuts,'" I read. "Do you need a doctor?"

"No. Just let me lie down in the grass for a minute," he gasps.

"Your face is red, and it's swelling," I gasp myself. "Let me get help." Too uncomfortable to lie down, he paces, puffing up like a blowfish. "Watch him," I say to the girls, then race inside for Marge.

Megan runs into the kitchen after me. "He can't breathe!" she yells.

"Call your doctor!" I shout, then run back outside to Clarke. He's delirious, gasping for air, and I help him inside while the others wait in the driveway for the doctor.

Twenty minutes later, Marge and Dick's family physician runs into the house. "That's quite an allergy you have, young man," he says after injecting five vials of adrenaline into Clarke's veins. When Clarke begins to breathe more easily, the doctor adds, "This could have been fatal. I'm glad I was home—I don't think my kids remembered that it's Father's Day anyway."

"Is it? Gee, we forgot too," I say.

"And we almost lost our head duck," Megan wails.

"Well, you didn't," the doctor says. "He was lucky. But he's not going anywhere today. At most, he's to walk around a little in the afternoon."

The doctor asks us a few questions about our trip while he monitors Clarke's progress as the adrenaline works through his body. "I think he'll be all right now," he assures us finally. "But it's possible that you may have a relapse," he speaks sternly to Clarke. "If so, take this medication." He hands Clarke a bottle of pills.

"What do we owe you?" I ask.

"Nothing. Just be careful on the rest of your trip, particularly you, son. I hope you like England."

After seeing the doctor to the door, I head for the kitchen. "I hope they don't think I gave Clarke the yogurt on purpose," Megan is saying to Kelly, unaware of my approach.

I don't comment on her concern, lost in my own fears. "Can you imagine the outcome if this had happened in some forest where we couldn't get help?" I say instead. "Or if we'd been in a country where we couldn't speak the language?"

"I can just see me going through a German dictionary," Kelly shudders, "trying to find a way to explain that Clarke is fatally allergic to nuts." Megan is silent.

"Megan," I say then, "don't feel guilty about this."

"I gave him the yogurt."

"But it's his responsibility to read labels. It's his allergy. You didn't knowingly give him nuts. After this, though, I imagine that we'll all read labels."

Clarke lies on the couch in the living room. "I feel like I have no bones."

Marge and Dick fold us back into their family. "Will you join us for lunch?" Marge asks.

"Only if you'll let us earn it," I agree, grateful. We're out of food. "Surely you have some chores we can do."

Kelly and Megan stem gooseberries and strawberries while I iron clothes, and the three of us water the lavish gardens with watering cans. "Normally," Marge explains, "it rains enough to keep the flowers going, but this year, with the drought, it takes four hours a day to water the garden." She looks sadly at her beautiful flowers.

In addition to lunch, Father's Day dinner is stretched to include us: lamb, Yorkshire pudding, gooseberries, spice cake and cider. That evening, as we pitch our tents again, Kelly and Megan happily discuss their first experience with above-and-beyond hospitality. "Do you think Americans would be so kind?" I ask them.

They think for a moment. "I don't know," Megan answers.

"I doubt it," says Kelly.

In the morning, Marge scatters feed for the chickens. "We're not letting Clarke eat anything until we're off your property," I call to her.

"How is he?" she smiles, her beautiful eyes bright with clear morning sunshine.

"Ready to ride. He's amazing."

After difficult goodbyes, we pedal away from the pretty farm, Clarke a bit shaky but determined. And instead of complaints about the hills and heat of England, Kelly and Megan's conversation turns to its wonderful, warm, generous people.

Marge had fixed us homemade bread and jam and tea for breakfast, telling us about nearby Warwick Castle. "I can't believe that we didn't take you there yesterday," she groaned. "But you must go today; it's only a few miles out of your way and is the best castle in England."

I call for a stop at the turnoff. "Anyone want to see Warwick Castle?"

"I do," Kelly says.

"Not me," Clarke responds. "We already lost a whole day of bicycling yesterday."

Megan looks at Clarke before answering. "It doesn't matter to me," she says hesitantly, "but will there be other castles?"

"There's one in Edinburgh," I answer. "So we have one yes, one no, and one neutral."

"So what do you want, Susan?" Clarke asks.

I want the girls to see the castle. I'd hoped to show them Longleat near London, but it was too far out of our way. For me, it doesn't matter, as I've seen English castles on other trips and Clarke and I have seen enough French *chateaux*. I vote no and regret it. Instead, I propose that we go on to Rugby to replace my broken odometer/speedometer. "What difference does it make how far we go?" Clarke asks. "We go as far as we go."

"I never thought I'd live to hear you say that. And no, it doesn't matter how far, but I still want to know the total. This isn't a challenge for you, but it is for me. And I bet Kelly and Megan would like to know how far they ride this summer too."

"Whatever," says Clarke. "But whatever it costs, we can't afford it."

It's our eleventh day with Kelly and Megan and already I can't remember what it was like without them. Life seems much more conversation than action now, and much more complicated. Like a short chain of paper clips, we wind up through the English countryside. Every once in awhile, someone drops off to fix a chain or to drink water or to take a photo, but for the most part, we stay clipped together, pulling and pushing each other up and down the steep hills. Traffic is light.

At a bike shop in Rugby, Clarke grumbles about buying a new odometer and I grumble about his having to buy new sunglasses because he left his someplace. Megan buys a handlebar pack so that she can help carry more food. At lunch in a tiny park, Clarke spreads out our large-scale map of England and Scotland. "We're still a couple of weeks away from Edinburgh," he estimates. "You guys allotted one month for England and Scotland. At the rate we're cycling, we won't have time to go much farther than Edinburgh, not counting the ride back to Dover. We'll have to take a bus unless we turn back now."

I'm more than unhappy. Everyone we've met has told us about the beauty of the Scottish Highlands. The terrain is difficult, they say, but well worth it. Now, not only have I given up Denmark, but also I'm giving up most of Scotland after pedaling all the way from Africa to get there.

"I vote for the bus," Kelly decides. "We haven't seen Sherwood Forest yet."

"Or Brontëland," agrees Megan.

"Can't we see at least some of Scotland?" I plead.

"Let's go downtown and check on bus fares to London from Edinburgh," Clarke suggests. "Susan and I promised two fox-feeding women we'd be back for a barbecue with two other mouths to feed—yours."

When we discover that English buses don't accept bicycles as baggage and that train and plane fares to London are seventy-five dollars each, ten days' allowance, none of us is happy with the news. Clarke and I spend a hundred dollars a week for the two of us for everything—food, bike parts and maps—and although the girls have brought extra money to make sure they have enough, they seem to be spending it too fast, even though the only things they've bought extra were a couple of teacups and some film in London. At one point, Clarke and I had wondered if some of their money had been stolen, but they were sure that they could account for it all and could stay within budget.

By the time we leave Rugby, we've spent four hours running errands but know that Clarke won't be content with a shortened cycling day even though he's agreed to let Kelly and Megan choose our start and ending times. Although it's blistering hot and we're all tired, neither girl calls a halt. When they finally do, there's no place to stop until we've ridden ninety kilometers.

It's nine o'clock and almost dark when we find a large, bare farm off a dirt road. In back, a man pitches hay up into a storage loft. "Hello," we call up. The man stares down at us. "We're Americans bicycling for the summer," Clarke explains hurriedly. "May we put two tents in your field tonight?"

Coming to the edge of the two-story hay pile, the man stares, pitchfork in hand. "You must be very wealthy," he says finally.

"Hardly," Clarke laughs. "We've sold everything we own and still can't afford a campground."

The farmer shakes his head. "Well, go around the front and put your tents on the grass," he says after thinking a moment. By now, four young men have joined him at the edge of the hay, looking curiously at Kelly and Megan. "When I'm finished with this," he continues, "I'll get you some fresh milk."

Major brings us milk and potatoes, explaining to Clarke that his wife left him and his four sons. "It's about all I can do to keep the farm running," he says. "I have a woman who cleans once a week and starts supper, but the rest of the time, we live very simply." No wonder there's no garden.

Kelly and Megan argue good naturedly about which one will return the empty milk bottle to the back door in the morning, each hoping to meet the handsome boys. "The way you two look and smell," Clarke teases, "I wouldn't bother."

Actually, they always manage to look great. Megan takes sponge baths out of her water bottle every chance she gets, and Kelly is always first to grab a shower when offered although the rest of us are close behind. Every now and then, Clarke refuses an offer to bathe, perhaps embarrassed by our eagerness or to prove his masculine disdain for such frivolity. "It's amazing how good you two look without makeup and hair dryers," I say honestly. "Especially today. Your clothes are clean, thanks to Marge."

Per instructions, the girls haven't brought much to wear. But like true Americans, they change clothes every day. In no time, everything they have is dirty and has to stay that way until they find a place to do laundry. Clarke and I have learned to wear one outfit for a week or two; then, when we find a place to wash it and us, switch to our other shorts and tie our newly-washed clothes on the bikes to dry. That way, we always have something clean when we need it.

When Kelly and Megan do laundry, they always have too much to tie on their bikes and put the wet clothes in a plastic bag, where they mold. Eventually, they wash only underwear unless they get hold of a washing machine. Most of the time, their clothes look pretty bad – in addition to wearing them, they use them for sitting mats, tablecloths and counter tops. Megan has already bought a new towel because hers is wet. Now both towels are wet, and getting heavier and smellier.

Tonight, it's dark before we get the tents up. Luckily, we'd stopped in Leicester after deciding that we were too tired to cook, eating greasy fish and chicken English style, out of newspapers, with mayonnaise instead of catsup on the fries. "We can't afford to keep eating out," I'd admonished us, chewing happily. "Before you guys came, Clarke and I only ate out once per country."

"That's what we liked best about your letters," Megan said. "They were full of strawberries and fresh bread beside a river. Your trip sounded very romantic and adventuresome."

"Then let's get back to it. We've found it hard to resist when you guys want fast food because we want you to have fun."

"Well, we won't be able to," Megan said logically, "if we're not even here because we're out of money."

In the morning, Megan is up first, fluffed and on her way to the farmhouse with the milk bottle before Kelly even stirs. "How'd you do?" Clarke crawls out of our tent to ask when she returns.

"Nobody around. I left it with the dog."

It's an incredibly hot and humid day, setting record temperatures all over England, and we're all overheated and irritable by the time we arrive in Nottingham. "I assume you want to see Nottingham Castle," I ask Kelly as we huff and puff into the city.

"Of course," she snaps.

"I don't," Clarke snaps back.

This time, I refuse to negotiate her out of her castle. "The Robin Hood stuff is the only thing Kelly's asked to see in England, Clarke. I want to see it also. How about you, Megan?"

"Sure."

"You can watch the bikes and enjoy the shade, then, Clarke, if you don't want to join us."

The castle is disappointing—nothing about Robin Hood, little of it open to the public, just a couple of rooms with displays about the city. The girls and I wander awhile, looking in vain for shady places to walk. "Let's go," Kelly decides finally, scuffing her tennis shoe in the dust.

Kelly has a terrific wit. When she's funny, she's a delight. When she's mad, she turns her wit to biting sarcasm and she drives us all nuts the rest of the afternoon, complaining about the hills and the heat and all the things that go wrong with her bike when she doesn't change gears correctly. We feel the weather also, and don't need to feel it again through her. Megan still tries to be super cyclist, keeping up with Clarke, and I'm jealous of her youth and stamina. Although Clarke enjoys the attention, he's irritated at all of us by the end of the day. In fact, we're all mad at each other and the blistering heat and humidity. "I'm pitching my tent right in the middle of this stupid road!" Kelly yells at five o'clock after less than fifty kilometers.

"Does that mean you want to stop?" Clarke matches her sarcasm. "Don't get mad at us—when we stop is up to you and Megan."

We end up at a pig farm. The owner listens to our request to camp, then looks around his garden. "Not here, because my dogs will bark all night, you know. But come with me. There's a soccer field at the school next door." His dogs, Bumble and Piper, never say a word. "You look hot," he remarks as he directs us to a flat spot in the soccer field. I'm sure we radiate heat. "If you want, go stand under my new irrigation equipment out there in the field. Bring your swimsuits and soap," he offers, then looks at Kelly and Megan, "or if you wait until I get home about nine o'clock, come nude and I'll watch."

"Okay," Clarke says with a straight face. "I'll be there."

Richard laughs and leaves the field shaking his head. Scrambling into our swimsuits, Clarke and I head for the sprinkler as a woman bicycles up. "I'm Richard's wife," she explains. "Wouldn't you rather have a real shower at our house?"

"Oh, yes," I say as always, and take the first one, dirt and sweat and stickiness washing down the drain with the soapy, cool water.

I talk with Julia in the kitchen while Clarke takes his turn. "Would you like to do some laundry?" she offers. Clarke and I didn't wash clothes at Marge's, so I gather up our dirty things while Kelly and Megan are in the sprinklers, no doubt wondering where we are. Julia takes us to the market in town, where we buy beer for us and cold soft drinks for the girls.

"Where have you been?" Kelly snarls when we return to the tents.

"Getting you cold drinks," I reply, then to rub it in, "and taking cool showers with lots of soap."

Too hot to sleep, I lie awake thinking about how little I'm seeing anymore and how uncomfortable it is to be around Kelly when she's angry at herself about not being good enough. Perfectionism, I've always thought, is something I have to pay for in my own life; I've never realized how much it can affect others. But watching Kelly on the trip, I see myself. And it's not a pretty sight.

Chapter 12

Deep in the sparse woods of Sherwood Forest, simple musical displays in a little group of buildings relate the fable of Robin Hood. By the time we fix lunch, the hot muggy weather turns overcast and windy. Not far from Budby, Clarke stops. "Look!" he points. "That mole can't get across the road. Let's help." While I hold up Clarke's bike and the girls hold up traffic, Clarke follows the little mole back and forth across the highway. Each time the fuzzy gray animal with pink feet and nose bumps into the verge at the edge, he wanders back into the traffic lanes to the other side, only to bounce off the other edge like a furry pinball; but when Clarke tries to nudge him over the weeds, the mole snaps blindly. "Whoops," says Clarke, pulling his hands away quickly. Finally, as the animal bumps up to one side again, nose snuffling, Clarke gently gives him a fast boost into the weeds, then waves on the patient motorists.

In Worksop, we mention the incident to half a dozen bicyclists, retired doctors who ride each Wednesday afternoon. "I tried the same thing a number of years ago," one tells us, "and damn near lost my fingers. Nasty little beasts, aren't they?"

By afternoon, it threatens rain and the wind comes up alarmingly. After only fifty kilometers, we ask to camp at a small farm near Tickhill. Earlier in the day, we'd discussed the cooking situation. Taking turns isn't working. "We don't know how to cook anything but fruit salad," Kelly finally admitted.

"Then let's plan meals and cook and clean up together," Clarke had suggested. "How about a taco salad tonight?"

When they arrived in Europe, Kelly had complained about her mother's cooking. "Dad only likes beef, so all we ever have is roast beef, baked potatoes, tossed salad and iced tea," she'd groaned.

Tonight, although Kelly and Megan do what we ask, mostly they watch us cook and then complain about the outcome. "I'll bet she'd kill for Jill's cooking now," I grumble, crossing the windy yard to the girls' tent to gather up their dirty plates.

"I hate green peppers," Kelly is wailing to Megan. "And onions and beans. Megan, what am I gonna eat? This wind is going to blow us to Siberia, except I'll be a bleached skeleton because of Clarke's gourmet cuisine. He's definitely out to get me. This looks like something out of the garbage disposal." She picks up momentum. "And then stuck into an army boot for a week while it sat in a marshy lake. Then moldered for three weeks in a dead man's grave after being basted in embalming fluid. Oh God, why are we even here?" Megan giggles and I pretend not to hear, miffed, thinking that they should be grateful for whatever they get since they can't get it themselves.

In the morning, we're invited into our hosts' house for coffee and tea. As we leave, Clarke peeks into the living room full of antiques and lovely paintings. "Forgive me for asking," he says to Maureen and David, "but this is such a lovely home. Would it be possible for us to see it?"

Maureen smiles. "Of course, but it's a mess. I'm right in the middle of spring cleaning." We could eat off the doorsills. Every room is perfect, spotlessly clean and decorated with fine furniture and fabrics. "Most of the furniture has been in the family for generations, just like the house," David explains. No wonder it fits so perfectly—it looks made for the house, or else the house was built around it.

An upstairs bedroom is full of sunshine and pictures of a lithe young girl on a horse. "Is this your daughter?" I ask.

Maureen's eyes lose their sparkle. "Her name was Alison—our only child. She died last year at twenty. She had multiple sclerosis for seven years. Much as I miss her, she suffered enough."

Maureen's pain is so acute that I can feel it, here in her daughter's bedroom. "I lost my father a year ago also," I tell her softly, "but I feel him every day on this trip. If he hadn't died, he couldn't be here with me." I continue, wondering if I'm overstepping my bounds. "Alison hasn't gone away. She just doesn't need her body anymore."

"I hadn't thought of it that way," Maureen says.

In Tickhill, we stop at a bakery for Cornish *pasties* and milk. Leaning on the building alongside our bicycle buddies to eat, the beginning of a migraine headache creeps behind my eyes as a steady stream of visitors crowd around us with encouragement and advice about where to go next. Clarke digs out my medicine, then goes for a second helping of *pasties* for himself and the girls. "Take all the time you need," he says when he joins me at the small town square where I'm trying to quiet my mind. "The baker says to stop by the church to listen to the bells before we leave."

"I'm okay now," I say after ten more minutes. "Let's go hear the bells."

At the simple church, a large alabaster statue catches my attention, the reclining figure of a young woman, the grave of the daughter of Lord and Lady Somebody, who had died at twenty-nine, two months after the death of her newborn son. Complications or sadness, I wonder, thinking of Maureen.

John and his handsome son Roger give us permission to camp under their apple trees just south of York. In the morning, John's wife supplies us with a map of the city and a little of its history as the oldest town in England. A beautiful place, York is full of tourists and narrow streets called snickelways, and we take turns watching the bicycles so that each of us can walk through the pedestrian-only areas and enjoy the architecture and the arty shops. After lunch, we pedal to York Minster, a giant cathedral begun in the year 627. "I'm churched out," Clarke declares. "You three go in."

"Clarke's gotta see this," I tell Kelly and Megan as we wander around inside. "This is more beautiful than St. Paul's in London. Do you want to go down into the crypt?" Crypts are Kelly and Megan's style—anything to do with the occult, the paranormal, the dark side, teenage angst. A tiny old lady gathers a tour group around her skirts, and the three of us trail along down the stairs. Then she locks us inside. "Oops," I say, wondering when we'll be set free.

Upstairs, the London Festival Orchestra is rehearsing for a concert in the evening. Thrilled by the beauty of the cathedral and the music, I run outside after we're disentombed. "I don't care how many churches you've seen, Clarke, you've got to see this one. I'll take care of the bikes."

He returns much later. "I think maybe this is the most wonderful cathedral I've seen."

"Let's see if John and Cynthia will let us stay another night so we can come back for the concert." The four of us hurry back to the farm. "If we'd known about this yesterday," I say as we lumber along the highway, "we could have left the tents and ridden into town without packs for a change."

It takes only ten minutes for all of us to wash our hair in cold water and change clothes. Back in my baggy cotton pants because my Paris dress looks like a flowered prune from being crammed into a pack, at least I have decent shoes after finally finding a pair in a tiny shop in northern France—silk espadrilles the perfect color and price, but a size too small.

Delighted to leave my thick, floppy blue rubber sandals in my panniers, I keep the silk shoes out of my toe clips as I pedal back to York. When the sweater tied around my shoulders keeps slipping off, I have no way to fasten it on my bike—usually like turtles, totally self-sufficient, we carry everything we own without a thought, stuffed onto the bikes in fat panniers.

After a hurried supper in a small pizza shop, we rush to the Minster after locking the bikes to a rack in the middle of town, and Clarke and I hold hands during the concert. For once, I just relax and enjoy, deciding that it's times like these that make the trip worthwhile—but jeepers, it's been tough since Kelly and Megan arrived. Halfway back to the bikes, my feet in agony from the too-small shoes, I slip them off, shredding my only pair of nylons. "I can't help it, Clarke," I say, feeling stupid, "it's either that or be crippled."

In the dark, we pedal back to Cynthia and John's, Clarke and my headlights merely a tiny warning to drivers, not bright enough to show the way. Neither Kelly nor Megan has a headlight. "We're backtracking a bit from here if you still want to see where the Brontë sisters lived, Megan," Clarke says. "Would you like to leave our packs at the farm tomorrow and spend more time in York? We didn't have time to see the Castle Museum."

"Or York Dungeon," Kelly adds, excited.

"I'd rather see the National Railway Museum," I say.

"So, let's split up," Clarke suggests.

"Did you bring your bike locks?" Clarke asks Kelly and Megan the next morning as we near the city.

"Nope," Kelly replies.

"How did you think you'd protect your bikes?" Clarke asks, sarcastically. "Or did you think that Susan and I would stay outside while you see the museum?"

"We didn't think anything–obviously," Kelly snaps.

After the Castle Museum, where we lose each other but not the bikes, we separate–the girls head to the dungeon, Clarke and I to the railroad museum. "Meet back here at two o'clock," I say. "Don't be late. We still have a long way to ride this afternoon."

Back to two of us for the first time in two weeks, Clarke and I chatter as we breeze through town, delighted with our compactness. We love the railroad museum. "Oh, my gosh, it's five minutes to two," I say, nose pressed to the window of a private car built for a European monarch a century earlier. The time has passed too quickly. "We don't dare be late." But we are. Kelly and Megan beat us to the bikes, but only by moments. It's enough. "Sorry," I apologize, embarrassed.

Kelly and Megan are quite a hit when they bicycle, sunbleached hair flying in the wind. Megan, eager for a suntan, wears short shorts and halter tops and looks ravishing, although she claims that she doesn't enjoy the attention. Her opinion of men isn't the best, to say the least. "Men are scum," she sneers after each encounter.

Clarke hoots. "If you don't want the attention, Megan, then don't dress like that."

Kelly, for some reason, never gets sunburned even though she used sunblock only for the first day or two. Before the trip, she only had to be outside for a few minutes to burn apple red. Now, she too is brown but sticks to t-shirts and longer bike shorts, ignoring the whistles. Once, after a particularly rowdy caravan of soldiers honks and hollers their way past, Clarke sticks out a skinny leg and yells, "Thanks!" He turns to Megan. "I know it's me they're waving at," he announces.

We stop in a village for groceries. When Clarke and I had been alone, we both went into the stores except in big cities, trusting that the bicycles could take care of each other. Anyone who could successfully pedal a bike loaded with a hundred pounds was welcome to try, we'd decided. But now, with four of us, one can easily keep the bikes company while the others shop for food.

All the stores along the street have large glass windows except for one brick building. Carefully leaning the bicycles against the brick, the others run across the street to the market while I keep an eye on the transportation team. "Young lady!" A woman stands at the door of the brick building. "This is a private residence. Remove your bikes."

"I'm sorry, ma'am—we were afraid they'd scratch the glass."

"I don't care. I won't have bicycles leaning against my house."

"Yes, ma'am," I reply as the door slams.

We get an early start for once and pedal sixty kilometers to Haworth in plenty of time for the girls and me to wander around the pretty town where the Brontë sisters lived while Clarke writes letters on a curb next to a service station. After collecting Clarke, we pedal through the moors and find a house with a flat yard late in the afternoon. A sign on the door announces: *No salesman, no phone, no petrol.* "That doesn't sound very welcoming," we decide, then choose another house farther down the road.

"Why do you want to stay here?" The man at the door is tall, in his sixties, with a rigid face and bushy eyebrows. His petite wife stands behind him.

"Because we need a place to sleep and because you have a flat field next to your garage," Clarke explains.

"But we didn't expect you," the man says.

I chuckle. "We didn't know your phone number or we'd have called ahead."

"Oh, dear," says his wife mostly to herself, "no one's ever asked this of us before."

"What will you use for toilets?" asks her husband, looking sternly at each of us.

"We always stop at a service station before we camp for the night. Some people allow us to use an outside toilet, but if not, that's okay. We'll just stop someplace after we leave in the morning." I don't mention that I always have to pee in the middle of the night and streak naked out of my tent to the nearest weedy spot.

"Why don't you stay in campgrounds?"

"We can't afford them. We hope to stay in Europe for a year."

We answer all of their questions as carefully as possible, reluctant to let these people get away when we know we won't hurt them. In France, of course, because of the language barrier, no one could ask many questions. They either trusted us immediately, or they didn't. Yet they always did.

The woman interrupts as her husband starts to form another question, his fuzzy eyebrows bunched together. "You can stay over by the garage," she says quickly. "If you need to use a toilet, just knock on the door." Her husband frowns but closes his mouth.

After dinner, a tiny old man with flyaway white hair appears on the other side of the crumbling stone wall next to our camping spot. "Do you have permission to stay here?" he asks Clarke in a horrendously broad English accent. Nodding, Clarke introduces himself. "My name is Dick," the man continues. "I originally owned this farm and lived in that house," he points to our hosts' home. "Sold it, though, when the farm got too much for me. Live in the little house yonder." By now, all four of us are at the fence and Dick reaches into his pockets to distribute a large handful of round white mints. "Don't give him any," he cautions Megan, nodding toward Clarke. "They're just for you."

As we tell him about our trip, he looks curiously at Clarke. "Your wife must have forced you into this," he says sympathetically. "You're crazy to spend your money like this."

Clarke laughs. "I wanted to come. Besides, it's her money."

Dick shakes his head. "No sane man would take this trip," he decides, giving Kelly and Megan another handful of mints. "Now, don't share those," he reminds them. "Do you want to put your bicycles in my barn? It may rain, you know. You're lucky—I hope you know that—any other year and you'd have drowned by now."

In the morning, our reluctant hosts appear together in the garden as we pack. "We apologize for being so nervous last night," the woman tells us. "Ralph and I are afraid of burglars." Now that he hasn't been robbed, Ralph visits for quite some time. A retired carpenter, he shows Clarke some of his work.

"He reminds me of my father," Clarke whispers as we roll up the tent. "He even looks a bit like him."

In the barn, the bicycles are lined up in stalls once reserved for dairy cattle, and after Dick replenishes our mint supply, we start toward the Lake District. "My front wheel sounds like it's full of gravel," I tell Clarke.

"It's probably your bearing."

In Skipton, Clarke leads us past a bike shop. "Shouldn't we see about getting my bike fixed?" I ask.

"It's your bike, Susan. You be responsible for it."

I picture myself in the middle of nowhere on foot. "Then I'm going back to the bike shop."

The young repairman immediately stops what he's doing to diagnose the problem. "It's a cracked bearing, all right, but I can't replace it because the bearings in your wheel are sealed. You can buy a new wheel but it won't be as good as the one you have, or I can rebuild your old one. That will cost about the same but will take all afternoon."

"What about the other bikes you're working on?" I ask.

"They can wait. I race a bit myself—won first place this weekend," he says proudly, showing me a magazine article about his team. "I know how it feels to need a bike fixed in a hurry."

As I ponder whether it's fair to delay everyone for the better repair, a deep voice whirls me around. "My God, look at those packs! You should be reported to the Society for the Prevention of Cruelty to Bicycles. If they were horses, they'd have to be put down!" It's the bike shop owner, headed to Paris to watch the Tour d'France bike race. While he chats with Clarke about our trip, I decide to buy the new wheel and get back on the road, not because I want to but because I know that Clarke does, although he hasn't said a word one way or the other.

"Good news!" the repairman bounds out of his storage room. "I've found a new wheel as good as your old one. It's more expensive, though." Here's my chance to get what I want, and I say yes before anyone else can offer an opinion.

On a long hill outside Skipton, it begins to rain for the first time since Kelly and Megan arrived eighteen days earlier. Although the girls had bought covers for their sleeping bags near London, it doesn't take long to discover that they aren't waterproof. I'd bought rain pants at the same time, and now pull them on over my shorts as I worry about Megan and Kelly in their inexpensive windbreakers that are neither waterproof nor warm. As uncomfortable as I've been in the rain, I know that the girls will be miserable, and I divide what's left of the orange rain jackets to cover the essential panniers on all four bikes—food, clothes, cameras. Usually, the tattered fluorescent plastic is tucked on the back of our packs like bunny tails to make us more noticeable to drivers. By now, there's not much left to divide.

After climbing toward the Lake District through dales and moors for the past two days, the bicycling is difficult again and the air is cold. In spite of the black sky and heavy clouds that blanket the rolling green hillsides as it rains harder and harder, the scenery is spectacular, washed by the gray, watery cast of rainsheets. Thunder rolls along the ground, welling up through the valleys and punctuating the hissing sound of our wet tires like heavy exclamation marks. We grow silent and soggy. Although the girls don't complain once, at a small village, hands shaking with cold, Megan asks to stop for tea, her legs rashed in purple goosebumps. Clarke and I readily agree, and we lean the bicycles next to the courthouse. While the bike seats get wet, we drip inside a café and sit in a corner by the window, getting four more seats wet, to drink tea laced with sugar and milk in hot gulps before wading back outside for another swim up the road.

Kelly and Megan manage fifty kilometers in heavy rain before throwing in the very wet towel. But we can't seem to find a house with flat fields or with anyone home. Finally, we see a little house with a tiny garden; smoke rises from the chimney in wisps. A woman with thin gray hair hanging in greasy strands over the shoulders of a threadbare chenille robe answers the door. "How much will you pay?" she says, eyes narrowed, after we request tent space in her garden.

"No one has ever asked us for money before," I answer, surprised, as I consider the picture we make: four shivering souls, soaked to the skin, hair stuck to our faces, rain washing off our fingers and clothes. How can she resist such a pitiful sight?

But she does. "My lease doesn't allow camping," she says, slamming the door.

Dejected and cold, we brush off our bicycle seats with freezing fingers and pedal down the highway as dusk joins the gray day. After many silent minutes, off to the left, two farms face each other like reflections in a pond. We knock on the door to the right. "Yes?" the man who answers asks politely, looking from one to the other of us as the storm continues without letup. After a long question-and-answer period, the man finally says, "Do you have any ulterior motives?"

"Only a place to sleep," I answer uncertainly. "What do you mean?"

"Are you Jehovah's Witnesses? Do you plan to convert me?" We burst into laughter and he joins us. "We've had a lot of trouble around here," he explains. "They're getting quite creative, you know. Well, since you're here and you're not Jehovah's Witnesses, we might as well make the best of it, don't you think? Let's see if there's room in the garage."

Gerald backs his car into the rain and strings up a light over our tents—for once, our day won't end with sunset. "If you guys had ever pitched your tent in a muddy field before," Clarke tells Kelly and Megan as we listen to the hard rain on the roof during dinner, "you'd appreciate this even more."

In the morning, Gerald arrives with a bottle of fresh milk along with a photograph. "This is the only picture of the garage I can find," he explains. "I thought you might like it as a souvenir of where you stayed last night."

It rains off and on all day. By now, we're in northwestern England, separated from the Irish Sea only by the Cumbrian Mountains. Kelly cycles extremely well, and Megan lags far behind when it's her turn in fourth position. Then Megan goes out ahead and Kelly, perhaps tired from her superb morning efforts, complains that Megan is going too fast.

In Kendal, we stop at a laundromat and find that it's affordable, unlike in France. Dumping the wet contents of our dripping clothes packs into the machines, we settle in a warm corner to make peanut butter sandwiches. "We'll shop for dinner if you'll finish the laundry," the girls offer after they get bored.

Long after the laundry is dried and folded, Kelly and Megan haven't come back. "What if they're lost?" I ask Clarke.

"If they are, they won't know how to ask directions. This laundromat doesn't even have a name."

I'm unsuccessfully trying to develop an emergency plan when Kelly and Megan return, out of breath and excited. "We thought we'd never find our way back," they exclaim together.

Now that we're in the famous Lake District, every house seems to be a commercial bed and breakfast and we worry about finding a private home where we can pitch our tents. "Can we stay at a campground tonight?" Megan asks. "I've been frozen solid for two days; I'd love a hot shower."

Studying the map, we locate a campground at Troutbeck, near the north edge of Lake Windermere. Pedaling out of Kendal, heavy rain meets us on an uphill grade and follows us up the steep roads, trying hard to wash us back down. Clarke gets a flat tire and we help him change it, squeezing us and the bikes in a skinny space between a tall wall and the narrow road as cars splash past.

Pitching the tents on the wet grass at the campground, we race for the showers but are cold and wet again by the time we crowd back into our tent to make tea and dinner huddled around the tiny camp stove. Kirkstone Pass is on the agenda for tomorrow, offering a sixteen percent uphill grade. "How steep are the highways over the Rocky Mountains back home?" Kelly asks.

"The interstate highways are limited to seven percent grades," Clarke explains. "Even the old mountain passes are only eight or nine."

Kelly and Megan get off to a bad start the next morning, already tired from little sleep. Their tent leaks and both sleeping bags are wet; being inexpensive, they aren't warm to begin with. It won't get much better for them either—when we suggested buying warm gloves or an extra sweatshirt or hat in London, they'd refused.

Rain and clouds obliterate the supposedly beautiful scenery. Once, climbing a steep hill, an abandoned manor house appears out of the mist and I shiver, half expecting ghosts to join us on the road. Silhouetted against the gray sky, the nearby forest hidden in foggy clouds, the mansion stares with the unseeing eyes of broken windowpanes that drip tears of cold rain. Caught in the mystery of the atmosphere, I submerge myself in my own experience, bicycling better than ever and letting Kelly and Megan fend for themselves. Even Clarke asks me to slow down. As Kirkstone Pass looms ahead shrouded in clouds, the girls pedal ahead, stringing out far apart on the difficult grade. In windbreakers and shorts with no gloves or hats, they're shivering uncontrollably by the time we meet at the top. An inn beckons. "Can we stop for tea?" they ask, miserable.

I hesitate. "I don't think so. I can't, anyway. If I warm up, my muscles will get too stiff to bicycle. I'm sorry."

"I have to go to the bathroom," Megan says. "Can't we just wring out our jackets?"

"Of course, but hurry, okay?"

Clarke and I stand outside with the bikes and watch tourists bolt from their cars into the warm inn. "Which way are you going?" asks a young man, and when Clarke indicates north, he replies quickly, anxious to get inside, "You're lucky. That side of the pass is a twenty percent grade."

Kelly and Megan are still inside after twenty minutes. "My knees are already stiff," I complain to Clarke. "I'm doing great today and can't afford for them to lock up. I'd better get the girls."

The restroom is empty, so I scan the dark restaurant for puddles of water under the chairs. Sure enough, huddled in a dark corner, fingers curled around large mugs, Kelly and Megan scrunch side by side in silence. They look stricken when I approach. "We can't come out yet," Megan wails. "We're frozen."

"The restaurant's out of tea," Kelly adds, "and we were so desperate that we ordered coffee." Since both of them hate coffee, the magnitude of the emergency is obvious.

"I wish you'd bothered to tell us so that we could have gone on instead of waiting in the rain. Look, I know how you feel, but believe me, going outside after getting this warm is going to be horrible. We'll wait at the bottom, but be careful—you won't be able to stop if you get going too fast." I remember my frightening experience in France coming down the road from the Chateau Quéribus, and that was only a seventeen percent grade on a dry road. "The highway may be slick, and the wind chill will eat you up."

"Don't tell us any more," they groan. "We'll find out soon enough."

Clarke and I race down the other side of Kirkstone Pass through dense fog and hard rain, braking to stay in control on the slippery road. Although I'm miserable, my heart is with Kelly and Megan, knowing that their experience will be much worse. At the bottom, we lean our bikes against a café wall to wait, thoroughly drenched and frozen ourselves. "I wonder what the view is on a clear day?" I ask to take my mind off my own discomfort.

"Let's get some tea," Clarke says finally, tired of waiting. "From here, the road goes up again—believe me, our muscles will warm up plenty fast when we leave here. By the way, I can't believe how well you cycled up that pass, Susan—the rain was horizontal! I couldn't keep up with you. How'd you do it?"

I shrug. "I concentrated on myself instead of everyone else for a change. I actually enjoyed the ride this morning—except for the cold and rain, of course."

We're on our second round of tea and scones when the door opens to two wretched wet faces, hair streaming water. One step inside the doorway and they stand in puddles, then collapse in the booth beside us with a groan. "Don't ask. We don't want to talk about it," Kelly says, putting her head on the table. Megan is silent as I wipe up the rainwater with a napkin.

Chapter 13

We're about to cross into Scotland, our fifth country after Spain, Morocco, France and England. Near the border, we pedal through a small village that has a distinctly different flavor from England—even the houses look different—and for the first time in a month, I feel like I'm in a foreign country. At a thrift store in Carlisle, Kelly and Megan buy sweaters, Kirkstone Pass still vivid in their memories, then call it quits for the day at a farm near Newcastleton.

A man with a ruddy face and tousled blond hair answers our knock in a ragged fisherman knit sweater, napkin in hand. "I'm just eating dinner," he says when we ask to camp, "but let me see if we can find someplace flat for your tents." Behind his strong, lilting brogue, the kindness in his voice is unmistakable and his ice blue eyes twinkle when he smiles.

"Eat your dinner first."

"Well, then come inside for tea and cookies. I won't be eating alone with you outside and hungry."

We gather in the living room with our tea while Jock gulps down his dinner in the kitchen, then stands in the doorway. "My wife Jean owns a restaurant in town and works fifteen hours every day. Our children are grown and gone, so I'll be liking your company."

Choosing a cement slab outside the barn for the tents because the fields are muddy, we tuck our bicycles under the roof in case of rain, then ask Jock if we can visit after our own dinner. He agrees eagerly, and as we scurry to prepare a quick meal, he showers and shaves. "Would you like to go into town to meet my wife?" he asks shyly after we tell him where we've been on the trip and where we're going.

Piling into a small van, Clarke and the girls scrunch on cardboard boxes in back and I ride in front with Jock, enjoying the different method of transportation as we bounce over the road into Newcastleton. At Jean's restaurant and antique shop, we file through the back door for dessert and coffee. Finally, business slows enough for a visit and she eases slowly into a chair with a sigh. "We bought this restaurant for our daughter," Jean explains, "but she moved to Australia. Now I have to run it, but really I'm interested only in the antiques."

"There's a traditional music festival in town this weekend," Jock tells us after a bit. "Why don't you stay?"

We've been asked to stay before, but always decline. This time, we can't resist—Clarke loves bagpipes, the girls want a rest, and I need to catch up on my writing. "We'll help in the restaurant," Kelly and Megan offer.

"I'll take you up on that," Jean says with relief. "I'm very short-handed for the weekend. Let's go home now. The competitions don't start until day after tomorrow, but I have a lot of baking to do before then."

Friday morning begins with a rainstorm. When Clarke and I get up, Kelly and Megan are already in the kitchen washing Jock and Jean's breakfast dishes, keeping warm. "Jean's at the restaurant," they tell us, "and Jock's cutting hay."

Unable to get the computer to work, I can't determine if the problem is me or the Scottish electrical current. Feeling worthless not riding or writing, I rattle around the house reading magazines, too restless to appreciate a relaxing day on my own two feet instead of on my bike. When the rain stops, Megan offers to pedal into town for lunch and dinner groceries, and after deciding on a pasta salad, we start a shopping list. "I use green olives and onions and cheese," I begin.

"I hate green olives and onions," Kelly interrupts. "Use black olives."

"I don't like black olives," Clarke says. By the time each of us eliminates the ingredients we don't like, not much comes back from the tiny market.

That evening, Clarke and I drive into town with Jock, who shows us around the village, introducing us to the locals in between impromptu jam sessions at the pubs where the festival musicians practice for the weekend. We meet an Englishwoman married to a boisterous man named Ian who wears a Johnny Reb hat and knows all about Colorado. Mary shares her views openly. "Twenty years ago," she tells us, "it was unacceptable in England to marry anyone but the boy next door. That's why

I married Ian. We weren't allowed to date anyone from the next county, let alone another country. But nobody would have wanted to—the Welsh hate the English and so do the French. If an Englishman buys a house in Wales, the Welsh burn it down, the savages."

"If a Frenchman bought a house in your town, would you burn it down?" I ask.

"I'd think about it," she says, eyes slitted.

"That's too bad," I respond. "Although we have different languages and customs, don't you suppose that all people are the same inside?"

"No," says Mary. "We all think differently."

"Yes we do, and that's what gets us in trouble. But we don't feel differently, and isn't that what counts?"

Saturday morning, I ask Jock if I can take a bath. As soon as I immerse myself in the deep clawfoot tub, the water turns black with travel dirt. I don't care—my last bath was in America. Hot water is hot water, whatever the color.

The four of us bicycle into town for the festival, stopping first at Jean's restaurant for Cornish *pasties*. As we walk to the first competition, Clarke and I recognize many people to whom Jock introduced us the night before; it's been a long time since we've seen a familiar face, and it's delightful to greet a passerby by name. We remember them all, and they remember us. We feel like locals. Kelly and Megan check with Jean once or twice to see if she needs help, but Jean is too busy to show them what to do.

Clarke studies the festival program. "All the winning performers are putting on a concert tonight," he says. "Let's eat at Jean's restaurant." Jock joins us for a drink after cutting hay for a neighbor all day, then insists on paying our admission to the concert. Afterwards, we go to a pub for one drink, but every time we start to leave, Jock and Jean's friends put another in our hands. Kelly and Megan stand around, bored, and at ten-thirty, Megan leaves to go back to the farm alone, insisting she'll arrive before dark.

Clarke has a fit. "She doesn't have a light on her bike, Susan. Kelly, see if you can catch her at the restaurant."

Megan is furious when Kelly brings her back. "Why can't you people just leave me alone?"

Kelly interrupts. "Jean says she's leaving the restaurant in a few minutes and will take us home in her car. We can put our bikes in Jock's van."

"Then it's settled," Clarke says, turning to talk with new friends as four young men crowd around Kelly and Megan. The tipsy boys are more than obnoxious, and Megan, angry to begin with, smolders.

"That's another thing," I say as Megan fusses about boys and their manners. "A lot of drunks are on the road tonight because of this festival. A female riding a bike alone in the dark is an invitation to be hassled, like it or not."

"I can take care of myself."

When we walk back to the restaurant, only three bikes fit in the van. "I'll ride back," Clarke volunteers. "I've got the only bike with a headlight now that Susan's burned out."

"If it's not safe to bicycle at night, why is Clarke riding?" Megan snarls.

"Because he has a light and you don't. And because he's bicycled more than you have. And because he's unlikely to get hassled by a carload of drunk men!" This is getting a bit old.

"So you think men are superior to women."

I spin around. "Megan, if there's anyone in the world who thinks that women are equal to men, it's me. Don't be stupid. His having a headlight has nothing to do with being a man; his being a more experienced cyclist than you has nothing to do with being a man either. The only issue that has to do with his being a man is the possibility of being harassed by a bunch of drunk men on the road; now if you think that makes men superior, then you're nuts." We turn away from each other, steaming.

At the farm, Megan goes straight to her tent along with Kelly while Clarke and I have a brandy with Jock and Jean. "If you don't enjoy the restaurant, Jean, why don't you sell it so that you can spend more time with Jock?" I ask as we rinse our glasses in the kitchen.

"Why should I? He never spent time with us when the children were young. He was always outside doing farm work. We've never been together; we even take separate vacations." I picture Jock sitting alone in the restaurant kitchen, scrubbed and dressed up, watching Jean work, hoping for a word or two, trying his best. I'm sad for them both.

Jean is already at her restaurant the next morning by the time we're ready to leave, and we find Jock on his tractor in the field. He rumbles and bounces to the fence where we stand in a sad row; his sweater smells like fresh grass when I hug him, and all four of us cry as we pedal to Newcastleton to thank Jean for her hospitality and buy one more round of her delicious pastries. She looks harried and tired, and as we bicycle away from the village, I wonder what these nice people will do next. Nothing different, I guess.

The road is narrow and quiet, a wonderful change from the crowded English highways. Open fields are dotted with fluffy white sheep and the emerald green landscape rolls past peacefully mile after mile. It doesn't rain, and this far north, the summer days last almost twenty hours. For those accustomed to being awake whenever the sun is, Scotland is a marathon. At least we don't need to cook by flashlight anymore if we have a long bicycling day.

Scotland is much less inhabited than England, and houses along our route are sparse. A refusal somewhere, we find, means pedaling miles to the next farm. That night, north of Galashiels, we have a difficult time finding a place to sleep. After four unsuccessful requests, we spot a large house up a short, steep drive near Bowland. A tall, stern man answers the door and gives us permission to camp along with a long lecture about how the world just isn't what it used to be. "There's no discipline anymore. People have no respect for each other. In my time, the things that happen in the world were not tolerated. Well. You go ahead and make yourselves comfortable. If you need a toilet, just knock on the door."

"He must live alone," I surmise.

After pitching our tents, Kelly and Megan head to the house to use the bathroom. "He's got a very nice wife named Mae," they report back.

In the morning, Megan washes the supper dishes while Clarke makes oatmeal and I go to the house to clean up. Kelly grabs the first bowl of food, and after breakfast, washes only her own plate. Clarke doesn't comment but is grouchy all day.

We've been cycling with Kelly and Megan a little over three weeks. Our plan now is to ride into Edinburgh, find a place to sleep on the outskirts, then go into the city and visit Edinburgh Castle before taking a train to London and pedaling back to Dover via our fox friends, Win and Jackie. By then, our four weeks together in England and Scotland will be over.

As we near Edinburgh, we stop in a parking lot for lunch. Clarke's still in a snit and the girls ask me what's wrong. "Why don't you ask him?" I suggest.

"Are you kidding?" they say in unison.

"Will you lead, Susan?" he asks after our silent lunch. "I could use a little help from the rest of the troops."

"Sure," I respond, "but I'm only wearing one contact lens today. I may need help reading street signs."

"Forget it," he snaps, pedaling away.

I walk to the corner, where Clarke waits, leaning against a wall. "What now?" I sigh.

"I just asked for a little help and you refused. Do I have to do everything for all three of you now?"

"I didn't refuse. But there's more bothering you than whether I'm wearing both contact lenses. You've been a beast all day—both Kelly and Megan have asked me about it."

"Why didn't they ask me?"

"They're afraid you'll bite their heads off."

"Screw you all." He rides off again.

Shaking my head, I walk back to where Kelly and Megan sit with the bikes, finishing off a candy bar. "Didn't I agree to lead?"

"That's my recollection," Kelly responds.

I plop down next to them. This time, I won't follow. It's Clarke's turn to return. He does, finally. "I said I'd lead, Clarke," I point out again, pulling away from the parking lot before he can respond.

Unfortunately, when someone other than Clarke leads the group, it never lasts long. Somehow, he always gravitates to the front of the line. The girls maintain that it's because he thinks they're not doing a good job; I think it's just habit. Today, though, every time he starts to pass me, I wave him back angrily. If you ask for help, buddy, you have to take it.

Our request to camp near Edinburgh is turned down three times. "Is it us or because we're so close to a big city?" I ask the group in general.

"Both," is the consensus.

After our first rejection, as we pedal past a pub, a young man runs outside to invite us in. Intent on our mission, we wave and continue on but return to lick our wounds after our second and third rejections. Once inside the tavern, the owner directs us to a fancier room reserved for tourists. We refuse. "We're in Scotland to meet Scots," we explain, "not English and American tourists."

As I nurse a beer, I tell one man of our inability to find a home for the night. He suggests a public park a few miles down the road. Another young man, overhearing, offers not his own yard, but the yard of his mother who's on vacation. We jump at the offer. "Finish your beer, Willie," I say, "while we buy food." Following his car to his mother's apartment, we wait while he checks with the neighbors.

After pitching our tents in the tiny backyard of the fourplex, we eat tuna and apple salad while a little girl named Claire practices gymnastics across the fence. After dinner, as Megan washes her hair with a garden hose, Claire drags a pail of warm water out her back door. "Here, ma'am, would you be needing this?" she asks Megan.

Inside our own tent later, we discuss Kelly and Megan's dwindling money supply. Although they've been frugal, it's clear that they don't have enough to last until August 21st, when they're scheduled to fly home. It's time to make some decisions. "Do you want to leave early?" I ask.

"No!" they say in unison.

"Even if you spend less, you don't have enough for seven more weeks. I don't understand where your money's going. Clarke and I still spend a hundred dollars a week. Are you sure you haven't lost any, or that nothing's been stolen?"

"We'll be fine," Megan insists. "We'll give up eating if we have to."

Clarke laughs. "That's the last thing you two would be able to give up."

"Well, then, let's just get more money," Kelly says. "Before we left, Mother said that this was the chance of a lifetime."

"True, but that money was given to you by your grandfather for college. What do you think he would say?"

"Go for it." Yes, he would.

Just before bed, Willie stops by with a friend. Punching his buddy in the shoulder, he points toward Megan. "See? She's pretty as a Christmas cracker," Willie says in a brogue that's as broad as the rolling countryside. Cheeks flaming, Megan scrambles into her tent. "You deserve a wonderful husband, lassie," he calls after her. "You wait for the right man." She doesn't answer. "Of course, I'm the right man," he continues, "but I already have a wife and baby. Oh, how I wish I didn't, lass. But you're still pretty as a Christmas cracker." Megan zips up the tent flap.

While we pack in the morning, Claire comes to the fence with pictures that she'd drawn for each of us. After we promise to write, Megan volunteers to lead but then stops when a bus in front of her stops. Pedaling past her and the bus, Clarke takes over the lead; shrugging, Megan goes back to the back.

At American Express, Kelly and Megan watch the bikes while Clarke and I check train schedules to London. "Bad news," Clarke announces after our quick trip inside. "There may be a rail strike at midnight, which means no late trains today. And, even worse, the ferry workers may go on a sympathy strike."

"So let's go all the way to Dover in time to take the ferry to France before midnight tonight," Kelly suggests.

Disappointed that we'll miss Edinburgh and its castle and our fox-sandwich friends, we can't suggest a better solution, so within the hour, Kelly, Megan and I are on the high-speed express to London with three-quarters of the transportation team while Clarke waits for the next train because only three bicycles are allowed on each train. The towns we've pedaled through flash past the train window at a hundred and twenty-five miles an hour, like a fast-forward movie, our three-week trip through England and Scotland reduced to five hours.

Arriving in London at four, we rendezvous an hour later with Clarke and a young man from Tennessee with whom Clarke has shared the floor of his crowded train. "You're all very brave," the American tells us. "Please drop me a card when you get home so that I'll know you made it back in one piece."

"We'll be fine," I say lightly. For some reason, I'm uncomfortable when people think we're courageous. Riding bicycles every day isn't a big deal.

The train to Dover has no conductor or baggage handler, so we load the bikes ourselves, all four of them, without having our tickets checked. In Dover, the only people in the station are our fellow passengers, and by the time we find someone to give us directions to the ferry dock, the last boat to Calais is leaving in ten minutes.

Now that we're getting out of England, we need to consider our arrival in France at midnight, a culture shock even more confusing than the fast train trip through England. "Let's use the radio phone on board the ferry to call Christine and Armel," Clarke suggests. "We stayed with them on our last night in France," he explains to Kelly and Megan. "May we sneak into your garden about one o'clock?" he asks after three unsuccessful connections.

"We'll leave the light on," they promise.

Chapter 14

The streets of Calais are wet with rain, and mercury lights on the boat ramp make shiny streaks on the black pavement as we hurry up the incline into the dark. Calais is deserted. It's midnight on the Fourth of July, Independence Day for Americans, a loss for the British, nothing for the French. Pedaling from streetlight to streetlight, we look unsuccessfully for the road to Frethun, eight kilometers southwest of the city. Finally, two young women come out of a house and Clarke asks them directions. *"Merci beaucoup, mademoiselles, bonne nuit,"* he says after they point us in the right direction.

"You only say *'bonne nuit'* when someone goes off to bed," Megan corrects him. "The proper phrase is *'bonsoir.'*"

"Why didn't you talk to them?" Clarke asks.

She shrugs. "You're the one who's lost."

"Here's your chance to bicycle without headlights, Megan," I say, changing the subject as we pass the last streetlight into the pitch black night. Clarke leads, his tiny headlight nearly useless, and I bring up the rear because Kelly and Megan don't have reflectors on the back of their bikes. Night blind, I see nothing but the white on Kelly's jacket and follow too closely, sure I'll fall into a pothole or ditch although more likely I'll crash into Kelly.

"We're near Frethun, I think," Clarke calls back after forever. Relieved to recognize Christine and Armel's house in the light over a garage behind an open iron gate, we move quietly across the gravel drive to the side yard, putting up our tents by feel. It's one-thirty in the morning. We started the day in Scotland?

During breakfast on the familiar patio, Clarke tells our hosts how much we missed French bread. "We bought you an extra baguette to take along," Christine smiles, then motions to the jar of French cherry preserves as I slather a spoonful on my warm bread. "Take the jar."

"Can't we buy this at any market?"

"Yes, but it won't be as good because this is a jar from my cupboard."

As we strap our tents onto the bicycles, Christine turns to Megan. "You speak French very well. You ought to live in France."

"I'd love to," Megan responds shyly.

"Come live with us for a year. I could use help with our new baby."

Racing back into Calais in time to exchange pounds for *francs* but too late to buy white cheese, onion and tomato for our famous fresh French bread sandwiches, we settle for peanut butter next to the Rodin statue by the town hall while Clarke spreads out a map of Europe on the grass. "It won't take a whole week to ride along the coast to Belgium," he decides, measuring distance with his fingers. "We're a few days ahead of schedule since we took the train all the way to Dover yesterday. So where to?"

The girls look at each other, conspirators. "Paris!" Kelly says.

I page through my daily journal. "It took Clarke and me nine days to get here from Paris." Now I measure the map with my thumb. "Even if we can pedal back in a week, by the time we reach Belgium, we'll spend two weeks in France. I thought you two agreed on just one." The last thing I want to do is go backward – Paris again, when there are so many places I haven't seen, has no appeal to me at all.

"We agreed to let Kelly and Megan choose the route this summer, Susan," Clarke reminds me sternly. "If they want to spend two weeks in France, we'll spend two weeks in France. Besides, we'll get to see Jo and Pierre again." This is true.

Determined to take a different route back to St. Josse, where Jo had eaten a hard-boiled egg so that Clarke and I didn't have to cook dinner, we pedal west past the Eurotunnel construction toward the beach, and after a brief swim, turn inland. "France isn't flat either," Kelly moans as we pedal up a steep pass in the hot sun.

"On bicycles, Kelly, nothing is flat," I sympathize. "Or not for long, anyway. Tally ho, we're at the top! Look out below!" Over we go, hurtling down the other side, taking curves with whoops and hollers, enjoying the hot wind in our hair as fields of cereal grains shimmer in the sun, then fade in mist into the horizon near the ocean. We gather at the bottom of the pass. "Where's Megan?" I ask.

"Last time I looked, she was right behind me," Clarke answers, then starts back up the hill on foot before spotting her near the top with several people gathered around. "Oh, shit," he says, starting to run. Kelly scrambles after him.

Twenty minutes later, Megan wobbles on her bike behind Kelly and Clarke, then pedals ahead when she sees me pacing back and forth. "I was going too fast," she explains as I gasp at her bloody right side; her tennis shoes are ripped, halter top torn, bicycle bunged up.

"Sit on this wall, Megan," I say. "You're lucky you didn't break anything."

"Can I sit on the ground? I feel faint."

Gently, I wash her cuts and abrasions. "Kelly, will you get the first aid kit?" It's not forthcoming. "Kelly?" I turn around. "Kelly?"

"I don't do blood," she whimpers, face faintly green.

"Me either," Clarke says, looking away.

"Oh, for pete's sake, you two. If you get hurt, you're on your own." After Megan is disinfected and bandaged, she staggers when she tries to get up, face chalky. "We're in no hurry," I tell her.

"But we don't have groceries for tonight."

"Don't worry about it," Clarke assures her. "We'll find a way; we always do."

Finally, the color in Megan's face improves and she stands, wobbly as a newborn colt. "If I don't ride, all my muscles will get stiff. They already are." Slowly, we pedal toward St. Josse, stopping at a market and then at a phone booth to call Jo and Pierre to ask if we can stay at their house the next night. "Can we stop now?" Megan asks after a few more kilometers, and while the rest of us cook dinner in a field next to the farm of a widower named Lucien, Megan goes inside to wash her cuts in hot water. In the morning, Lucien leaves her a large bucket of water at the pasture gate and Megan leaves a thank you note in French on his doorstep.

About eleven o'clock, at a quiet intersection on a tiny road, we're stopped by a family who once visited America. They invite us to their home for lunch; normally, we would jump at the opportunity, but they live twenty-four kilometers in the wrong direction and we already have a dinner date for the first time. Unwilling to let us go without offering some kind of hospitality, they present us with a big, round loaf of bread for which they'd just driven to a nearby village. "Wow," Kelly says. "The French are really friendly, aren't they?"

"Unlike what everyone says in America, eh?"

By early afternoon, however, the heat has stripped Kelly physically and mentally. "Anyone low on water?" I ask after a long hill.

"I don't give a damn about water," she snaps. "I'm through! Enough!"

"Jo and Pierre are expecting us in St. Josse tonight," Clarke reminds her. "Just rest for a few minutes and we'll get water in the next village."

"I don't want rest. I don't want water. I want to quit. I can't ride in this blasted heat." After a long break, we convince her to go on. Megan lags too, stiff and sore and weak.

As we pedal up and down steep hills in the stifling heat, Clarke and I discuss whether we should continue. "Megan's cuts need more than soap and cold water and our little antibiotic cream, Clarke. They're getting infected." I call back to Megan, who looks like a bloody combination of Raggedy Ann and Daisy Mae, "Do you think you can go on?"

Megan nods as Kelly pedals away growling, exploding into curses when her front tire goes off the road into sand. "I'm not good enough!" she screams. "I hate this! I don't even want to be here!"

"Kelly, calm down," I say. "It's blistering hot and these hills are brutal. Don't be so hard on yourself."

"Shut up, Susan."

We reach Etaples at two o'clock, stopping at the gift shop where Jo works. "Pedal on to the house and help yourselves to showers, *cheries*," Jo says. "Pierre and I will see you later."

"Pedal?" Kelly snarls after Jo goes back inside her store. "Pedal where?"

"Their village is ten kilometers from here," Clarke sighs.

"I thought these people lived here."

"They don't." Clarke is losing patience. "Look, Kelly, we can't cool off the weather or eliminate the hills or move Jo and Pierre's house. But we've found you a wonderful family who has offered you a home-cooked dinner and a cool shower. That's the best we can do, and if you ask me, that's pretty damn good. What are you doing to contribute to the rest of the group today?"

"Just what, Clarke, do you have in mind?"

"You could fill the water bottles instead of feeling sorry for yourself. The rest of us are hot and tired too, and I have to stop at a bike shop. You're not the only one who wants a cold shower."

As Clarke disappears inside the bike shop with his French dictionary, Kelly snatches the water bottles off her and Megan's bikes and stomps across the street to a brick house. I follow with Clarke and my bottles as she rings the bell without a word. "I don't speak French, you know," she growls in a low voice, hearing footsteps inside.

"Neither do I."

A young woman answers the door. Kelly holds up the bottles. "Uh, water, *s'il vous plait?*" she says tentatively. The woman looks at us curiously.

"*L'eau?*" I hope I remember the word for water. I still have one foot in Scotland.

"*Ah, oui, madame, mademoiselle. Entre.*"

We fill our bottles at her sink, but the woman won't let us leave without a cold glass of grape juice. "Here's your water, Clarke," Kelly snaps when we return to the bikes.

We pedal in silence to St. Josse. "I get the first shower," Kelly announces, taking over the bathroom before anyone else can locate a towel.

"You're the one who needs cleaning up, Megan," Clarke says. "I'm worried about all the dirt in your cuts."

"It doesn't matter."

No matter how many times we disinfect and bandage Megan, she seems to get dirtier, particularly her hands. Holding her handlebar grips turns Megan's palms black and scrunches the bandage over her deep cut into a string. Already, her wounds bubble with yellow puss.

Emerging from the house, Kelly plops down by the lake with clean hair and dirty clothes. As Megan goes inside to shower, I sit by Kelly but don't speak for quite awhile. "What would it take for you to think you're good enough, Kelly?" I ask finally.

"I don't know."

"If your friend Melissa were with us, what would you tell her if she were mad that she couldn't keep up with you?"

Kelly sits quietly, then shrugs as if the answer were obvious. "I'd tell her it's okay just to do her best. I wouldn't mind waiting for her."

"And we don't mind waiting for you. Why can't you say the same thing to yourself?"

Kelly thinks for a few seconds. "I have higher standards for myself than for other people."

"Ah. On a scale of one to ten, how would you grade yourself so far on this trip?"

"Seven."

"Why not higher?"

"I'm not fast enough." I wonder if fast enough to Kelly means keeping up, or passing everyone. Passing everyone, probably.

Dinner's for thirteen; with one day's notice, Jo and Pierre throw us a party. It's a wonderful evening, but very different from our first dinner-for-four because Jo and Pierre's son Patrick can translate after living for a year in New York. In our desire to communicate, we let Patrick do most of the talking, and although we get more said, we feel less connection between us and Jo and Pierre. Limited as our French is, we find it more satisfying than perfect translations. Megan says little, which surprises us. We expect her to be the most communicative because of her five years of French class; according to Kelly, her teachers think she's quite gifted in the language.

"Where do you go now?" Pierre asks.

"Back to Paris," I sigh.

"Ah, to the Bicentennial?"

"No," I say quickly. "We will leave the city long before then." In Calais, Kelly and Megan agreed to spend only one or two days in the city; we plan to be in Paris no later than Tuesday and the Bicentennial celebration, Bastille Day, is Friday, the 14th of July.

"Ah, no," Patrick says. "It is a pity. The two hundredth birthday of the French Revolution will be very special. Where will you stay in Paris?"

"Last time, we stayed at the campground in Bois de Boulogne."

"You will never find space because of the celebration," Patrick shakes his head. I perk up; maybe we can avoid going backward after all. Patrick turns to Pierre. "Papa, how about Coco? Could they stay there?"

"Ah, but of course," Pierre exclaims. "*Superb.*"

"My father's brother lives south of Paris," Patrick explains. "We'll ask him if you can camp in his yard, okay?" "Okay" is one of the international words we've discovered, along with "Coca Cola" and "*kaput.*" Our favorite phrase, though, is "no problem."

Megan leaves the party early while Kelly stays up to listen to a conversation impossible to follow, drinking too much wine. Finally, we can't keep our eyes open another minute. "We will talk some more tomorrow, yes?" Pierre says.

"Only for a moment in the morning. We must leave."

"No, no, no! Please stay for the weekend, *cheries*." It was hard to leave them the first time, even though we knew that we might come back through Calais, but now we know that our paths won't cross again unless they travel to America or we return to Europe. This time, leaving will be unbelievably difficult.

Morning comes too early–because we stayed up too late the night before, because we drank too much wine, because of a thunderstorm that woke us in the middle of the night. "Please do not leave," Jo and Pierre plead as they leave for work.

"It won't be any easier to say goodbye if we stay, will it?" Clarke asks, wiping his eyes as I pet their chubby white dog that I've dubbed the *petit mouton*, or little sheep.

"No, my friends," Pierre says, kissing us one more time. I have a feeling that they'll come home for lunch with special groceries anyway, just in case we change our minds.

It's Clarke and Megan's birthday; he's forty-one and she's sixteen. "What do you two want for your birthday dinner?" I ask.

"French onion soup," they decide.

"I don't like onions," Kelly reminds us.

"It's not your birthday," we remind her.

We stop to buy groceries just as rain tears open the clouds once again. An overhead awning does nothing to protect the bikes from the slanting downpour, and Kelly and I shop quickly, buying Clarke a bottle of white wine and dashing across the street to get pastries for dessert. While the girls go into a pharmacy for more bandages, I spot a flower shop and buy three huge pink daisies, delivering them to Megan as she comes out of the store. "*Merci beaucoup*," she says, kissing us on both cheeks, French style. Arranging the floppy flowers in one of her water bottles, she pedals off in the rain as if the day were full of sunshine.

Downpours alternate with gray humidity all day. By late afternoon, we're all drenched and out of sorts. Even the flowers droop. When the girls decide to quit for the day, I'm in the lead and don't stop at the first available garden, deciding instead to wait for inspiration. I continue on in the rain, aware that a mutiny is no doubt brewing behind me. We ride past a wall, then I pause. Turning around without a word, I pedal back just as a Jeep comes out of the gate. "What's behind that wall?" I ask the driver in English as if I'm sure he'll understand.

"My house," the man responds in the same language.

For the first time in Europe, I don't explain who we are. "May we camp on your property tonight?" I ask instead.

"Of course. Just tell my wife Helene that you've already spoken with me."

Behind the wall is a *chateau*. The girls gasp. "Is a castle good enough for a birthday celebration?" I ask smugly.

After we knock on the ornate front door, a pretty woman with shining blond hair sticks her head out of the kitchen window and seconds her husband's hospitality. "This is a special treat for us," I tell her. "It's Clarke and Megan's birthday."

"*Bon anniversaire*," Helene says to them both and calls her son Arthur, who shyly wishes them the same and then disappears back into the kitchen behind his beautiful mother. "One moment, please," she says in English, "the telephone, it is ringing." She returns after a moment. "That was Marc. He thinks you'd be comfortable at the farm." She points to a rectangular building built around a courtyard next to the main castle. "I must get ready to go out to dinner now," she says after escorting us over, "but I'll see how you're getting along before we leave."

The farm is perfect. We have shelter from the wind, barns to store the bicycles, all the water we need, and even a toilet in a remodeled horse stall. The sun comes out for the first time today. "Ah, nature is finally making an effort to give you a good party," I say to Clarke and Megan as we spread our wet tents on the grass to dry. "Let's take advantage of what sun we have to hang up our laundry."

Although we washed clothes at Jo and Pierre's, everything is still wet and we drape shorts and underwear and t-shirts up and down the rusty barbed wire fence that separates the farm from the sheep. Helene and Marc and Arthur march across the grass with a birthday tart in a pink box wrapped with ribbon, a red rose for Megan, fancy chocolates for Clarke, and a homemade card from Arthur. "Will you join us for dessert after your dinner party?" ask the birthday boy and girl.

"It will be too late, I think," Marc says.

"Let me dry your clothes while we are out," Helene offers. "They will not dry in this weather."

While Helene and Megan pick ragged underwear off the sticky barbed wire, Marc tells us the story of the *chateau*. "My great grandfather was very wealthy and bought houses for everyone in the family. This *chateau* was built in the sixteen hundreds, and my brother and I inherited it jointly. The house is divided in half. Unfortunately, our wives do not get along, so Helene and I may move."

"What a shame," Clarke says. "It is very beautiful."

"Yes, but it is not so beautiful when our wives do not speak."

The onion soup turns out fine, even for Kelly, and after gorging on the pastries plus the tart and chocolates and wine, we decide to explore the barns to settle our fattening dinner. The rooms have been used recently for a party; huge pink bows still hang on the walls, and upstairs in the loft a long table is strewn with empty candy cups across its snowy white cloth. "I'm sleeping up here," announces Kelly from the second-floor hayloft.

"Not me," says Megan, "but I'm moving our tent inside the barn. I've had enough rain for one day."

Clarke and I stay in the courtyard. We don't mind the rain because our tent is waterproof and our sleeping bags stay warm and dry. We like being outside.

En route to the bathroom in the morning, I discover two bright pink bags full of dry and folded laundry propped up against the barn door. Attached with a pink ribbon is a note inviting us back and wishing us a safe journey. How many times now have rich people turned out to be just as loving and generous as everyone else? In my opinion, it's the best birthday present Clarke could have. After we say goodbye, Helene runs after us up the driveway. "I have a small gift. It is a picture of our house, as a souvenir. Perhaps you will remember us, no?"

The day after the birthdays is Clarke and my first wedding anniversary. A year ago today, we were married by the municipal judge above the Buckhorn Trading Company in Ouray, Colorado, a month before our meadow ceremony. In honor of the occasion, Kelly and Megan offer to cook dinner.

Before lunch, Clarke decides to stop at a bike shop to borrow tools to repair his lower bracket again, and Megan needs a new derailleur chain. Arriving in a large village minutes before the markets close, Kelly and I run for a bakery as Clarke and Megan head into the bike shop. As Clarke and Megan work on their bikes on the sidewalk, Kelly and I fix lunch while our bikes lean against the wall of a house next door. An elderly woman sticks her head out the window as we slather vinaigrette on long loaves of still-warm bread. "Uh-oh," I whisper, remembering the woman in

England who chastised me for leaning bikes against her house. "*Bonjour madame,*" I say quickly.

"*Bonjour,*" says the Frenchwoman, then chatters amicably through the window about this and that as we work.

"May we have some water?" I ask after a bit, hoping to fill our bottles from her garden hose.

"*Oui, madame,*" she says and disappears, returning with bottled water and four glasses.

"*Non, non, madame,*" I protest but don't know the French words for garden hose or kitchen sink.

Megan sits on the pavement, covered with grease. "Come inside and wash," the woman suggests in French after looking at her for a long minute. "Have some tea."

Clarke is still working on his bike–the new part that the girls brought from America doesn't fit properly. "Go on," he says, grumpy. "I'll join you if I ever get finished. There isn't anything you can do to help anyway."

Joan and Roget prepare a place for us to wash in their tiny, bright flower garden–hot water and soap and turpentine and towels. Hands clean, we crowd inside their cozy kitchen for tea and cookies while I run in and out to check on Clarke's progress. When he joins us after determining that the part won't fit, Roget opens a bottle of wine, then drinks only a sip after pouring Clarke a glass. "Because of my health," he apologizes, tapping his heart with a finger.

Joan and Roget lived in a fashionable neighborhood of Paris for years, they tell us, but moved to the country because of Roget's health. "We do not like it here," she says in French. "Country folk do not welcome Parisians. All our friends are still in the city."

In their late seventies, perhaps, they seem a happy couple nonetheless, frail but full of life, obviously careful to take care of each other as well as they can. After helping us find L'Hay-les-Roses on our map, the suburb where Pierre's brother Coco lives south of Paris, they send us on our way at four-thirty with the opened bottle of wine for our anniversary dinner.

Kelly and Megan have apparently decided to ride at least fifty kilometers a day to get to Paris, so we pedal up a surprising number of hills before they choose to stop. My knees ache from the thirty-mile afternoon, and it feels like bicycling is now breaking me down instead of building me up.

"Clarke," Kelly calls ahead, "there's something wrong with my bike. It sounds awful in low gear."

"Be more specific than that, Kelly. It's your bike."

She doesn't respond. Near the small village of Grandvilliers, we pitch our tents far apart in the large grassy yard of a pretty house and are invited for drinks on the patio. "Where's Megan?" Clarke asks Kelly.

"Cooking. She doesn't want anything."

Again, I wonder why Megan seems to avoid her beloved French but forget about her as clouds that have been building all afternoon disintegrate into a downpour and we run inside the house to finish our wine. "Take your time," Kelly offers. "I'll help Megan. We'll let you know when dinner's ready."

A heart-stopping scream interrupts all conversation, and Clarke and I bolt outside to discover that Megan has dumped a whole pan of boiling water on her foot. She insists that she's all right, but dinner is in ruins after all the commotion. The French family comes to our rescue, sharing their own food, and we chatter merrily using their daughter Marie Laurence willingly and Megan reluctantly as interpreters, plus our own meager French. When we compliment France and the French, the father looks puzzled, then distressed. "But isn't America wonderful?" Ronnie asks.

"Of course it is," we respond. "But so is France. So is everywhere."

Ronnie shakes his head, still confused.

"Would you like to sleep inside tonight?" his wife asks after dinner. "The girls can sleep on the floor and you two can have the couch because it's the anniversary of your marriage."

"If you won't make too much noise," Ronnie chuckles.

Clarke smiles. "We'll go to our tent to be alone and then come inside to sleep." But we end up having an argument about Kelly and Megan instead of making love and stay in the tent all night, preferring our individual sleeping bags to a double bed. Joining the family for breakfast, everyone assumes that we made mad, passionate love all night, and we say nothing to disappoint them.

Kelly calls Jill from Beauvais. "We're having a wonderful time!" she bleats into the telephone, chattering happily about Dick and Marge, the family in England who took care of Clarke when he was sick, and Jo and Pierre and the dinner party.

Sitting on the curb in front of the phone booth, Clarke and I look at each other, amazed. "Did you know she was enjoying herself, Susan?"

"Nope."

South of town, Jean Marie and his wife Lilian offer their patio table for our dinner, complete with real dishes and fresh radishes from the garden. Their daughter Delphine has studied a little English but Frederick is too young. Again, Megan hardly speaks but seems to enjoy our struggles to communicate, snickering or grimacing at each error. Frederick, however, doesn't care whether he speaks English or we French; following us everywhere, he examines our tents and bikes and packs with little-boy interest, offering to escort us on his bike to the next village in the morning, where he'll visit his grandmother.

The next day, we wave goodbye to Frederick at the next town and continue under sunny, blue skies along a tiny road that winds around fields and farms north of Paris. Kelly and Megan's excitement grows as we near the famous city; with good luck, we might arrive today. "Stop, Kelly!" Clarke suddenly calls from behind her. "Your freewheel just fell apart."

She stops and glares at him. "I told you I was having problems yesterday."

He ignores the comment. "You're lucky Susan brought a spare freewheel from America—if she'll let you have it."

I shrug. "If you'll buy me a replacement, assuming that we can find one to fit, of course."

"We need a vice." Clarke is all business. "Come on, Kelly, let's walk back to the last town and try to borrow one."

"Me?" Kelly says. "Take Megan; I don't speak French."

"It's your bike." They walk back down the road, wheel in hand, while Megan and I lie in the grass and make small talk. They return an hour later. "Frederick helped us find a man with a vice. We're all set," Clarke reports. As we pedal off, he calls ahead to Kelly. "It would certainly be nice if you thanked me for my help and Susan for the spare part."

I cringe, waiting for Kelly to erupt. Instead, she says, "Oh, my goodness, yes. I'm sorry, both of you. I don't know what I was thinking of, but thank you for helping me. Susan, I'll get you a new freewheel in Paris."

It's lunchtime and we haven't found a market; now, even if we do, it will be closed for two hours. At a picnic table in a roadside rest area, we dig deep in the food pack for a little of this and that. "We're not that far from Paris," Clarke says as we split part of a candy bar four ways. "But to get to Coco's, we have to ride all the way through the city and to his village to the south. Let's make it a short day and then go in tomorrow." We agree. "I'd like to mail some things home," he adds. After five months, we've accumulated lots of used maps and more than a few gifts.

"We've got some extra stuff too," Megan says.

In St. Ouen, we stop at a new post office. Clarke and Megan wait in line to buy two boxes, but after the cartons are carefully packed, the postal clerk insists that the boxes are too big to go by boat. "Air mail!" I whoop. "If cars can be shipped by boat, for heaven's sake, why not a small box?"

"She refuses to send them for anything less than a hundred and twenty-five dollars," Megan explains.

"Let's find a rational postal clerk somewhere else, then."

As we struggle to attach the bulky boxes to our bikes, sleeping bags and tent and laundry spread all over the pavement, a tall young woman stops on the sidewalk. "You are American?" she asks in English. "Where are you going?"

"Paris," I answer with a sigh, "then Belgium and Holland and Germany and Austria and Italy and Greece."

"And where have you come from?"

"Morocco and Spain and England and Scotland. France, of course. We stayed seven weeks and liked it so much that we've come back," I say with a glance at the girls.

"Are you going all the way into the city tonight?"

"We'd rather go in tomorrow. We've been camping in people's fields all through Europe." I smile, brightening. "Do you have a garden?"

"No," she smiles back, "but my boyfriend's sister does. If you'll come home with me for a drink, I'll find you a place to spend the night. I'd love to hear about your trip. I teach English and I've traveled in your country." Delighted, we follow her car through rush-hour traffic, first this way and then that, then into a driveway behind a wall just as I'm sure we'll lose her in the stream of autos hurrying somewhere or other. Devouring nuts and cakes and cold juice, we chat about Monique's trip to America.

"I'd like you to look at my English textbooks," she says after awhile. The lessons seem more practical than the language lessons we study in American schools. In British English, they're based on words and phrases which one might actually use rather than just on verb conjugations. When the next country's language starts only a few kilometers away, I decide, the incentive to speak it is much greater than in America, where English is understood for thousands of miles. I wonder what it would be like to have to learn Wyomish, or New Mexican, in order to travel to the next state. It's an appropriate comparison.

Monique's boyfriend, a dark and handsome young man, arrives with a shy greeting in French. "Dominique would like to make you *crêpes* for dinner," Monique translates, smiling at him proudly. "He's a fabulous chef."

"How far is his sister's house?" Clarke asks. "We need to be there before dark."

"We have decided that Dominique and I will stay at his sister's. We want you to sleep here, in our home. We have a double bed upstairs, and this couch will be fine for Kelly and Megan."

"No, no," Clarke protests. "Why don't we just put our tents in your driveway?"

"Absolutely not. Dominique and I hitchhiked through America and we'd like to return the hospitality given to us by your countrymen. We know how much a bed will mean to you. We insist."

"You don't even know us but you're willing to leave us in your home alone?" I ask.

"Yes," Monique replies simply.

Clarke and I go to the market with Dominique and Monique. Driving with Dominique is an experience, and Clarke and I cling to each other in the tiny back seat as he careens around each corner. "He drives a car just like his motorcycle," Monique explains with a sigh, putting her hand on his shoulder. Inside the shopping mall, we find a giant food store with a better selection of food than anything we've seen in our own country—three or four dozen kinds of cheeses and sausages, for example, and Dominique knows about each one.

"Will you teach me how to make *crêpes*?" Clarke asks after we survive the trip home. Dominique demonstrates and draws pictures, and Clarke tucks the recipe into his money belt before settling down with the rest of us to dinner *crêpes* filled with ham and cheese and raw eggs—the warmth of the thin pancakes cooks the egg at the table—and another whole meal of dessert *crêpes* with ice cream and chocolate sauce.

"Megan," Monique says sternly after dinner, "your French accent is excellent, but you do not speak many words to me. It is the custom, you know, to speak in the language of the country you are in. You should always speak French while in France.

In America, I will speak English with you." Megan ducks her head. "Come decide what sheets you want on the bed," Monique turns to me with a smile. "I will get you all fresh towels for a shower and then Dominique and I must leave. Perhaps I'll return before you go in the morning."

Words can be totally inadequate sometimes. Would I move out of my house to let four strangers spend the night in comfort? I would now, I hope, but would I before this trip? Would it even have occurred to me?

Clarke and I sleep late the next morning. As we dress, Kelly knocks at the bedroom door. "I've brought coffee. I hope it's okay; we don't know how to make it very well." It's lovely.

One Christmas before I met Clarke, Kelly and Megan had come to visit me in the Colorado mountains to ski for the first time. Although I was too busy at work to join them, I put them in lessons and retrieved them at the end of the day. It was snowing and cold and almost dark by the time we finished our hot chocolate in the lodge and I heard of their exploits on the slopes.

On the way back to the main highway, my car broke down. Hitchhiking to the nearest pay phone, we called for a tow truck that didn't come for several hours because of the blizzard. By then, it was too late for dinner out and the movie we'd planned, and I was totally depressed about my car, which I was told only a new engine would resurrect. I'd promised to drive the girls home to Denver the next day, Christmas Eve.

After a restless night, I was awakened by Kelly and Megan carrying a breakfast tray decorated with a sprig of evergreen tied with a red Christmas ribbon and dusted with sugar to look like snow. "You need cheering up," they explained.

Instead of feeling sorry for themselves for not having a way home for Christmas, the fourteen-year-olds were worried about me. But they weren't cooks. They scrambled the eggs just fine, but since the rest of the meal wasn't ready, reheated them later in the microwave. "I think they're a little rubbery," Megan apologized as I dived in with a fork. They were, but they were also full of caring.

"How do you make coffee?" Kelly had asked at the time. After I explained, she laughed. "We've never made it before, so we spooned a bunch of coffee into a paper towel and held it over the pot. Is it too strong?" It was like mud, but I wouldn't have thrown it out for the world.

Monique arrives as we're packing the bikes. "I must write down what you should see in Paris," she declares, then writes out a list of her favorite places.

"I've wanted to hear an organ recital in a big cathedral ever since we arrived in Europe," I tell her. "Would there be anything in Paris?"

"There's a free concert at Notre-Dame every Sunday evening. Don't miss it."

"We won't be there that long," I reply. "We'll be gone by Thursday or Friday."

"But Friday is the beginning of the Bicentennial celebration," Monique exclaims, eyes wide.

"All the more reason to leave," I insist. "Crowds and bicycles don't mix."

Megan fiddles with her hair, which hangs in her eyes. Long ago, her brown rinse had faded and the sun had bleached and dried out her long hair. "I look a mess," she complains. We all feel better about our looks when we don't have mirrors.

"I get my hair cut at a famous salon in Paris," Monique tells her. "If you allow them to use you as a model, they will cut your hair for free. Do you want me to make you an appointment?"

"What if I don't like it?"

"Then you've got the rest of the summer to let it grow," I say. "Come on, I'll do it if you will."

Monique calls, but because of Bastille Day, they can't fit us in. Monique then turns to me. "Suzanne, you must at least go to the Muslim mosque called the Hammon. They have a fabulous steam bath which women are allowed to use on Thursdays. In fact, I will go with you. You need to do something special for your body; it's been working very hard for quite a few months, no?"

I glance at Clarke for his reaction to spending money on just myself. "Is it expensive?" I ask Monique.

"No," she says. "Besides, you're worth it."

"Go on, Susan," Kelly and Megan say, assured of their second day in Paris if I go to the Hammon on Thursday.

"I think it's a great idea," Clarke agrees. "You've been worried about everyone else now for over a month."

Before we leave, Monique calls Coco to tell him that we'll be at his house by seven in the evening. "He speaks no English," she tells us when she hangs up the phone, "but says that you are not to worry about your tents. He will have beds for you."

"Then we can't possibly stay more than one night," I say. "We'd better cancel our plans for the Hammon."

"No. Come back here, then. You must go to the baths."

We arrive at the northern outskirts of Paris at four, just in time for rush hour again, and have trouble keeping everyone together through the busy streets. Megan and Kelly are so enthralled to be in the enchanting city that they can't decide whether to watch us, the traffic and stoplights, or the buildings and people. Megan, it seems, is always two blocks back in the heavy traffic, without a care in the world that she might lose us. Maybe she wants to. In any event, it makes for a nasty bit of cycling for the rest of us, lurching through the bustling city in fits and starts, waiting for her to catch up. She doesn't seem to see us, lost in another world, one of her dreams.

Earlier in the day, Megan and I had found ourselves alone outside a bank while Clarke and Kelly exchanged dollar-denominated travelers' checks for French *francs*. "Why don't you want to go back to Paris?" Megan asked.

"It feels like going backward. Doing something twice – and now three times – has no appeal to me. When Clarke and I were in Paris a few weeks ago, I didn't have a very good time sightseeing because not much was new. This time, I'm afraid, will be more of the same, showing you and Kelly all the famous landmarks instead of discovering anything on my own."

"You don't have to show us anything. But thank you for letting us come. I've always dreamed of seeing Paris, especially the Louvre."

How selfish I am, I'd said to myself. Who could guess whether Megan would ever return to Europe? And after five years of studying French, a trip abroad with only a day or two in France and no time in Paris would be a crime. "Megan," I said after a long moment, "going back will be good for me. If I can't enjoy an incredible city like Paris three times, how can I enjoy wherever I live every day?" There are no accidents. If I can't learn things on my own, someone else will throw the lessons in my lap.

Chapter 15

Paris the second time has little to do with Paris but a great deal to do with Parisians, in particular a man named Coco and his devoted band of buddies. After our rush-hour race through the city, through the Place de la Concorde, its famous periphery stacked with temporary bleachers for the Bastille Day celebration, and down the Champs-Élysées behind a two-column row of red-coated riders on horses with rumps shaved like checkerboards, we finally find our way out of the fabled city to the fashionable suburb of L'Hay-les-Roses. Old and narrow and crumbling, Coco's house sits like a wedge between million-dollar new homes, stubborn as a thistle.

Leaving the bikes at the street, we climb a narrow staircase to an open door. At our hesitant knock, a short dark-haired man with a thin mustache joyously waves us inside, where half a dozen men sit companionably around a long kitchen table piled high with papers and bread, each with a glass of milky liquor. The air is filled with cigarette smoke, the sink stacked with dishes. Scrambling up to greet us, they redeposit themselves at the table to continue their animated conversation while Coco leads us through the living room to the back stairs.

The house is one room wide, a two-story shoebox that attaches a rooftop patio over a garage to the kitchen and living room and toilet. Built into a hill, the back of the second floor is flush with the ground. Going forward, doubling back the way we'd come one floor higher, are a storage room, a tub and sink, and the bedroom. "*Pour Clarke et Suzanne,*" Coco says. It's obvious that this is Coco's bedroom, and we protest. "No problem," he cuts us off, pushing Kelly and Megan to an attic ladder, where another double bed tucks under the eaves. "*Pour Megan et Kelly,*" Coco smiles.

"*Et Coco?*" we ask. Motioning us to follow him down the stairs, he points to the living room couch. "*Non, non, non,*" we say in chorus, but Coco raises his hand for silence and instructs his friends to carry our bicycles upstairs to the overrun back garden, then delivers us back to the kitchen table and pours a good measure of the clear-colored liquor into a glass which he ceremoniously deposits in front of Clarke; adding cold water from an ice bucket with a silver ladle turns the liquid milky white. Tasting the strong anise flavor, I make a face and decline a *pastis* of my own.

Coco settles back with his friends. One young man named Fabrice speaks a bit of English, and with our bits of French, we're able to communicate reasonably well. Coco makes sure that the glasses stay full, and none of the men seems the least inclined to go home for supper. By eight o'clock, I'm starved, and wondering what to cook for so many people, ask Coco where to find the nearest market. He springs to his feet, gesturing wildly. He has much food in the house and he will prepare us a feast. We're not to cook; his father had been a chef, Coco can cook too, and we are his guests. Period. Then he sits back down to have another drink.

All evening, the room swells and ebbs with men of all ages who gather around Coco like bees around a sweet flower, and when Coco finally prepares dinner, he seems to do it by instinct, moving about the kitchen in an intricate dance with his pans without neglecting his guests for a moment. The meal is fabulous—fresh asparagus and a delicate and tender roast. "It is *cheval,*" Fabrice tells me. "The English word is horse. The French, we are cannibals, no?" Mentally apologizing to the horse, I wonder why it should be any harder for me to eat than a cow or a lamb.

As Fabrice washes dishes, Coco's son Didi and his girlfriend Natalie arrive, confiding that the doctors have just found a malignant tumor on Coco's throat. He must go into the hospital in ten days for treatment. "The family is very worried," Natalie tells me, "but Coco's morale is *superb.*"

We visit until very late, then crawl into bed upstairs and listen for several more hours to the happy laughter of Coco and his friends as they stay up all night to drink and play cards. He's still asleep on the couch when we get up in the morning, so Clarke goes for croissants, buying enough for an army. By the time he returns, Fabrice is offering to escort Kelly and Megan on a sightseeing tour of Paris and Megan accepts with enthusiasm, taken with this shy, blond eighteen-year-old. Kelly has her eye on Jean Luc, a dark and handsome twenty-two-year-old who had come after dinner the night before.

After Coco arranges a patio umbrella in a flowerpot on the balcony to give me shade, I record memories on my computer, referring frequently to the tiny pocket journal where I keep mileage, expenses and our photo log. Clarke spends the day with Coco and his friends as they drift in and out for a glass of *pastis*, then plays tennis with Didi, Jean Luc and Fabrice. "Well, ladies, what did Fabrice show you in Paris?" I ask after the boys leave for their game.

"Everything!" they reply, eyes shining.

"Isn't Sacré-Coeur a beautiful church?"

"We didn't see it," Megan admits, "but we did walk past Notre-Dame."

"You didn't go inside? What about the Louvre?"

"We didn't want Fabrice to wait in line."

Dinner is crab and rabbit, and when Megan hears about the rabbit, she looks stricken and leaves the table. Concerned that Coco might be hurt, I tell him that she's tired from her tour of the city. "The Metro was very warm," Fabrice agrees. But when Jean Luc arrives to suggest that he and Fabrice take the girls into the city to see the lights, she miraculously recovers and skips out of the house as the boys solemnly promise to have them back by twelve-thirty. They roll in the door at three—they'd been drinking. Although I can't imagine how any sixteen-year-old American girl could resist ordering her first drink in a Paris bistro with two handsome Frenchmen, I'm still a bit miffed.

Because of my appointment at the Hammon with Monique, the four of us decide to ride the Metro into Paris on Thursday and eat lunch and dinner in the city so that Coco won't have to cook. Although Fabrice and Jean Luc seem to be his marketing and cleanup crew, nobody will let us do anything and we're worried about Coco's health.

"Have you seen my money belt?" Clarke asks after breakfast. "I've looked everywhere." So I do also. Kelly and Megan haven't seen it either. "My passport's in it, plus all of our travelers' checks and most of our cash. We can't leave in the morning without it."

On the Metro, something occurs to me. "Clarke," I whisper, looking over my shoulder at the girls a few rows back, "do you think that Kelly and Megan might have hidden your money belt so they can stay in Paris an extra day because of Fabrice and Jean Luc and the Bicentennial celebration?"

"Surely they wouldn't do that." Clarke looks incredulous. "Would they?"

I could never have suspected Kelly of such a trick until this trip. But after hearing stories of her and Megan's exploits at school the year before, I've realized just how much more trouble two can get into than one. "I guess I'm suspicious because they haven't asked if they can stay for Bastille Day."

"Let's not ask them about it yet, Susan. They're liable to decide to go off on their own again if they think we don't trust them."

At the Metro stop nearest the Hammon, Kelly and Megan disappear into the crowds and Clarke drops me off at the Muslim mosque. "Get a massage," he tells me. "You deserve something special for yourself."

"Your husband is so romantic," Monique sighs as we enter the baths. I nod absentmindedly, struggling to enjoy the special occasion instead of worrying about Clarke's passport and our money.

No one at the Hammon speaks English. After paying the fifty-eight *francs* for entrance, less than ten dollars, Monique inquires about a massage. "They have what they call a scrub," she translates. It's another fifty *francs*, and I wonder why I'm thinking of spending two day's allowance on myself after we just lost two hundred dollars and our travelers' checks—then do it anyway.

Once inside the mosque, I'm in another culture, another century, another lifetime. Around a large ornate room, mats are arranged on platforms around a fountain. Above is a dome with a walkway around the inside, like a viewer's gallery. After we take off our clothes and lay our towels on mats under a row of dusty horizontal windows, I follow Monique to the baths, large white marble cubicles built on platforms. Each has a fountain at the back with running hot and cold water.

Naked women surround us in ones and twos. Some wash each other with large sponges; others cover their bodies with a muddy substance; some rinse each other's hair with henna. Although it looks like a faintly wicked religious ritual, none of the women seem even slightly self-conscious about their nudity or their ministrations, and to me, their bodies are beautiful although they're all shapes and sizes and ages. One woman, with only one breast, is just as lovely as the others. "Let's go see what the steam bath is like," Monique suggests after awhile. It's so hot that we have to pour cold water from a hose over ourselves every few seconds.

When I'm called for my scrub, I lie on a cool table next to the shower room as a woman rubs my body with a large, rough sponge; it's invigorating, and layers and layers of dark skin peel away, covering my skin like tiny slugs. There goes my suntan, I think, but it's too deep to scrub off. Although the leftover skin is soft and smooth, I wish that she'd worked on my muscles.

While Monique is in another room, I lie on my mat and enjoy the rare peace of being alone. Later, walking slowly, lightly touching my new soft skin, I enter the steam bath one more time. A beautiful young woman perches on a ledge. Taking a cold water hose in her hand, she cools herself off with sensuous movements, with no thought of anything but her body, I am certain; her ablutions seem both natural and wholesome.

"Let's take a short nap before we go," Monique suggests, and we stretch naked on our mats without speaking, content to enjoy each other's proximity before slipping back into the real world. "If you like, I will call Dominique and see if he will meet us in the city for dinner," she offers as we dress. "I have some things to do yet, but we can meet you at eight o'clock." Although I want to save Coco from cooking, I'm not sure whether we should spend our last cash on a restaurant dinner. Explaining our dilemma to Monique, I decline to give her an answer until Clarke arrives.

Distraught over the loss of his money belt, instead of sketching the streets of Paris, he's gone back to Coco's to look once again. "I'm angry at myself for suspecting the girls," Clarke says, "and angrier that my suspicions might be true." But we decide not to ruin our time in Paris because of a practical joke and get directions to the restaurant before starting off down the street, hardly noticing the architecture as we discuss the lost money belt.

Arriving at the restaurant at eight, we find a long line of customers. When we finally reach the front, I tell the maître d' that we expect two more people. "Wait outside," he instructs us, and we step out of line to wait near the entrance. Monique arrives at eight-thirty, Dominique at nine. When Monique tells the maître d' that we're finally ready for a table, he gestures toward me brusquely. "I told you to wait outside."

"I am, aren't I?" I respond, looking up at the sky to prove that there's no roof over my head.

"Outside the courtyard, madame," the man says in English, gesturing to the end of the long line that winds around the corner.

"We've been waiting over an hour," I say slowly in French. "I am sorry if I misunderstood you, *monsieur*." The man sighs, then smiles and seats us right away.

During dinner, I spend too much time thinking about what I'll do if the girls have hidden Clarke's passport. Lying is something I won't tolerate, and Kelly knows it. I even consider sending them home, imagining my telegram to Jill: *Your daughter and her friend are thieves. Please pick them up at the airport and lock them up forever.*

"What will you do if Kelly and Megan took your passport, Clarke?" I ask as we leave the restaurant.

"First, I'd ask why they did it."

"Not me. I'd go straight into my revenge mode."

"Come with us to visit our friends," Monique suggests. "We can attend a *bal*, what you call a street dance. They are all over Paris tonight because it is the eve of Bastille Day." While Kelly and Megan stay home, I think vindictively, we'll celebrate the Bicentennial. "Clarke and I will take the Metro," Monique continues, "and you can ride with Dominique on his motorcycle."

Remembering how fast Dominique drives a car, I think a long moment before answering. "Without money, the trip is over anyway," I joke. "He can't be worse than riding through the Arc de Triomphe on bicycles." But he is. The streets are jammed with people screaming and staggering and laughing and drinking and throwing firecrackers, and Dominique races through the crowded streets as if they're deserted, crossing lanes, cutting off cars and motorcycles and pedestrians, driving on sidewalks or between rows of vehicles, playing chicken while I cling to his back like a suction cup. Shutting my eyes, I pray to the god of first-time motorcycle riders that I won't make a fool of myself, or die. Dominique takes the scenic route, pointing out the Bastille and the Hôtel de Ville and other places of interest as we streak by each one, the architecture a blur.

Arriving at Monique's friends' apartment long before Clarke and Monique, Dominique locks his motorcycle to a lamppost, then strides across the street to the apartment building. Unable to remember the people's last name, however, he can't get us in and paces back and forth outside, too shy to visit, perhaps embarrassed that his English isn't as good as Monique's. It's light years better than my French, so I can't reassure him.

By the time Monique and Clarke arrive, Monique's friends are ready for bed. They invite us up for a drink, but we soon realize that we can only get part way to Coco's because the suburban buses have stopped for the night. If we don't leave immediately, the inner city Metro will be closed also. Coco assures us on the telephone that he will send someone to pick us up at the station. Kelly and Megan, he mentions, are at the local *bal*, having returned to his house before five. "They just wanted a free dinner," I hiss. "They don't care about Coco; all they want is more time with the French boys."

By the time we get to the Metro station near L'Hay-les-Roses, it's one-thirty. Coco arrives with Gerard and his wife Gigi, who take us home for a drink and then to the local street dance. Frustrated and tired, I'm not in the mood to celebrate the 200th birthday of Bastille Day or any other day, except maybe the one that Kelly and Megan go home, but when we arrive at the park, Kelly is dancing with Jean Luc and my heart softens just a bit. Megan is alone. Fabrice, as shy as she, dances with no one.

Everyone in the community seems to be at the park, and Coco floats from one group to another, enjoying this celebration as he seems to enjoy every moment of his life. Almost everyone dances; no one seems tired except me. The French certainly know how to love life, I think for the thousandth time, trying to get into the spirit of the celebration. At four-thirty in the morning, I ask Coco's daughter for a ride to the house. Patricie agrees. "I am just taking my children home to bed."

We make the rounds to say goodnight and Kelly and Megan reluctantly agree to come with us. We thank Gerard and Gigi for rescuing us from the Metro. "*S'il vous plait*, will you eat lunch with us tomorrow?" Gigi asks in French.

"We can't leave until we find or replace your passport, Clarke," I say quietly, "and this will at least relieve Coco from cooking another meal for us." We accept Gigi's offer with gratitude.

If we have to stay until Monday to replace Clarke's passport, I think as we pull up to Coco's, at least I can see an organ recital at Notre-Dame on Sunday, but the thought gives me little comfort. We still haven't confronted the girls, but since neither of us looks forward to it, we decide to put it off for a few more hours and crawl into bed at dawn. But when Clarke gets up at ten, he finds his money belt on a chair under some papers. "We suspected that you two took it as a joke," I tell Kelly when she gets up, "or as a way to stay for the Bicentennial."

Kelly looks straight into my eyes. "If we'd wanted to stay in Paris for Bastille Day," she says, "we would have asked rather than make you worry about something that important."

"But why haven't you asked? I know you want to stay, yet you haven't said a word."

Kelly looks thoughtful. "I don't know. For some reason, both of us were sure that we'd be here for Bastille Day."

I believe her. If they had taken the money belt, I'm sure they'd have a much better story than this. "I apologize for suspecting you," I say, wondering about myself. "Since we've already accepted an invitation from Gerard and Gigi and today's Bastille Day, I guess we're staying."

Lunch at Gerard and Gigi's lasts five hours. Megan declines to join us, hoping instead to see Fabrice. Exasperated at her manners, I make up an excuse about her not feeling well. Outside on the patio, we enjoy much food, wine and conversation, although without Megan or Fabrice to translate, the conversation is more gestures than words. "We will take you into Paris for the parade tonight," Gerard offers.

When we stop to pick up Megan, she's not interested. "I'd rather watch it on TV with Coco," she announces, glancing toward Fabrice. Jeepers, I think, what women deny themselves for men—why doesn't she just invite Fabrice to come along?

In the center of Paris, floats from countries all over the world assemble on one of the streets that feeds into the Champs-Élysées, lining up one after the other, ready to march in the same direction for the same purpose. As the simple American float passes, our French friends help us cheer for our flag. It's the first time we've seen it in five months, and as it moves next to the Russian flag under the Arc de Triomphe, I wipe tears from my eyes.

As fireworks burst over the Arc de Triomphe, we drive home in time to watch the end of the parade on television before going to bed at two. "My throat hurts," Clarke complains. "I'm not used to sleeping inside."

He tosses and turns, making it impossible for either of us to sleep for more than a few minutes. "Do you want me to get some aspirin from your pack?" I ask at three-thirty. "If we're going to leave in the morning, we need some rest."

"Is that an offer?"

I get dressed and put in my contacts, then tiptoe downstairs to find Coco playing cards on the patio with a group of friends who arrived after we'd gone to bed. This man has cancer?

"*Non, non, non,*" Coco says with real disappointment as I come down the stairs the next morning with clothes for my pack.

"*Je regrette*," I say. "We must leave today."

"*Non, ma cherie.*" He turns to speak with the ever-present Fabrice, who's washing drink glasses.

"He says that you must stay until Monday," Fabrice translates.

Upstairs, we gather in the bedroom. "How can we stay?" I ask. "Coco refuses to let us cook and he's not well enough to work this hard. He also can't afford this— neither can we." We've contributed two hundred *francs* a day toward food, much more than we usually spend but not nearly enough to cover the wine and delicacies.

"But he seems to love being surrounded by people, more than anything," says Clarke. "Kelly and Megan, what do you want to do?"

"Stay!"

"I'm still not caught up with my writing," I admit, "and I'd love to hear the concert at Notre-Dame tomorrow."

We traipse downstairs all in a row to tell Coco that we'll stay the weekend if he's absolutely sure that he wants us. His eyes sparkle with joy. "The man is nuts," we tell Fabrice, laughing.

It's a lazy day, which we need after four nights of parties. Clarke washes clothes in Coco's bathtub while I write on my laptop until its monitor turns into a jumble of characters like a test pattern. Coco's son Didi and a friend try unsuccessfully to help. "I will help you call the computer store on Monday," PhiPhi offers in English. "Maybe they can tell you how to fix it over the telephone. If not, I will take you there. It is difficult to communicate about something as complex as a computer when you don't speak the language, no?"

"So I've found out. *Merci beaucoup encore, mon ami.*" PhiPhi's girlfriend works at the post office and has already shipped our boxes for substantially less than an arm and a leg.

"Ship the damn computer home," Clarke grouses when he comes outside.

Lunch is pheasant, another gourmet meal seemingly put together without effort by Chef Coco. Again, Megan declines to eat and Coco frowns with worry and hurt. "That's how she stays so slim and beautiful," I explain lamely.

After lunch, Clarke sketches a lively little cartoon of Coco. Tears brimming, Coco lovingly tacks the paper to his wall. From then on, when someone comes to visit, Clarke draws a portrait.

PhiPhi offers to take everyone into Paris for the fireworks display at the Eiffel Tower and I write in longhand until we leave. In spite of the loving care of Coco and his friends, I feel out of sync with my own life. Ever since the girls arrived, we don't bicycle far enough to suit me and our mileage is so concentrated in the afternoons that my knees ache continually. Still grouchy about allowing Kelly and Megan to control our route, I feel trapped, unwilling to convince myself that their choices are fine with me. I also don't like having to be in Munich by August 21st, preferring to set my own pace without limits. Although Clarke seems to be accepting everything, I'm fighting it all. When Clarke comes into the room, I share my thoughts. "I hear what you don't want, Susan, but what solutions do you have?"

"Allow me the luxury of my emotions, okay? If I think of any solutions, you'll be the first to know. Just let me feel sorry for myself for awhile."

Everyone but Coco joins a caravan of cars that leaves before dark, driving part way into the city for a transfer to the Metro, where we scatter to find room on the overcrowded subway. As the doors of my car close, I realize that I'm separated from the rest of my group and have no idea where to get off—but there's no need to worry because the train empties all at once, and like hot, sticky lava, the passengers flow from the subway onto the platform and run off down the stairs. "Hold hands," PhiPhi orders, gathering us together to snake through the streets toward the Eiffel Tower, raising clasped hands over people's heads in order not to interfere with others' progress.

Lighted, the Eiffel Tower looks like gold filigreed wire. One by one, the lights go out and the tower dissolves into the night sky and music and fireworks celebrate the story of the French Revolution. Although I don't understand the narration, the emotion of the occasion is unmistakable. Afterwards, unable to find a Metro with space for any of us, we walk two hours to our cars, glad for Coco's sake that he decided to stay home.

When we arrive at his house at two-thirty, he's waiting on his balcony like a deserted puppy. The railings are decorated with candles, now burned down to stubs, and with red, white and blue spotlights, the colors of the French flag. My eyes fill with tears to see him alone. We're no more up the steps than food arrives on the table—pheasant, ham, sausages, pickles, cheese, mousse, yogurt, bread and wine. Staggering to bed at three-thirty, we learn the next day that Coco played cards the rest of the night with his friends.

By the time Clarke and I get up at noon, Megan has already gone to the *boulangerie* for croissants, bringing Kelly roses that grace the rickety breakfast table with the same class that Coco does his tumbly house. Soon the balcony is filled with friends and Clarke finishes portraits while I call about the organ recital at Notre-Dame, discovering that it's been canceled because of the Bastille Day festivities. Not surprised, I go upstairs to mope and listen to Clarke outside the window.

He's the star, the center of attention. Prior to meeting Coco, his drawings and photographs were all of scenery. Now, they're of people. "You and Clarke are very different," my secretary had told me once. "You have dozens of friends. Clarke has one—you. He doesn't need anyone but you in his life." Yet here he is, falling in love with a group of Frenchmen as if he just discovered the human race for the first time.

Although I'm thrilled for him, I feel left out, then decide to cheer myself up by wearing the flowery dress I'd bought on our first pass through Paris. I'd washed it the day before to wear to the organ recital. Adding hose and my silk shoes, I pull my hair up in combs. "Gosh, you look beautiful." Megan meets me on the stairs. "I have some earrings which would look great with that dress."

As I emerge onto the porch, I'm greeted with applause and whistles and given a place of honor across from Clarke and his sketchpad. Fabrice looks at me shyly. "Your hair is very pretty like that," he says.

Natalie arrives wearing green tennis shoes with bright pink polka dots and laces. "Those are wonderful shoes," I tell her.

"What size do you wear?"

"*Trente-sept*," I say, six-and-a-half American.

"That's my size," she says with a grin. "Here, take them. I have another pair."

"Heavens no, Natalie."

"I insist. I want you to remember us."

"How could I ever forget? May I buy them?"

"Of course not. Take them, please."

I slip them on with my fluffy dress, no longer glamorous but feeling even more lovely because of the gift. Pirouetting about the porch, I kiss Natalie on both cheeks, and she seems as delighted about the gift as I.

Claude, a retired Paris bus driver, arrives with regulation bus driver ties for all four of us and a regulation blue shirt for Clarke. Then he takes a fifth tie and solemnly knots it around Clarke's neck, then cuts off the ends, giving the wide one to Coco and tucking the small one in his own shirt pocket. There are tears in his eyes. "We will meet again," he tells Clarke in French. "When we do, I will sew the tie back together." Coco quietly puts his piece of tie into the bag he'll take to the hospital.

Dinner is roast *cheval* again because it's a special occasion, our last night. All of our new friends come, and the goodbyes are almost more than we can bear. We've never stayed this long anywhere, and leaving is like pulling up our hearts by the roots.

PhiPhi is unable to take me to the computer store in the morning, so Clarke agrees to go with me on the Metro. "Stay one more night," Coco pleads.

"Only if we can prepare dinner," Clarke says sternly in French, as unable to let go of Coco as Coco is to let go of him.

"Okay, no problem," says Coco.

At the store, we're told that it will take until three-thirty for the technician to diagnose the computer's ailment. Clarke invites me outside the store. "Ship it home," he says through gritted teeth. "It's been nothing but trouble."

"No. I'll come back myself." I have to get my way about something, I decide.

Back at Coco's, Kelly offers to come with me to pick up the computer while Clarke and Megan shop for dinner. We've decided to serve Dominique's *crêpes* and a big green salad, American style. At the computer store, Kelly and I are told that the technician is out for another hour and a half. For the first time on the trip, we have a chance to talk by ourselves. "So tell me why you and Megan ditched school so often last year," I begin.

"We were bored. The classes were so remedial that they were a waste of time."

I chuckle. "Not everyone is as smart as you and Megan, m'love, but I guess it doesn't matter what you do as long as you're willing to pay the price for getting caught. I hope it was worth it."

"It probably wasn't, but it was fun at the time."

At six o'clock, the technician announces in marginal English, after I apologize for my less-than-marginal French, that the problem is the software, not the computer, and he's somehow able to put me back in business. By the time we return to Coco's at eight, Megan and Clarke are up to their elbows in *crêpe* batter and the guest list is growing—Coco, Gigi and Gerard and their daughter, Fabrice, Jean Luc, PhiPhi and Nellie, Coco's son Didi and Natalie, his daughter Patricie and her two children.

While I play hostess to seventeen guests with sign language and suffer quiet embarrassment that my American salad is too elaborate for French taste, Clarke bustles in and out of the kitchen serving steaming hot *crêpes* with theatrical flair, then joins the group with a *crêpe* of his own amid a standing ovation.

Again, we say goodbye—this time, for good. I write a letter to Coco, which Natalie translates after everyone leaves. "He wants me to make a copy of it," she says quietly, "in case he ever loses it. He will treasure it always."

We visit alone with Coco until one o'clock, when PhiPhi returns with a photograph of himself and his girlfriend. With tears in his eyes, he tells us that he's sorry we're leaving. "Coco says that he will cry when you go," he adds in English.

"Tell him that we will too," Clarke says, "but it is time. Each day gets harder."

At breakfast, Coco begs us to stay until after lunch. "*Non, monsieur,* we cannot." I kiss him on both cheeks and tell him I love him. He cries as we pedal away from the little house wearing Claude's ties—Clarke wears the one that was cut.

Chapter 16

We stop at a bike shop so that Kelly can replace my freewheel cassette. After locating the part at a competitor's, the owner locks up the store to fetch it, thrilled to help, while we wait outside on the curb, hearts in tatters, wondering if we will ever see Coco or any of his friends again, praying for a cure for his cancer. The shop owner returns with the part, but it doesn't include the core, the broken piece we need, and we try to express our appreciation for his extra efforts as well as we can. Several kilometers down the street, hearing a honk, I turn to see the shopkeeper on his motorcycle, waving my sunglasses, which I'd left on his counter.

As we pedal through Paris in silence, I realize that the city to me is now Marie Claire and Coco – not the Eiffel Tower or the Louvre – and I'm sure it always will be. Perhaps we're America to some; I hope that we represent our country well enough.

North of Paris, Kelly calls home. "Megan and I are out of money," she says, direct as always. "We've spent more than Clarke and Susan somehow. Can we each have another five hundred dollars? Megan promises to pay back the extra."

Jill's response is exactly what Kelly expected. "How will I get it to you?"

"I'm proud of you for telling Jill that you and Megan are spending extra," I tell Kelly after she hangs up.

She shrugs. "It's the truth, isn't it?"

We get an early start the next morning and Megan leads at a fast pace through deep, cool woods. After a few kilometers, though, she balks. "I won't lead anymore."

"Why not?" Clarke asks.

"I don't like to lead."

"Neither do I. So what?"

"I don't know how fast to go. Kelly just yelled at me because I was going too fast, but how would I know? She's right on my tail."

"Kelly," I say, "if Megan's going too fast, don't worry about it. Just go at your own pace. She'll either slow down or wait up ahead when she notices you're not right behind her."

"I won't lead anymore," Megan reiterates.

"Kelly, how about you?"

"No way."

"Then I will. My knees are so sore from your seventy-five kilometers yesterday that nobody will have trouble keeping up. We rely on Clarke too much."

All day, we crisscross back and forth across the main route north from Paris toward Lille, pedaling thirty kilometers before lunch, as we had prior to Kelly and Megan's arrival. In theory, I'm much happier; in reality, my knees ache painfully after the week off. The girls don't call a halt until we've ridden eighty kilometers, and their new-found stamina bewilders me until they explain that they'd heard me griping in Paris about not getting enough mileage and vowed to ride fifty miles a day, no matter what, just to get back at me.

At a ragtag farm owned by a widower named Roget who happily consents to have us, Kelly and Megan wash their hair in a garden hose while Clarke and I cook dinner surrounded by a circle of Roget's curious neighbors. Instead of visiting, Megan crawls into her tent. Earlier, when Clarke asked Roget if we could camp, she'd made fun of his struggling French. "Why don't you ask if we can camp, then?" Clarke had asked Megan as we pitched our tents.

"That's your job," she replied loftily. "You and Susan obviously did fine before I came."

One of Roget's neighbors, a spry woman proud of her eighty-one years, now asks what time we'll leave in the morning, then the group disperses with wishes for a safe trip and Roget offers us coffee before bed. Kelly and Megan decline, leaving us to be ambassadors. The next morning, we discover why the neighbors wanted to know our departure time. Led by the eighty-one-year-old, they run across their yards en masse to wave goodbye.

"Why don't we take turns leading?" I suggest at the first turn.

"Okay," Kelly says. "You go first."

"I led yesterday and Clarke led the day before. You decide between you."

We wait in silence while the girls look glumly at each other. "All right, all right," Megan says finally.

Mid-morning, we stop at a service station to top off our tires with air. "Thank you for liberating France," the mechanic says in French after he sees the "U.S.A." sign on the back of Clarke's bike.

"*Pardon?*"

"During the war. If it weren't for your country," he shudders, "we would be Germans."

"I need to find a village big enough for a pharmacy," I announce before lunch. "I'm low on medicine for my knees." At this new pace, I can't afford to run out. And, of course, we need a *boulangerie* for bread and a market for groceries. With four of us, we shop for food twice a day. Although we find a village, there's no bakery. At the market, we're told that bread is sold at a corner café, but they're sold out. A woman walks up the street with a loaf of bread under one arm. "Megan, would you please go ask where she bought that?"

"Why me?"

I'm exasperated.

"Because you supposedly speak French. Why else?" I run after the woman, and although I'm able to ask where she bought the bread, I can't understand her long answer. Staring at her dumbly, feeling stupid, I stutter my thanks and trot back to the bicycles. "Forget bread," I snarl, "because I couldn't understand what she told me. Unlike someone else I know, I haven't taken five years of French."

Megan says nothing and the rest of us decide to eat cheese and tomatoes in the park because we're too hungry to look for another village. "Let's go to the pharmacy first," Clarke suggests. "They're about to close for lunch."

"Do you have a prescription for these?" the pharmacist asks in careful English when I show him my almost-empty box of pills.

"I thought we could buy them over-the-counter all over Europe," I answer.

The pharmacist smiles gently. "I would advise you to get a prescription before you get to Germany. The French are strict but the Germans are even more strict. I will give you two months' supply so that you will have time to get a prescription from your American doctor." The handsome man smiles. "I am Libyan. I will help you because I want you to know that I am not Qaddafi. You are not your President Bush either," he chuckles.

Across the street, I divvy up our sandwiches-sans-bread. "I'm not hungry," Megan says, then walks away to sit alone. We save her yogurt and an orange but eat everything else and cycle on in silence.

"Let's get some wine," Clarke says after an hour. Although the next village has a wine cooperative, it won't open for twenty minutes. Megan flops down on the curb, sullen, and I decide it's time for a conversation.

"I'd like you to think about what you're contributing to this trip," I begin, "to us, to Kelly, to the people you've met, particularly in France. But most of all, to yourself. Just what have you learned by making fun of our French instead of practicing it yourself? By staying in your tent instead of getting to know the people who help us? What do you suppose the French think of Americans when they offer you shelter and you won't even talk to them?" Megan stares at the street. "You're not a snob," I continue in a softer voice. "You're just shy. But you're letting that interfere with your learning about yourself and others—and in no small measure, with us too."

Megan huddles on the sidewalk, fighting tears. "None of us can afford the luxury of one of us not contributing," Clarke adds. "You can't afford it either; your life is much too important for that." I try to kiss her on both cheeks, French style, but she won't move her fists from her dirt-streaked face.

As we pedal through the hot afternoon, I wonder if anyone has the right to challenge someone else for his actions or whether we should just learn to accept what others do, no matter what. What right do I have to tell Megan that she should act differently? *Dear Megan's Mother,* I should write, *I have totally destroyed your sixteen-year-old daughter's self-confidence because I think she should speak more French although I can't speak it at all.* Jeepers.

We're nearing the Belgian border. A beautiful red brick house with immaculate gardens looks imposingly down on the road. Around the back, we tether our bicycles to a low fence and approach the back door as a man dressed in work clothes comes around the corner of the house. John rings the back bell and speaks rapidly to a woman in a maid's uniform after Clarke asks in French if we can camp. The woman disappears into the house, then emerges out of the gloom of the long dark hallway as a white lace curtain parts in the window, gnarled fingertips grasping its edge. "Yes,

Madame says you may sleep here tonight," the maid says in French as the owner of the hands on the curtain appears behind her shoulder.

"*Americains?*" the old woman asks sternly as her employee politely steps aside and cups her hand protectively under the woman's elbow.

"*Oui, madame.*"

"Have you seen the cemeteries?" she demands in French. "That is what you must see in France." She goes on to speak of World War II, but we aren't able to understand her words, only the pain of her memories as they erupt from her throat in a gravelly rush. Was her husband killed? Was her farm taken? We could not know.

She sends John to open two rooms for us in a barn-like dwelling in back of the main house. "The soldiers slept there," he explains. Which ones?

The rooms are filthy; perhaps they've been locked since the war. But they're safe from rain and we have a level place to put our cook stove. Clarke and I eat dinner outside next to the garden in the fresh air while Megan and Kelly eat inside propped up against the dirty walls. I don't know what to say to Megan, but I try to treat her gently. We'll be in France only one more day; it's too late for her to participate anyway, at least with the French.

While everyone else shops for groceries the next morning, I sit on a curb with the bicycles, allowing the sunshine to warm my tanned face. A group of school children pass by with their teacher, and I wave and say a few words in French. Pointing to our heavy bikes, they engulf me with greetings and smiles as an old lady approaches and pats my head, saying gentle and encouraging words that I don't understand. After all my reluctance about returning to France, my love for it has grown even more. It feels like home.

Tomorrow, we'll be in Belgium and I begin to feel my usual qualms about entering a new country. At least Belgians speak French, I console myself. We may have to learn a new currency, but not a new language.

After finding a park for lunch, we tease the girls about a group of workers who watch their every move. As we gather up orange peels and yogurt cups, a man carrying a large trash can approaches from a nearby house. "Please, if you would like, here is a can for your rubbish," he says in French. "Would you like to come into my house and wash?" We look at each other, surprised. Normally, we carry our trash in a plastic grocery bag until we find a city trash receptacle, our sticky hands smelling like onions until we sweat off the remains of our lunch. After leading us across the grass, Jean introduces us to his daughter while we take turns in the bathroom. "I was ten years old during the war," he explains. "I will never forget the Americans who died to save France."

As we pedal away, the man's daughter runs after us. "Would you send my father a postcard from America?" she asks. "It would mean a great deal to him." We take down his address, as anxious to touch this man's life in some small way as he has ours.

I've been thinking about the girls' leaving. Today is July 21st and they're scheduled to leave in a month. "Okay if we call a travel agent today, Clarke?"

"We don't have time."

"Why not? Do we have dinner reservations somewhere? Look, if we wait until the last minute to book their flight, airfares will probably be higher than with thirty days' notice. They're using Kelly's college savings, you know."

"So call. You're going to anyway, so why ask my permission?"

In a fair-sized little city, we cycle to the town hall for directions to the nearest travel agent. There aren't any, and we're several days from Antwerp. "I think we'd better call Jill and have her reserve something," I tell Clarke.

"Just hurry up."

Ignoring his impatience, the girls and I crowd into a stifling phone booth to get Jill out of bed and ask her to check on flights out of Munich. "But don't book them if there's a penalty if we cancel or change dates," I tell her. "We have no idea if we can get there on time. We'll call you back in a few hours to see what you've found out."

When we do, Jill reports that any flight that can be changed costs three times what the girls paid to fly into London. "If we have to pay that kind of money, we might as well book at the last minute," we agree. "Let's all look for something better in the meantime."

We're close to the border. "Anybody want a French pastry before Belgium?" I call back to the troops.

"Yes," Kelly and Megan say together.

"No" says Clarke, still snarly, but it's three against one, so we stop. It's been three against one all day—I'm relieved that Megan is speaking to me again, although I have no idea what's gotten into Clarke.

We sit on the curb in a row and munch cream pastries while the bicycles lean in a row against the bake shop window. Slender Megan goes back for seconds. "You're going to get fat," I tease, writing down her purchase in my little journal. Every Sunday, I tally up all the expenditures to figure who owes what. It's a pain, particularly when we change currencies; this week's expenses in French *francs*, for example, will have to be converted and paid back in Belgian *francs*.

"Belgium's just across the river," Clarke announces later.

"Can we stay on the French side tonight?" Megan asks.

Clarke looks at the map. "Sure. We can follow the river for another ten or fifteen kilometers."

"What about stopping here at this house?" she asks.

The red brick house that sits next to a small pond has an owner whose son speaks some English, but they won't allow us to stay on their property. "We are afraid that our dogs will attack you," they explain. As usual, I surmise that the tension between the four of us puts the people off. Why blame the dogs? It's never overt. When we come to a house, we try to put away our frustrations, using the same words as always and being as polite and friendly as any other day. But somehow our own conflicts must show. It's too coincidental that our difficulties in finding a yard to sleep in come on the same days that we have unresolved differences between us. "Father says that maybe you can sleep in the soccer field next door," the young man tells us. "Wait here, please, while he telephones for permission."

Remembering our last night in France at Chrisine and Armel's before we'd picked up Kelly and Megan, I'm disappointed that this last night in France will be spent without the French but follow the father next door to a large soccer field in shouting distance of Belgium. As Clarke and I unpack our cooking supplies, I wonder why he's in such a bad mood. Lately, it seems like anytime anyone wants to do anything, we have to ask Clarke and he always says no. No one seems to be getting along very well.

At dinner, Clarke comments about how difficult it is to get Kelly and me up in the morning. "Maybe you should resort to my father's tactics when I took a semester off from college." I suggest, smiling at the memory. "I wrote poetry until three-thirty in the morning but had to get up for work at five so he brought me hot coffee and lit a candle on my nightstand." I laugh. "Of course, a candle would probably burn down the tent and we have no way to make decent coffee, Clarke, but still it's a nice idea."

Clarke says nothing, then crawls into our tent after dinner. When I follow, he scrambles out, rebuffing me without a word. After a few words with our host family, who brought us a bottle of wine, he returns to the tent. "That really hurt to be compared to your father, Susan. Tell me, do you think your father did that for you out of guilt?"

"Guilt? He did it out of love, Clarke. Some people do things for others because they want to, believe it or not. Why is it so hard for you to imagine that someone would want to be nice to me? If you're jealous, that's your problem." Clarke doesn't respond and then we bicker for a few minutes, resolving nothing.

"If you keep talking, Susan, I'm sleeping outside." Clarke pulls back the tent flap to drag out his sleeping bag.

"Oh no, you don't." I yank the bag back inside, hoping he'll come with it. He doesn't. "If you choose to sleep apart, Clarke, do it in the dirt!"

He leaves the tent wearing only bike shorts. Hurt, I lie awake, and at one o'clock in the morning, look for him in the cold, misty night, then return to the tent and toss and turn until six, searching again in the lightening day. He's nowhere to be seen, but I can't imagine that he's gone far because his shirt and shoes are still in the tent. Frustrated and angry, feeling very empty, I begin to pack. "Clarke's gone," I have to tell Kelly when she gets up at seven. Megan hasn't seen him either.

While the girls pack their bikes, I walk all over the playing field looking for red bicycle shorts. Finally, as the mist lifts, I spot a black lump on the far edge—Clarke, curled up into a ball in his black sweats, his jacket pulled over his head, a water bottle at his side. He'd gotten into his clothes pack on my bike. I'm relieved for an instant, then furious. "Wake up, Clarke." I stand above him, murder in my eye, then poke him with a foot. "Wake up!"

"Go away. I didn't get any sleep last night after you threw me out of the tent."

"You threw yourself out of the tent. I didn't have such a great night either."

He curls up into a ball again, arms wrapped around his chest, jacket hood pulled tightly over his hair. I pull loose an arm, and he flings off my hand, curling up tighter. Anger and hurt turn me into a monster—I pick up his water bottle and pour the whole thing on his head. Uncoiling like a snake, he jumps up, grabbing my arm hard. Shoving him away, I advance when he retreats. "You bitch," he says finally, "You had no right to compare me to your father."

"I didn't, Clarke. I just told you about something nice he did. So what? Why did you walk out?"

"I don't care anymore about resolving issues before we sleep, and I don't think we should say what we feel all the time—sometimes it's just too painful."

"Of course it is. Neither of us likes to hear when we've screwed up."

He keeps his distance. "If you can't accept me like I am, then I'm going to do whatever it takes to protect myself."

"So it's all right for you to say whatever you want and to tell all of us what to do all the time, but if any of us has an opinion, then it's too much for your delicate feelings?"

"That's right." We argue for a long time, circling each other like boxers, looking for openings. "Maybe we should go home," Clarke says.

The verbal uppercut takes me by surprise and I plop down on the grass, arms wrapped around my aching knees. Ever since Kelly and Megan arrived, I've been tense and irritable, pulled between two factions that change almost hourly. Why wouldn't I want to go home, back to comfort? "Going home won't solve the problem, Clarke," I say finally.

"What problem?"

"I feel totally controlled every minute. I need to be able to say what I feel and want without your handing me my head."

Now it's Clarke's turn to think. "That's fair, I guess," he agrees reluctantly, "but I'm still going to do whatever it takes to take care of myself."

Too exhausted to discuss our differences any longer, we walk back to Kelly and Megan, seated like spectators at a soccer match, cross-legged on the grass, empty yogurt cups scattered about like flowers. "We've been to the store twice already," chirps Megan.

"I liked it when you poured water on his head, Susan," Kelly says, licking her spoon. "That was good."

"But we cheered for you too, Clarke," Megan adds hastily.

Clarke and I look at each other, embarrassed. "The first time you get up at a decent hour, Kelly, and we still aren't ready to leave until nine," I groan.

"I wouldn't have missed this for the world," she giggles.

Chapter 17

MEGAN LEADS US INTO Belgium. "Let me read the map," she offers. Delighted that she's taking more responsibility, Clarke hands it over. But tiny-scale maps take a little getting used to, particularly when one reads, interprets and bicycles at the same time.

After several turns, I pull alongside Clarke. "It feels like we're going back toward France," I say quietly.

"I agree, but I'm not going to hurt Megan's feelings by saying anything yet."

Eventually, Megan asks for help. Indeed, we're headed toward Paris. "You just want to see Fabrice again," we tease, making light of her blunder. Laughing, Megan pedals off in the right direction, hair flying in the wind, abrasions healing nicely after a week of soap and hot water.

It's noon when we cross the border into Belgium, our sixth country, sixth currency, and it turns out, fourth new language—Flemish, the Belgian dialect of Dutch. When Clarke asks a woman for water in French and Megan asks again in much better French and the response both times is unintelligible, we're back to communicating in gestures. After the woman finally goes inside to fill our bottles, I attempt to visit with her husband by showing him on our map that we're cycling to Antwerp. The man looks astounded, and when I point out, laughing, that we started in North Africa, he takes a step backward, open-mouthed. I hardly believe it myself. Clarke and I have pedaled 6800 kilometers, over 4200 miles, and the girls have ridden over a thousand miles already.

Although the terrain is mostly flat, the weather is blistering hot and humid. Bright sun glares and glitters across the fields like a mirror, and the tiny roads are deserted. By two o'clock, we need water again and stop at a neat, square house surrounded by flowers. Clarke and Megan speak to the tiny old lady in French, Kelly tries out her high school German, and I hold up a water bottle from my bike. Between us, the woman understands, and after looking us over carefully, gestures for Megan to follow her into the house. "I'm amazed that people this near the border don't speak French," I comment to Clarke and Kelly.

"Maybe they just want us to try their language." Clarke pulls out our European phrase book, which includes Dutch but not Flemish.

The afternoon stretches into an endless ordeal of heat that feels like pedaling across a giant frying pan. At four, we spot a small market, abandoning the bikes to get a cold drink. "I do not have much right now," a voice speaking English says from the front of the store. "I am closing next week to go with my family on holiday."

Drawn by our own language, we gallop to the cash register. "You speak English!" Clarke says.

"Not very well," the attractive woman laughs. "I learned it by watching American television programs. I listen to the words and read the Flemish subtitles."

"You speak perfectly," I tell her, amazed.

"It is nice to have a chance to practice. It is very hot today, no? Would you like a cold drink? I have some at home behind the store." We accept gratefully, then Nicole invites us to camp on her lawn. "My daughters would love to meet you," she says, seating us at a patio table in her back garden, bringing cold drinks and buckets of cool water for washing up.

Nicole runs in and out of the market, tending to customers and us while Kelly and Megan offer to make grilled cheese sandwiches for dinner and Clarke washes his and my clothes. Suddenly, Nicole's words are drowned out by horns. "Come!" She leads me to the front of the store. Transport trucks roll down the street, their cabs filled with waving children. "These children are handicapped," she explains. "Each year, the truckers take them on a tour of four or five towns." I wave at each truck, a hundred and fifty of them, knowing how much it's meant for us to get encouragement along the way.

It's a national holiday in Belgium. In this town, Westrozebeke, there are religious and secular celebrations, a Catholic Mass with a procession and a carnival. "Would you like to attend the Mass?" Nicole's fourteen-year-old Margy asks. Kelly and Megan decide to stay behind to fix dinner and recover from the heat while Margy and two friends escort Clarke and me to the church, where the service is already in progress. Afterwards, she scoots us out the door. "The procession is only about two kilometers and we visit each chapel in the town." Men and women carrying brightly colored flags representing each neighborhood lead the parade, followed by the priest and the congregation and a truck which broadcasts religious and classical music. At the end, a tractor tows a cart of flowers surrounding the church's statue of the Virgin Mary. We walk down the road, gathering more and more people from each home we pass.

The procession and the music stop abruptly at the first chapel, a tiny shrine at an intersection of two roads. A person from the congregation reads a prayer, then the priest says another prayer and the music and the walkers continue on. We stop at six or seven chapels, each with fresh flowers and lighted candles, each with a beautiful, freshly starched hand-embroidered altar cloth. Each is a shrine to the Virgin Mary, but the last is for Jesus.

Margy's two friends had slipped away to the carnival, but Margy stays with us, explaining everything in English. Walking ahead of us is a neighbor whose oldest daughter was hit by a bicycle at Christmas and may never walk again. In bike shorts, feeling guilty, I watch the woman's seven-year-old stare at me with open curiosity, then I take her hand. Clarke takes her other hand, and the little girl happily marches through the streets with Americans of her very own. The priest catches my eye and winks.

At the end of the parade, Margy presses a few coins in our hands for the offering as everyone files past the priest to kiss his ring. Clarke and I, not Catholics, look at each other questioningly, then I file past like everyone else and kiss the ring. Clarke and the priest exchange smiles and winks and leave it at that.

We go to bed at eleven, not a cloud in the sky, clean clothes drying on the line, my computer recharging inside the house. Two hours later, the world explodes in thunder as lightning strikes daylight into the tent. Clarke and I scramble upright. "Are you guys okay?" we call in Kelly and Megan's direction as another bolt of lightning flashes so close that we smell ozone, setting off earsplitting thunder. The town fire alarms wail as rain pours from the sky like a waterfall, eliminating communication between the tents, and Clarke and I huddle together, waiting for the storm to pass or to be hit by lightning, whichever comes first. It's a long night. At dawn, Nicole is in the back yard. "I was awake most of the night worrying about you," she tells us.

"You weren't the only one," I reply with a shaky laugh as Kelly crawls out of their tent dragging a wet sleeping bag.

"There's a foot of water in there," she groans, pointing toward the tent with a dripping finger as Megan emerges, hair dripping, to wring out her own bag.

"We would have drowned if we hadn't sat up all night," Megan adds.

"Let me hang up your sleeping bags to dry," Nicole offers. "I've moved your laundry into the garage." Inside the garage, we discover a homemade breakfast on a little table set with a pretty cloth, and as we finish our coffee, Nicole and her family sift in and out to visit as they go about their morning chores, bringing us a newspaper with pictures of a horrible airplane crash in Iowa. Unable to read the Flemish captions, I feel a million miles from home.

When we leave, Nicole says in perfect English, "I will never forget my time with you."

"The secondary roads have been deserted," Clarke says later, studying the map. "Let's try the big roads to Brugge." Traffic is light, but it doesn't matter—the main highway boasts a bicycle lane separated from the roadway by a parking lane, and we pedal fast, two by two for the first time, safe and secure.

The first thing we find in Brugge is a whimsical fountain filled with more people than we've seen since entering the country. Babies paddle under the spurting waterfalls, elementary school kids splash and scream, teenagers sit on the edges to socialize. A young man walks up to Clarke as we cool our own feet in the fountain. "My name is Ian," he says, "and I'm a Canadian on a year-long bike trek. I just broke down outside of town and hitchhiked in on a truck," he continues, staring at our healthy bikes. "You're certainly carrying a lot of stuff."

"We're camping. How about you?" Clarke asks.

"After eighty to a hundred kilometers a day, all I want to do is eat out and sleep in a bed. I stay in hostels every night." Although our record is still 118 kilometers, we've been pedaling eighty kilometers a day since Paris and I feel proud of our accomplishments, particularly since we're camping and cooking ourselves, then wonder if Ian is lonely.

Jo and Pierre's son had told us that Brugge is the most beautiful city in Europe, but we still aren't prepared for its Middle Ages magic. Twelfth- and thirteenth-century buildings crowd together in pastel colors along the narrow streets and canals like watercolor brush strokes, and lace, music and church bells tie the city like ribbons as we pedal, enthralled, through the streets and over the waterways. At a tiny corner shop, I buy decals for my bike from every country on our itinerary in silver, gold, red, yellow and blue. They don't have a sticker for Morocco; Morocco is another world.

"This is without a doubt the most beautiful city I've ever seen," I say, leaning over a bridge to watch the reflection of pale-colored buildings shimmer on the still waterway like an impressionist painting. "This whole city is a museum, one giant canvas." Engrossed in Brugge's loveliness, unwilling to break its spell by focusing on anything less than the sum of its parts, we pedal along the narrow streets, looking up, and all around the main square, absorbing the grace of the eight-hundred-year-old buildings.

"You guys want to try to get to the beach tonight?" Clarke asks Kelly and Megan, studying the map.

"I'd love to sleep on a beach," Kelly answers.

"We can probably afford to spend a whole day," Clarke says. "The way you two are cycling, we'll have no problem getting to Germany in a month."

"We'll probably be there in two days," I groan, massaging my sore knees. The girls smirk.

We can't find an open market on the north side of Brugge and finally stop at a *frituur*, buying burgers and fries for fifteen dollars. "Nobody gets to eat at all tomorrow," I say half seriously as we watch Clarke count the Belgian *francs* that will have to last until we reach the American Express office in Antwerp.

Arriving in De Haan on the North Sea, we find "no camping" signs along the beach and the town crowded with vacationers celebrating the national holiday weekend. Belgium seems to tuck its people into pockets; in between, there's no one. "I think we'd better go inland," Clarke decides finally.

"I thought we were sleeping on the beach," Kelly complains.

"Not if the police might make us move our tents in the middle of the night," I say. "We can't just hop in our car and go somewhere else."

Farther and farther inland we pedal, looking for somewhere–anywhere–we can ask to stay. Finally, a house in the middle of a rose garden beckons, and we knock on the front door, phrasebook in hand. "*Goedenavond*," Clarke tries in Dutch although Nicole had told us that often Belgians refuse to speak either French or Dutch even if they know how.

"Why?" we had asked.

"Pride. I don't understand it either."

The young woman at the door looks carefully at each of us as we look at each other, wondering what to say next. "Are you British?" the woman asks in English, "or American?"

"How did you know?" we breathe a sigh of relief, saved again from ourselves.

The woman laughs. "Your accent," she says. "I teach English."

As we build our little tents among the roses, Anne and her husband bring us fresh coffee, cookies, and big ripe strawberries dipped in sugar. "You are very courageous to travel like this," Anne tells us. We start to protest. "No," she interrupts. "Traveling is dangerous. My uncle was just murdered in front of his pregnant wife and children in Kenya." Anne's eyes fill with tears. "He tried to stop someone from stealing their car. He was like you, always wanting to experience new places and see new things. I admire you, but please be careful."

Anne invites us for breakfast and says that we can leave our packs in their garage while we go to the beach. "Can I sleep in the garage tonight?" Kelly asks. "I forgot to finish drying my sleeping bag at lunch."

In the morning, as I unload my bicycle in the garage, Kelly asks to wear my clean shorts to the beach. "Why didn't you and Megan do laundry at Nicole's? What did you do while Clarke and I went to the church procession?

Kelly shrugs. "We were tired."

I'm torn between sharing what I have with her—as others have done repeatedly with us—and wanting her to learn to be responsible for her own things. Grumbling, I give her my other pair of shorts, with conditions, although no one has imposed restrictions on their generosity to us. "I want those back washed. I don't see why you have to wear clean shorts to a beach anyway."

After breakfast in Frank and Anne's sunny kitchen with their three-year-old daughter, we strike out for the ocean carrying only the laptop and towels. As Kelly and Megan run for the water and Clarke hikes up the beach to admire the topless women, I set up the computer, ready to catch up on my writing once and for all. It won't work, and frustrated and disappointed, I pack it away, checking my warranty booklet for a computer store in Antwerp.

Stretching out in the hot sun in my swimsuit, I notice my suntan. Although part of me is nicely browned, my feet and ankles are perfectly white, as are the top halves of my thighs—but my hands are the most exotic. Because of my fingerless bicycle gloves, my fingers are only brown from the tips to the second knuckles and I have a round brown spot on the back of each hand; the rest is bone china white.

Mid afternoon, we leave the beach and eat lunch on the curb outside the market because we have no panniers to carry the food we just bought. Back at Anne and Frank's, we pack hurriedly and Anne comes outside to see us off. Clarke and I hug her tightly, American style, trying to show our sympathy for her uncle's death. "Thank you for staying," she says. She has reminded us to value each day, each moment, each person, each experience. And we need to be reminded, based on my hesitation to loan my own niece a pair of shorts.

We pedal back toward Brugge to exchange money, Megan in the lead poking along at fifteen kilometers an hour. Although I worry that the banks will be closed by the time we get to the city, I keep quiet because I don't want to hurt her feelings, and we arrive in Brugge with only ten minutes to spare. The girls and I get into a tussle in the bank lobby about something or other. "We don't need you here, Susan," Kelly says.

Hurt, I go outside. "I was only trying to help," I explain when they come out of the bank.

"We know," they say, looking at each other. "You always are."

Kelly, who thinks she can't bicycle well, leads the sixty kilometers to Antwerp the next day at twice Megan's pace, and we get to Antwerp much earlier than planned. "If we can find a place to stay," Clarke proposes as we near the outskirts, "Susan and I can strip our bikes and ride into the city to exchange money and pick up our mail and get the computer looked at – again." He glances at me sternly. "You guys can come with us – it's about thirty more kilometers round trip – or you can stay and start dinner."

"We'll stay."

After a few more kilometers, we find a farm near the highway. The owners are on holiday in Switzerland, but their daughter and son-in-law from the Netherlands, Griet and Johan, along with their two small daughters and infant son, are at the house with Griet's grandfather and let us camp behind the barn. Clarke and I unload our bikes except for Clarke's back panniers, which support the computer pack, and leave Kelly and Megan and the two beautiful little girls in charge of the tents.

Because downtown Antwerp is on the other side of a large river, we have to go through an underground tunnel. The elevator down to the tunnel isn't working, so we take the bikes down four long, steep escalators. With the added weight of panniers and the computer pack, Clarke has trouble holding his bike on the moving staircase; I have trouble too—my bicycle apparently wants to race me to the bottom. "I'm glad we don't have full packs," I call down to Clarke, who's holding fast to his front and back brakes. And then, of course, after walking through the tunnel, we have to hoist the bicycles up the other four long, steep escalators on the other side, an even harder feat. But when we see a man pull his lightweight racing bike on the escalator without a thought, no doubt a commuter, we decide that practice must make perfect.

Antwerp is paved in cobblestones, and we bump and joggle through the old part of town slowly, careful of our tires and our teeth. It turns out that the computer store and American Express are on the same street, so we split up for efficiency. "Um," I say to the computer store receptionist, not sure which language to try. I obviously don't know Flemish or Dutch and don't want to offend anyone by speaking French. Holding up my computer, I say one of those wonderful international words, "*Kaput.*" Then, "I'm sorry, but I don't speak Flemish. Does anyone speak English?"

"A little," says the receptionist, gesturing to her manager. I hold out the computer, embarrassed as always to be restricted to my own language.

The manager shakes his head. "I am sorry, but we are not able to work on this type of computer." Smiling sympathetically at my frustration and disappointment, he continues. "But I will see if I can find someone who can." A few minutes later, he returns, triumphant. "I have found a company in Deurne that will look at it. They are open until five o'clock."

It's four-forty-five. "How far is Deurne?"

"Only ten kilometers."

My face falls. "We are on bicycles."

"Ah. One moment, please." Moments later, he's back. "The technician who works on these computers will be at his office in the morning between eight and noon," I think he says.

Clarke arrives with money and mail, including ten letters from America and two from France and England. Back through Antwerp we pedal, down the escalators, through the tunnel, up the escalators, and back to the farm to find Kelly and Megan inundated with little girls. "They're darling," says Kelly, "but what a handful! Do you want them now?"

"Absolutely not," I laugh. "I'm reading letters!"

Griet offers homemade soup and a patio table for dinner, and we gather with her family to share strong Belgian beer and conversation until after midnight, feeling fortunate to find another English-speaking family after trying in vain to greet Griet's grandfather in Flemish. "We need to get an early start," I say finally. "It's twenty-five kilometers to the computer place, and the technician will only be there in the morning."

For some reason, Clarke decides to do laundry in the morning although the rest of us are ready to leave at eight, and I worry all the way to Antwerp that we'll miss the technician. If the elevator at the tunnel hadn't been working, we'd never have gotten the bikes on the steep escalators with full packs. We'd probably still be outside Antwerp, in a heap at the bottom of the first escalator covered in dead bikes and panniers.

There's no time to sightsee, and we bump along the cobblestone streets as fast as we can, worrying about our tires. "We shouldn't be riding this fast," Clarke warns.

"We should have left the farm at eight," I point out.

Once, crossing an intersection, Kelly spots a window full of fluffy wedding dresses made of extravagant Belgian lace. "Look!" she screeches, craning her neck for one last glance as we jostle along the bumpy stones through a yellow light, too rushed to stop.

After two wrong turns, we find Deurne, and it's eleven-fifty-five when I run inside the computer company. "I am sorry," Patrick says in English after introducing himself. "Mark waited until nine-thirty for you but then had to go to Brussels."

"It is my fault," I reply. "I thought he would be here from eight until noon, not eight until nine. I am the one who misunderstood. Could he see me when he returns?"

Patrick smiles. "I'm sure he will make time for you. He is due back at three-thirty."

"Just ship the damned thing home," Clarke snaps when I report to the troops.

"If you want to wait, Susan," Megan says, "then let's wait. It's your computer, not Clarke's."

By four, Mark still isn't back from Brussels, but Patrick comes into the lobby with a smile. "I found another engineer who can look at your computer," he announces. "Wait, please." Clarke and I sag onto the hard bench in the waiting area, me with relief and Clarke with resignation, while Kelly and Megan write letters outside with the bicycles. "Come in, please," Patrick finally sticks his nose out an office door. "Andre wishes to speak with you."

Andre shakes my hand politely. "I cannot find anything wrong with him. He malfunctioned once, but now he is working fine."

"Turn it off and start up again," I suggest.

"I have, many times. He works every time except for the first time. I do not know how to fix him if he is not broken."

"Of course not." I feel more than stupid. "He's like a sick kid who miraculously recovers when his mother takes him to a doctor for a shot."

The engineers laugh politely. "Well, we are sorry that we found nothing to fix but hope that he works for the rest of your trip," Andre says.

"What do I owe you?" I ask.

"Nothing. Just have a safe trip and send us a postcard. Are you going to Nederland?"

"Yes."

"They have much better bicycle paths. These in Belgium are no good."

It's my turn to laugh. "These in Belgium are the only ones we've seen in five months. We think they're fabulous."

The homes northeast of Antwerp are beautiful, spread out in luxury under large trees and formal gardens. They all have room for us, but although it's five o'clock, we've ridden only twenty-five kilometers from Griet's farm, so we wind around the narrow roads north toward the Netherlands for another forty kilometers before we quit for the night when our bike path disappears and we're clipped by a Citroën. Two houses, one large and one small, share a tall hedge. Behind the small one, we see two teenaged girls. "Let's try here," Kelly says.

"I am sorry," the oldest says in English, "but my parents won't be home until nine-thirty. Try next door at my grandmother's."

The old woman calls for a grown daughter who speaks English. "Of course you can stay here. Do you need water?"

As we put up our tents in back, I say to Megan. "I've been thinking about whether I had the right to get mad about your not speaking French. It's just that I know how much you're missing—notwithstanding that we could use your help—and I want this trip to be wonderful for you. But I shouldn't have told you to do anything different."

"Don't worry about it—I'm glad you said something. But I feel left out sometimes because the rest of you are family."

"You?" says Clarke. "With three women, I'm the odd man out!"

I laugh. "You are odd, Clarke. But most people would say you're a lucky dog to have three women trailing after you every day."

"Ha."

Our conversation is interrupted by one of the teenagers. "My parents are home now," Katrine explains. "Mother would like you to come for coffee." Inside the little house, the four teenagers compare notes about life in their respective countries. "I'm crazy for anything American," Katrine admits, then answers my question about school. "I want to study law. But I'm not the student my sister is—she wants to be a doctor. She's only thirteen and already speaks Greek."

Her parents Denise and Paul had owned the big house next door at one time, they explain, but lost it when he got sick and quit his job as a well-known chef. He's starting all over in the house restoration business. "Paul's parents don't even recognize his existence now," Denise says bitterly.

"You're right next door and don't get along?"

"Not at all."

In the morning, after saying goodbye to Paul's family, we knock on his mother's door to thank her for the use of her garden. A tiny little thing, she motions us inside for coffee, tea and cookies and I can't imagine her being angry with anyone. But when she shows us her photo album, she points to her daughters and grandchildren with pride but not to her son. Finally, I point him out in one group shot. "Paul?" I ask.

"*Ja*," she says stiffly. Her husband, a large, lumpy man, comes into the room to sit with a thump on a kitchen chair, arms folded across his chest, saying nothing. When we leave, the old woman hugs and kisses us with tears in her eyes, but when I try to embrace her husband, he pushes me away.

Chapter 18

IT'S MY DAY TO lead and I'm looking for Holland and its famous bike paths. I find Holland, but the bike paths are another story. Along the roads, little bicycle signs point toward a specific village, and a bike path meanders off by itself through the fields, safe and peaceful. But I can't find on the map the villages where the paths lead, and if we don't know where we're going, at least we need to know where we are. We skip the bike paths.

At Zundert, we exchange travelers' checks for Dutch *guilders*. "I'm still trying to mentally convert French *francs* to Belgian *francs*," I groan. But getting used to a new currency isn't hard once we get a conversion ratio into our heads. We only need to convert one way, from the new currency to our own, and only if we want to understand the price in American money. If so, we take the foreign price and divide by however-many-whatevers there are to a dollar. In France, for example, we divided the French price by six; in Belgium, by thirty-seven. Now, in the Netherlands, we divide by two. In England and Scotland, we had to multiply.

The trick is not to need to convert, to understand what prices mean in the currency of whatever country we're in. After awhile, we can think in its own terms, money or language. Each time we cross a border, we mentally convert our daily allowance into that currency and make budget decisions based on a hundred and twenty French *francs* or ten British pounds or whatever. Dollars become irrelevant.

The same for language. Instead of thinking the English word and then translating, we just think of the French word, or the Spanish. Conversation is getting quite odd among ourselves, sprinkled with whatever foreign word comes to mind. A new language is much easier to learn in its midst.

Now, newly in the midst of Dutch, we stop for groceries in Breda. A woman stands behind a counter, vegetables at her back, and it's up to us to tell her what we want. With no idea how to ask for a tomato in Dutch, or any other vegetable for that matter, we point and gesture and name vegetables in German and French until a woman standing off to the side translates one of the languages into Dutch.

Self-service markets aren't necessarily easier. Most have computerized scales that price vegetables—after pushing a button with the name and picture of the vegetable, out pops a sticker to attach to the bag, noting the name of the vegetable and the total price. But the faded pictures on the scales don't always resemble the vegetables, and the written description is helpful only if we know the language. Once in Spain, Clarke went in for plums and paid for dates. Another time, Kelly was turned back at a checkout stand in France for pricing mushrooms as garlic and carrots as beans; mortified, she vowed she'd never buy another vegetable in a foreign country.

About seven o'clock, I see after studying the map that we'll be on a major highway all the way to Rotterdam, so we decide to stay somewhere along the small farm road leading away from the noisy highway. After knocking at the door of a dairy farm, thirteen-year-old Carin and her friend Chantal give us permission to camp. "What about your parents?" I ask.

"They won't be home until very late," Carin answers, scrambling over the pasture fence to move a horse and two calves to an adjacent field so that we can park our tents near the house.

After dinner, Carin and Chantal invite us in for soft drinks. "I'll join you in a few minutes," I say. I've just pulled out the computer, determined to work on my journal. It's taken several tries to make it function and I'm not about to quit while I'm ahead. I write until after dark, holding our tiny flashlight in my teeth.

Joining the others in the cozy living room, I find four girls and Clarke comfortably scrunched in overstuffed chairs. Carin and Chantal seem totally at ease with strangers in the house, oblivious to possible danger, unselfconscious about speaking English. As we crawl into our tents at midnight, I wonder what Carin's parents will think when they come home to see an open gate to the pasture where they usually keep animals.

In the morning, we wave to Carin's father as he crosses the field to water the horse. He waves back cheerfully. As we pack the bikes after Kelly and Megan shower inside the house, Carin comes along to say that her parents want us to come in for coffee. "No, thank you," Clarke says, grumpy that we're already getting a late start because of the girls' showers. Two minutes later, Carin returns with her father. Although Joop isn't tall, his presence is commanding. Uncommonly handsome, a Paul Newman look-alike with startling blue eyes, he says two or three words to make it clear that he wants us to accept his invitation, then turns to lead us into the house, assuming victory. We follow like lambs, even Clarke.

Joop leans back at the breakfast table, nodding satisfaction that he performed his mission. And then he smiles at me, nodding again, and the sparkle from his eyes tumbles like waterfalls in sunshine. I melt into a big, fat puddle and compose another postcard: *Sorry, folks, I've left Clarke for a Dutchman who already has a lovely wife.*

Although Joop claims not to speak English, forgotten words return after a few rusty sentences. "Where are you going in such a rush?" he demands as we finish our coffee and biscuits.

"Rotterdam," I respond. "We haven't decided about Amsterdam. Everyone tells us that it's very dangerous to take bikes there, but that hasn't stopped us before."

"It should this time. Amsterdam is very beautiful and you must go, but you must not take your bicycles. Go by train for the day." Not used to moving fast, we hadn't planned on deciding about Amsterdam for another day. On bicycles, route decisions can be mulled over for miles without missing anything. Joop senses our hesitation. "I will call about the fare. Sit."

Round trip for four is fifty dollars, but we justify the expenditure by saying that it will cost that much in food to bicycle there. "Too bad we didn't decide this before we took down our tents," Kelly says.

"You will manage," Joop declares. "We will take you to the station now."

"Isn't he gorgeous?" I whisper to the girls as we walk our bikes to the barn.

"For an old guy, I guess," Kelly concedes, "but he must be forty."

Joop gestures us toward his car as we lean our bikes against a trailer filled with windsurf boards. "My family is going windsurfing tomorrow. Do you know how?"

"No," we admit.

"You must learn. You will come with us."

At Rotterdam, an announcement in Dutch is made over a public address system inside the train, and everyone moves toward the doors. We look around helplessly. "There is something wrong with the train," a woman stops to tell us. "You must get off and take another one."

"How will we know which one?" Megan asks Clarke.

"Beats me," Clarke replies, but we follow some people from our car when they get on another train.

As the express train pulls into Amsterdam, we discover an old city of beautiful canals and architecture and graffiti. Although its central train station is reputedly the most dangerous place in the city at night because of thieves and drug dealers, during the day it's a kaleidoscope of young people traveling in and out of Amsterdam to gather big time fun. Like a Club Med for students, Amsterdam is an international hodgepodge of every language and style. The kids have long hair, ponytails, mohawks, no hair and hair of every color, particularly purple and orange; beads and leather and short skirts and baggy pants and rags; earrings and nose studs and tattoos and chains; boots and bare feet. They carry backpacks and satchels and string bags, and go in and out of the station in droves.

Out in the sunshine, we pass through crowded streets of sex shops, souvenir stands, punk clothing stores and American fast food joints, looking for a real bank to exchange money. At a small takeout shop, we buy sandwiches. Two well-dressed American women wait in line ahead of us. "What will that buy?" one woman says, pushing a fistful of guilders into the waiter's hands. "I can't wait to get back to the States," she turns to her friend. "I just can't deal with foreign currency." I resist the urge to tell her to divide by two as the young man patiently gets her sandwich and returns most of the money with a shake of his head.

We find the Anne Frank house on a beautiful, quiet canal in the middle of town, the international teen jet set left near the station. A steep flight of Dutch stairs takes us to where this brave Jewish family had hidden for two years during the Holocaust and a thirteen-year-old girl immortalized their fear in her diary. At the end of the tour is a room with pictures of Anne and her family, the SS roster where their names were listed when they were captured and a photo of a pile of bodies at the concentration camp where Anne and her sister died of typhus.

Quiet and introspective, we spend another hour walking the crazy streets of Amsterdam. I groan as we pass yet another herd of teenagers. "I've never felt so old in my life. The only two other people over twenty-five in this city are the women who tried to buy six dollars worth of sandwiches with a hundred bucks."

Back at the station, the swarm of young people veers past a body lying prostrate on the cobblestones. Judging from his face and balding head, it's a middle-aged man, although his body looks much younger, hard and trim and tan. Wearing only a cloth wrapped like a turban around his loins, he lies motionless on the stones, eyes closed, expression peaceful, arms crossed over his chest. "What a place to meditate," Clarke says with admiration.

"Are you sure he's not dead?" I ask.

The next day is warm and sunny, and the windsurfing lesson is a great change from sweaty bicycling. Kelly is first to try, on a broad board with a big sail. "She should use a smaller board at first," Joop's wife Ineke tells me as Carin and Joop give her instructions. The big sail pulls against the wind and Kelly; she falls into the water, sputtering, then crawls up onto the slippery board, standing to pull up the heavy, wet sail. Then down she goes again. It's hard work, but she sticks to it, determined to give it her best shot. Usually, like me, if she doesn't get it right the first time, she loses interest. We both hate learning curves, thinking we should have been born perfect.

Megan grabs hold of a smaller board and does well, no doubt to Kelly's dismay. Clarke takes a short ride too, but seems more interested in watching a topless young woman try her own luck on a board near the shore. Then I give it a try, nervous about looking clumsy in front of Joop and the girls. "Come on, Susan," Kelly says as if reading my mind. "I made a fool of myself. You can too." But I quickly balance on the small board, pull up the sail and walk around the mast. "I hate you," Kelly shouts from the shore.

But I don't have a clue how to catch the wind to navigate. At the mercy of the windsurf gods, I'm taken to the far end of the lake with the ducks. Finally, Joop comes to my rescue on his big board, expertly tacking back and forth in front of me, moving swiftly, demonstrating, coaching, laughing when I becalm myself, which is always.

After the day of being clean and wet and exercising different muscles, we offer to take the family out to dinner. "It is not necessary," Joop answers, but we insist, then discover that ordering Chinese food in Dutch is more than a minor challenge. Finally, Joop points to what he usually orders. "Try it, it's *goed*," is all he'll say. I end up ordering chicken and cashews, which isn't nearly as good as Joop's pork. "See?" he points out, blue eyes twinkling as he gives me a taste from his fork. "I am right."

After three nights with this warm, fun, generous family, we know that our goodbyes will be difficult and we pack in silence the next morning. I feel lonely, thinking of pedaling off to strangers yet again, and am pleased when Joop comes to help me take down the tent. He fills our water bottles, then helps me pack my bike. As we gather to say goodbye, Joop kisses me gently and looks into my eyes as if we've known each other forever. After kisses and photographs all around, the family stands in the driveway waving until we're out of sight, and although it feels like my heart has been broken again, I know it's because it's too full to hold all of my happiness.

At breakfast, we'd decided to head toward Germany. "You must go to Maastricht," Joop had commanded. And of course we agreed, allowing him to plot a route back into Belgium, then to Maastricht in a little finger of Holland that points down between Belgium and Germany.

It's raining lightly when we go into a café for meat rolls because the markets are closed; by the time we finish our small meal and pedal a few kilometers, the rain explodes into a downpour. Unable to find shelter, we pedal on, soaked and frozen. At times, it rains too hard to see and the wind pelts the rain into our faces like needles. When Megan has trouble with her freewheel, we pull under some trees for adjustments as rain soaks through the branches and falls in great blobs on our heads. We manage seventy-five kilometers before stopping. "Look for a barn," I say, teeth chattering. "I refuse to sleep in the mud tonight."

"There's one," Kelly says finally, and we ask for permission to put our tents inside.

"Of course," Eddie says after conferring with his father. The barn is filled with automobiles instead of hay, Clarke and his allergies are relieved to discover, and we have plenty of room for our tents and to string bungee cords from post to post for our wet clothes.

I couldn't be Kelly and Megan on this trip. Their tent leaks, their sleeping bags aren't warm and get wet every time the tent does. Megan has no sleeping mat. And they always manage to leave things out in the rain at night. But then, why not? It's just as wet inside their tent as under a waterfall, come to think of it. Megan's clothes have been damp, dirty and stale for weeks. One day, I'd asked her why. "No washing machine," she shrugged, apparently thinking that anything larger than underwear or a t-shirt can't be washed by hand.

When I sit on the ground, I try to sit on one of our tattered fluorescent raincoats to keep my shorts clean as long as possible; the girls just sit, and use their jackets as cutting boards. Even when they do wash something, they forget to hang it out to dry on the bikes or at our next stop, leaving it in plastic bags to mold.

Kelly would arrive complete with wet sleeping bag at someone's house on a warm, sunny day. Instead of spreading out her bag to dry, she'd leave it rolled up until bedtime and then get mad when she had to sleep in a soppy bag another night. But in spite of all their discomfort, much of it self-imposed, they seem to survive amazingly well and to keep their amazing senses of humor. "How come you didn't invest in better gear?" I had asked soon after they arrived. "You could have stayed less time but been a lot more comfortable for the same money."

"How were we supposed to know it rained in Europe in the summer?" Kelly had replied.

In the morning, Eddie's father arrives at the barn with hot coffee and a dozen huge tomatoes from his garden, ripe and perfect, and we pedal away from the farm in light rain. At lunchtime, we spot a bridge over a canal. At the moment, the sky is dry. "Let's duck under there to eat before it rains again," Clarke suggests. As I make tomato sandwiches on the ground, bicyclists pass us along the canal, waving and ringing their bike bells. Another group passes along the other side. "These are bike paths," Clarke exclaims. "Let's see if they go where we're headed." They do, and we follow them the rest of the day, flat and straight as arrows. Container boats float up and down the waterways, long barges made home by white lace curtains and hanging plants and flowers in the pilots' cabins. One has a big tomato plant tucked behind the front window.

Late in the day, Megan gets a flat and ruins her inner tube trying to fix it. "Why didn't you ask for help?" Clarke asks, irritated.

"Because you're always telling us that you're tired of doing things for us. Make up your mind."

As we pedal off, Megan's freewheel starts to rattle again. We've left replacing my freewheel up to Kelly since she used my spare outside of Paris, but anxious to get to Germany, she'd decided not to look for a bike store in Belgium. Now it looks as if Megan will need one of her own.

"We're ready to stop for the night," they announce after sixty kilometers, choosing farms off the canal as likely candidates. None of them is accessible from the canal, however, and I get tired of their grumbling as we pass each one.

"So why don't we get off the canal?"

"Quit telling us what to do, Susan," Megan snaps, but takes the next road off and finds a small group of houses. "Let's try here," she says. "This house looks like my grandmother's."

The woman who comes outside smiles as she wipes her hands on a threadbare blue apron, but acts frightened when we ask for permission to camp. It's the first time we feel totally unable to communicate with someone–in retrospect, of course, the four of us hadn't communicated well for the last couple of hours so we shouldn't be surprised. It's clear that the woman wants us to leave, and I lead the way down the block, secretly blaming our failure on Megan's poor choice of houses instead of on our own negativity.

I choose another house, and luckily the owner speaks English. "I am sorry," the young man says, however, "but my wife and I are leaving very early in the morning for a bicycle trip of our own. I have a neighbor who might take you in, though. Wait here, please."

"We should be asking for ourselves," Clarke says, and we hurry down the block after the young man. But we've already been accepted, sight unseen–it's probably just as well–and find that we're to be given not only flat, soft grass for our tents and a shed for the bicycles, but also a kitchen and a bath with shower.

"We built a separate house in back for university students through the school year," Gerard explains in English. "We would give you bedrooms too, but the students have left their clothes behind for the holiday."

Grouchiness forgotten, we hurry to put up our tents, hang wet clothes and sleeping bags on the line, and prepare dinner in our very own kitchen complete with real plates, glasses and silverware, pans and a four-burner stove. It's our first kitchen in five and a half months, and we take turns making omelettes so we can each enjoy the luxury of modern cooking. Gerard's handsome son bursts into the kitchen several times–first with eggs that we boil for the next day, then with an offer to use the barbecue, and last with an invitation to the house after dinner. And, of course, all three times, to flirt with Kelly and Megan.

Reluctant to give up our comfy kitchen, we go inside for Belgian chocolates and beer and an opinion from Gerard about the best places to visit in Germany, complete with leaflets for our later perusal. When we ask about where Bavaria is located, Gerard says, "That place is not in Germany, although I may have heard of it. It must be in the Far East somewhere, or in Holland, where people are very sneaky."

We mention how much trouble we've had communicating in Flemish and Dutch. "Even when we think we've learned a word," Clarke explains, "no one seems to understand our accent."

"Ah," says Gerard. "It is because Belgium has many, many dialects. Even Belgians can't understand each other. We all study ABN, which is like a BBC Dutch, but no one will speak it."

"Why not?" I ask, amazed.

"Village pride. My wife and I came from villages five kilometers apart and cannot understand each other's dialects. With each other and our children, we speak ABN."

Back outside, we discover that it's been raining. Kelly's almost-dry sleeping bag is now soaked. "While you screech," I say, frustrated that my own clothes are wet, "I'll take a shower so there'll be more time in the morning for everyone else." When I come out of the shower, Kelly is curled up on the hard floor outside the bathroom.

The next morning, Megan comes outside wearing her jacket, which is dripping water. "I left it outside in the rain last night," she explains, "so decided I might as well wash it."

"Where to?" Clarke asks.

"We're hungry," Kelly announces.

"I think we'd better think about a bike shop today," I say.

Clarke studies the map. "We can be in Maastricht in about an hour."

"I can't wait that long for food," Megan says.

"Then we'll have to leave the canals and go to Genk," Clarke sighs. "It's out of our way, but you guys are the bosses."

By the time we wind through Genk in heavy traffic, exchange Dutch *guilders* for Belgian *francs* again, buy groceries, then find a bike shop, it's closed for lunch. "Let's wait here and eat lunch," I suggest. "We've ridden this far out of our way, we might as well accomplish something." I've planned egg salad sandwiches with Belgian waffles and jam for dessert. As I unpack the food, planning that we'll each peel our own egg to speed up the preparations, Kelly and Megan pounce on the waffles. "Can't you two wait five minutes for lunch?" I snarl. "Why can't you help fix it, anyway?" Kelly and Megan stop chewing to look at me with big eyes.

"What difference does it make if they eat their dessert first?" Clarke comes to their defense.

"Because I'd like a little help. While they're eating dessert, I'm the one who's making lunch. Can't they each peel a stupid egg?"

"I'll do the dishes," Megan says to appease me. It doesn't.

Piling lunch in front of the others, I sit alone on a low wall. "So eat," I order.

Kelly spills a quart of milk on the sidewalk, and we use all of our water to clean up the mess. "Now I can't wash the dishes," Megan announces smugly.

"Oh, yes you can," I reply, stomping off to the nearest house for water. Our entire morning has accomplished only one more feeding frenzy. Eating is getting to be a pain, I decide, then wait in silence, crouched against the wall, for Megan to clean up the dishes.

When the bike shop opens, Clarke buys freewheels for Kelly and Megan while they write and sketch in their journals. At this point, I won't do anything for either one of them, even if it means helping Clarke, so I stay outside, muttering, and compose another mental postcard: *Free to good home, two teenaged American women. Housebroken but untrainable, immediate delivery.*

Because Clarke had signed all of the travelers' checks in Antwerp, the girls had asked us to take care of their finances, so I write everything down in my little journal, grumbling. Finally, at three o'clock, we're on our way again, tool kit complete and no one complaining about hunger. Instead of it taking an hour to get to Maastricht, it's taken a day, and we pedal in silence through the beautiful city on the western edge of Holland's apostrophe between Belgium and Germany.

At a dairy farm just short of the German border, we stop for the night. Unfortunately, the rains from the past few days have made the pastures a mire of mud and manure but the young farmer offers a tiny shed for the bikes. Megan squishes through the slimy manure wearing the tennis shoes that had split when she fell from her bike near Calais. "Eeeeoo, eeeeoo, eeeeoo," she groans. "There's cow shit oozing between my toes."

Tucking the bikes in the shed filled with old farm implements, dusty hay, wood, plastic tarps and spider webs, Kelly and Megan announce that they're starving again, so we hurry to set up camp. As Clarke and I put up our tent, Kelly screams. It's a dead blackbird, stuck on the electric fence behind the girls' tent. But when Kelly and Megan move their tent away from the carcass, strong winds bounce it down the mucky hill like a tumbleweed, and by the time the girls rescue it, its green sides are camouflaged with muddy manure. When it begins to rain again, hard, Clarke and I scramble inside our tent. "Can we come in too?" Kelly asks meekly, peeking through the flap.

"No," I say, still angry about the detour and lunch. "You're muddy and wet and I don't want our tent smelling like yours." Clarke looks at me sharply, and I shrug. "They've got to learn to take care of themselves, Clarke. Why should we pay for their leaving their stuff outside in the rain?" Poor Kelly and Megan slosh to the shed, heads down, miserable.

"Dinner!" I call and they run to get it, squishing through the muddy field back to the shed to eat under a roof. Finally feeling guilty, I trudge through the rain to take them second helpings. They're standing up. "Why don't you sit down?" I ask.

"Because there may be awfuls under the woodpile," Kelly says, shuddering.

Chapter 19

IN THE MORNING, AS they roll up their dripping tent, Kelly and Megan watch us stuff our dry sleeping bags into their waterproof pouches. "A shark circled our tent all night," Kelly says.

When we cross the German border mid-morning, the road bends uphill after flat cycling in northern France, Belgium and Holland. No more seventy kilometers after lunch, I bet, realizing that it's time to get better organized—it's August 2nd, and Kelly and Megan plan to leave from Munich on August 21st.

In Aachen, we transition into country number eight by exchanging money—this time, Belgian *francs* for *deutschmarks*—memorizing the new exchange rate, learning part of a new language before grocery shopping, buying new maps. Kelly and Megan cash the last of their original travelers' checks. "We'll use this money for our personal stuff," they decide, "if you'll still keep track of our joint expenses every week."

Clarke's digging in his pack when Kelly and I go into a market, expecting him to follow with our cash. He doesn't. Finally, I find him outside. "What are you doing?" I ask.

"Looking for something," he snaps, rummaging through his disorganized packs.

"We'll need you before we can pay for the groceries, Clarke. What kind of fruit do you want for lunch?" He ignores me and I return to the store. When he still hasn't come in by the time we're ready to pay for our food, I go back outside, working up a good snit in the process.

"He walked down the street," Megan tells me.

When he returns ten minutes later, I ask through gritted teeth, "If you didn't want to help buy groceries, why didn't you give us some money?"

"It doesn't take three people to buy groceries."

"No, but it does take money." I bite out the syllables. "It's too complicated for all of us to carry cash—I'm the one who has to keep track of expenses. Why do you always have to make everything so difficult?"

"Why does everything have to be your way, Susan?" Why can't this trip be fun, I wonder as we eat lunch on a bench.

"After just a year of German, I can actually read some of the signs in the shop windows," Kelly exclaims, ignoring our fuss.

"Good for you," I reply. "The rest of us don't know a word." Burrowing my way through a fat sandwich, I change the subject. "Does anyone mind if I take a few minutes to write?" I'd bought a spiral notebook a few days back after the computer refused to work again.

"Are you sending the computer home?" Clarke asks hopefully.

"I haven't decided."

We leave town at three o'clock after trying in vain to call Jill about Kelly and Megan's airline reservations. "Why would we get a busy signal?" Kelly asks. "It's seven in the morning in Denver."

It's my turn to lead and I have a devil of a time with the new German map. Near the edge of Aachen, I ask Clarke for help. "It's not my day to lead," he says, refusing. We're both still angry about the grocery store stupidity. Now I know how Megan had felt about her flat tire; the message from Clarke seems to be "ask for help so that I can say no." I pedal on, frustrated at our pettiness.

An hour later, still somewhere on the outskirts of Aachen, Kelly's bike breaks down on a bridge over the railroad tracks. It's her lower bracket, the same problem that plagued Clarke in Spain. While Kelly looks up words in her German dictionary, I stride off to look for someone who can speak English, into efficiency instead of language practice. By the time Kelly puts together a question in German, I have directions to the nearest bicycle store. Unlike Megan in France, Kelly is trying to participate but I don't give her the chance. "I'll meet you at the bike shop," Megan announces. "I'm going to the post office."

"What if you get lost?" Clarke asks. "You don't speak German."

"I'm not going to get lost," she replies, offended.

Kelly's bike is fixed in twenty minutes. While we wait for Megan, Clarke shows the bike mechanic his own cracked bracket. "There is nothing wrong with it," the German says.

"Yes, there is. See the crack?"

"It is fine."

"What could be keeping Megan?" Clarke asks, giving up.

"She's lost, of course," I predict. "I can't believe we turned her loose in a strange city where she can't speak a word of the language. She may think she's hot stuff, but that doesn't mean that she is."

"I'll ride back to the post office." Clarke offers after another half an hour. "You two stay here in case she shows up."

There's a pay phone on the corner, and Kelly and I try again to call Jill without success. Then Clarke pedals up with Megan. "She was lost," he tells us. Megan shrugs, apparently unconcerned about our wait and worry. It's six o'clock; it's taken all day just to dip our toes into Germany.

We'd been told in Belgium that Germany has few bike paths, so I try to find safe passage away from the major highways, looking for a small road marked on the map as scenic. Unfortunately, the roads don't seem to match the maps and we finally run into a group of hikers at the edge of a forest. Kelly asks them in German for directions to the road we want, and each of them talks to each of us all at once. At our looks of confusion, they talk louder, gesturing and yelling directions. Clarke, Megan and I nod dumbly, totally lost, knowing that we've understood all we can, which is nothing. Further explanations are lost on us. "I think we're on the right road," Kelly says finally.

"Now what?" Megan asks after the hikers trot off.

"It's about twenty kilometers to Langerwehe," I reply.

"Let's stop here for the night," Megan says.

We pedal back to the last houses we passed and pick a tidy little home with a flat garden. All four of us go up to the front door. "*Dürfen wir in deinem Garten schlafen fur ein nacht?*" Kelly asks.

The middle-aged man looks from one to the other of us, then shakes his head no. "I live alone," he explains in German and English, "and leave for work in the morning at six. I'm sorry, but it is not possible for you to stay here."

We explain a bit more about our trip and he reconsiders. "Please, do not say yes unless you want to," I tell him, sensing his discomfort.

He looks relieved. "I am sorry."

"Let's go back to the house on the corner," Clarke suggests as we regroup on the street. "The one with the Mercedes in the garage."

"A few months ago, Clarke, you'd never suggest staying at a house with an expensive car," I note, surprised at his change of heart.

It's a big house with a swimming pool in back, and Clarke goes to the door with Kelly happily in tow. The owners listen patiently to Kelly's request to camp, then call their daughter, a tall slender nymph with masses of auburn hair. Dressed in purple, she's breathtaking. "My father says you may stay here as long as you like," Astrid translates. "He will take his car out of the garage so that you can put your bicycles safely inside, and we have a summer house in back that has a table. We have a toilet and shower that you are welcome to use too, and Mother wants to know if you would like some beer."

Our spirits are instantly elevated, the stress of a new country forgotten, and as we tuck into the little summer house to enjoy eating at a table instead of in our laps, Astrid brings her older sister outside. "Mother told me to come quickly because there were four Canadians in the backyard," Susan laughs, then invites us in for tea after dinner.

"We are not Canadians," I explain to Hans and Ursula, Susan and Astrid's parents, when we go inside. "Is it still okay if we stay?"

Hans laughs uproariously when Astrid translates my question. "*Ja!*" he exclaims, then apologizes for not being able to speak English. He asks many questions about us and our trip; several times, as we describe life on the road in strange countries, Ursula's eyes fill with tears. "You have much courage, great spiritual strength and a great love for the people of the world," Hans says finally. "This trip is a very difficult undertaking."

Always when someone compliments our courage, we start to protest. Then something stops us. "Thank you," Clarke says simply.

"We don't mind being strangers in the world," I add, touched by the German's comments, "because we're able to make friends with people like you."

When I explain that I may write a book about our journey, Hans asks a question. "Father wants to know if you knock on doors at night as a trick to see what people will do," Susan translates, "as material for the book."

I look directly at Hans. "We knock on doors so that we can meet people and so that we can afford to live on our bicycles for a year."

Tears well in his eyes as Susan translates my answer. "You have great love," he says again.

The next morning, as I walk through the garage to the bathroom, Kelly is curled up on the cement floor. "Sleeping bag still wet?" I ask.

"Three guesses."

Breakfast is compliments of our hosts—cold cuts, cheese, tomatoes, juice, rolls, tea and coffee—and as we finish, one by one the family asks permission to join us for more conversation. Too soon, we're ready to leave, and after delaying our departure with photographs and hugs and kisses on the front porch, goodbyes are said with tears all around.

It's a glorious morning and with Megan in the lead, we ride through a beautiful green forest, pedaling through several kilometers of tiny green frogs that hop back and forth on the road as we pass. They remind me of the chicken feet in Spain, except that these guys are still attached to their bodies.

Megan keeps getting lost, and after Clarke's refusal to look at the map the day before, asks for my assistance. "It's the blind leading the blind," I laugh, but we get from one place to the other in spite of Clarke's complaints that we'll never make it to Munich if we don't make better progress. Trying to find a direct route is almost impossible. The Germans may have built the *autobahns* for efficiency, but these little roads go around and about like scribbles. "Let's skip Köln and turn south to Bonn," I suggest finally. Big cities always seem to take up a day, no matter what, even if we don't sightsee.

"As long as I get to ride along the Rhein," Kelly says.

"Coming up," Megan replies as she and I try to back into a route to the river.

Late in the afternoon, we discover a medium-sized road that parallels the famous river, and turning south, pedal a few kilometers without seeing water. In Widdig, a man directs us to turn left, and sure enough, there's the Rhein, all ours, with no cars, compliments of a perfectly lovely paved bicycle path right next to the water.

Pedaling back up to town after seventy kilometers, we look for shelter. Nothing looks right—perhaps after our perfect evening the night before, nothing can. We ask a couple walking down the street about a place to stay and they suggest that we camp by the river. Eager to share the evening with another family, we try to explain that we try to stay with families each night. Kelly, anxious to understand and be understood, uses infinitives when she can't conjugate her verbs, not caring how she sounds, only that she communicates. Megan watches her in silence. Finally, the man offers to ask for us at a nearby farm. It isn't his own house, but we appreciate the gesture. We're refused, and go on. We find a woman in her garden who will hardly speak to us other than to say no. "This is a bad place," she says.

Disappointed and tired, we decide to try one more house before going back to the river. "There's a farm in those trees," I point. "Let's try there." The girls and I pedal off, then turn to find Clarke making word pictures in the air in front of a middle-aged man. We pedal back.

"I know of a place you can stay," the man says, pointing to an empty field next to a fenced pasture a few doors from his own unoffered garden.

Trying to find a level spot in the vacant lot for our tents, we lean our bikes into the spindly bushes. It looks like rain. "We're getting spoiled by garages," I say, hanging the clothes I'd washed in the morning on twigs, hoping they'll dry a bit before the storm. Kelly and Megan fling things about in their usual abandoned style, and I know that if it rains they'll never get their stuff inside without everything getting wet.

Across the fence, a man sits near a small stable watching us with amusement. Finally, he comes over to the fence, and in a mixture of German and gestures, explains that it's going to rain. "*Ja, danke,*" I say to him. So what do you suggest we do about it, I say to myself.

"You had better stay in my barn," he continues.

By the time we stow our packs in an empty horse stall, Sepp returns with his wife Sepella. Building a bench in front of our tent with crates, he arranges himself and his wife on it with a smile. Neither speaks English but they want to visit, and Kelly rises to the challenge, her desire for perfection apparently forgotten, asking them to repeat words or to say things another way until she understands, giggling when she makes a mistake of her own. Sepp and Sepella love her.

It's getting dark. Megan's not happy; she can't understand a word of the conversation and doesn't seem to care to communicate in any way, perhaps jealous of Kelly's willingness to converse or realizing how much she missed in France because of her own reluctance. Another neighbor, Wilhelm, appears—then another, an East Indian Sikh named Bobby who, he said, had left his country because of religious persecution. Megan withdraws even more. I feel little sympathy; after all, the rest of us are doing just what we came to Europe to do. Why had Megan come?

Bobby translates into English a question from Sepella. Would we like wine? Taking pity on Megan, I ask him to explain that we have to prepare supper before dark. Sepella answers that she will bring the wine to us and it will take only a minute to drink. As they leave, we dive into the food preparation, chopping vegetables, discovering that we've lost the German sausage on which we splurged at the market. "I hope we don't find it in Megan's moldy clothes en route to the airport," I smile.

"Eeeeoo, eeeeoo, eeeeoo," Kelly answers, thrilled with her success in communicating with real Germans in their own language.

Wilhelm returns with a gift of his own, explaining that the fresh eggs are special. "They're from happy chickens," I say finally, understanding at last that they're from hens allowed to roam instead of being confined in coops. Wilhelm laughs, nodding that I'd understood.

Along come Sepp and Sepella, arms full of bags. In addition to German white wine and mineral water which they mix half-and-half for Kelly and Megan and themselves, they bring crackers, and for Clarke and me, cognac. And six real glasses. The rain holds off until they leave us with goodnight kisses and an invitation for breakfast.

Early the next morning, breakfast is waiting inside their small house—breads and homemade marmalade, tea and coffee. Eating hurriedly, we walk Sepella to the turnoff for the train station and watch her run down the path, kindness streaming behind her like a bright ribbon.

Although the morning is cloudy and gray, we enjoy pedaling along the quiet bike path. At Bonn, we take a ferry to the east side of the river to have a better view of the famous city. Then, we pedal through a giant greenbelt park with miles of separate bike paths and pedestrian walks, cars distant as a memory, the silence a blanket of peace.

A family of white swans nestles next to the path. As Kelly passes first, one of the birds reaches out its neck and hisses, ready to grab her foot. When Megan pedals by, the swan strikes at her bike like a snake. "Ride by again, Megan, so that Clarke can take a picture," I call ahead.

"That's not fair," Clarke admonishes me. "He's just trying to protect his family." So Clarke and I, talking softly to the swans, make a wide berth around as Papa glares and hisses under his breath.

It's a glorious afternoon. Clouds tatter across the sun to make light and shadow checkerboards on our day as tour boats from Holland and Belgium and Germany bob down the Rhein like tall white blocks, and gray container boats and military craft slide flat and silent in the water. A family of ducks cuts the current like tiny boats one after the other.

"Stop!" Clarke yells, and we turn to find him in a blueberry thicket. Half an hour later, we return scratched and bleeding to the bikes with blue tongues and teeth and a plastic bag of dessert, stopping at the next town to buy cream. There, Megan decides that she wants to quit for the night. "It's only four o'clock," Clarke complains.

"I'm hungry," she answers.

"How many blueberries did you eat half an hour ago?" I ask. "Instead of stopping the whole circus for the night, why don't you just eat another snack and we'll go on?"

Megan agrees reluctantly and she and Kelly wolf down crackers and cheese from lunch. I'd planned to eat my crackers while cooking dinner but decide they won't exist by then, so Clarke and I join in the little feeding flurry while tourists detour around us on the crowded sidewalk. Megan's angry when we pedal off, and stays that way. Three hours later, I apologize for not letting her stop. "We broke our word, Megan. I'm sorry." She grunts.

Next to a cooling tower, we discover a scruffy farm with no visible means of support except for a large room full of stale bread rolls. The place is like Dogpatch, rundown and ragtag, totally unlike the pristine cleanliness that we'd found so far in Germany, but we're allowed to pitch our tents in a vacant field behind the house under the watchful eye of the tower. "I'm sure it's nuclear," Kelly says. "We'll all be dead by morning."

I consider putting a postcard under my sleeping bag like a suicide note: *We were killed by a nuclear accident. Our purple tongues are not evidence that will be helpful in investigating this matter.*

"I've lost an earring," Megan announces after dinner.

"Oh, my God," Kelly mimics horrendous panic, "the girl's lost an earring! Call out the light brigade!" Immediately, Kelly's teasing deteriorates into impromptu theater. "What is it about you, earring, that makes you not want to participate today?" she continues, striding around like Clarke. "I'm Susan, earring. Please, please, don't get upset and leave us. We like you, honest!"

For an hour, we play each other's parts, laughing and screaming and throwing things around the vacant lot. Both Kelly and Megan portray me as Miss Fluffy, backing up whatever Clarke says, fluttering about to keep the peace. Clarke, on the other hand, plays me as a control freak, a strong Type A, male-dominant personality, and I wonder if he accuses me of being controlling to encourage me to be a compliant wife to his authoritarian husband. If his ploy is working, no wonder I'm so frustrated most of the time.

In Koblenz, the market is closing for lunch, but a customer directs us to a store up the street that stays open another half hour. "After that store closes, nothing will be open again until Monday morning, you know."

We look at each other, horrified. "If the stores close at noon Friday in Germany," Kelly groans, "we'll starve before Monday." Normally, we shop for food twice a day except for weekends, when we have to buy enough for a day and a half on Saturday. It isn't easy.

Racing up the street, we load up with everything we can carry. The bikes look like elephants; every corner and crack is filled to overflowing; plastic bags hang from our handlebars and packs in the back; the bucket over my front tire is filled with fruit and vegetables. Pulling my little calendar notebook from my frame pack, I start to write down the cost of our purchases. "It's not Friday. It's Saturday."

"Oh boy, more to eat," Kelly says happily.

Whatever day of the week it is, it's beautiful. The sky is clear, bright blue and the warm sun on our backs pushes us along like a gentle hand. As we wind through riverside villages, our path threads through pocket parks like a needle and thread tying town to town at the edge of the Rhein. We stop at a chessboard laid in stone patterns in a little overlook. Two-foot-high chessmen are lined up on each side, ready to play, so Clarke and I start a game while the girls look for a public restroom.

Late in the afternoon, outside Oberwesel, we find a terraced garden leading up the mountainside and knock on the door of a white two-story house set with its back against the hill. A woman sticks her head out of an upstairs window, stern and suspicious. "*Einen Augenblick,*" she says, just a minute, after Kelly attempts to communicate a request to camp. Closing the front door carefully behind her, she comes out on her front porch and Kelly's sincere attempts to converse win her over. "*Ja, das ist okay,*" she agrees with a smile and turns to go inside, stopping, her hand grasping the doorknob. It's locked. Cheeks pink, she turns, hands over her mouth, eyes wide with embarrassment.

Clarke races to her rescue, jogging down the stairs to retrieve a mostly-toothless twenty-foot ladder that he'd seen by the road. Leaning it against her balcony, he climbs up as far as he can, then Megan climbs on his shoulders to reach the two remaining rungs and crawls over the balcony, careful not to upset the potted flowers as our hostess watches, hands clasped in her starched white apron. In a flash, Megan is down the stairs to fling open the front door, earning us an invitation for coffee.

Around Irene's kitchen table, we learn German words. Kelly and Irene get along famously, and Megan joins in too, her appetite for participation perhaps whetted by her good deed. After coffee and biscuits, we go outside to find places for the tents. As we eat dinner, Irene's son Hans invites Kelly and Megan to a local disco. "What'll we wear?" they ask, looking at each other and their dirty legs. Neither has clean clothes, par for the course. I'm sure that they would love to wear my Paris dress, wrinkled or not, but which one will I loan it to? Besides, I think, whatever I loan them will never come back clean. Kelly had returned the shorts she'd worn to the beach without washing them. After Megan appears in a brief halter top, Hans gives her one of his own t-shirts to pull over it, and Kelly goes dirty but decent.

As Clarke and I climb into our tent, alone for once, I start a conversation. "I'm too tired to talk tonight, Susan. Besides, most of our communication is meaningless."

The next day is the first anniversary of our meadow reception, the party we'd given a month after we were married by a judge in Clarke's hometown. I have a bottle of wine in my pack that I'd hoped to save for the occasion because the stores will be closed, but when Clarke reaches for it, I keep quiet, certain that I know his response: "What are you afraid of?... Are you into scarcity?... Anniversaries don't mean anything anyway.... We may be dead tomorrow." These days, he seems to psychoanalyze every word out of our mouths. So do I.

As I retreat into my own thoughts about our uncomfortable marriage, Hans stops by our tent on the way to the disco to extend an invitation for a glass of wine with his mother. "Sure!" Clarke says enthusiastically.

"I thought you were too tired to talk," I say.

"This is different," he replies.

At this point, my German consists of, "I'm sorry, but I do not speak German. Do you speak English?" While Clarke draws Irene's portrait, I struggle with gestures and pictures and body language, too tired and hurt to enjoy the evening.

In the morning, Clarke is making a new "U.S.A." sign for his bike when I wake at seven. Kissing his shoulder, I wish him a happy anniversary. He doesn't respond. Disappointed, I write instead of reminiscing about our wedding party. As it begins to rain, I remember that I have a leak in my front tire, and since my hands aren't big enough to squeeze both brakes with one hand while I unhook the cable with the other, I ask Clarke for help. Without a word, he jerks my brakes off, then crawls back inside the tent.

While Kelly and Megan join Irene for coffee, Hans takes my tube inside to run it under water in order to locate the leak, but I have trouble with the repair. From inside the tent, Clarke watches me work and finally offers a hint or two. "Thanks," I say, frustrated. "I'm not Megan, you know. I don't mind receiving help. My self worth isn't based on being able to fix a tire in the rain."

"You want more help? I thought Hans already rescued you."

"Yes, I'd appreciate help, Clarke."

But instead he goes inside to have coffee with the others as I continue to struggle with the tire in the rain. "Irene wants you to come in for coffee," Clarke comes out to tell me.

"When I'm finished. Why did you go inside when I asked for help?"

"Because I wanted to be with Irene, of course." Angrily, he helps me finish and I go in for coffee while he and the girls pack. When I return, Clarke announces that Megan has done the dishes. "Wasn't that nice?" he says sweetly. "What an incredible woman Irene is," he continues.

Yes, I think, but what am I, a slug? "I'd hoped to spend some time this morning remembering our wedding day," I comment.

"Maybe later."

"We may be dead by then," I mimic.

It's my turn to lead, and the gray, dreary day reflects my own unhappiness as I pedal off, wrapped in misery, ignoring the others. Feeling controlled and rejected, I decide that it takes too much energy to be myself with Clarke–the price is too high. Remembering our skits the other night, I wonder if I'm allowing Clarke to perpetrate a huge manipulation. By constantly telling me to operate out of my heart instead of my mind, is he trying to get me to let him control both of our lives? When I try to express my true feelings, Clarke refuses to listen, claiming I play word games when I think I'm just trying to communicate honestly.

Keeping as much distance as possible between me and the others, I set a blistering pace, too hurt to listen to Clarke tell Kelly and Megan jokes in a British accent when he won't even be civil to me on our anniversary. "Stop! I have a flat," he yells up to me once.

Remembering his reluctance to help with my own tire that morning, I take my time going back. Why do the rest of us have to cater to Clarke just to keep the peace? "What do you want me to do?" I offer without enthusiasm.

"Nothing. Megan is already doing everything I need."

"I'm the nurse," Megan says brightly.

Goody, I say to myself, walking back to my bike to wait for the others, feeling very alone. The girls were right to characterize me as a wimp, I decide. The day before, I'd suggested that we stay in a hotel in Wiesbaden for our anniversary because on our wedding night we'd stayed in a hot springs spa in Colorado with the same name. "Too expensive," Clarke had dismissed me, and I'd dropped it. Now I don't care if we even pass through Wiesbaden; the coincidence of our being there exactly a year after our wedding seems suddenly meaningless.

As Clarke and the girls round the corner, I pedal off, still keeping space between us, unable to bear their chatter, rain washing tears from my cheeks. The bike path turns to gravel and then to mud which flies up from our tires onto our legs. We string farther apart to keep from splashing each other. It's cold. Then Clarke gets another flat and pulls into a tunnel under a road. I stand shivering, leaning against the cement wall as far from him as possible without going back into the rain, pedaling off before everyone is ready, keeping my distance, miserable. Why am I here, I ask myself over and over and over.

We arrive in Wiesbaden about six-thirty, pulling under an overhang. "Where do you want to stay tonight?" Clarke shouts over the rain.

"I don't care," I shout back. And I don't. Sitting all night in a deluge is fine with me; the last place I want to be is with Clarke, either inside a tent or in a hotel room. More than anything, I want to be left alone.

As Clarke and Kelly go inside a bar to find out if there's a cheap hotel nearby, Megan sits beside me on the curb. "You're having a pretty bad day, aren't you?" she asks gently.

"Yes."

Clarke and Kelly return running, as if they aren't already soaked to their bones. "There's a Greek hotel down the street," he tells Megan. "Let's check it out when the rain lets up." I sit on the curb, still-unchecked tears running down my face with the rain while Clarke ignores me and I ignore everyone. Finally, the rain lets up just a bit and Clarke and the girls pedal off.

"Rooms are seventy-five *deutschmarks* each, about forty dollars, including breakfast," Kelly announces when they return.

"What do you want to do, Susan?" Clarke asks, impatient.

"I said it doesn't matter and I meant it." I'm too unhappy to care. "As far as you and I are concerned, Clarke, I could spend our anniversary right here on the curb. Our marriage isn't worth a celebration." Jumping on my bike, I pedal down the street toward the hotel.

Eventually, Clarke and the girls follow. "We've just been hearing about the world according to Clarke," Megan explains when they catch up.

"Lucky you."

We check into the hotel, each pair with a room at opposite ends of a hall with a communal bath. As I soak in the deep tub, my second bath of the trip, Clarke brings me a glass of wine, then leaves without a word. Tears fall into the dirty water, now cold. "So what's going on?" he asks when I return to our room.

"I've become a doormat," I answer, "and I won't stand for it any longer. I'll give up this marriage before I'll give up me. You're not worth it."

"I won't let you leave me, no matter what. Regardless of what you think, I don't want you to give yourself up, for me or anyone else."

"It feels like you want me to accept everything you say as fact, Clarke. You hate it when I think for myself and try to make me stop by saying that my mind doesn't serve me. Well, I have a very fine mind, thank you very much. I agree that I may need to pay more attention to other areas of my life, but I don't want to get in balance by letting someone else do all of my thinking."

"Don't be ridiculous, Susan."

We don't work out any differences; instead, I just make threats about what I'll do if we don't. But at least I say my piece and he listens.

We offer to pay for the girls' dinner, and although Clarke is silent during the meal, I feel better, mostly because I'm clean and dry and warm and don't have to cook. At the moment, that means more than anything. We agree to meet for breakfast at eight-thirty although I know that the girls and I could happily sleep until noon. Wondering why we always have to hurry along just because Clarke wants to, I'm too tired to argue, emotionally drained, tired of being wet and cold, and just plain tired. Actually, I could sleep for a week.

After two bottles of wine, Clarke and I crawl into a real bed for a change and I suggest making love, hoping to bridge the distance between us. "I'm too sleepy," Clarke says, turning away.

Clarke is silent again during breakfast, and I decide to focus on something other than his moods and our problems, visiting with Kelly and Megan as if he weren't there. But when the hotel owner's son unlocks the storeroom where the bicycles spent the night, Clarke is instantly full of conversation and friendship for this stranger.

We pedal to a large shopping center to look for bike parts. "I'd like to buy a cassette player," Clarke announces after leaving Kelly and Megan in charge of the transportation team.

"I'm not interested," I reply, certain that music will give him another excuse to tune me out. When we return to the girls empty-handed, Kelly explains excitedly that they've found a travel agent.

"We asked how to sell our bikes," Megan interrupts. "We want to use that money toward our air fare home since we've spent so much. She told us to take them to the U.S. military base here."

"How on earth could you deliver them here from Munich?" I ask.

"We wouldn't have to," Kelly exclaims. "We could leave now!"

Clarke and I look at each other, dumbfounded. Kelly spent the whole summer bicycling to Germany, and now she wants to leave after only five days? Is it because of our fight? "Are you sure?" I ask.

"Absolutely."

"Then find out about air fares while we watch the bikes," Clarke tells her. He and I begin to communicate again, perhaps because we have a situation that needs our joint attention or because it's an excuse to talk without either of us having to admit that we've been less than wonderful to each other.

"Let's get two cassette players," I say when Kelly and Megan return to report that they can take a bus to Luxembourg, then fly from there to New York with three days' notice. "Something will have to keep us company if these two desert the ship." Racing back into the store, we buy the players and two tapes, classical for me and jazz for Clarke. Outside, I listen to Mozart, crying and dancing on the sidewalk, then wonder if I'm celebrating the music or the possibility of less stress because the girls are leaving. Will this help my marriage?

In a small park en route to the military base, we stop for lunch. Hunched up against a tree with my cassette player, I cry again—partly because of the beautiful music, partly because I'll miss Kelly and Megan, partly because I'm homesick myself. Kelly writes down German phrases and I tearfully thank her. "*Bitte*," she says softly, you're welcome.

Clarke keeps telling the girls that it's dumb to go to the military base to sell the bikes, but I'm delighted that they want to handle the sale themselves. As we pedal along the highway, I think about how much I'll miss them both. Much as we've been at each other for the last two months, Kelly and Megan are a part of the trip, and I cry all the way to the base. There, the soldiers tell us that they can do nothing to help and the girls decide to sell their bikes at home if they have to. "Let's make our plane reservations," Kelly suggests, but the travel agent is closed. "Mom can do it, then—it's eight hours earlier at home." Now that the decision is made, the teenagers don't want to waste another day, or another minute, and call Jill from the first pay phone. "We want to come home," Kelly says.

"The twenty-first?"

"Now."

"Is something wrong?" Kelly's previous calls have been full of their enjoyment of the trip.

"We're just homesick." Jill, no doubt bewildered, agrees to make reservations and asks Kelly to call back in the morning.

We're in downtown Wiesbaden. "Can we eat at that Burger King?" Megan points, mentally already back in the land of fast food and shopping malls. Besides, if they leave early, they'll save two weeks' expenses.

After dinner, we find our way to the edge of the city and turn right at a nature park. Deeper and deeper we pedal, with no end in sight. After sunset, we pitch our tents as inconspicuously as possible, hiding the bikes among the trees in a deep thicket. Late walkers pass as we wait to be caught trespassing. Noting the bunching clouds as we pitch our tent, Clarke and I bring all of our packs inside and suggest the same to Kelly and Megan. They ignore us, and by morning, rain has soaked everything they own—again—and they're furious—again. We pedal back into Wiesbaden to call Jill. "I haven't heard back from the travel agent," she says.

"How about taking a train to Frankfurt?" I suggest, knowing that Clarke hates inactivity. "It may be easier to sell the bikes there and maybe Jill can get you on some sort of a charter flight for a better fare than this Luxembourg deal."

"I don't want to take a train," Clarke says. "I'm here to bicycle."

"Why don't you two go on to Switzerland?" Megan suggests. "We'll stay here until we hear from Jill."

"I don't care whether we go or stay," I announce, "but I'm not leaving you two until your bikes are sold or boxed and you're on a plane or bus. You couldn't even carry bike boxes by yourselves, let alone your other stuff. How would you handle your bicycles if we left?"

"I don't know," Megan admits.

"So we're not splitting up. End of discussion. Let's just ask Jill to make all of the arrangements out of Frankfurt and hope her travel agent hasn't already confirmed reservations from here. If so, you can always take a train back, I guess." I turn to Clarke. "I know you want to ride today, but I don't think we can afford that luxury. There's too much to do, particularly if the girls have to leave in the morning." I sound like a drill sergeant, but at least I'm thinking for myself.

"Okay, okay," Clarke concedes. "I don't know how much more I'm willing to do, but I will do that. At least we have the names of those people we met at the castle in France. They live near Frankfurt, and maybe they can give us advice about selling the bikes."

Arriving in Frankfurt in the afternoon after rolling our fat bicycles just like they're people onto a passenger car of the eastbound train, we're assured at two bike shops that although mountain bikes are worth a great deal in Germany, it is necessary to sell them privately. "But we have no way to run an ad," Clarke explains. "We have no home, no phone number."

Disappointed, we take the train to Christa's village. "I don't know why you two think that these people will help strangers," Kelly grouses. "Why don't we stay in Frankfurt?"

"We promised we'd look them up and Christa speaks English," Clarke closes the discussion.

We call from the village train station. "It's the Americans," Christa calls to Bohus. "Yes, of course you can stay. We have room for two inside the apartment and the others can stay outside in our garden."

"We get dibs inside," Kelly says, suddenly delighted about our decision to find these people.

"No, you won't," I growl. "You'll soon sleep in a bed every night while we'll be on the ground for another six months. Respect your elders, missy. Our bones won't hold out forever."

But when Christa arrives to lead us home, she insists that it's too dangerous for the girls to sleep in the garden. "They will sleep inside," she announces. "You and Clarke will sleep in the garden."

Kelly and Megan snicker viciously. "We've been sleeping outside every night for months," I tell Christa, trying unsuccessfully to save face, "and we've had no trouble. But we will accede to your wishes although I'm sure that Kelly and Megan would be fine outside." Christa and Bohus give their bed to the girls and sleep on the couch, and I'm furious that the teenagers allow it until I find that refusing Christa's kindness is like arguing with the Berlin Wall.

The garden is several blocks away, a community plot of fenced parcels inside another locked fence. Christa insists that Clarke and I sleep inside the tiny shed next to their vegetable garden. "There's not enough room inside," Clarke says. "We're happy to put our tent on the grass—we've slept in forests and fields for months." He laughs. "This is the first time we'll have a locked fence around us."

"No," Christa says. "It is unsafe. You will sleep inside the shed. It locks from the outside only, but you will lock it and then climb in through the window and latch it from the inside."

"Christa," I laugh, "we never lock our tent!" But we're overruled. The shed is just big enough for one to sleep on a narrow cot and the other on a chair with a footstool. It promises to be a long night but we're grateful, of course, for any place to stay. At least if it rains, we'll be dry and warm.

Christa and Bohus allow us to stay until Kelly and Megan leave. Each night they gather us around their table for a wonderful dinner and each day take us sightseeing or help with errands. Bohus has a friend with a bike shop who installs Clarke's new headset for nothing and offers to consider buying the girls' bikes.

The best that American Express in Frankfurt can do is eleven hundred dollars each for airfare; in a week, the fare will drop to nine hundred, still twice Kelly and Megan's fare coming over. "Jill needs to be involved in this," I decide. "If I were she, I'd at least make you wait until the fifteenth."

Outside, we split up. I want a haircut and Kelly and Megan want to shop for souvenirs for their families. "Call Jill before we meet you here at four o'clock," Clarke says to Kelly.

He and I enjoy our day together on the wide pedestrian mall, buying pastries, listening to music and window shopping, our anniversary conflict conveniently forgotten. I walk into a beauty shop and come out looking like a totally different person—my long, curly hair is now short and blown dry. "I told her to cut just a little," I say. "It's a good thing I didn't tell her to cut it short! My German's lousy—we'll never survive without Kelly."

"You look great," Clarke says as we buy wine and flowers for Christa and Bohus.

Kelly sits on the steps outside the American Express office wearing high-top tennis shoes with a Batman t-shirt, and Megan has on a short, tight white skirt and purple blouse. "I thought you were buying gifts for your families," I say.

"Mom said not to make reservations," Kelly replies, ignoring me. "She wants to handle it from there."

During dinner, as Christa talks about her past travels, her stories are full of fear and caution. No wonder she gave us mace in France—yet why does she seem to trust us? Bohus, the man she's lived with for fourteen years, explains that he escaped from Czechoslovakia in 1968 at the time of the Russian occupation, swimming across the river to Austria and leaving a wife and eighteen-year-old daughter. He's never been able to go back.

In the safety of their home, Christa and Bohus are almost overwhelming in their love—all directed toward what they feel we'll enjoy most. It's difficult for us because we aren't used to plans ahead of time, but we try to accept their caring gracefully although we certainly don't approve of the teenagers having the bedroom while Christa and Bohus sleep on the couch.

When we call Jill after dinner, she's made airline reservations but the tickets have to be picked up in Frankfurt the next day. She also has other news. "Your CPA says that your taxes are eight thousand dollars more than he thought."

I gasp, and when I get off the phone, whisper the bad news to Clarke. He just shrugs, uninterested, then back at the garden hut, accuses me of ruining everyone's evening by being grumpy. "I always ignore my own feelings to make everyone else happy, Clarke. But that's more than our whole trip will cost! Obviously, the taxes mean nothing to you because it's not your money, but they mean something to me."

"So now it's your money again instead of ours."

"I've tried to think it's ours, Clarke, but it isn't. I earned it and I saved it and it's mine. I don't mind using it for us, but it was mine long before I met you. And it bothers me that I seem to be the only one who worries about our finances."

"I don't worry about things I can't do anything about." He changes the subject. "But I can do something about missing my kids. I want them to live with us when we get home."

I'd felt that one coming ever since Kelly and Megan arrived. Much as I care about Christopher and Jennifer, after a summer with two teenagers I have very mixed feelings about my abilities as a stepmother. "That's fine," I say, "but I'd like some input into the decision rather than you and your ex-wife deciding as if I don't even exist."

"Don't you want me to be able to live with my children?"

"Of course I do, but it will be quite an adjustment for me, and quite a responsibility. I'd appreciate it if someone at least recognized that."

The next morning, we decide to spend some time alone together. While Kelly and Megan pick up their airline tickets, Clarke and I enjoy each other's company for a change, tinkering with the bikes, installing new cables and brake pads, cleaning and polishing the frames. Finally, my bicycle is clean enough for the pretty country decals I'd bought in Belgium, and I line them up one after the other behind the "U.S.A." sticker like flowers along the frame—Spain, France, England, Scotland, Belgium, Holland, Germany—saving those for Austria, Italy and Greece to add later, unwilling to cheat.

When Kelly and Megan announce that Bohus's friend bought their bikes for a hundred and fifty dollars each, I'm amazed that they could part with their bicycle buddies for just a fraction of their airfare. I'd swim home before I'd sell my bike—but then lately it seems to be my only friend.

At dinner, Hungarian goulash prepared by Bohus, Christa announces that it's too dangerous for Clarke and me to sleep all locked in the garden hut. "Susan, you and Kelly and Megan will sleep on the couch. And Clarke will sleep on the floor." We agree because it means that Christa and Bohus will get back their bed.

Our last supper is an early one because Christa wants us to get up in the morning at four-thirty in order to leave for the airport at five-forty-five. "You must pack now," Christa tells Kelly and Megan right after dinner.

"We're already packed," Kelly responds, "except for what we still need tonight." Christa looks dubious.

"When you carry everything on a bike," I explain, "you don't carry very much." Besides, most of their stuff has gone into the trash— notably, Megan's moldy clothes and towels that she's carried since June.

"We must all be in bed by eight-thirty," Christa announces then. Kelly looks at me helplessly and I know that they're much too excited about seeing their families and friends to go to sleep that early. Promptly at eight-thirty, Christa and Bohus go to bed with stern admonitions for us to follow suit, but instead we talk quietly among ourselves, engulfed in a wide range of emotions both happy and sad. Christa comes into the living room at eleven-thirty. "You are keeping us up," she says crossly, "even the dog. Go to sleep."

At four-thirty, Christa pops up to prepare breakfast, giving each of the girls souvenir books and huge chocolate bars before packing us all in the car for our five-forty-five departure, arriving at the ticket counter at six-thirty, exactly as planned.

We aren't allowed to accompany Kelly and Megan to the gate. This is it, the end. I look at my niece, my throat constricting into a knot, words melting somewhere inside my stomach. Turning, I hug and kiss Megan first, then cling to Kelly. "I love you," I say.

"I love you too," she whispers. Then they're off. I ache to have them back, to do it over, to do it better this time. As they walk away, I long to call after them, "Do you want to borrow my shorts? Here, take them!"

Chapter 20

It's our thirteenth day in Germany and all I know about it is what it takes to dispose of two bikes and two teenagers and that the Rhein is a beautiful river. It's our eighth country and currency, our sixth foreign language, and we've been gone a week short of six months.

"We will take you to a German bath," Christa announces later as Bohus pours coffee and passes crispy German breads. They've invited us to stay one more night.

I change into my Paris dress. I'd washed it earlier in the week, along with everything else we brought, pressing its ruffles with my hands as they dried. Tanned arms and legs protruding from the flowery flounces, I feel awkward in my slender silk slippers instead of heavy bicycle shoes as the four of us set out for the baths at Bad Nauheim.

Unlike the thermal springs near our home in Colorado, which are just underground caves, this *bad* is modern and spotlessly clean, bereft of personality. Christa loans me the required swimming cap and we each take our required full shower with soap before entering the first of three pools of different temperatures. The final and hottest pool is my favorite, but an attendant behind a window frowns when I stay in longer than the five-minute recommended limit and I obediently return to the cooler pool before taking another required shower before leaving.

At an outside café, we all order ice cream and sacher torte, then attend a classical concert in a park filled with flowers and sunshine. Eyes closed, I immerse myself in the music, thrilled to be still for once. Clarke and I doze.

After returning to the house, Clarke slips into the bathroom where I'm washing up for supper and makes hurried love to me in my Paris dress, both of us giggling like teenagers. After hours of conversation with Christa and Bohus, we go to bed late – Clarke and I in the bedroom, no matter how hard we try to refuse. Once in the double bed, I want to make leisurely love but Clarke isn't interested. "Why do you always refuse when I suggest sex, Clarke? I never refuse you." He starts to reply, but stops, and we make gentle love, then sleep wrapped in each other's arms.

After breakfast the next morning, after Christa says goodbye and leaves for work, Bohus watches with sad eyes as we pack our panniers. Walking into the bedroom, he returns with an oversized jacket, handing it to me. It's much too heavy to carry, and my Gore Tex is waterproof, warm and lightweight. "*Danke, nein*," I say, shaking my head. He holds it out farther, passing it to Clarke.

"*Nein, Bohus,*" Clarke says, showing him his own jacket. Bohus nods, then disappears into the bedroom again. This time, he emerges with a large briefcase and empties its contents onto the floor. Putting Clarke's sketchpad inside, he holds it up proudly. "*Ja, Clarke?*" he asks hopefully.

"*Nein, Bohus.*" Clarke attempts with gestures to show that it's too bulky to carry on his bike, unwilling to take something he's unable to use. Bohus has already given us each bicycle shirts, and the day before, tried to give me his watch after I'd temporarily misplaced mine after the baths. While Clarke finishes packing, I write in my notebook; my laptop had gone home with the girls. Hearing music upstairs, I discover later that Bohus has given Clarke his harmonica as a gift small enough to come with us. He also gave him a dress shirt after seeing Clarke pack the Paris bus driver shirt that Claude had given him at Coco's.

After one last phone call to Christa, hugs and kisses to Bohus and last-minute instructions – again – on the correct route out of town, we start down the street, our bicycles clean and shiny for the first time in six months. I turn to wave one more time to Bohus, who's taking just one more picture, and almost fall off my bike. "My bike's so heavy that I can barely push the pedals down, Clarke!"

"Hurry up!" he snaps, pulling ahead. "You've gotten soft."

On a slight incline near the train station, I'm forced to get off and push my bicycle up the hill, much to my embarrassment and the amusement of the railroad workers who cheer me on. But when we stop to ask directions, I discover that my back brakes are clamped in a death grip against the rear tire because I hadn't loosened the cable when I installed new brake pads. It's the same as driving a car with its emergency brake on. Impatiently, Clarke loosens my brake cable, grumbling.

We call it a day after sixty-five hot kilometers. "Where's that piece of paper Kelly gave you?" Clarke asks. "The one with the German phrases we need."

Rummaging in my pack, I find only a German dictionary. "Damn."

No one is home at the first two houses we try, then we spot a one-armed man working in the garden outside a small apartment house. "*Guten Abend*," I stammer, desperately casting about for another German word. "*Amerikanisch*," I say, pointing to Clarke and me.

"*Nein*," says the man, looking up, then runs away with his one arm above his head. Clarke and I look at each other.

A voice drifts down from the balcony above us. "I am married to an American soldier," it says in English. "Do you need something?"

Here we are in the middle of Germany, unintelligible. "Neither of us speaks German," I explain, terribly embarrassed, "and our traveling partners who did flew home yesterday. Forgive us, but would it be possible to put our tent in this yard for one night?"

"I'm sure that will be fine," Veronica replies.

"We've got to learn some German tonight," I whisper to Clarke, ready to shoot myself for not working on basic phrases with Christa and Kelly. In Spain and France, at least one of us knew sentence structure and pronunciation rules when we looked up new words in a dictionary. Phrasebooks, while great for most tourists, have little value – knowing how to make dinner reservations or to call a taxi aren't the sentences we need.

Morning brings breakfast and showers in Veronica's spacious apartment. She and Ed have lived in both America and Germany and she has many opinions about how the American army should be run. "The Germans laugh at the Americans," she explains, "because they are not organized. The Americans are always calling Ed to come to work on his days off because they can't remember the schedule. I wish he were with the German army so we could plan our lives."

We ask how she liked living in America. "It was very nice," she replies, "but I did not like the schools for my children. Here, the children are expected to know what they are taught. They have quizzes many times during the week, without planning, and only have announced tests twice during the term. They must study continually to keep up." I remember all the times I'd crammed for a test at the last minute, only to forget everything after I'd gotten my 'A' on the exam.

Veronica continues. "In my country, we must learn much more than in America. For example, grocery store clerks are required to memorize prices of everything and are regularly tested for their speed and accuracy. We are required to be much better at math and must learn to do long sums in our heads. We do not use calculators in school. American schools are much too easy."

"We've heard that workers are allowed to quit their jobs only six weeks before the end of each quarter in Germany," Clarke tells her.

"Of course."

In Aschaffenburg, we finally find waterproof bags to cover our packs after almost 5000 miles on the road. Their only drawback is that we have to completely unwrap our panniers each time we want to get into them. Rewrapping them is difficult too, as the bags are much too big for our packs and the extra fabric must be tied up out of the way of our wheels.

We leave town at two o'clock, ready for rain, then spend the next five hours pedaling uphill in hundred-degree heat under a cloudless blue sky as rolling hills heap themselves one after another like green grassy building blocks and dark forests edge the hillsides in geometric shapes like puzzle pieces.

Soon, the heat absorbs all my thoughts into its shimmering vacuum, sucking all my energy into its void, and I think of Kelly and Megan in air-conditioned America with a stab of jealousy. Breathing requires intense concentration, and we each drink two bottles of water every hour—ten minutes after refilling them, the water burns our mouths. Worried about heat stroke, I feel dizzy and wobbly as we wind up through the blistering countryside. Finally, where our small road threads under an *autobahn*, we find a service station and dunk our heads under a water faucet. "Can you go on?" Clarke asks, as dehydrated as I.

"If I don't die." I shake my wet hair into tangles as Clarke studies the map.

"How are your knees? We've climbed about thirteen hundred feet in the last two and a half hours."

"It's not the hills, it's the heat and the humidity."

We pedal only forty-five kilometers that afternoon, averaging nine kilometers an hour. Once, gasping by the side of the road, out of resources, I almost give up. Listening to a cassette tape that we bought in Frankfurt, I try to forget where I am and what I'm doing. Suddenly, the music captures my spirit and sends energy into my legs, and I pedal with its cadence, lost in its dance, somehow able to push away the misery of the heat and steep terrain. I look back once—Clarke is far behind.

Finding a bike path off the main road, we follow it to the next village. "That one," I announce, pointing to a large white house with terraced rose gardens. We knock on all the doors but no one answers. "This house is wonderful, Clarke. We have to stay here." Something about the house draws me—its shape, the mounds of pearl onions on the back porch, its slightly funky personality, all its doors, whatever. Tiptoeing through a back kitchen to an outside staircase, I knock on the door at the top. A tall, white-haired man with bushy eyebrows steps outside. "*Guten Abend,*" I greet him. The man nods. "*Uh, das tut mir leid, ich spreche kein Deutsch. Sprechen Sie Englisch?*" I have done my all, saying the only two sentences I learned from Kelly: "I'm sorry, I do not speak German. Do you speak English?"

"*Nein.*"

I gesture between Clarke and me. "*Amerikanisch.*"

"*Nein.*"

Now what? "*Bitte, ist okay schlafen en Garten ein nacht?*" I make up a sentence that I hope means something like, "Please, is it okay to sleep in your garden one night?"

The man beetles his eyebrows and says something totally unintelligible. I turn to Clarke, who shrugs and says, "*Petit camping gaz und wasser.*" The German speaks several more unrecognizable sentences, then turns to go inside.

"*Ist okay?*" I ask hopefully, desperate not to let him get away. "No problem?"

"*Ein minuten,*" he says over his shoulder, holding up a finger.

"*Petit camping gaz* is French," I hiss to Clarke after the screen closes.

"*Wasser* is German," he replies defensively.

The door fills with the shadow of the tall man, then it opens and sunlight floods his large features. "*Das ist gut, ist okay,*" he says with a smile.

Clarke and I grin with relief. I put my hand on my chest. "Susan," I say with what I hope is a German accent, gesturing toward Clarke with a flourish. "Clarke."

Our host's eyes twinkle. "Alfred," he says, putting his own big hand on his chest, then follows us back to the garden where Clarke chooses a flat place for the tent under a huge old willow. "*Nein,*" says Alfred, pointing to large black rain clouds gathering in the distance.

"I think he's afraid that tree will fall on us," I tell Clarke.

"It's probably only been here a hundred years," Clarke says, but paces away the distance of the height of the tree and chooses another flat spot by the woodpile.

"*Ja, das ist gut,*" Alfred bellows after he rechecks Clarke's measurements with his own eye.

A short, gray-haired woman appears. Elsa is Alfred's *Frau*, she explains. "*Mein Mann,*" she says, pointing to Alfred, teaching us the word for husband.

A beautiful young woman and her son trot around the side of the house, greeting us in English. Apparently, Elsa has called for an interpreter. "Alfred thinks you should put your tent under the porch roof," Irmgard translates. "It will rain tonight."

Alfred rolls Clarke's bike into an inside workshop off the porch and I follow with mine, finding it hard to believe that clouds can grace such a blistering hot day. Nevertheless, as we put up our tent, the clouds fatten and darken, rolling closer in the sky. At a table on the back porch, we gather to learn as much as we can about each other through Irmgard's translations, with beer for the men and apple juice mixed with mineral water for the women, and chocolate cookies all around. "Elsa and Alfred want to know what time you get up in the morning," Irmgard says.

"Seven-thirty or eight," I answer.

"*Gut.* Coffee at half after seven, Alfred says."

Clarke disappears into the workshop to adjust his brake cable under the luxury of a light while I prepare a small meal of bread and cheese and yogurt. About midnight, a hot wind comes up with a rainstorm. We can't feel the rain on our tent because of the porch roof overhead, but we can see the lightning—even more strange, because the house is built over a river complete with inside water wheel, we can't hear the rain over the sound of the rushing water beneath the porch. It's like watching a storm on television with the sound turned off. We're not used to being cut off from nature.

At seven the next morning, we wake to muggy heat and are packing the bikes in the workshop at seven-ten when Alfred arrives to inform us that breakfast will be ready in *zehn minuten*. At exactly seven-twenty, Elsa announces "*Kaffee!*" and we follow her upstairs to a spotless kitchen and a hilarious breakfast of mispronunciations and pantomimes, then Alfred shows us the water wheel inside the hundred-and-fifty-year-old house. At the end of a wooden sluice which froths and churns with cold water, its old wooden paddles creak and groan as it turns in the cool dampness, now just an ornament but as well cared for as when it was used to mill the villagers' grains.

Elsa and Alfred watch us pack, amazed at how quickly our household folds around the haunches of two bicycles. As I roll mine onto the back porch, Elsa holds out a huge coral rose, tying it with orange twine in a beer bottle into the basket on the front of my bike. Pointing to herself and to me, she says, "*Schwestern*," then points to Clarke and Alfred. "*Brüder.*" With gestures, she invites us to stay, certain that we'll learn each other's languages if we just stay the weekend. As we pedal away, I turn to see Elsa wiping her eyes with her apron.

The rain has washed out some of the heat, and cycling is easier. My rose bobbles and tips, filling the air with its heady perfume all day. The countryside looks like France, full of fields and rolling hills, tiny villages with red tile roofs and flowers spilling everywhere, and lots of dairy farms. Our plan is to follow the famous *Romantische Strasse* to Augsburg, then turn east to Munich, or Munchen, as we learned to call it the first time we used the American pronunciation with no response.

Just north of Rothenburg, Maria gives us immediate permission to park our tent next to her house and her son Gerhard brings us beer. "You seem a bit down in the mouth," I say to Clarke while we fix dinner. "Are you homesick?"

"No." Then he thinks a few moments. "I don't feel like I'm taking risks anymore."

"Maybe I'll feel the same after we learn some German, but I still feel at risk every time I open my mouth." Clarke doesn't respond and I leave him alone with his thoughts.

Gerhard serves us breakfast in the morning inside the house, his mother either too shy or too busy to join us; she and her husband eat in another room no matter how hard we try to get the five of us together. After homemade coffeecake and streusel, Gerhard shows us their pigs and dairy cows and rabbits, which live in the barn attached to the house, eliminating the need to go outside in bad weather to tend to the animals.

Rothenburg is a charming town too quaint to be spoiled by tourists who somehow in my imagination look like shadows of the people who lived there when the city grew up during the Middle Ages. At an interesting bookstore, I can't resist the urge to find a book in English, choosing one by Milan Kundera, a Czech writer from Bohus's hometown. As we eat lunch in an elaborate park next to the river, I thumb through the first book I've touched in six months while Clarke munches his sandwich in silence. "Maybe you just miss being afraid," I say finally.

"I don't know," he responds and I wonder why he can't be happy unless life is hard. For me, life is plenty difficult—the hilly bicycling again, another new language, Clarke and my struggling relationship. I'm not even close to being too comfortable.

As we backtrack through the streets, we spot two bicyclists, Americans from Los Angeles on a three-week trip through Germany. Avid cyclists in the U.S., Gary and Karen are committed to riding a hundred kilometers a day compared to our sixty- or seventy-kilometer pace now that we're back in the hills. "How's your marriage faring?" Karen asks when she hears how long we've been on the road.

I grimace. "This hasn't been easy."

Clarke is telling Gary that we stay in people's gardens or fields every night. "When we bicycle at home," Gary says, "no one will even give us water."

"Do you think Americans would be nicer to foreigners than to their own countrymen?" I ask.

"The Germans haven't been all that nice to us," Karen complains.

"Really? Do you speak German?"

"Gary does, very well."

I wonder if we've been lucky or if we just take more time with people because we don't need to travel a hundred kilometers a day. We don't even have a destination in mind when we leave in the morning.

Gary and Karen have been following a bike path along the *Romantische Strasse* and explain how to watch for the signs. We say goodbye, knowing that we won't see them again because of their faster pace, sorry that we can't spend more time comparing notes. Although the bike route is no longer a path of its own, it follows tiny roads through quiet villages, beautiful and peaceful. Late in the afternoon, as the path intersects the main route, Gary and Karen appear on the main road. "Why aren't you on the bicycle route?" we ask, surprised to see them again.

"It meanders too much," Gary explains. They haven't been away from Los Angeles long enough, I decide. Or maybe we've been gone too long. Seconds later, the Californians pull away out of shouting distance, hurrying to the next town. This time, we're sure we'll never see them again.

"Let's cook dinner before we find a place to stay for the night," Clarke suggests that evening. "That way, if we find a family to visit, we won't have to juggle food and friendship at the same time." We stop at a roadside park to fix dinner, then camp in the backyard of a new house.

After washing clothes the next morning, I take a sponge bath and wash my hair in a faucet in the garden. As we pull out of the driveway, here come Gary and Karen! This time, they stop long enough to tell us that Gary is a minister, Karen a painter, and then are off to Donauwörth for lunch. "That's probably where we'll end up tonight," we laugh before saying goodbye forever for the third time.

A bit later, I turn around to see bicycles behind me. But it's another couple, Canadians, and we cycle together awhile, pacing the same speed. Bob is a semi-retired designer, Ione a social worker with a passion for nature photography. "We stay in small hotels and eat our meals out," she explains as we pedal side-by-side. "I would never want to cook and camp after bicycling all day."

"Sometimes I feel that way too," I admit, "but we get the people this way as well as the scenery. I wouldn't trade the experience for the world."

They pull ahead when Clarke and I stop for water and we wave, hoping to see them along the road again. In Nordlingen, as Clarke and I make sandwiches in a park, Bob and Ione bump up the curb to join us. "We've been looking for you. Can we ask about your route?"

After showing them our favorite parts of France, the four of us discuss how our experiences have changed our outlook on life and agree that we need more time to share stories. "Let's meet in Donauwörth for a beer at the end of the day," Bob suggests as they put on their helmets. "We'll stop at the first café with tables outside."

We find no cafés in Donauwörth. It's a pretty town, but the streets are almost empty, most of the businesses closed. Clarke and I go to the tourist office to ask about an outdoor restaurant but its doors are locked too. Pedaling slowly out of town, we search in vain for our new friends, feeling lonely and cheated.

"We haven't been by ourselves one night since Kelly and Megan came," Clarke says later as we snack on cheese and crackers in a woody park. "How about hiding in the woods tonight and not talking even to each other?" Leaving new friends day after day is getting harder and harder, I acknowledge, realizing how mentally tired I am. We can't find a place to hide, however, and end up at a dairy farm near Meitingen, visiting with Paul and Elizabeth until bedtime.

Once in the tent, we fall into exhausted silence, stretched beyond our capabilities to be friendly American ambassadors. "This is the pits, Clarke," I say finally. We're making cheese omelettes for dinner.

"What now, Susan?"

"We save all of our energy for strangers. We never talk to each other any more."

"I'm sick of this conversation."

"Of course you are. So am I. I'm sick of our whole marriage. It's boring."

He looks at me strangely, as if seeing me for the first time in months. "Yes, it is boring."

"Our egos are so well-fed by others that we don't need each other any more. Each night, we show up on someone's doorstep and I say something, then you say something else—it's always the same because we know so few words. We get praised and taken care of, and in return, give back love and friendship. But not to each other."

"I don't need to talk to you, Susan. I already know everything you think. Talking to you takes up energy I could use talking to someone new."

I feel the same way. Maybe our marriage is over. Maybe it has been for months, based on the way we've been treating each other. I cut up bread, wondering how it would feel to be alone again, to go home now, to start over. My stomach hurts. "Our marriage is boring because we make it boring," I say finally, hoping that admitting our feelings, getting them out in the open, will allow us to move forward. "Do you want our marriage to work, Clarke?"

He concentrates on his omelette for a long time. "I want it to work," he says finally.

"So do I."

In the morning, we kiss and get up early, scraping wet slugs off the tent after accepting the bottle of fresh milk that's offered as soon as our heads pop out into the misty daylight.

Our short ride to Maisach, where we plan to catch a train the few kilometers into Munich at Christa's insistence, is a fairy tale. The sky is so bright that it's luminous, and deep green forests and quilted fields are bathed in yellow light. The roads are almost silent; perfectly smooth, they flow up and down the gentle hills like silken ribbons. The villages shine in the sun, all quiet, although dazzling white laundry already hangs in the yards. We hear a dog bark, and bird songs in the forest, but that's all. It's time to be kind to each other again.

At the train station in Maisach, we're trapped at the bottom of a long flight of stairs, but help arrives in the form of an American soldier and his German wife. "We'll carry them up," the German woman announces after assessing our dilemma.

"They're too heavy," Clarke warns her, but she lifts the rear of my bike so I grab the front and the six of us arrive on the platform along with the train. Once inside, we introduce ourselves, discovering that Jacob and Celine live in one of the villages that we pedaled through the day before. They'd met while Jacob was stationed at a U.S. Army base in Germany and Jacob never went home.

At the Munich station, they help carry the bikes up three escalators. "If it weren't for you," I say gratefully, "we'd never have gotten out of this station."

"If it weren't for us," Celine says with a broad smile, "you'd still be in Maisach."

With a fat mail packet happily in tow—another pair of contact lenses, the prescription for my pills and a bundle of letters—we buy a six-month supply of medicine and pedal through Munich along the Isar River, intrigued by the nude sunbathers along its banks in the middle of the city. "I can't stand it, Susan. I'm filthy. Let's join them," Clarke suggests.

After a moment's hesitation, I agree. Stripping off our sweaty clothes, we ease into the cold river. Surrounded by Germans of all shapes and sizes, I realize that no one pays any attention to anyone else and soon I'm spread nude on my dirty towel, reading the mail, refreshed but feeling a million miles from home as I write postcards to unsuccessfully bridge the gap.

We leave about four o'clock, continuing up the river for another three hours before stopping to make supper, then get into an argument about what kind of wine Clarke bought for dinner. I insist on retrieving the bottle out of the trash to prove that he's wrong. "You absolutely have to be right all the time, don't you?" Clarke snaps.

"Only when I am," I defend myself.

The argument spoils the day for me, and we sleep in the forest alone for the first time in four months. With no one but each other to talk to, we continue our conversation about the state of our marriage. "Are you sure you want this to work?" I ask again.

"Maybe not," Clarke replies slowly. My stomach lurches. "Let's make love," he suggests after our words go nowhere.

"No. I don't know you anymore."

"Then I won't make love to a stranger. I've already done that enough in my life." Clarke turns away from me and I lie awake, lonely and sad.

In the morning, I hardly notice the indirect light curling through the tall forest trees and the soft animal sounds around us. Will Clarke and I do what it takes for our marriage to survive this trip? Individually, we're experiencing tremendous growth, but will the trip cost us life as a couple? *Dear Families,* I write sadly in my mind, *remember our year long honeymoon plans?*

At Starnberger See, a large lake southwest of Munich, we discover a bike path that edges its sunny banks and pedal along the shoreline past magnificent houses that we assume are vacation homes until realizing that they're easy commuting distance by car from Munich. Half a day by bicycle is half an hour by car.

At noon, we stop at a little picnic area for lunch. "Let's not be in such a rush all the time," I suggest, thinking of Gary and Karen and their mandatory hundred-kilometer days. We bathe in the lake, wash clothes and lie naked in the hot sun. Although it's relaxing, all I can feel is a hole where my marriage has disappeared from my life. South of Penzberg, in a field next to a forest, we make sandwiches for dinner, polite and solicitous of each other without being connected at all.

"Susan, look!" Clarke says as we pedal silently in the soft light of early evening. To the right, in steely silhouette, bordered on the bottom with soft green fields and on top by pale sunshine, are the Alps. I stop, amazed, caught by the incredible sight. The Austrian Alps! The breathtaking, distant cut-cardboard fantasy shapes inspire a jumble of emotions—awe at their beauty, gratitude that we've made it this far, fear that I can't pedal over them. I feel Clarke's emotion too, connecting us once again with a common goal and a common experience. We can't give up now.

A big yellow farmhouse sits like a hen in a meadow nest just up ahead, the Alps a watercolor backdrop to its fields. Trailed by a dirty, naked little boy, a young woman is cleaning up the last balloons of an outdoor birthday party. Elfriede welcomes us in English, tucking us in an empty garage, a pedal-in hotel just big enough for our tent and our bikes. "Join us for supper," she says.

"Thank you, but we've already eaten."

"Come up anyway. I would love to practice my English."

Elfriede and her husband Michael scoop us large dishes of rum topf—liquor-soaked fruit—which we wash down with champagne and orange juice, then schnapps. Elfriede immediately comments on the strength of our relationship. "You must love each other very much to be together under this stress twenty-four hours a day."

"Yes, we do," Clarke says, looking at me.

Elfriede's house is a jumble of toys. "In the part of Germany where I come from," she tells us, making a face, "the women clean house all day, every day. Their marriages are measured by how clean their houses are. I'd rather spend time with my family."

Inside the cozy garage for the night, Clarke and I can see lightning through the windows and hear thunder. But we and our bicycles are warm and dry thanks to the generosity, once again, of strangers who give more than we need.

Refreshed and rested, we roll the bikes outside in the morning sunshine as Elfriede bounds out of the house to invite us for breakfast, eager for more conversation. Over fresh bread and coffee, our friendship grows and parting is difficult. Elfriede has been a friend to us, more than she knows, helping us acknowledge our love for each other, and it feels like part of her comes with us as we pedal through the cool morning air back to the highway. It's our last day in Germany.

We pedal up a long pass that looks like intestines on the map, steep winding roads that rise eight hundred feet in four kilometers. On either side are lakes, seen from breathtaking lookout points along the way when we stop to gather strength from the beauty and the clean air. At the south end of Walchensee, we stop for lunch and then pedal to Wallgau, Krün, and Mittenwald, Germany at its finest—tiny whitewashed villages with red tile roofs and brightly-colored wall murals and church steeples, sometimes with red or blue clock faces contrasting with the clear, quiet air and bright sky; clean farms in velvet meadows; flowers bunched around every window and in baskets and jars and gardens.

We spend the night on the German-Austrian border, building our tent behind a work barn set in a perfectly-groomed field of grass, the cuttings stacked by hand on shelves to dry in the sun. The eight cows are milked by hand twice a day.

Sitting outside our tent after dinner, we watch light fade from the sky. The beauty is staggering, too big for words. Above the pale meadows the Alps fade into the distance in jagged layers of lighter and lighter shades of blue, pointing to the pale gray sky like gnarled old hands. A train passes next to the field, red and silver, its whistle echoing like a song, and the sound makes me homesick. I hear cowbells.

We wake early to a misty morning, but not before the dairy farmer arrives to begin his day. Cool clouds hang low on the mountains, obscuring our view in mystery, and we cross into Austria without a border check.

Chapter 21

In Scharnitz, we exchange *deutschmarks* for *schillings*, thirteen-plus to the dollar, grateful that our arrival in country number nine doesn't include a new language. Our German is just barely communicable: "*Ist okay Toilette?*" somehow works, in spite of us.

The road up to Innsbruck is a five-to-fifteen percent grade, but after six months on bicycle, I can at least enjoy the scenery instead of obsessing on the hill. In Austria, not a rock is out of place—the grassy meadows are as smooth as fur, bordered by straight lines of tall, old pines that look like prickly shortgrass against the rugged Alps blue with distance. White villages huddle in the valleys, low and cozy except for the red church spires that poke at the bright sky.

At the top of the pass, a sign says "no bicycles" but there's no other route, so we plunge over the edge, hurtling down a sixteen percent grade as fast as the cars, pushed to our limit by gravity and our heavy packs. Runaway lanes break off the highway at intervals, giving us and the traffic a margin of safety, but we keep it together and plummet down the mountain to Innsbruck like diving hawks in the late August sunshine.

After buying expensive groceries for a light lunch in a tiny park off the town bike path, we pedal along the river toward Salzburg, from village to village through fields and meadows, the long way from one place to the next but full of quiet beauty. My knees ache from the morning's climb, and I'm disappointed that they aren't stronger. Clarke keeps pushing me to talk about it, irritating me into silence. Finally, in the middle of a cornfield late in the afternoon, I decide to dance to a lively tape on my cassette player, and rocking my bike back and forth in time to the music, I hold my face to the sun and laugh out loud. "I'm okay now, Clarke. It had nothing to do with you."

In that perfect slanting light of just-before-sunset, we stop for dinner at a bus stop bench next to a railroad track, then ask to spend the night at a farm across the road. A young teenager named Petra and her friend Brigga help us put up our tent in a sheltered spot next to an outbuilding, and we practice each other's languages until Petra's father arrives home to welcome us with a firm handshake and very adequate English. After conversation and coffee on the patio and a great commotion over Petra's new beagle puppies, her father offers us breakfast. "If it's not too much trouble," we reply, anxious to continue our conversation in the morning.

Our host disappears without a word and Clarke and I look at each other. We wait awhile, then go to our tent hoping to repair over morning coffee whatever social blunder we've made. Suddenly, Petra's father bursts from the house with a plate full of pancakes—but instead of accepting his hospitality, we commit the further mistake of explaining to Petra that we thought his invitation was for morning and have already eaten. "That's okay," she says. "My friends and I are starving." But it isn't okay. Petra's father, clearly offended, says stiffly that he will leave for work long before we wake up.

In the tent, we nurse our embarrassment as Clarke gently rubs my sore knees with lotion warmed on our stove. "Your knees are always cold, Susan. You need to find a way to increase your circulation; no wonder they hurt all the time."

When we get up the next morning, no one is about except the new puppies, and we leave a note on the door, ashamed that our inadequate German has hurt someone's feelings.

Petra's father had suggested that we turn southeast at Salzburg and go through Yugoslavia to Greece instead of to Italy because that route over the Alps is easier. Although Clarke and I are both concerned about my knees, we decide to put off our decision because going south from Salzburg will eliminate Vienna and the possibility of a visit with Bohus's daughter in Czechoslovakia. "The weather may decide for us," I say. "I'm not crazy about crossing the Alps in snow." The weather, although sunny, feels crisp. Summer had ended at the Austrian border.

We spend the afternoon lost. After lunch and a dip in a cold river, we continue along our tiny road. The pavement narrows to gravel, then the gravel disappears into dirt, and the dirt washes into an impassable stream. "Oops," Clarke says, unconcerned that we have to backtrack several kilometers to start over. Who cares where we are when the scenery is this beautiful?

"Let's go to Kitzbühel," I suggest at Wörgl. Turning down a narrow highway, I hit the edge of the pavement and spill into the road with a crash. Four middle-aged hikers in *lederhausen* run to assist as I scramble up, embarrassed, ignoring my scrapes to pick up my bike—the front wheel has come loose, along with my left panniers. Nothing is damaged except my pride, but I realize how easily I could have been injured if there'd been a car in my lane when I fell. "Look for another *radweg*," I call up to Clarke.

The bicycle paths take longer but are safe and quiet, and soon the view steals my attention again as we pedal up through soft, green grass meadows at the base of jagged peaks, a contrast of overwhelming proportions, like velvet and steel mixed together. The light softens to gray and the scant air turns cold, reminding us of our own mountain climate in Colorado. Maybe we need to turn south after all.

A young woman sticks her head out of a farmhouse window as we stop to consider where to stay for the night. Why not here? She motions us inside to meet her husband Simon and their children and three other visitors whom they'd met only two days earlier while on a walk—Heide, a beautiful German woman, and her daughter and son. "I thought you were your daughter's friend," I tell Heide as she greets us in English.

She laughs like jingle bells. "I am thirty-five," she says. "Sandra is fourteen. But thank you."

Clarke and I put up our tent in the field and cook dinner crouched around our little stove for warmth. Afterwards, Katherine and Simon invite us for wine on the back porch, protected from the wind by the house. "What part of Germany are you from, Heide?" we ask their German guest, wondering if we'd bicycled through her town.

"West Berlin. But originally East Berlin."

"How were you able to leave?" Clarke asks.

Heide shrugs. "Knock on the right doors," she replies and I wonder whether the doors were in East Germany, or West. "My husband is still in East Berlin," she tells us. "I cannot return for five years. But I wouldn't, even if I could."

Simon refills our glasses every time we take a sip, and we write down each other's birthdays, determined to stay in touch, three families who've known each other two days and five hours, respectively, and who are German, American and Austrian,

Communist (or ex-Communist) and democratic and whatever the government is in Austria. We don't talk politics; we talk people.

It rains during the night, and freight trains pass one after the other next to our tent, brakes screeching as they round the corner above the farm. Once, after yet another howling train wakes us, Clarke mutters something about having to re-think our practice of following the train routes, then we toss and turn back to sleep until another goes by. We don't wake until eight and move slowly from too little sleep and too much wine. At nine, we're still tying our packs under their cumbersome waterproof covers when Simon emerges from the house dressed in full Tyrolean costume. He's driving to Augsburg for a festival that day. "It took us a week to bicycle from there," we say as Simon poses proudly for a photo.

The tiny road flows through soft, high meadowland that climbs higher and higher on the shoulders of the Alps. Birds sing in the cool, thin air, their voices shrill and crackling in the altitude. The landscape is washed in early morning light; the mountains are cutouts pasted on a backdrop, gray on gray, and morning sun on the dew-damp grass hazes its rich green to filmy wetness.

Emerging from an ageless mountain trail into the resort village of Kirchberg feels like a slap in the face, like waking to a nightmare. Although the village is beautiful, it's crowded and noisy and expensive, full of people bustling and pushing as if they don't have time or money enough to do it all. Where did they come from? It's as if the buildings and cars and people arrived by helicopter and haven't touched the countryside at all. Buying as little of the expensive food as possible, we eat yogurt and bread, then pedal out of town after a brief walk through an expensive store to get out of a thunderstorm.

Near Kitzbühel, we stop under the roof of a train shelter for lunch and then pedal into the beautiful town. When I see the sign for McDonald's hamburgers, I keep pedaling. "Don't you want to stop?" Clarke asks.

"Nope." Unfortunately, Kitzbühel is just another charming, quaint, crowded tourist town.

"Let's look for a campground, Clarke," I suggest late in the afternoon. "I could use a shower to warm up." It's rained on and off all day. Near Steinpass, where we'll cross into a finger of Germany before going back into Austria near Salzburg, we find a campground for seven dollars and look sadly at each other. "That's a pretty expensive shower," I say.

"And we'll have to put all our wet packs in the tent." We've gotten used to leaving our packs safely on the bikes at someone's house.

"Maybe we can find a barn for the bikes instead," I suggest, then wonder when they had become a higher priority than our own comfort.

We tell the campground owner that we've decided to go on and he gives us directions to the bike path to Salzburg. Following his instructions, we cross the border into Germany with a wave from the Customs officer, then cut onto the dirt road that leads under the highway. Soon, the tiny forest road opens into thick meadows edged with deep woods that warm the feet of crystal blue mountains like fuzzy green slippers. It's stopped raining, and everything smells of pine and sunlight.

Two farmhouses share the meadow. We stop at the first one and the farmer's wife shows us where to camp with the help of her puppy, who grabs her foot in his mouth every step of the way while Clara pretends that she doesn't notice.

In the morning, a tractor rumbles up to the door of the tent and I stick my head into the sunshine to discover that Clara's husband is delivering homemade cake on a blue china plate for our breakfast. "It's amazing how friendly people are after surviving the night without being robbed," Clarke observes. As we finish the cake, Clara stops by on a clunky black utility bike on her way to church in the next village.

Shortly after we leave, we discover a cold waterfall splashing into a tiny pool in the shadowy forest. "Here's your bath, Susan," Clarke says with a smile.

"I'm not that dirty," I shiver. "It was a hot shower I was looking for. I have my limits, you know." But still it's tempting.

Following forest and river bike paths all the way to Salzburg, we jump back to the highway only long enough to cross back into Austria. Rain again threatens; the cool trees drip and I imagine what a cool and shady route this would be on a hot summer day.

In Salzburg, we eat lunch on the river and watch black clouds churn overhead. "Maybe we'd better not sightsee," Clarke says, eyeing the approaching storm.

I look at the blackening sky behind the cold, jagged mountains. "Which way, south or east?"

Clarke considers only a moment. "South. Why go to Vienna when we enjoy the countryside so much more?"

As the wind rises, we hightail it down the river bike path as large raindrops tick loudly on our waterproofing and the soft rush of heavy rain sweeps up from behind. The sky is black as night. "Head for shelter!" Clarke shouts as the thunderstorm overtakes us, drenching us with cold rain as lightning and thunder crack and boom on all sides. Scrambling into a bus stop enclosure, we decide to wait it out. Usually, we keep cycling in rain, but this storm is too big—too much lightning, too much wind, too much cold. After an hour, the storm hasn't let up and we agree to wait thirty more minutes before continuing—as if we have an appointment somewhere.

Boom! Thunder crashes as the sky lights up like an explosion. After counting our fingers and toes, we take perverse pleasure in seeing that the television in the little house across the road has gone dark. I picture the headline: *Two Americans and one television electrocuted by lightning bolt. Joint funeral service to be held at Salzburg TV and Appliance Repair.*

"Maybe when that guy can't watch TV," Clarke says, "he'll see us and let us inside his garage." Our fantasy grows to include his warm house and an oven-cooked meal, but we only feel worse; and when the half-hour is up, we pedal into the finally-diminishing storm, splashing through puddles, dodging the leftover rain squalls only in our minds.

Somehow, we manage seventy kilometers, but between Kuchl and Golling, our frozen bodies call a halt at a little farm where a young woman milks cows inside the barn. Nodding assent to our teeth-chattering request to camp, she goes back to her work as we slosh through the mud to find a flat place to roll out our tent in the muck, cold and tired and wet, as the storm revs its engines again.

We sleep little, worried that the tent won't hold in the wind, but at seven in the morning, doze for two hours before draping the tent over a tractor to dry while we pack and eat bread, folding the tent damp in a driveway full of cow dung. On our way out of the farm, an old woman wants either to know how much our trip cost or whether we'll pay for her muddy field; we finally assume the former, thank her, and ride on as black clouds bundle together in big blobs, crowding each other until they fill the sky to overflowing. Knowing that they'll burst sooner or later, we race to the nearest village to buy rolls for breakfast. Our clothes are still wet and cold from the day before, and we take turns going into the market for warmth.

From Golling, it's uphill and cold and rainy. At Bischofshofen, we buy small, inflatable camping pillows at a sporting goods store—after 8500 kilometers, six months and nine countries. Mostly, the stop gets us out of the miserable weather. Shop windows display beautiful woolen clothes and I fantasize about being warm and dry and dressed up.

Gems of fancy tourist towns are strung together by silken meadows and tiny ski slopes, but as the afternoon gets older and we climb higher, the rain increases and the temperature drops. Bones frozen clear through, we find a home for the night in between splotches of slimy cow manure in a muddy yard hung over a cliff, too tired to stay awake for the storm.

"We have tunnels today," Clarke announces in the morning.

"Fine. We may get run over, but at least we won't get wet."

After scraping off as much manure as possible, we pack our dripping tent. The owners of our yard are already gone, so we say goodbye to their rabbits and follow the road down to the river in a heart-stopping fall that numbs our fingers and faces. The road ends at an aluminum plant. "Now what?" The last thing I want to do is pedal back up the mountain.

Clarke points to a group of workers who gesture to a steep flight of stairs leading up to a railroad track. One at a time, Clarke and I push and pull the bicycles up the stairs, our frozen hands slipping on the wet packs. "Be careful!" he yells, clutching his handlebars as my feet slip on the icy metal steps. At the top, we follow the tracks through the plant, waving to the cheering workmen. A little road connects the factory to the main highway; we climb five hundred feet in less than two kilometers, up a fifteen percent grade, walking the bikes at least two-thirds of the way. "Are we having fun yet?" I wheeze, lungs aching from cold and exertion.

"No, but at least the exercise warms us up."

Once on the highway, a long tunnel gives us a break from the horrible weather but it's dark and clammy and full of fumes. Our eyes water and sting, and passing cars sound like freight trains. Unable to see the potholes and curbs in the darkness, I follow Clarke too closely, breathing hard, frightened. Mid-tunnel, the road turns slightly downward and we shoot out, fast as we can, gasping for clean air, thankful for daylight and even the rain mixed with snow.

At Badgastein, at the end of a string of pristine postcard villages, I buy tiny bells for the bikes and make tomato and cheese sandwiches with numb fingers while Clarke fixes a flat. Snow is on the mountains and even my bones feel brittle. My knees throb. A young man stops to chat, explaining that we have to go by train through the next tunnel. "If you hurry, you can make the two-thirty train; it's only five kilometers from here."

But the five kilometers are straight up. The wind pushes us, chasing us with another storm. At the top, we find the station. "Go around back and wait," the ticket seller tells us. "You must get on the end of the train."

Already at the station, the train is a series of open cars on which motorists drive their autos like a ferryboat. "How can we manage the bikes, Clarke? There's no way to even tie them down!" I imagine us clinging to a flatbed rail car speeding through a ten-kilometer tunnel to freeze or be pitched off into the blackness and mashed like slugs.

Then we see the boxcar, and a passenger car at the end. Inside the boxcar, six little stalls with gates will keep the bikes wooly warm and snug. Tying them up, we pat their rears and climb into the passenger car for our own cozy ride through the tunnel across the top of the Alps, laughing at our fantasy of doom on the open rail cars.

When we pull into the station at Mallnitz, it's snowing lightly and strong winds tousle the trees into a frenzy. As we unload the bikes, I imagine them kicking and pulling, unwilling to leave their warm stalls. But we've done it. We've crossed the Alps. The next eight kilometers of hairpin turns are twelve percent downhill grades with a strong tailwind, and we race down the mountain almost too fast. It's taken four hours to pedal thirty kilometers up the mountain in the morning and only two and a half to ride down fifty in the afternoon.

Morning brings only cold and wind. Because we haven't had a real shower since the day after leaving Frankfurt two weeks earlier, we pull into a rest stop to wash our hair in the freezing alpine water of a drinking fountain. My head aches from the cold, and I wonder if my hair will freeze before it dries. It does.

In Villach, on the border of Austria, Italy and Yugoslavia, we stop for maps and to mail postcards. I'm cranky, tired of the cold and rain and worried about the mountains to come instead of congratulating myself for pedaling over the Alps. We're about to cross another border into the unknown, to a new language and a new currency. Whatever country we go to next–Yugoslavia or Italy–looms like yet another black abyss. The few words of German we've painstakingly learned are about to be of no value, and even Clarke's knees hurt. A flat tire further holds us back in late afternoon, and fifty-five kilometers into the day, we cross the Italian border after hesitating only a moment at the junction between Italy and Yugoslavia.

Chapter 22

Italy, the country I most want to see, is night and day different from Austria. As if crossing an invisible line, I can immediately feel the change in the air, see it in the scenery, hear it in the people. As always, crossing a border means a new language and a new currency, but the change this time is much more than that. Italy is a $33^{1}/_{3}$ record played at 78 rpm.

In the first town, Tarvísio, a speeding truck runs me into a curb. "I need wine," I announce, my heart beating fast from the near-miss as we exchange our few *schillings* into many *lire*, fourteen hundred to the dollar, and buy a big bottle of cheap Italian red to ease our transition into country number ten after more than 5300 miles. It's the last day of August.

While we cook dinner behind the loading docks in a shopping center parking lot, we discuss the fears that express themselves as irritation with each other every time we cross a new border. "At least you can speak Italian," Clarke says.

"A one-semester class more than twenty years ago."

That night, Danny and Sylvia gather us around their kitchen table with bread and wine and cheese. "*Tutti é possibile in Italia,*" Danny says, gesturing wide with his arms, refusing to let his no-English and our no-Italian prevent us from communicating. Everything is possible in Italy.

The next day, I fall head over heels in love with this country as we fall 2000 feet down through the mountains, tumbling with the river past villages like tattered lives whose shambling architecture shows the loving neglect of many years. Although the air is cold, the sun warms our backs as we freefall through mile after mile of mountain valley, down out of the Alps into the land of joy and gestures, *vino e vita*, wine and life. A perfect blue sky stretches overhead from mountaintop to mountaintop, the depth of its color extending back to infinity above jagged white-and-gray granite crags with slopes grudgingly giving hold to the stubborn pines that etch a soft ruffle between sky and rock.

As I listen to Mozart on my cassette player, my spirit takes flight, white wings flapping. Italy! A place only in my dreams for twenty years—now it will be in my memory forever. Unlike Germany, it takes only a moment to experience this country. I can feel it by seeing it; its soul infuses the countryside, the villages, the people…open and rambunctious and glorious. Words bubble up inside my mind and bounce like moths flying into light.

When we pause for water, a tiny brown-and-white butterfly flutters around my legs before flying to Clarke and across the highway into the grill of a passing truck, then lies motionless on the road, its greeting still and silent. Clarke lifts it gently, wings fluttering like a tiny breeze. Leaving the butterfly in the hollow of a large leaf, we're reminded once again that the life we take for granted can turn into death in a moment.

We're dirty. After days of rain and steep alpine passes, the discovery of an icy stream churning under an ancient granite bridge sends us scrambling down the embankment to plunge everything we own into the river—clothes, sleeping bags, tent, bicycles and bodies—spreading the dripping fabrics and ourselves among the warm rocks to dry in the sun while we eat lunch and drink wine cooled by the river. Back on the road, new people in body and spirit, we float and bob downhill next to the river between villages strewn across the hillsides like breadcrumbs scattered for the birds.

Italy is like a woman with her makeup on crooked—ragtag, disheveled, scruffy, but full of life and exuberance, moving quickly through each moment to capture them all.

Late in the day, we're kidnapped by another bicyclist that Clarke says waited for me after passing us earlier. The Italian buys us a beer at an outdoor café, and after a hurried conversation full of gestures, leaps up to resume his own ride as if possessed. "Do not go to Napoli," he shouts as he pedals away, his face crowded with concern. Danny and Sylvia had told us the same thing the night before.

That night, near Osoppo, Luciano and Rita agree. "Anything south of Rome is not Italy. It is Mafia." We're sitting in their warm kitchen drinking wine and coffee. Stella the white rabbit is curled on my chest, warm-eared and happy, but Buk the dog is relegated to his pen for the night in spite of our protests. Daughter Donatella is too shy to try out her English, which she's just begun to learn in school, but shows us her English lessons and her scrapbook while her father, eager to communicate, helps me with Italian words and his wife pushes plates of prosciutto and salami and bread onto the table.

The next day, leading the route we agreed on the night before, I stop after thirty kilometers. "Let's cross the river," I say, pedaling across the almost-dry stream that looks like a collection of wet and dry ribbons tangling south under the bridge. "I know we decided to stay on the east side, but this feels better."

At the first intersection, a car pulls alongside. "Where are you from?" the driver asks in English.

"Colorado," Clarke replies.

"I'll be damned," the handsome young man says, then explains that he lived in New York for two years and invites us home for a glass of wine. "I live only a few kilometers from here," Alexandro adds when Clarke hesitates. "My family has a small winery."

"I knew there was a reason we changed our route," I whisper. "Sometimes we scare me."

The winery turns out to be an eighth-century palace. "Do you actually live here?" I ask.

"Yes," Alexandro laughs. "My father bought the *palazzo* a few years ago and we've been restoring it ever since. Ah, Mama," Alexandro turns as a short woman with copper hair emerges from a side door. She shakes our hands gravely, then smiles with twinkling eyes. Close behind follows Franco, Alexandro's father, who greets us in Italian with warmth and courtesy. When he turns to say something to his wife, his eyes shine with adoration. "My parents invite you to have lunch with us," Alexandro translates.

We consider our usual cheese and tomato and onion sandwiches on the ground, then hurriedly accept. "*Grazie, Alexandro, mille grazie.*"

Alexandro and his father show us the *palazzo*. Upstairs in the ballroom, an old French painter is restoring murals, teetering up on a tall scaffold resurrecting cherubs and flowers. "My father wants to use this room for art exhibitions for the village," Alexandro explains.

The wine is stored on the lower floors. Franco describes in Italian the different varieties, pouring a golden wine from a cask for each of us. It's full-bodied, smooth and sweet; we nod our appreciation and Franco accepts our acknowledgment with a dignified dip of his head.

Around a long table off the kitchen, in a room filled with pictures and books and an old bottle collection, we're served a leisurely lunch of eggplant parmigiana, marinated red peppers, fresh bread and cheese, along with wine and *grappa*—liqueur made from grape skins—and then rich, strong *espresso*. The meal is superb, the company better: Franco and Nella; Alexandro and his brother; and Mario, the French painter, who's a little deaf but full of opinions about everything. It's obvious that Nella and her sons adore Franco, and he obviously feels exactly the same about them. As we finish our coffee, Nella disappears from the room. "Mama has had a room prepared so that you can rest," Alexandro explains when she returns.

Ignoring our protests and gently refusing my offer to help with the dishes, Nella sends Alexandro to show us our room. The king-sized bed looks as big as a meadow, each side turned down to expose crisp blue sheets and soft, puffy pillows. The beamed ceiling floats high over the icy white room like a cloud, and a massive wooden armoire and dresser stand like ancient trees against the walls next to a chair and footstool upholstered in flowers. From the window, sunshine streams through thick walls to cast a square that starts on the carpet and turns up the side of the bed. To my right, the bathroom is filled with gleaming brass and thick white towels. All this, I realize, because we changed routes. I turn to Alexandro. "I don't know what to say," I begin.

"Don't say anything. Just take a hot shower and sleep as long as you like. You and your husband have been on the road a long time."

The luxurious caress of the cool, ironed sheets is too pleasurable for sleep; instead, I listen to the church bells and the birds and the workers in the vineyard outside the open window. The square of sunshine has crossed the bed before Clarke wakes and stretches, yawning, his sun-browned body a ripe olive against the clean blue sheets. We sit naked by the window. "I wonder if we could ask to spend the night," Clarke says.

"We've never asked for a bed before."

"I'll ask, Susan."

We dress and go downstairs, where Alexandro sits at a large desk full of papers, telephone to his ear. On the walls are photographs of village streets filled with white-clothed tables. "My father hosts a charity wine-tasting each year," Alexandro nods toward the pictures as he hangs up the phone. "He loves to do this. It is tradition now."

Clarke and I fumble with words for several minutes, too timid to ask if we can spend the night after so much has already been given us. Clarke's nerve melts completely, and out of embarrassment at our embarrassment, I ask if we can stay. "Of course. We were going to invite you anyway."

The next morning, we leave the winery with five bottles of wine—two have replaced the water bottles on Clarke's frame. "Next time you come, stay a week," Alexandro translates his mother's invitation.

"We may stay forever," Clarke laughs.

Not far from town, gray clouds bunch overhead and then settle, gathering determination for a storm similar to the one brewing inside my own mind. The night before, after experiencing so much love from Alexandro's family, I'd hoped to take advantage of a bed and bath and extra time to make love with Clarke, or at least to snuggle together. I miss sleeping in his arms. Clean and shining and relaxed, I'd crawled into bed expectantly but Clarke curled up in the armchair to write, slipping out of bed early the next morning to continue his journal. Clearly we're growing apart, I think now, so involved in discovering others that our own relationship doesn't matter any more. Bicycling under the leaden sky, filled with the love of strangers but not of my own husband, I make the decision that I'm not willing to live my life without an open, honest, intimate relationship. If we both want it, it can happen; but if that isn't what Clarke wants, there's nothing I can do but wish him well and be on my way. The relationship we have now isn't enough, not for me.

Loading up on crusty, fresh rolls at a *panetteria*, we find shelter in a covered picnic area in a public park. All of the warmth has gone from the day and we eat our bread in silence, shivering with cold as rain bursts from the sky, surrounding our enclosure with silvery curtains, clamoring a drumbeat on the metal roof above us. Still we sit, and the rain comes down harder as we argue once again about our marriage, blaming each other for our problems instead of taking responsibility for our own actions.

Before the trip, one of the best ways for us to understand each other's feelings when we disagreed was to take turns arguing the point from each other's perspective; our natural inclination to win any argument allowed us each to present the other's case convincingly, which led to understanding and compromise. This time, we don't even try to comprehend each other's feelings. Finally worn down, we slump, cold and lonely, farther apart than ever. The rain comes down harder. "I wonder if we should just pitch our tent under this roof," Clarke says finally, gazing mournfully at our still-dry clothes and bicycles.

"There's no one to ask for permission," I respond miserably. Digging into the clothes pack, I pull out long pants, a sweatshirt and full gloves for each of us. Zipping up tightly, we pedal into the storm at five o'clock and bicycle through the downpour for two hours. Although I'm warm enough, water running from my hair stings my eyes from the dirt on my face and it's difficult to see through storm-streaked sunglasses. The rain pelts my skin like tiny pins, and every time a car approaches, it and I seem to hit a puddle at the same time, sending waves of water to drench my already-soaked shoes and socks.

For the first time in Italy, our request to camp is turned down – four times in a row. I begin to panic, certain we'll drown if we have to travel much farther. *"Buona sera, signora,"* I say wetly to the woman who comes to the door of the next farm. *"Mi chiamo Susana e questo é mi marito Clarke. Siamo Americani sopra bicicleti per un' anno."* The woman stares as we crowd closer under the eaves. I continue in marginal Italian, "Is it possible, please, to sleep here for one night? We have a small tent and need only water." How many times have we tried to translate that same speech into Spanish, French, Flemish, Dutch, German and now Italian – two hundred?

The woman looks from me to Clarke, explaining that she doesn't have an extra bedroom. Unwilling to let number five get away because she doesn't have something we don't need, we keep talking – me in fractured Italian, Clarke with gestures – hoping that she has a garage or barn where we can get in out of the rain. Finally, she understands our request. *"Ah, sì, signor e signora,"* she laughs, and pulling on a sweater, runs through the rain to a wide doorway at the end of her house which opens on to a room full of chickens and rabbits. "Okay?" she asks.

"Sì, signora, é buono." Yes, this is good. Very good indeed, especially when Carmela allows our dripping bicycles inside and insists that we come in later for dinner. We accept gratefully, presenting her with a bottle of Franco's family wine.

As we set up our tent, a dark figure appears in the doorway with a rag to polish the light bulb over our heads. *"Mi chiamo Isaia,"* he introduces himself, then sets out to teach me Italian. Discovering that I catch on quickly to the beautiful language, Carmela's husband redoubles his efforts, gesturing broadly and exaggerating his inflection, which I copy with the same great gusto until we're howling with laughter. After a wonderful meal, warm and dry at last, with more than enough wine and hot food to keep us insulated during the night, Clarke and I return to the contented hens as they trundle about their coop next to our dry bicycles, then fall asleep holding hands.

The sun shines through scattered clouds the next morning as we crisscross south toward Venice through fields and villages clean but unkempt like a person just getting up in the morning. At Casale, we stop in a café for *cappuccino*, then pedal out of town past two young bicyclists whose girlfriends perch facing them on their handlebars, Sunday skirts spread like fans across their knees.

Alexandro's brother had told us that bicycles aren't allowed in Venice, so we hope to store them at someone's house near the causeway. Skirting Mestre after seventy-five kilometers, we pedal to the last town on the shore, but locked fences surround every house. Clarke turns down a ragtag lane facing the lagoon that surrounds the island of Venezia. "Let's try just one more street," he suggests, knowing that our only choice is to keep looking until we find what we're looking for.

The last house has no locked gate; in fact, it has no gate at all, nor a fence. Instead, a construction crane guards the front yard of the dilapidated home, along with an old German shepherd who doesn't bark, perhaps because the crane doesn't. The house is full of people. *"Buon giorno,"* we call through the open window. A young woman appears, accompanied by a small dog and an older man wearing a red stocking cap, and we're immediately offered an open garage for the tent and our bicycles. Rolling them under cover, we rummage for our camp stove.

"Per favore." The young woman stands politely next to her father. *"Caffè?"* Her father beams his own invitation with a smile, and we obediently follow them inside the house, where eight or ten people crowd around the kitchen table playing cards and an enormous woman sits by the window stringing white beads on a wire. As we sit, cookies and wine and coffee appear on the table and we're officially introduced to

the family: Lucia, her father and mother Danilo and Giocanda; Giocanda's mother and her cousin and her sister; several friends, two dogs and ten cats.

When Lucia's husband and young son arrive, along with Danilo's brother, who's celebrating his birthday, Danilo and Giocanda invite us to dinner. Good and plentiful and crazy, this bunch; the table overflows with laughter and wine and good food, generously shared. At ten-thirty, I thank the family for dinner, wanting to return to our tent for a good night's sleep. Clarke reluctantly follows, chastising me for my abrupt departure. "I'm tired, Clarke. Sometimes I need time for myself instead of everyone else. We had plenty of time for conversation tonight, to learn new Italian, to talk with the family."

After morning coffee, our bikes safely tucked in the garage, Danilo's brother escorts us to the bus stop, giving us tickets and schedules to Venezia. There we discover a jumbly five-hundred-year-old city suspended in a lagoon, full of color and cracks and cats and pigeons. "No wonder there are more cats than people here," I say as a white kitten looks up into Clarke's camera lens. "No cars and lots of fish."

After sniggling our way through tiny streets and alleyways from bridge to bridge across the huge Piazza San Marco full of pigeons and people, past the gondolas filled with tourists and produce and garbage, and through students and posters and art, we thread our way back to the bus, returning to Danilo's at five o'clock.

The whole family gathers for photos as Giocanda's cousin holds a huge white goose away from the playful jaws of the German shepherd, then Danilo emerges from the back of the garage with a giant oil can, drenching our derailleur chains with black, oozy oil that splatters all over our legs and the bike frames as we pedal away from the loving house, certain that Venice to us will always be Danilo's family as much as the beautiful canals.

When we stop at a small farm twenty-five kilometers east, Giovanni invites us to stay before we can ask permission to camp, then his wife asks us for dinner. "I have only two eggs," she explains in Italian, insisting nonetheless that we join them.

In America, if we don't have something lovely to give—a fine meal, a perfect guestroom—we hesitate to give at all. Maria and Giovanni give all that they have, unconcerned whether or not it's enough; and two eggs and a flat place in front of the door are more than enough. As we settle our tent next to the farm animals, I wonder if I'll be able to remember back home that it's the giving that matters, not the gift.

In the morning, Maria and Giovanni gather us inside for coffee and juice and salami sandwiches, and although worried that our breakfast would have been their dinner, we also know that their gift is too important to refuse.

Near a tiny village late in the day, my bicycle seat falls apart, spreading pieces of bolt and bracket all over the highway. As we search for my seat parts, an old man helps us find the sheared bolt and then bicycles home to find another—but it's too short. "Use my seat," Clarke offers. "Let's hope the next town has a bike shop." We attach Clarke's seat to my bike, but the post is too slender so the seat slips to its lowest position and I pedal through the village, knees pumping high but certainly more comfortable than Clarke, who stands up the eight kilometers to Lúsia.

Within minutes, the whole village congregates at the bike shop to hear who we are and ask about our trip. After the shop owner refuses payment for his repair, one bystander races home to get a bottle of *prosecco*, and we celebrate our ability to continue our travels, thanks to this town. The villager hands me the opened bottle to take with us. *"No, no, signor,"* I protest, thinking he's already been too generous. Misunderstanding my refusal of the sparkling wine, he goes inside for an unopened bottle, insisting that we take it instead.

Whole again, we continue west into a huge red setting sun and stop after seventy kilometers at a vegetable farm, where for the first time since we crossed into Italy, we prepare our own dinner, speaking English to each other instead of Italian to strangers. As we wash our plates, Mario invites us in for coffee and wine with his family, insisting that my Italian is excellent. Already, I understand a great deal of what I hear and my inflection seems natural, unlike French or German, which grate on my nose and throat. At each house in Italy, I've learned a few more words, thrilled with the language and the Italians who teach it to me.

In the morning, after washing clothes and my hair with the garden hose, we start off about nine-thirty; Mario and his workers are already rinsing vegetables in huge concrete ponds, lettuce heads bobbing like green apples in a giant tub. An hour and a half later, we stop for directions in Lendinara, and I take a picture with my memory: Clarke, feet planted firmly on each side of his bulbously-baggaged bicycle, bending over his map next to the church steps, his long brown body like the stem of a mushroom under his white bicycle helmet— surrounded by a dozen chattering Italians, each wanting to help pick the best route to Cinqueterre, near La Spezia on the Ligurian Sea.

I have my entourage also, another baker's dozen who are more interested in who we are than in where we're going. As Clarke gestures and smiles and tries to speak Italian with his hands, I'm once again filled with amazement at the ease with which we're accepted by strangers.

Two days earlier, we'd discussed how difficult it is to knock on doors every night. "Take the normal stress of being a houseguest, Clarke, and add the permanency of being a houseguest every night for a year. Then be guests of strangers, arriving with no invitation whatsoever, dirty and tired, having to convince someone who has never even heard of you to let you stay. If that's not enough, do it in a foreign language!"

Clarke had thought for a moment, then added, "You forgot the part about our being the only Americans many of these people have ever met. The way we act influences the way they may always view our country."

"And the frustration that our ability to communicate is so limited, Clarke. We spend so much time repeating ourselves—who we are, where we're from, what we're doing."

"Maybe it's time to have everything, our new friends and each other, Susan. Maybe it's time to slow down, to talk with each other about more than routes and groceries and where we'll stay for the night. You're right—all of our real conversations are with strangers." I'd looked up, surprised. "It may be inexpensive to travel this way, but it's not easy. We still have half a year left and we've been to ten of the dozen countries we considered to begin with. How far have we ridden so far?"

I had consulted my little journal. "Almost nine thousand kilometers, fifty-six hundred miles."

I let the conversation drop. Clarke needed to work this out for himself so that he wouldn't feel slowed down by my own fatigue and stress. We'd continued on in silence, but I knew that he was considering our words long after we left them vibrating on the side of the road. Could it be that we would take care of our relationship after all?

Sure enough, in Lendinara, an hour and a half after leaving our last temporary home, we allow ourselves to be kidnapped twice—first by Carlo and his daughter Silvia. "My father would like you to have coffee with us," Silvia explains in Italian mixed with English. She and her father are in my chattering cluster and I waddle my bike up to Clarke, parting the sea of gesturing Italians to forward the invitation.

Without a moment's hesitation, Clarke agrees, and abandoning our bicycles outside a tiny *ristorante*, the four of us file inside for *espresso* and a bilingual language lesson.

Vito meets us outside the door—he'd been part of Clarke's crowd. He speaks a little English, he explains, because he spent six years as a prisoner of war in Africa and Egypt in World War II. Now, with thumbs in his pants that ride high on his stomach, he tips back and forth and says in English, "Come. You will eat at my house." Clarke and I look at each other. "My wife, she has prepared a meal already for you." He must have run home after we'd gone into the café for coffee, issuing orders or requesting permission to have guests, depending on his relationship with Mama.

Vito and his friends escort us in a long procession home, where a long table in the dining room is set for twelve with a tablecloth and napkins, beautiful dishes and fine glassware. I'm amused and embarrassed; my bath had been in a hose that morning. Giavanna rushes in from the kitchen, a flowered apron tied around her middle, gray hair falling in wisps about her worried face. "*Buon giorno, signora,*" I greet her. "*Piacere. Come sta?*"

No doubt surprised that I speak a few words of her language, she responds, smiling, "*Molto bene, grazie,*" then excuses herself to go back to the kitchen.

We share a giant lunch of lasagna from fresh homemade pasta, pork stuffed with artichoke hearts, green beans and onions, cheese and fruit and wine and *espresso*. Giavanna scurries back and forth between the kitchen and the dining room, making sure that her meal is perfect. It's more than perfect; it's divine. "Giavanna, sit down and eat with us," I plead.

Smiling, she brushes aside my entreaties, darting back to the kitchen for another plate of pork. Finally, she sits down at the end of the meal. "The food was wonderful," I say in Italian, and Clarke adds his thanks. Giavanna ducks her head, embarrassed at the attention although clearly pleased with the compliments. Her eyes fill with tears as we include her in the conversation and rave about her cooking. I feel guilty, knowing that this woman had bustled about her kitchen all morning to make a fabulous meal for people she'd never met while her husband told war stories in rusty English outside in the sunshine.

After lunch, more ready for sleep than for bicycling, we gather around our coffee cups as Silvia's mother arrives to give us a large book, a limited edition about an Italian artist who was born in their village. As we stand in the doorway surrounded by villagers, Vito speaks for us all. "You will stay with me, in my heart." Tearfully, he leads us out of town on his heavy black bicycle, no doubt proud of entertaining the special guests, proud of his English, proud of his village. Pausing at the edge of town, Vito poses like a soldier for photographs with each of us, shakes Clarke's hand and then mine, hugs and kisses us both, then pedals away, turning to wave once or twice as he goes home to Giavanna, his old bicycle wobbling precariously when he looks over his shoulder to salute one more time.

Just outside of town, a car has hit an old woman. She's not hurt but her bicycle is smashed. How lucky we've been – nine thousand kilometers, and this is the first accident we've seen although we're on the highways eight to twelve hours every day.

Five kilometers from Lendinara, a young woman stops to help with our route, then motions for us to follow her, pedaling back the way we've come. I wonder if Vito's friends are kidnapping us one more time, but she turns into the driveway of a small factory and disappears inside after directing us to wait. A stunning young woman dressed stylishly in black comes outside. "I am Chiara," the chic woman says in perfect English. "My sister says that you are lost. My husband is a bicyclist too, and he just returned from Austria, Hungary and Romania. You must come home with me for dinner."

It's four o'clock and we've bicycled only fourteen kilometers for the day. Stuffed to the gills with Giavanna's amazing lunch, we look at each other. When we discussed slowing down, we hadn't meant grinding to a halt, but if we've learned anything in this country, it's that one doesn't say no to an Italian. "May we put our tent in your garden for the night afterwards?" Clarke asks.

"Certainly," Chiara replies, leading us to her pretty apartment, leaving us with a bathtub all to ourselves so that we can relax and clean up while she returns to work.

"You're willing to leave two strangers alone in your house?"

"Of course."

This is my third bath in seven months that hasn't been in a river, and I wash and wash again until the water turns cold, drying my hair with a hair dryer for the first time in Europe while Clarke takes his turn in the tub. Unable to resist, I dab a tiny bit of Chiara's cologne behind my ears, then feel like a thief. When we emerge from the bathroom an hour later, shiny and clean, Chiara and Maurizio are preparing pasta and meat and salad. "I wonder if I can gain ten pounds in one day," I whisper to Clarke, suspecting that I surely can if we continue to spend more hours eating than bicycling.

We may be only three miles from Lendinara, but this progressive young couple is light years in lifestyle from Vito and Giavanna. Chiara, thirty-four and pregnant with her first child, owns her own clothing manufacturing business, has a beautifully-furnished flat and looks like a million stylish bucks. Each summer, she travels with friends all over Europe while her husband takes solo bicycle trips. Maurizio holds a doctorate degree in nuclear engineering and teaches high school physics, is an accomplished musician and speaks fluent English, French and German. He's in charge of cooking pasta while Chiara prepares the sauce. I can't picture Vito in Giavanna's kitchen for one moment. "Where did you learn your perfect English?" we ask Maurizio during dinner.

He shrugs. "I wanted to read English engineering textbooks, so translated them with a dictionary and an English grammar book. Then, after university, I took private schooling to learn how to speak your language correctly." Immediately, the Italian I've been so proud of disappears completely, embarrassed at its own inadequacy.

We discuss politics and travel. Europeans, we've noticed, particularly teenagers, often know as much about American politics as we, whereas we know little about European governments. At Franco's winery, Alexandro had told us that Mussolini had no choice but to ally with Hitler. "It was the only way to keep Hitler from taking over our country," he explained. "Mussolini hated Hitler too, but he loved Italy more."

"Who's the president of Italy?" I ask Maurizio now, embarrassed not to know. "Or does Italy even have a president?"

Maurizio laughs. "Do not worry, most Italians have no idea who's president either. Anytime someone doesn't like what's going on, they call an election. Our president has very little power—he's never in office long enough to do anything."

Clarke and I prepare to put up our tent in the little garage already inhabited by our bicycles. "No, no, no," Chiara protests. "You will sleep in our bed."

"Absolutely not."

"We will sleep at my parents' house. You deserve to be spoiled for one night."

Maurizio breaks in. "Remember, I know what it is like to ride bicycles and camp."

We sleep so well that it's hard to give up the bed in the morning, but by the time Maurizio and Chiara arrive with pastries for breakfast, Clarke and I are happily washing the supper dishes, humming. Chiara is horrified. "If you only knew what a pleasure it is to wash dishes in a sink with hot water," I laugh. "This is fun."

Pedaling through the capital of the province, Réggio Nell'Emília, we get lost and stop at a bookstand to buy a map. The owner refuses to sell us one, preferring instead to give us free directions by pointing a hand with long fingernails to the highway out of town toward the scenic route to La Spezia.

At the next village, after consulting with her father-in-law, Patricie gives us permission to camp in the field behind a white stucco house with a large, tiled patio. When I return for water out of the hose, the old man comes pounding outside, and after long and thoughtful examination of me, invites me to get water from the kitchen tap. Tall and distinguished and authoritative, he escorts me back to our campsite, studying the clouds, then presents us with a ground cloth in case it rains, explaining importantly that was how it had been done when he was in the army during the war. "*Mi chiamo Marco*," he tells us, introducing himself finally.

In the middle of the night, we wake up in a lake. It's raining hard, and instead of the water soaking into the ground as usual, Marco's ground cloth gathers it under the tent, where it seeps inside. "Now I know how Kelly and Megan felt all summer," Clarke says as he piles the contents of his packs in a mound to keep at least some of the stuff from submerging.

In the morning, around the corner of the barn, we discover a large, dry opening where we could have spent the night high and dry. As we pack, Patricie invites us for tea, but when we arrive at the house, Marco offers coffee. "I am sorry," I say in Italian, "but we are having tea with your daughter-in-law."

Patricie and her husband live on the third floor of the house. As we gather around her table, Marco's wife climbs the stairs from her apartment on the first floor, puts a pot of coffee on the table without a word, and then leaves. "No one refuses Marco, do they?" I smile.

"Who?" asks Patricie.

"Marco, your father-in-law."

It's Patricie's turn to laugh. "That isn't his name," she says. "His name is Ultimio. It means 'the last.' He hates the name because it makes him sound like an afterthought." After a moment or two, she continues. "My husband and I live on the third floor because Ultimio doesn't approve of our not having children. My husband's younger brother gets the second floor because he has three children already."

"Marco" meets us on the front porch as we leave. I can't resist. "Ultimio," I smile, shaking my finger at him, "ah, ah, ah." Grinning sheepishly, he gestures for us to follow him to a metal building next to the house, a shop for building wooden pallets which he operates with his two sons. Pointing to a huge furnace at the back, he builds up a roaring blaze with wood chips and sawdust so that we can dry our dripping sleeping bags and tent, but by the time our equipment is dry enough to pack, rain oozes out of the flat gray sky, and then pours.

Ultimio trots into the shop, followed by his wife. "You cannot bicycle in the rain," he announces in Italian.

"It warms us," I assure him.

"You must have a meal first," Alma insists.

Inside their small apartment, we devour a huge bowl of buttered spaghetti with fresh parmesan cheese after Alma demonstrates the correct way to cook Italian pasta. As Patricie translates, Alma keeps her eye on a small television. "*Televisione Americana?*" I ask.

"*Dallas!*" Alma exclaims, her eyes lighting up with pleasure.

"*Dallas* is the number one television program in Italy," Patricie tells us. No wonder Europeans think Americans are strange.

We're finally ready to go at two-thirty and Ultimio and Patricie pose for a picture on the porch. On his way into town to play cards, the old Italian looks dapper in a sport coat and hat. We motion for Alma to join the photo but she shakes her head, indicating her plain dress and apron and clunky shoes. "You are beautiful," I say in Italian, and mean it. Finally, she peeks at Clarke's camera from behind her husband, wrapping her hands in her apron after smoothing her hair.

From Réggio Nell'Emília, the road climbs 6000 feet over the next seventy kilometers, forty-some miles. We pedal only twenty-five kilometers that afternoon because of the rain and difficult grade, stopping at six o'clock to buy groceries. At the market, we meet an Italian on the home stretch of a two-month bicycle trip. Surprisingly, we've seen few people touring on bicycles—three North American couples, and two or three German groups in Spain.

Cold wind and fading daylight convince us to stop at the next town, but there isn't one. An old brick building is deserted, and we pedal on, up and up, frozen inside and out, until a tiny group of houses and a café stuck to the hillside give us someone to ask. The next morning, finally breaking through the mist, we continue to climb in the cold, humid sun, inching up the mountainside that stretches on its tiptoes and spreads valleys and treetops like skirts to its ankles. "How are your knees?" Clarke asks when I signal a break.

"They hurt. How are you doing?"

"Believe me, I can feel this climb."

At each turn in the road, we're treated with a new view of the mountain monster whose chest we climb. We snatch another quick break near a solitary house hanging over the road, but the cold wind freezes our sweat and we decide to continue before we've caught our breath. "*Buon giorno!*" a woman calls from the balcony of the house.

"*Buon giorno, signora,*" we call back.

"*Caffe?*" she offers.

"We can't," Clarke says to me. "We don't dare let our muscles cool off in this weather. Sorry. It sounds good to me too."

"*No, grazie, signora. É impossibile,*" I call up to the woman, explaining in Italian that I can't let my knees get cold.

"Ah!" she replies, understanding. "*Un minuto, per favore.*"

"Come on, Susan, let's go."

"She said wait, Clarke."

Bounding out of the house, the woman holds out a pair of striped woolen legwarmers from her daughter's dance class. Clarke grins as I pull them on gratefully, and we follow Rosanna inside to bundle Clarke's knees into woolen socks that Rosanna cuts off from their toes. While we enjoy coffee and strawberries in the kitchen, Rosanna goes outside, returning with another unusual gift—flower seeds. "Will you plant these when you get home?" she asks shyly in Italian. "Perhaps you will remember me when they bloom."

"We will remember you anyway," I assure her, carefully folding the seeds in a tissue.

Warmed by the hot coffee, we retrieve our bicycles from the garden wall where they huddle against the wind, then pedal off into the damp mist. Near the top of the pass, we run out of energy. It's almost seven o'clock, and the air temperature is dropping too fast to keep warm, no matter how hard we pedal in our new legwarmers. "The nearest town is another twenty-five kilometers," Clarke announces after studying the map while I rub my knees and jump up and down.

"I can't make it."

"We'll just have to go on, then, and look for shelter in the trees somewhere. How's your water?"

"Almost gone. But I'd rather go without than ride fifteen more miles today."

Slowly we pull ourselves up the mountain, pushing and pulling with every muscle we have or can invent until a narrow road cuts off the highway to the left. Two young girls stroll toward us, arm-in-arm. "*Buona sera, signorine,*" I greet them. "Does this road lead to a village?"

"*Sì, signora, due chilometri,*" they answer and walk on, looking back once to wave.

Clarke and I look dubiously at the road hunching up the mountain like an inchworm. "If I can't make it, Clarke, just leave me to die by the roadside."

When we finally reach town, the houses hang like starfish on a cliff above the river. At the very top of the village, however, we locate a tiny flat patio next to a house across the street from the church and are given permission to stay if we'll be careful of the flowers that march around the patio like the rococo frame of a mirror. After our tent is filled with packs to keep it from blowing away in the high wind, Auclide suggests that we move it in front of the shed next to his patio. Assuring him that we won't need the windbreak, only because we're too tired to move everything, we ask instead if we can lean our bicycles against the little building, wanting us to accept his additional hospitality. They end up inside the shed, warm and dry all night.

Huddled in our tent out of the cold, we cook dinner; then Auclide and his wife rush us inside to warm up, giving us coffee and *grappa* by the hot stove while we discuss Italy and America and World War II. Toasty warm with heat and liquor, we bid the elderly couple goodnight and set out in the cold for our cloth bedroom. "If it rains," Fidalma calls after us, "you can sleep inside by the stove." She's already confiscated our damp laundry to hang in the house to dry.

We spend the night listening to the church bells across the street. They ring the hour; and on the half hour, ring the hour plus a different-toned note. We always know what time it is, because we're always awake. At seven the next morning, as the church bells play "Santa Maria"—all four verses—we're invited inside for *caffè con latte* and French brandy.

Gathering up our dry laundry, we push our bicycles into the wet morning to ride to the top of the pass, refreshed if not rested. "You two are spoiled," I whisper to the bikes so that our hosts won't hear. "How do you manage to stay inside while we sleep out in the tent?"

It starts to rain again, covering in clouds the mountaintop toward which we've struggled for three days. In fact, everything is lost in clouds, including Clarke, who cycles only a few feet ahead. "I hope there aren't any cars close behind," I call up to him, my voice echoing in the fog.

"Stay close to the edge of the road."

"I can't see the edge of the road."

We know we've reached the top only when it's easier to pedal, then we pick up speed, rocks from a mountain sling shot, racing the wind and the rain and the clouds down the mountain's back, dropping almost 3000 feet in eighteen kilometers. Glimpsing a view here and there through tattered cloud curtains fluttering in the wind, we mostly watch the road and try to ignore the fact that we're freezing.

In Fivizzano, we come out of a market to another downpour and pack our food with wet, shaking hands, then continue until the rain stops. In a suburb of La Spezia, we eat lunch in a park and then wind through the busy city looking for the coast highway. A wrong turn near the port sends us two kilometers out of the way, up a fifteen percent grade; the correct road, when we find it, spirals up above the city like a tightly-coiled spring. After eighty steep, wet kilometers, we find a house clinging to the edge of the mountain whose owners let us sleep in their garage.

After a late dinner, we walk along the shelf highway overlooking La Spezia. The port city looks like a double handful of gold and silver stars reflected on a mirror surrounded by black velvet. "I don't know which I like best, Clarke, Italy or the Italians," I say as we tuck into our tent, grateful to be prone and warm.

Chapter 23

THE MORNING AIR ABOVE La Spezia is thin and watery, washed clean and pale by the rain. As we pedal higher, villages cling to the mountainsides like stone masks to a mossy, ancient wall and vineyards march up the mountains in dusty brown rows, holding on to each other and the rocks, defying gravity.

We're looking for the five villages of the Cinqueterre. After several long tunnels, a sign directs us to a narrow shelf road crossing the mountain cliffs by the sea. Up we go, walking and pedaling by turn, hot and tired, unable to understand the logic of a high road that doesn't string villages together—every few kilometers, a fork in the road plunges down the side of the mountain to a town on the rocky coast. "Why are we climbing up, when civilization is down?" I complain, sweat dripping down my back. As we climb, my stomach grows more and more queasy, and after a clunkety old truck bounces past billowing exhaust fumes, I almost throw up. "I'm not sure I can go on, Clarke. I'm about to pass out—whether from my stomach or the heat, I don't know."

"How's the food supply?"

"Don't mention the word. But to answer your question, we're out." While I rest, Clarke rummages through my food pack to find chocolate, cherry marmalade and mayonnaise. "If I can't make it to Monterosso, you're going to have a horrible dinner," I say, my stomach churning.

"If you can't make it to Monterosso, you're going to have a horrible time getting help if you need it."

Narrowing, the road turns to dirt, and we bump along for hours between potholes filled with rainwater. The weather is brutally hot and humid and there's no shade along the mountaintop, just dusty vineyards and occasional farms strewn uphill like dead leaves tossed from a huge hand. The road continues to climb until we reach the road to Monterosso, which falls from the sky in an exuberant rush to the village which crowds against the sea in a puzzle of pale colors: ocher, salmon, slate, red and brown.

Monterosso's one campground doesn't allow tents. After six exhausting hours of bicycling, we can't stay, and all the houses that might have garden space are high above us. We've looked forward to a couple of days of sun and ocean, but not to running up and down a fifteen percent grade once or twice a day. Regardless, I'm too sick to pedal back up the mountain. "How about taking the train to the next village?" Clarke suggests.

"You cannot take your bicycles on the train except as baggage," the clerk explains in Italian while Clarke waits on the street with our bikes. "You must remove all of your packs and check them separately. I do not advise it. It is very, very expensive, much more than passenger fare." And the three flights of stairs to the station from the street seem insurmountable at the moment. We don't have it in us.

As we pedal up and down the quay discussing our alternatives, or lack of them, a loud voice erupts from the open door of a *ristorante*. "Stop!" it hollers, then is followed by the restaurant owner. "It's illegal to camp anywhere but in the campground," Andy tells us after we explain our dilemma, "but I will help you find a place to stay if you're not fussy. Come back at five-thirty." When we return two hours later, he directs us to put our bikes in the garden behind the restaurant. "Eat dinner," he says. "Then I'll find you something."

Of all times to have our one Italian restaurant meal, this is the worst. Tired and discouraged and still nauseated, I only want to resolve the sleeping problem, but 31,000 *lire* later, two days' allowance, Andy still hasn't come up with a solution. "Go sit in the bar," he says, scooping our money from the table. "I will see you as soon as I can."

"He wants us to spend more money first," I snarl at Clarke.

"Stop, Susan, the man's busy. At least he offered to help."

"Sorry. I just want to be done with today."

Clarke nurses a beer while I scrunch on a barstool, dirty and tired and bitchy. Two hours later, Andy offers a corner of the garden behind the restaurant after closing. Whenever that is, I think sullenly, hunching down farther like a gnome. A young Scot enters the bar with his bride, he and his father friends of Andy's from twenty years of vacations in the Cinqueterre. After they exchange news for awhile, Andy asks if they have an extra room in their flat for us. "Of course," Caspar replies, "but first let's have another beer." We buy drinks for Caspar and Susan for two hours. Perhaps noticing that my eyes are shut every time he turns to me, Caspar finally says at midnight, "Why don't we just give you a key to the flat? We're not ready to turn in yet."

My eyes pop open. "Thank you," I reply quickly before Clarke decides to wait. "You don't know how much we appreciate this." I'm more than happy to be a party pooper; Caspar and Susan are twenty years younger and haven't bicycled sick from La Spezia in blistering heat.

Leaving the bikes to their own devices in back of the restaurant, we find the flat, and by twelve-thirty, I'm sound asleep in a real bed, finally appreciative of the generosity of these two Scottish strangers and the help of their Italian friend.

"Let's go up the coast to Levanto," Clarke suggests the next morning. "Andy says there are a couple of campgrounds that allow tents."

"Fine." Still physically drained, I'm unwilling, really, to stay or to go, but back up the mountain we pedal, taking our minds off our physical pain with a heated discussion. Politically, Clarke and I are worlds apart. "Andy is a really nice guy," Clarke starts in, "but he gouges the tourists just like in Aspen at home."

"You don't have any idea what his costs are," I defend the man I'd been angry with the night before. "Can you imagine how expensive it is to get food delivered to this place? He probably makes the same net profit as every other Joe in the restaurant business. Our dinner with wine was only twenty bucks!"

"You always defend business just because you were a stockbroker. Why don't you ever see the other side, that of people?"

"Business is people, Clarke. What do you think Andy is? Corporations are owned and run by people, not by things. It's you who are criticizing people. Government is people too; you always act like it's some artificial entity."

We haggle and pedal all the way up the mountain, then streak down into Levanto in time to get a campsite and spend the afternoon at the beach. I lie on the sand and think of nothing, tired all over—mentally, physically and emotionally. Sometimes, I decide, nothing matters. Writing, riding, talking, loving, being loved.

It's not a negative feeling; it's no feeling at all. Half listening to the monotony of wave after wave and to children's games that are the same as in America, I wonder about the futility of reaching higher and farther.

As the sun dips behind a gray haze, the sea flattens to slate, its glitter disappearing into bumpiness, its light flat and unshadowed. The beach people leave in couples and small bunches, trailing cold seawater over the sand, their brightly-colored swimsuits disappearing into the village to leave the sand and ocean a monochrome of gray and white. I feel detached from everything, including myself.

After dinner in our tent, we have another rip-roaring fight about our relationship. Same song, twelfth verse. It gets pretty brutal.

It rains in the night and a little stream washes through our tent, soaking everything. We get up without words the next morning, straggling back to the beach to be alone with our despair, exhausted. We hang on, but tenuously. I feel like a room full of shattered old glass, empty and fragile, like someone without skin. What should I do? For now, I can't even begin to think about it, and I lie on the sand, absorbing the sun, aware of Clarke lying next to me, a million miles away.

I'm coming apart at the seams, I think, mentally lost on a sand beach with the long horizon surrounding me like the rim of a cereal bowl, flat and unending. There's no flavor to my life, only hard-baked earth and a glittering sunshine that fills my eyes with so much light that I can no longer see. My feet burn as I try to walk up and down the beach to find a new view, but all I can see are miles of endless sand broken by dirty foam and scraps of slimy seaweed. All the shells are broken, in the process of grinding themselves into sand, their whorls and colors lost forever. Thrown from beyond my cereal bowl rim like leftover milk, my heart is obliterated in the sunshine.

Neither of us is ready to tackle the mountains between us and anywhere else, so we stay two more nights, eating ice cream each afternoon, reading, writing, listening to music and the surf. I buy a bottle of cologne, *Noire* by Bic, the cigarette lighter people, for 4000 *lire*, less than three dollars. It's the only stuff cheap enough to buy and small enough to carry—and it smells like lighter fluid.

The second night, we eat pasta salad on the beach, and as the sun sets, Clarke makes a life-sized sand sculpture of a reclining female and I mold the face of a man. In the morning, after washing the tent and us and our clothes, we meet a twenty-year-old Brit who just walked to Italy from England, about 1400 kilometers, and I wonder if he'll ever be happy with a settled life after tasting travel on such a basic, important level. Will we?

Because the banks are closed, we have no cash for the boat back to La Spezia and pedal out of town just before one o'clock, having resolved nothing about our marriage. As hot September sunshine broils my body, I think of all we've done the last thirty weeks. I'm exhausted.

As we pedal next to the seawall at Viaréggio in heavy traffic the next afternoon, a car bumps a pedestrian, who turns to kick the vehicle as we pass. "I wonder what this place is like in August, the big vacation month?" Clarke asks, evading the flung leg. Shopping malls with glitzy stores crowd the road along the shore. I feel displaced, crowded myself. "This road stops up ahead at a nature park," Clarke says after consulting the map. "We'll have to take the national highway into Pisa."

At the south end of the nature park, a tiny secondary road loops off the national. Black women in tight, short skirts and plunging necklines stand here and there along the road, watching us pass without a word. They look like the prostitutes we saw in the Bois de Boulogne in Paris.

An old woman sits under a tree at an ancient farm. She allows us to put our tent next to her stone barn, watching from her chair as we fill our water bottles from the hand pump above the rock laundry tub in the garden. Clara tells us in Italian that she can't believe that we're bicycling all over Europe. "I am ready to die," she says. "I am eighty. If you return here in two months, I will already be *mort, dormire.*" Dead, sleeping. We believe her.

"Life is so short, Susan," Clarke says as we pedal away the next morning after yet another argument about money, communication and control. "Why do we spend it fighting?"

"I don't know." I feel bitter, desperate, without hope.

It takes four hours to get in and out of Pisa just to take a picture of a tipsy tower. The traffic is horrible—ancient narrow streets only wide enough for horse-drawn carts now must accommodate cars, parking, and our fat bicycles. At the Piazza di Miracoli, we fix lunch on the grass next to the leaning tower and speak briefly with an Australian family doing a whirlwind tour of Europe as a scruffy young man edges closer. "My name is Charlie," he begins, and I wonder what he wants.

"Hello!" says Clarke, as usual happy to talk to anyone but me.

Charlie turns out to be an honors student in statistics from the University of Melbourne who's taking a six-month round-the-world tour. He looks like a deadbeat but is intelligent, witty and interesting. As we compare travel notes, we forget all about visiting the tower, parting with promises to let each other know when we arrive home safely.

We're turned down twice that evening. Finally, just west of Empoli, we're given permission to stay behind the house of Asmaro and Gina, Italians who'd lived in France for forty years, and we welcome the big dose of Italian/French hospitality after the coldness of Pisa. Their dog spends the evening munching on a bone as big as he, too busy and happy to bark. "It's the knee of a bull," Asmaro explains.

We're drifting east toward Florence, stopping for lunch in a small park in a tiny village west of the city. As I slice off a chunk of bread for sandwiches, Clarke pours a black plastic cupful of wine from our almost-empty bottle. "I feel like I'm slowing down, Susan. I've felt that way since Cinqueterre."

"Maybe our intuition is just telling us to take more time for ourselves, like we discussed after leaving Franco's house." I polish off a carton of yogurt, then lick my spoon clean and put it back into Clarke's side pack.

We sit for a long time, mostly in silence, then I write while Clarke walks around the woody park, returning with a question. "How about going back to Spain after Italy or Greece? It was a beautiful country, but we missed something there."

"People?"

"Yes. We didn't really start getting to know families until France."

"I've thought a lot about that, Clarke." Then, after a very long moment, "What about Morocco?"

"Could you handle it again?"

"I don't know. But I don't want to miss Greece; it will be our greatest challenge language-wise, particularly since Greek doesn't use our alphabet. How will we read maps?"

After talking all afternoon about what might be next in our lives, we pedal out of town into early evening hoping to be kidnapped by friendlies. Nothing happens. Turning down a dusty road to a few small houses after two hours, we wave at two young boys as we pass the last barn. The boys chase our bicycles, and soon every bike in the neighborhood surrounds us like a litter of aluminum puppies. A dozen parents fold into the throng, deciding that we should camp for the night at the home of Domenico and Margerita and their son Leonardo.

Domenico offers a drop light on a long extension cord along with a bottle of local wine. "What a luxury to be able to see after dark," Clarke says as he leisurely slices vegetables with our dull Swiss army knife.

"*Signor*," a small voice filters through the tent. Leaning over the plate of vegetables, Clarke sticks his head out the doorway. Leonardo hands in a bowl of ice.

"I wish we could save this for tomorrow afternoon," I say, remembering the blistering heat of the last few days, then add the ice to our water bottles and our wine after we rub our faces with it. Slowly, the crystal cubes left in the dish turn to slivers and then melt, and we use the last icy drops to wash our hands after dinner.

"*Signor, signora.*" It's Leonardo again, with fresh fruit for dessert and an invitation to come inside for coffee and brandy. As I slip my naked body into my light sleeping bag several hours later, I wonder why we can't just let people like these teach us to love generously again.

Near Florence, we stop at a computer store to inquire about the cost of printing my journal, thinking it might hold a key to what we do next. I'd kept my disks when Kelly and Megan took the computer home, unwilling to trust them to anyone else. Alberto offers to print it for free, but after two hours' work, including converting their Italian computer to English, we discover that without my printer disks, their printer can't read my program in any language.

Pedaling into Florence, we find the city center full of Americans; when we cross the river Arno, the Ponte Vecchio off to the right looks like a dollhouse bridge full of tiny shops balanced on the span like child's blocks. We pedal through narrow, crowded streets in the old part of the city, then at a pretty church, pour water into my wine cup for a hot black dog that droops down the stairs like a charred rag. He won't drink until his mistress returns to give him permission. "I'd like to spend some time in Florence without the bikes," Clarke says as we walk around the church. "Let's find a place to stay on the outskirts and take a train back tomorrow."

It's rush hour, and we pedal furiously through the fast cars rushing out of the city, darting in and out of near misses, getting lost, then dive in again, swimming north through the traffic current through industrial areas until we find a large old house off the road near a suburban train station. There, we're given permission to camp and to leave the bikes the next day by two young couples, two sisters and their husbands who are restoring the old house together. Although the Italians speak excellent English, I'm glad that I'm able to communicate in their country in their language.

As Clarke and I build our home for the night, Franco invites us for dinner. He and Angela remind me of Chiara and Maurizio—sophisticated, liberated, interested in the world. "You need more than one day to explore Florence," Angela tells us.

"May we camp one more night then?" I ask, imagining how nice it would be to just get up and leave our "house" like everyone else in the world.

"Of course," Angela smiles. But on the way back to the tent, Clarke reprimands me for asking to stay another night, and I reluctantly agree to leave after just one day in the city.

The first thing we do in Florence is shop. After seven months of sleeping in private gardens, I decide I need a nightshirt—one of these nights I'm going to pop naked outside the tent to pee and get caught. Then we tour the Uffiti Museum (which overwhelms me with its enormous collection of large paintings—I always have to see everything and it's always too much); the Cathedral of Florence (stunningly beautiful on the outside but dark and uninspiring within); and then crowd across the Ponte Vecchio along with everyone else in the city.

Mostly we just enjoy the feeling of the architecture and the novelty of being on foot. Clarke buys some new drawing paper and I look for a small piece of gold jewelry to commemorate pedaling over the Alps. The memory is too big for a souvenir, I finally decide, buying nothing.

Sitting on a curb with wine and pizza, we philosophize about this and that for a couple of hours, enjoying ourselves immensely. It's a nice change. "We have no bike to pack the rest of this wine on," I point out, at my limit or a shade beyond.

"Guess we'll have to finish it up," Clarke replies, taking a long pull from the bottle.

By the time we return to Franco and Angela's around six o'clock, we're acutely aware of the different muscles involved in walking. "I'm not sure I've got it in me to ride around looking for another place to stay, Clarke."

"Me either."

We knock on the door and I explain to Franco that we'd planned to leave because we felt guilty asking to stay another night. "But we are very tired. Would it be all right to put up our tent again?"

"Of course. We wondered why your bikes were all packed this morning." Hurriedly, we build our tent and disappear inside so that the families won't think they have to ask us to dinner again, and when we say goodbye to these generous Italians in the morning, I'm both sorry that we haven't spent more time with them and embarrassed that we asked as much from them as we have. "You are welcome to stay another night," Franco says.

"*Grazie, no*. It is time to go south, toward Rome."

"We will meet again," he says gently. "The world is a small place."

Retracing our circuitous route to Florence, we stop at a small shop to buy underwear. Although I find what I want, I'm unwilling to squander a day's allowance for a pair of panties, opting to continue in rattiness. "I'll just ruin them anyway, scrubbing them on river rocks," I tell Clarke.

A boy of seven or eight steps up behind me as I pull my bike away from the wall. Spreading a newspaper over the handlebars, he turns his grimy face up to mine. "Buy a newspaper!" he demands in Italian.

"*Grazie, no*," I reply, smiling.

"*Per favore, signora*," the child pleads. The paper isn't even current.

Suddenly, a passerby yells at the boy, who runs away into the crowds. "Be careful, *signora*," the man says to me in Italian. "That boy," he indicates with a jerk of his head where the boy disappeared, "he was trying to get into your packs while he covered his hands with the newspaper."

"*Grazie, signor*," I smile, "but we don't have much to steal." The most he'd have gotten for his trouble was a handful of my tattered underwear.

We pedal into the hills of Chianti on a small road that winds around and around through ancient Tuscan stone houses set high up in the mountains. Early in the evening, we look down into a valley from the top of a steep pass; the road winds down the mountain like a dirty lost ribbon with nothing at the end. Finally, we spot an old church, and leaning the bikes inside a small shed full of scorpions and praying mantises, zip ourselves inside the tent and listen to church bells most of the night.

As always, we awaken to the birds and the breezes and the weather, whatever it is. We're part of nature and live it, not just as observers but as participants. This morning, the air is crispy, like crackers, until the pale sun bakes its edges to soft gold.

The road to Siena seems silent but is full of the sounds of nature—the wind in the trees, tittering birds, the tiny rustling of animals hidden in the dry leaves. The bicycles lumber along the small Italian road, fat with faded packs, tires softly rubbing along the pavement like quiet breath. As the morning sun touches the treetops, the road merges into my private thoughts about the beauty of the world.

"Stop!" Clarke says from in front. Together, we listen to the silence of man, the noises of nature, the rustles and the tremblings and the scratches, the flapping of wings, the skittering of insects, the passage of air. "Wouldn't it be wonderful if man hadn't come along to ruin all this?" Clarke announces finally.

I think for a long moment before responding, having decided long ago that man's ability to reason has to be for a purpose. "Maybe if we can just…," I begin.

"Why do you have to debate everything I say?" Clarke flares like a struck match. "Can't you ever agree or just keep quiet?"

"Who says that we talk only when you want, Clarke? You interrupted my quiet without a thought." The serenity of the morning falls next to the dead grass along the edge of the road, and we swing our suntanned legs over our metal mules, urging them forward around the next turn, and then the next.

In Siena, Clarke gets into an argument with some teachers at a private school because they won't allow us to eat lunch on the grounds, then we find a picnic bench in a park downtown and spend half an hour discussing our route to Rome and wondering how to check in with Jill and the kids because Italian phone booths don't have telephone numbers for anyone to call back. After lunch, distracted, we forget to explore Siena and pedal southwest toward the front laces of Italy's boot.

Why do we go from one place to the next, I wonder as we pedal uphill. Why, when we find someone or something special, don't we give it more time? If we'd been in a car, we could have covered the same distance in three weeks. Have we seen that much more, or are we too busy just trying to keep moving?

From Siena, the national highway shoots straight toward Grosetto, bypassing the villages instead of wandering from one to the next like the secondary roads we usually choose. Hour after hour we pedal, through dark tunnels, up and down steep passes. No one lives in this part of Italy, I decide, wondering where we'll get food for the night. Clarke signals a halt at the entrance to a tunnel near dusk. "This one's long, then there are two more short ones before a town called Civitella. Hopefully, we can get there before the markets close."

"We've already ridden sixty kilometers."

"I don't think we have a choice unless you see a village somewhere." Clarke gestures toward arid hills and scrub brush as he attaches our tiny flashlight to the front of his bike. His headlight is out now too. Earlier in the day, he'd scavenged a broken taillight from the side of the road and now fastens it to his packs in back while I make sure that my leftover orange fluorescent bunny tail covers as much of my rear packs as possible. Then we enter the black hole.

I can see absolutely nothing after the first few feet of uphill pedaling and follow Clarke by sound, breathing fast and shallow in the stale exhaust fumes. Suddenly, a truck enters from the far end, its engine reverberating from both walls to fill the entire space around us. In the blinding headlights, Clarke points to the right, his arm a black shadow; rats run alongside the bikes, jumping down into storm drains along the curb. Keeping my eyes on the faint glow of the tiny reflector stripes on the back of Clarke's pedals and breathing through my mouth, I pedal as fast as I dare, trying to keep up, imagining myself spilling in front of the truck if I hit the curb or a pothole. As the truck echoes out of the tunnel behind us, we're engulfed again by total blackness and clouds of diesel fumes choke my lungs and burn my eyes. Tears stream down my face and I try to wipe them away with the back of my dirty bicycle glove, blinking hard to re-center my contact lenses.

Engines again! This time, a car and truck enter from either side of the tunnel and the car veers around us just in time to get back in our lane as the truck passes, honking. "Hurry!" I scream, but even I can't hear myself. Hoping for another vehicle to illuminate our way but terrified of falling into an occupied traffic lane, I try to follow the sound of Clarke's tires but the noise is obliterated by the sound of the next truck, and the next car and the next, until they careen past with a deafening roar and a blast of exhaust fumes. Panting, my heart beating fast, I spot a glimmer of light up ahead and can just make out Clarke's dim outline. The end! Bursting out of the tunnel, we drink great gulps of air and dusk. "I couldn't decide whether I'd be run over or die of asphyxiation," I gasp when I get enough air to talk. "How long was that thing?"

"Two kilometers," Clarke replies between deep breaths.

"And you say we have two more?"

"They're shorter."

I only have enough energy for a short note: *Leave my body to the rats.*

After eighty kilometers of mountains, we find the turnoff to Civitella, a small village at the top of a long, steep road. It's almost dark, and although my legs are shaking with fatigue, we need to push on immediately unless we want to bicycle in the dark without headlights. After a grueling climb to the top, we locate a tiny market with little food and buy a jar of antipasto and some noodles, then coast back down the hill to look for a house with a level space big enough for our tent. An English-speaking Italian directs us to a small public park after greedily eyeing our packs. "Did that guy make you nervous back there?" I ask Clarke as we look for the park.

"Yes, but maybe I'm just imagining things."

Pitching our tent under a little party shelter at the back of the square, we uncharacteristically lock up the bicycles, then cook a terrible dinner by waning flashlight and struggle with a cold water sponge bath before shucking ourselves into our smelly sleeping bags, wishing that our bikes were watchdogs.

Still nervous, we wake early the next morning, riding sixty kilometers before lunch at a beach near the island of Monte Argentario. "I keep thinking about the book, Clarke."

"What about it?"

"This is an incredible story, whether or not I'm good enough to write about it. But where does it end? Every night seems to be the same—knock, explain, camp, become friends, leave. Our Italian is good enough now that it's not even a challenge to communicate. I almost feel lazy—the bicycling, although it's still hard on my knees, is just another part of my life, like sleeping in a tent on the ground every night. It's like breathing. I don't even think about it any more. Bathing and washing clothes in rivers, the same. It's gotten too easy—and too hard."

"The hellos and goodbyes?"

"Yes."

"I know what you mean." He studies the map. "Look, there's an island just off the coast. Let's camp there for a few days and decide what to do. There's even a monastery on the top of the mountain. Maybe we can ask to stay there."

"Skip the monastery. I don't need any more people to visit right now."

Chapter 24

If a seagull were flying off the western coast of Italy north of Rome, Monte Argentario would look as if a tiny mountain had slipped into the sea and was holding on to Italy for dear life with two arms, five-mile causeways, with a little town at the elbow of one. There are two roads on the island, one around its circumference to Porto San Stefano, the only village, and the other up the mountain to the monastery. That's it, except for a radio tower above the monastery.

Bundled against the sea at the foot of the mountain in a clutter of soft old colors – pale yellows and creams and ochers, everything roofed in red tile – the village of Porto San Stefano boasts a harbor full of fishing boats and yachts. Spotting a Gucci store, we decide that this isn't what we need. "Maybe one of the boat owners needs crew," Clarke suggests.

"I might have to chop heads off fish."

Inquiring at a small market about the road up the mountain, we're told that visits to the monastery are allowed. "But the road is very steep," the owner explains in Italian, eyeing our heavy packs. "It would not be impossible to ride up on bicycles, but it would be very, very difficult."

It takes an hour to pedal the seven kilometers up to the monastery under gathering black clouds. Although the grade is horrendous, I don't pay much attention because I'm busy thinking of the best way to ask in Italian for shelter at a Catholic monastery, hoping we aren't making an unacceptable request, fluorescent modern Americans encroaching on ancient, holy walls, offending everyone.

Strolling into the two-hundred-and-fifty-year-old chapel like normal tourists, we're too uncertain to pound on the door of the main building even after months of asking families if we can sleep in their fields, then sit on a wall in the deserted courtyard hoping to be rescued from our dilemma. Sure enough, a monk in black robes and blue tennis shoes ambles down the hill, spots the "U.S.A." sign on the back of Clarke's bike, and makes his way over to confirm that we speak English. "Thank God I've someone to talk to!" he exclaims.

Father Brendan is a seventy-five-year-old Irish monk on his way to Rome. The monastery, he explains, is the founding house for his order, the Passionists. "No one inside speaks English and I don't speak Italian," he says sadly. Too bad they can't speak Latin to each other, I say to myself. After we explain our request, Father Brendan shakes his head. "I cannot ask for you because your Italian is much better than mine, but it might be possible for you to stay. There's another sanctuary farther up the mountain—maybe you can find help there."

The storm breaks then, sending sheets of rain in rivers over the ground as the three of us huddle next to the wall and a monk comes outside to kick a small shivering kitten with runny eyes away from the door. Clarke retrieves the dripping cat and deposits him in my arms, where he falls asleep, purring, keeping both of us warm. "That cat should be killed," Father Brendan announces with disdain.

"This cat should be healed," I hiss as the Irish monk knocks on the door to get inside, leaving us and the cat in the downpour. Rain washes across the courtyard, and lightning and thunder are the only commentary to our misery. Thoroughly drenched and cold and feeling as unwelcome as the cat, we pound on the door and are told that the monk in charge is away. "What about the other convent up the mountain?" I ask in Italian.

"The Superior's name is Padre Vittorio," the old monk answers, shutting the door in my face as the cat scurries under a woodpile.

Tired and discouraged and wondering what steep, muddy field we'll sleep in if we're again turned away, we labor in the rain up an even steeper half mile to another very old building. "He is sleeping until four," a young woman announces in Italian when we ask for Father Vittorio.

Two young men appear with their hands full of wild mushrooms. Like the woman, they're dressed in work clothes. "May I help?" one asks in English.

"We have slept on the ground for eight months," Clarke explains. "We are very tired. May we find shelter here for one or two nights?"

Paul smiles kindly. "I will ask Padre Vittorio at four," he promises, then leaves us in the rain. Pulling my jacket collar more tightly around my neck in a futile attempt to keep out the water, I slump on the ground in silence. Clarke sits in the mud next to me. Twenty minutes later, Paul pokes his head out the door to invite us into the kitchen for tea. As we sit at the large marble table in the big kitchen, the room feels like home, for this moment at least, and with freezing fingers curled around a hot cup to keep them from shaking, tears of relief slip down my cheeks to mix with the rain dripping from my hair.

Paul is telling Clarke about the monastery. "We have about twenty people here," he explains, "men and women. Some are religious, but many have come here for help with drug and alcohol problems and disease. We don't worry about burglars," he smiles. "They're all on the inside."

At four o'clock, Padre Vittorio decides that we can sleep in an adjoining building. "Nothing will be required of you," Paul explains as he shows us around the grounds. "You may take whatever you want from the garden and are welcome to join us for meals or not, as you wish."

"Hello!" We turn to see the Irish Father Brendan, accompanied by a monk from the other monastery. "We came for a tour and understand that you speak English, Paul." He turns to Clarke and me, eyes twinkling. "Hello again, Americans."

"Come along, then," says Paul, introducing us to Father Brendan's companion, the other monastery's youngest inhabitant at seventy-five. "This order was founded in seventeen-twenty by Saint Paul of the Cross," Paul explains. "We now have monasteries all over the world. This building was the original prayer house for the larger monastery below. It had been abandoned for ten years before it was turned into a place for healing—no one wears robes here, even the monks; the people are young and everyone works."

Later, after the two older monks stroll back down the hill, Paul continues his explanations. "The other monastery is very traditional and doesn't really understand what we do here. It is full of old monks who want only to give the sacraments."

"They certainly didn't seem to know what to do with us," Clarke comments.

"No, I would guess that they didn't," smiles Paul, scanning our wet clothes and dirty faces. "If you like, put your bicycles in this storage room." He opens a first-floor door. "Sometimes we use it as a nursery, but there are no children here at the moment." Dirty, ragged toys are scattered about the floor and dusty cobwebs form a thin brown sheet over the sparse furniture. Grabbing an armful of wet packs, we start up the stairs to our room. "At this end of the hall are three men from Rome who are restoring our chapel. You will share the bathroom with them." Paul opens the door to a small dirty room with toilet, sink and open-stall shower.

Overlooking the monastery and its gardens across an earthen courtyard, our room has two bare bunk beds and a small dresser. "This means a great deal to us, Paul," I say as we dump drippy packs in the corner.

"Yes, I can tell. You've been traveling a long time. I will leave you now."

"Why don't you take a nap?" Clarke suggests after the door closes gently. "I'll bring up the rest of our stuff."

"Would you mind very much if we didn't eat dinner with the people here this evening?"

"I'm sure we can find some lentils and rice in the bottom of your pack."

Closing my eyes, I imagine my body emptying of everything—cold, rain, fatigue, uncertainty, my marriage. My mind floats away. Suddenly, men's voices erupt in Italian and English at the end of the hall, then Clarke tumbles back inside our room. "I'm sorry, Susan, but the men who are working on the church insist that we have dinner with them. I explained that we were tired, but they want to help us rest by cooking for us. My Italian isn't good enough to refuse."

Salvadori, Sabatino and Luigi are gathered around a small table when we arrive after washing our faces. Jumping up as we enter, the three men usher us to the small table with a gallant flourish, then pour wine all around and fill the table with pasta and salad and bread. Our conversation is in Italian, Spanish, German and French—but no English. "A Frenchman we met felt that wine was the most important thing in life, followed by food and then women," Clarke tells them. "What do Italian men think?"

Salvadori responds immediately. "Food is number one in Italy, and then wine. Women are three, four and five!"

As we wish them good night, the three men are already planning our meal for the next evening, ignoring our protests with louder and louder protestations of their own, falling all over themselves like big puppies to be perfect hosts. I hug and kiss each of them, and their laughter echoes inside me long after I curl up in my sleeping bag on the lumpy mattress of the bottom bunk across from Clarke.

Although it's raining lightly, we keep the window open, used to fresh air, unused to being warm when it's cold outside. In the middle of the night, lightning fills the room with eerie blue light and we jerk awake, confused. Outside the window, the black trees on the mountaintop behind the chapel are silhouetted by jagged waves of light, one after the other, then suddenly a storm explodes and thunder echoes and re-echoes around and around the tiny island. Mesmerized, we watch in silence as rain pours out of the sky in great curtains, drenching everything once again as if the day's storm hadn't been more than enough.

Clarke leaves for a walk early the next morning while I take a steaming shower, and after shaving my legs, feel human again, thoroughly spoiled and pampered. Although the facilities are meager and not very clean, they're worlds better than an icy stream. Returning to our room after cleaning the bathroom, I discover a cup of fresh purple grapes on the windowsill, compliments of Clarke, then go out for a walk of my own. Looking over the bay 1200 feet below the flower garden, I name the vegetables that grow alongside the monastery and watch rainwater drip from the branches of the trees above the lookout point. Everything is cool and wet and gray. At the bottom of the garden, I sit below a small white statue of Jesus, closing my eyes.

Walking deep into the woods, I eat a row of chocolate from the previous day's candy bar, then write a long letter home, blue page after blue page of cramped words explaining where we are and why. As I write, the sky brightens to blue and the sun dapples to bright coins the ground around the old wooden bench where I sit in the forest.

Putting away my letter, I turn my face to the sunshine. It's noon and I'm not sweaty yet. I miss Clarke. Ten or twenty white butterflies race through the sunshine every which way like flying flowers, each to its own direction but part of a happy dance. I try to sketch the chapel and can't even begin.

Slowly, I walk through the gardens to our room. There are coins spread all over Clarke's mattress. He's probably thinking of his children—we've been accumulating change for a week, to call. I leave my letter home for Clarke to read, along with a spray of tiny white flowers. My hands smell good, of soap and cream and flower petals instead of sweaty leather.

Walking back to the garden, I rub my face, accidentally killing a mosquito, its body and my blood filling a fingernail, then sit on the stone steps of the little chapel, my back against the hard cement, grateful for somewhere to lean. Clarke is near the lookout point, and I ache for his nearness, knowing that as he's spotted me, he's gone another way, as I would have. It's time to be alone and apart.

I listen to the symphony I played in the park in Wiesbaden, Germany, when I thought about how much I'd miss Kelly and Megan when they left. They'd just decided to go. My throat aches as I remember my niece, excited to return home, writing down German phrases that I lost, understanding my tears. I cry again, alone at the back of the garden, homesick beyond words for my family and friends, torn between my love for foreign adventure and the cradle of American love that's been mine for forty-two years.

Clarke is with Paul at the lookout point when I stop to say good morning. "Did you rest well, Susan?" Paul asks, looking down with a smile.

"You look wonderful," Clarke adds.

"I feel great, but the storm was an interesting experience. How nice that we weren't outside in a tent, thanks to you," I say to Paul.

"Some of the people here think that the storm came last night because of you, that it's a sign of some kind. Indeed, it was a most unusual storm for this island."

Clarke eats lunch with the monks while I sit in the cool breezes, looking over the bay, a zillion miles from home, whatever that means. A bee, a thin little species, flies around my fingers, attracted to the bright pink writing on my t-shirt. The ocean merges with the mainland in mist, and the tiny houses of Orbetello are strewn at the water's edge like miniature golden sugar cubes, each with a red hat. A ferryboat cuts a thin white wake into the gray water as sea breezes ruffle the trees below.

Scenes from the last eight months, like snapshots scrambled in an old box, tumble through my mind, one after another, a potpourri of amazing experience. Not knowing what questions to ask, I kneel in the church, meditate in the chapel, let go of my thoughts like raindrops falling into a river, flowing away. "It doesn't matter where you go," my intuition finally says, "it matters how you live. All that you seek, you already have, and if you touch your own heart, you will touch the hearts of others."

Idly, I wonder about the book. "No, there is no conclusion," says the voice inside my heart. "There never is, when it's a true story. Life is not a destination anyway, it's a journey. Your book doesn't need an ending."

So. It doesn't matter if we stay or go home, if we go on to Greece or back to Spain or Morocco.

Somehow, we both know that our trip to Europe is over, after thirty-three weeks, ten countries and 10,000 kilometers. We don't debate it like we do everything else. We just know.

The next day, we leave the monastery during Sunday services, perhaps afraid that we'll stay forever if we have to say goodbye to Paul and his friends face-to-face. After packing our beloved bicycles, we walk the grounds separately. Standing by the little chapel to Jesus at the edge of the forest, I'm torn, almost literally, by the cumulative sadness of all of our European goodbyes and by the incredible joy that caused such sorrow. Silently, I join Clarke in front of the church and we slip with a lifetime of memories through the gates as the bells from the old monastery below fill the bright air with music.

About the Author

A third-generation Coloradoan, Susan Musgrove was raised in Denver and majored in creative writing and speech pathology at the University of Redlands, California. After a number of years as a stockbroker in Dallas, she moved to the Colorado mountains, where she met and married Clarke.

Although she and Clarke are now divorced, Susan still hung onto her bicycle. She currently lives in Denver, where she is a financial advisor for a major brokerage firm. She loves to travel and, after thirteen orthopedic surgeries over the years, continues to add to her list of "things I've at least tried once." This year, after surgery for a torn rotator cuff from rock climbing aggravated by mushing dogsleds (and a re-do of a previous fix from unhappy incidents involving racquetball, water skiing and her horse), she decided to skip sea kayaking and attend a travel writer's conference in Italy—where she broke her ankle the first day.

Susan's idea of balance is experiencing all of the extremes—sleeping in a tent on the ground, then staying at the elegant Connaught in London; working like crazy all week, and then curling up with a good book and her sheltie Katy all weekend. Happiness is great friends and family, a little hiking, good fiction, bicycling, meeting friends for coffee, one great trip every year.

Her dream is to own a one-room cabin in the forest by a stream.

www.ingramcontent.com/pod-product-compliance
Lightning Source LLC
Chambersburg PA
CBHW022049160426
43198CB00008B/168